Praise for The Essential Thyroid Cookbook

"Jill and Lisa have made *The Essential Thyroid Cookbook* as beautiful as it is beneficial for those with hypothyroidism. It respects and honors that each of us has different journeys, experiences, and preferences, and it's a must-have for anyone with Hashimoto's."

—**Frank Lipman,** MD, founder and director of Eleven Eleven Wellness Center
and *New York Times* bestselling author of *The New Health Rules*

"A monumental achievement! This book belongs in the kitchen of not only every person with a thyroid problem, but in addition, all of their genetic relatives. Great nutritional information, at last."

—**Richard L. Shames,** MD, author of *Thyroid Power* and *Thyroid Mind Power*

"You will savor the simplicity and deliciousness of these food as medicine recipes that are designed with your thyroid and immune system in mind."

—**Kathie Madonna Swift,** MS, RDN, LDN, Integrative
Clinical Nutritionist and author of *The Swift Diet* and *The Inside Tract*

"With all the noise surrounding health and wellness, *The Essential Thyroid Cookbook* provides a clear message for optimizing the health of your thyroid and immune system. Lisa and Jill have overcome their own struggles with Hashimoto's by using food as medicine and these challenges have allowed them to create this tool to help lift and guide others on their wellness journey. With this cookbook, food can be your medicine, too."

—**Michelle Robin,** DC, creator of the Small Changes,
Big Shifts podcast and founder of Your Wellness Connection

"If you struggle with hypothyroidism, this is your ultimate cookbook. These 100-plus recipes will empower you to live each and every day with joy, energy, and balance. The authors are superstar nutrition professionals; savor their insights and let their wisdom nourish you!"

—**Gregory Plotnikoff,** MD, MTS, FACP, author of *Trust Your Gut*

"What a relief it was to read Jill and Lisa's *Essential Thyroid Cookbook*. It echoes my approach to a functional nutrition approach to thyroid health—honoring not just the fact that we each have different and unique dietary needs to start, but also to maintain, on our healing journeys. I'll be using and recommending this cookbook regularly."

—**Andrea Nakayama,** Functional Medicine Nutritionist & Educator

"There is no one right way to eat! This is what I tell all my nutrition clients and what I love most about Lisa and Jill's cookbook. *The Essential Thyroid Cookbook* is just that—essential. It's full of great science-based information that reviews nutrition guidelines that work for everyone with thyroid and immune imbalances. But it also presents various concepts along with delicious, practical recipes to help tailor which way of eating works best for you."

—**Maggie Ward**, MS, RD, LDN, Nutrition Director at
Dr. Mark Hyman's UltraWellness Center

"Lisa and Jill take a practical approach to the evidence and the kitchen. People with hypothyroidism who want to use food as medicine need to know the 'why' and the 'how to.' This cookbook is it!"

—**Leigh Wagner**, PhD, RDN, Integrative Dietitian

"As a chef of over 20 years in some of North America's top kitchens, I can confidently say that Lisa has a real understanding for how to use whole food ingredients that not only capture great flavor, but also nourish the body. These remarkable recipes are clearly written and use easily attainable ingredients and techniques that are approachable for any level of cooking experience. This cookbook is sure to be a pillar for strengthening health in anyone, but particularly for those with thyroid conditions."

—**Michael Magliano**, Executive Chef of the SOHO House, West Hollywood

"As someone who has been there, and self-healed naturally, this is a pivotal resource for anyone suffering with thyroid and autoimmune disease. This is not simply a cookbook; it's a guidebook to beginning your self-healing journey in an empowering, digestible way."

—**Heather Dubé**, Functional Nutritionist, e3 Energy Evolved

"People with thyroid issues—like me—need to pay special attention to what we eat. But no one wants to think about nutrition all the time! We want to eat. Live happy lives. And enjoy our food. The magic of this cookbook is that the recipes are designed to improve your health and support thyroid function—but that's all invisible. You can just eat, drink, and be merry."

—**Melissa Joulwan**, author of the bestselling *Well Fed* cookbook series

"After seeing thousands of clients over the last decade, it became obvious that foods were the primary cause of their autoimmune thyroid diseases. When junk foods were replaced by whole foods, and reactive foods like gluten and dairy were eliminated, antibodies would often normalize and autoimmunity would vanish. It's refreshing to see that Lisa and Jill have come to the same conclusions while conjuring up some wholesome and tasty solutions in *The Essential Thyroid Cookbook*. There's nothing more powerful or effective for thyroid disease than delicious medicine!"

—**Tom Malterre**, MS, CN, Certified Functional Medicine Practitioner
and author of *The Elimination Diet*

Gluten-free
&
Dairy-free

THE ESSENTIAL
Thyroid
Cookbook

OVER 100 NOURISHING RECIPES FOR THRIVING
WITH HYPOTHYROIDISM AND HASHIMOTO'S

Lisa Markley, MS, RDN & Jill Grunewald, HNC

Foreword by Aviva Romm, MD

BLUE WHEEL PRESS™

Published by Blue Wheel Press, LLC
PO Box 6755
Minneapolis, MN 55406
www.thyroidcookbook.com

Copyright ©2017 Blue Wheel Press, LLC

All rights reserved.

Distributed by Greenleaf Book Group

For ordering information or special discounts for bulk purchases, please contact Greenleaf Book Group at PO Box 91869, Austin, TX 78709, 512.891.6100.

Design and composition by Greenleaf Book Group, Courtney Sullivan, and Anthony Magliano
Cover design by Greenleaf Book Group, Courtney Sullivan, and Anthony Magliano
Photographs (food) ©2016 Kenny Johnson
Food styling: Anne Fisher

Library of Congress Control Number: 2017933693

Print ISBN: 978-09911-7050-0
ebook ISBN: 978-0-9911705-1-7

17 18 19 20 21 22   10 9 8 7 6 5 4 3 2

First Edition

BLUE WHEEL PRESS™

This cookbook is dedicated to the millions who have suffered or are suffering from hypothyroidism and Hashimoto's thyroiditis. May you be adequately tested, acknowledged with empathy and understanding, and compassionately cared for.

Contents

Part Two: Essential Thyroid Kitchen

Authored by Lisa Markley, MS, RDN

Part Three: Essential Thyroid Recipes

Authored by Lisa Markley, MS, RDN

Part Four: Appendixes

Authored by Jill Grunewald, HNC

FOREWORD

By Aviva Romm, MD

While medical doctors possess a wealth of knowledge and go through intensely rigorous training, I often find that I learn more from my patients struggling with specific conditions about what truly works for them and what doesn't than medical training ever taught me. In fact, my patients often, out of necessity prior to finding an integrative, functional medicine doctor like me, had to become their own personal health detective to find a proper diagnosis and solutions beyond the medications offered to them by their conventional physician, too often accompanied by the statement, "This is something you're just going to have to get used to living with."

As a result, many people with specific conditions become very knowledgeable about cutting edge alternative research, buried or ignored but important scientific findings, and natural alternatives. I have found this to be true nowhere more than for women with thyroid problems, particularly Hashimoto's thyroiditis, most likely because thyroid problems are amongst the most overlooked, yet prevalent conditions that impact women's health today.

It was my unique background as a midwife and herbalist for 25 years, combined with my training as a Yale medical doctor specializing in integrative women's health, that led me to develop specialized knowledge in the conventional and natural treatment approaches to thyroid conditions. And it was my unique background that has led women with fatigue; inexplicable weight gain and inability to lose weight even with proper diet and exercise; hormonal problems including irregular periods, infertility, and miscarriage; depression and anxiety; chronic constipation; aching joints; hair loss; and more—all of which can be symptoms or signs of a thyroid problem—to seek my care.

These women were seeking answers and often had a suspicion that they might have a thyroid problem. Most often, their suspicions—or my own when they shared their list of symptoms with me—were spot on; they had Hashimoto's or, in fewer but nonetheless important numbers, non-autoimmune hypothyroidism. It was the need of women to have Hashimoto's answers, and in such great numbers, that led me to specializing in this area.

While many women do benefit from a thyroid medication, for some it is unnecessary; some are able to avoid it and others to go off of it, and all are able to maximize their overall health and energy by getting to the root causes of their illness—what led to the immune disruption in the first place. Topping that list is usually a diet that contains triggers that can lead to chronic inflammation and that often lacks the important nutrients the body so desperately wants to stay in health and balance.

One of my most oft repeated sayings is that, "The body has the ability to heal beyond what we've ever been told." But for that to happen, we have to remove the obstacles to the body's innate healing potential, while providing the body with the building blocks it needs to produce health. Though eating the right foods is one of the biggest needle movers toward health, one can practically get whiplash trying to keep up with the latest food trends and food science; and when it comes to what to eat for thyroid health, it can be unclear what information to trust.

Enter Jill and Lisa. First, and most importantly, like so many of my patients, they had to become their own health detectives to solve the case of what to eat to support their own selves back to health in the setting of each having been diagnosed with Hashimoto's. Both have learned to manage it with sound nutrition that helps them to also reduce inflammation and support immune health. They know what you're going through first hand and they're committed to helping you get your life back—and in a way that doesn't overwhelm, since you're likely already struggling with fatigue and with it, overwhelm.

But Jill and Lisa didn't just write from their own personal health experiences; they took a well-researched approach to this book to bring you the best possible food science on the subject. Jill brings with her many years of successfully coaching women with hormonal imbalances, primarily hypothyroidism/Hashimoto's, and has added a substantive educational component to this volume—a thyroid health book within a cookbook.

Lisa, a Bastyr-trained Registered Dietitan Nutritionist, who has been teaching culinary nutrition classes since 2009, has written and developed most of these outstanding recipes, with the exception of the three noted. Her passion is translating healthy eating to the plate and empowering others to reclaim their health by getting back in the kitchen.

The thyroid is highly nutrient dependent for health, and most Americans are deficient or low in many of the very nutrients the thyroid requires to maintain (and restore) proper functioning. In a non-dogmatic way, Jill and Lisa take a fresh approach to helping you eat in a way that reduces your exposure to common contaminants found in food, including pesticides, heavy metals, and plasticizers like BPA that damage the thyroid while creating

delicious, "food as medicine" inspired recipes to help you meet your specific needs.

My goal as a physician specializing in natural approaches to women's health is to help women take back their health. One of the fastest, most effective, and most empowering ways to do this is to take back your kitchen by preparing whole foods-based, fresh, unprocessed meals that satisfy and delight your taste buds while healing your body. This book is an important step in that direction. To enjoy good health, enjoy good food. Bon appetite. Bonne santé.

Aviva Romm, MD
Author of *The Adrenal Thyroid Revolution*
August 28, 2016

ACKNOWLEDGMENTS AND GRATITUDE

This cookbook was made possible because of the love, enthusiasm, and encouragement from a great number of people. Without all of the unwavering support we received throughout the writing and creation of this book, it may have never come to fruition.

Firstly, Lisa and I would like to thank our spouses, Jim and Mark. You are two of the coolest dudes on the planet. You held space for us—and cared attentively and lovingly for our young children—as we brought this vision to life; manically obsessed over every detail; took evening, weekend, and holiday time to collaborate; turned our home kitchens into test kitchens; turned our dining room tables into writing dens; and left home to write in solitude.

You repeatedly and patiently listened to us marvel at how long it took to make this cookbook a reality. Most importantly, even with our full and busy lives, you wholeheartedly believed in us and what we were capable of.

There's no way we could've written this book without the extra love and support we received from Lisa's parents, Rory and Jerry, and my in-laws, Moureen and Charles. Without their help with extra childcare, our husbands would've struggled finding the time they needed for themselves, the dishes would've piled up, and the mountain of laundry would still be sitting there.

We would like to thank Lisa's brother, Anthony Magliano, and his wife, Christen Edwards, for opening up their home for a multi-day food photography shoot. We realize the leftover morsels of food you

On a working vacation in the backwoods of Minnesota in 2013, at the start of our journey writing this cookbook.

Lisa's son, Evan, and Jill's daughter, Harriet (2013).

willingly received were not enough to convey how much we appreciate everything you did for us.

I would like to thank my good friends who are fellow "word nerds" and grammar and punctuation enthusiasts. Thank you for your dedication to one of my favorite things: the written word. We live in a world of hapless abbreviation and carelessness with one of the things that makes us human and your sisterhood is immeasurably meaningful and buttressed me through this journey. You helped create this cookbook, whether you know it or not: Laine Bergeson, Angelique Chao, Courtney Helgoe, Kristi Kohanek, Karen Olson, and Jen Sinkler. Karen Olson, journalist and editor extraordinaire, deserves an additional thank you for consulting with us, on many occasions, on the finer points of writing and layout.

Lisa and I would like to thank our friends who've gone before us—those who've published books, including cookbooks, and who've negotiated the Wild West of publishing. Thank you for making yourselves so willingly available to answer the long list of questions that we barraged you with along our journey: Jenny Breen, Pete Dulin, Melissa Joulwan, Tom Malterre, Ana Gabriel Mann, John David Mann, Tess Masters, Sarah Moran, Jim Norton, Therese Pautz, Dr. Aviva Romm, Alissa Segersten, and Amie Valpone.

Thank you to the creative team who helped us establish Blue Wheel Press™: Annie Einan, Judd Einan, and Kevin Fenton.

Thank you to the legal team who helped us establish Blue Wheel Press™ and who helped expertly guide the creation of this cookbook: Katie Feiereisel, Ernest Grumbles, and Leita Walker.

Thank you to the friends who helped me hide away in a writing hermitage when I needed it by offering their homes and cabins: Elizabeth Frost, Martha Hotchkiss, Kate Rime, and Diana Tollerson.

Thank you to our attentive, passionate, and lovingly merciless manuscript editor, Laine Bergeson, and to our talented recipe editor, Nicole Fallon Croes. Thank you also to my friend and colleague, Heather Saam, Certification Manager for Food Alliance, for reviewing our chapters that reference sustainable agriculture.

Thank you to our incredibly competent design, photography, and layout team for capturing our vision and bringing it to reality. Without them, we wouldn't have this beautiful book that we're so very proud to share with you. We're enormously appreciative of the talent of designers Neil Gonzalez (of Greenleaf Book Group), Courtney Sullivan, and Anthony Magliano; photographer Kenny Johnson; and food stylist Anne Fisher.

Thank you to marketing experts, Jennifer Kane and Diana Needham, for helping Lisa and me authentically and thoughtfully create a marketing plan for this cookbook. Thank you to Simone de los Santos for going cross-eyed with me, re-reviewing the detailed nutrient springboard chart for this cookbook with one final fine-toothed comb, just prior to publishing, and to Courtney Sullivan for refining that chart for our website (www.thyroidcookbook.com). Thank you to Loma Huh for editing and finalizing our notes/citations. Thank you to our indexer, Erica Caridio.

Thank you to our team of recipe testers for test-running Lisa's recipes along with their family and friends. Our work would not be complete without the important feedback we received from Joy Goodwin, Monica Hansen, Paula Iturra, Stacy Karen, Stephanie Kelly, Shannon Kinney, Marcy Lawless, Chris and Kylee Leatherman, Stephanie Lecovin, Candice Leibert, Rory Magliano, Jane Markley, Kelly Mason, Tina McGrew, Natalie McLaws, Rachel McTarsney, Dana Meier, Laura Minns, Kerry Moon, Krista Moore, Emily Newbold, Julie Schmieder, Amanda Stolba, Brooke Tarkin, Jennifer Ward, and Coral Wert.

Last but not least, we would like to thank the thousands of clients and students who we've had the pleasure of teaching, mentoring, coaching—and in Lisa's case, cooking for—throughout the years. You've taught us more than you could ever know. You've mirrored, enlightened, and humbled us. You've made us laugh and you've made us cry. We stand in reverence of each of your paths toward wellness. This cookbook is largely dedicated to you.

A SPECIAL THANKS
TO MELISSA JOULWAN

I f you're familiar with the Paleo and AIP diets, you're likely familiar with Mel Joulwan.

She's the author of the best-selling *Well Fed* cookbook series and the blog, www.MelJoulwan.com, where she writes about her triumphs and failures in the gym, in the kitchen, and in life. Her newest cookbook is *Well Fed Weeknights: Complete Paleo Meals in 45 Minutes or Less.*

I'd admired Mel from afar, due largely to her funny and poignant writing and also her discoveries post-thyroid surgery. And at the onset of the journey in creating this cookbook, I longed to connect with her about her cookbook publishing process. She was living in Austin, TX at the time. I live in Minneapolis. And just about the time that I was going to ask our mutual friend, Jen Sinkler, to make an email introduction, I ran into Mel. Here in Minneapolis. So weird. And magical.

I stared at her from across the room—Is that her? Is that really Mel Joulwan? No, I don't think it is. Wait, it is her . . .

A couple of weeks later, we had a meaty, cards-on-the-table conversation about the wild and wooly world of self-publishing. In the years following, as we inched our way toward publishing this cookbook, she continued to be a sounding board and member of our cheerleading team. Mel holds nothing close to her vest and Lisa and I have benefitted immensely from her advice, wisdom, experience, and kindness. She has been invaluable in helping to bring this cookbook into the world.

More about Mel

After a lifetime of yo-yo dieting and food as the enemy, Melissa found the Paleo diet in 2009 and has been happily following it ever since. That year, she also underwent a thyroidectomy. In the aftermath of the surgery and recovery, she became particularly interested in how diet affects hormones, body composition, mood, and motivation. These days, Melissa's workouts are just as likely to include yoga and meditation as lifting heavy things and sprinting to stay ahead of the stopwatch.

Well Fed 2 was named one of the best books of 2013 by Amazon.com and was a *Washington Post* best seller. Her first cookbook *Well Fed* appeared on the *Wall Street Journal* bestseller list, and she's the author of the recipes in the *New York Times* bestselling book *It Starts With Food* by Melissa and Dallas Hartwig. She writes a column for *Paleo Magazine* and her recipes have been featured in print in *Low Sugar Living*, *Inspire Health*, and *Where Women Cook*, and online at Buzzfeed.com, FoodNetwork.com, Nylon.com, PopSugar.com, and Men's Journal. She has been a featured chef for U.S. Wellness Meats and Lava Lake Lamb, as well as an instructor at Whole Foods Market.

INTRODUCTION

Given our shared passion for sustainable agriculture and the power of nutrition to heal the body, it was a foregone conclusion that Lisa and I would write this cookbook together. The idea came late one evening as I was wrapping up the last teleclass in my multi-part *Fire Your Thyroid* educational series, of which Lisa took part. Three minutes after the last class, Lisa emailed to say, "This was a fantastic series. As soon as you're ready to begin translating your nutritional suggestions to the plate, let me know." I slapped my forehead and immediately emailed her back, "Let's do it."

Thus, our cookbook journey began. It had never crossed my mind to write a cookbook—perhaps a hormone health and autoimmunity book, but never a cookbook. Because you see, being in the kitchen isn't my comfortable habitat. I'm not a "natural" in the kitchen, but I make it work. Unlike my husband, I'm not someone who can whip delicious meals together based on whatever random ingredients are in the refrigerator. (Yes, I'm lucky to have him.) And I'm not one to simply toss cereal in a bowl for breakfast or make mac and cheese for dinner, as you might guess.

I need recipes. Or I need to have made a dish so many times that I have the amounts of this and that ingredient memorized. I can improvise in my life in many other ways, but my relationship to cooking mirrors my relationship to my piano playing. As a child and young adult, I was an accomplished pianist, but I needed that sheet of Chopin or Brahms in front of me. If there were a piano at someone's home or in a hotel lobby and someone said, "Jill, sit and play something for us," I'd freeze. Get me home with my printed music, and I could go to town.

The kitchen is, however, Lisa's habitat. She and I are the yin to each other's yang. She's a master recipe writer and developer and has been cooking for others, including teaching cooking classes, for many years. I've relished Lisa's creations on many occasions and she never ceases to inspire me. Her dishes are simply delicious. This cookbook will not disappoint.

Lisa has written and developed all of these original recipes, with the exception of three. I simply had the "task" of testing many of them (darn!) and creating the nutritional springboard that is the foundation of this cookbook. (See the chapters, *Our Springboard* and *Our Methodology*.)

Although we're as excited about this cookbook now as we were the night we agreed to create it, my biggest fear was someone saying, "This is just another cookbook."

I was afraid our readers would see these delicious, easy to prepare, original, and thoughtful recipes without the context of why they help to support thyroid and immune function. Thus, in addition to providing you with satisfying recipes, Lisa and I:

1. Provide context for how we chose our ingredients; and

2. Educate you about the true healing power of nutrition in overcoming hypothyroidism and Hashimoto's.

While this cookbook was written for those with hypothyroidism and Hashimoto's, Lisa has ensured that her recipes are well received by a wide variety of palates. One recipe tester had this to say about the Quinoa Meatballs: "I cannot believe my child knowingly ate quinoa and loved it! These were easy to make, looked like 'traditional' meatballs, and tasted delicious! I will definitely make again and freeze some next time."

Although we know many readers will jump to the recipes—and rightfully so!—we hope you'll take the time to read the educational component of this cookbook. The information will help you understand some of the primary causes of hypothyroidism and Hashimoto's and provide you with additional steps you can take to get your thyroid working for you versus against you.

Additionally, we've written *The Essential Thyroid Cookbook Lifestyle Companion Guide*, where I address factors associated with hypothyroidism and Hashimoto's beyond what was appropriate for this cookbook. You can download it for free on our website:

www.thyroidcookbook.com/companion.

Will this cookbook (and our companion guide) be the "cure" for hypothyroidism and Hashimoto's thyroiditis? No. But given that diet plays such a significant role in nourishing and supporting both the thyroid and the immune system, getting the right nutrients is a critical step in healing. (See Appendix A, The Nutritional Springboard for This Cookbook, for more information on our exhaustive research that is the basis for the ingredients in Lisa's recipes.)

Without the right nutrition, all other approaches in supporting thyroid function and mitigating the autoimmune response will fail.

In fact, I've seen it over and over with my clients—they come to me having worked hard to "fix" their thyroid, often with the instructions to simply take thyroid hormone replacement (which I'm not categorically against) or to take a fistful of supplements, with, by no fault of their own, little attention to diet or digestive function.

Not surprisingly, many get only minimally better. And often, they feel worse than when they started.

Again, I'm not necessarily against thyroid hormone replacement. I'm not a doctor, but I feel that thyroid drugs should be taken in the context of dietary and lifestyle modifications and in the right dose for the shortest amount of time. That's right, contrary to prevailing myth, thyroid hormone replacement doesn't have to be a "for the rest of your life" prescription.

Supplements should be just that—they should *supplement* a sound, whole foods diet and give us what we're deficient in or what we can't get from our food. Sure, there's some non-negotiable supplementation that should be taken during an immune modulatory, therapeutic phase, (glutamine, for example) but most of what I recommend can be taken relatively short-term.

The only supplements that I feel everyone can benefit from in perpetuity are: Vitamin D, a multi-strain probiotic that includes a soil-based organism like Bacillus subtilis, and an Omega-3 fatty acid in the form of a molecularly-distilled fish oil. (See the chapter, *The Nutritional Heavy Hitters* for more on each of these and also Appendix B for supplement recommendations. You can also find links to all of these supplements at our website: www.thyroidcookbook.com.)

The approach I take with each client is a four-legged stool of:

1. Diet and nutrition, including addressing digestive function, healing leaky gut, and balancing blood sugar (approximately 60 percent)

2. Lifestyle modifications (approximately 15 percent)

3. Addressing body burden/toxic load (approximately 15 percent)

4. Supplementation (approximately 10 percent)

Many come to me heavy on supplementation—much of which I suggest they stop taking. If someone is taking hundreds of dollars of supplements each month but their digestive issues rage on, many of the benefits of those supplements won't be absorbed anyway.

Once these previously over-supplemented clients (who are also frustrated—no one wants to take that many pills) start thinning out their daily supplement regiment, begin focusing on nutrient-dense, thyroid- and immune-supportive foods, and begin healing their digestive system, things begin to change pretty quickly. Our bodies are always seeking homeostasis or balance

> 66 Without the right nutrition, all other approaches in supporting thyroid function and mitigating the autoimmune response will fail."

and for the most part, the body will begin responding to sound nutrition and to being well cared for in a matter of days.

It's been widely reported in the functional medicine* community that 70-80 percent of our immune system is in our digestive tract. The right nutrition—as well as the critical importance of identifying food sensitivities—is your first line of defense in not only supporting thyroid function, but also mitigating a hypervigilant immune response and taming autoimmune conditions.

While this book isn't about healing digestive problems specifically, I've provided simple Elimination Provocation diet instructions (see the chapter, *Elimination Provocation Diet Instructions*) and address the thyroid/gut connection in the chapter, *The Thyroid/Digestion Connection*. Sleuthing out your unique dietary triggers that can cause a systemic inflammatory response and fan the flames of autoimmune antibodies is critical in supporting your thyroid and managing Hashimoto's. I suggest that anyone with Hashimoto's walk through an Elimination Provocation diet—it's a non-negotiable for those with any manifestation of autoimmunity.

This cookbook is gluten-free and dairy-free. (See the chapters, *Gluten and Your Thyroid* and *Dairy and Your Thyroid* for thorough explanations.) All gluten-containing grains and milk products have been omitted, with the exception of ghee, which is an optional ingredient in many recipes. Read more about why we feel it's fine for most people to include ghee in our *Pantry Staples and Ingredients* chapter.

If you're unfamiliar with the term "functional medicine," I believe it's best summed up by internationally recognized functional medicine doctor, Dr. Mark Hyman, who said, "What is functional medicine? It's the opposite of dysfunctional medicine." He also calls it, "The medicine of why."

It's an approach to medicine that addresses the root causes of disease instead of administering prescriptions for symptoms. In other words, investigating the "why."

Dr. Hyman states that functional medicine is grounded in systems biology. "Systems biology seeks to understand how systems in the body are related and interconnected as a network rather than seeing them simply as a series of organs and body parts that have no relationship to one another. The perspective of medical specialization—organizing medicine by organs and diseases—is a flawed view that has placed modern medicine at a crisis point."[1]

OUR STORY

This cookbook is a collaboration of two very close friends who recognized the crucial need for a whole-foods cooking resource for the millions suffering from hypothyroidism and Hashimoto's. As Annie and Judd Einan, two members of our creative team, say, "If it doesn't exist, create it." So we created it.

First and foremost, Lisa and I are dear friends. Second, we're colleagues with a deep respect for each other's work. Third, we have a deep passion and respect for time-honored, sustainable farming practices and the way that food was meant to be grown and prepared. Fourth, we've both suffered from Hashimoto's.

Lisa and I met in 2006 in Kansas City. I had just returned to my home state of Missouri after graduating from nutrition school in New York and Lisa was recently back to the City of Fountains after graduating from Bastyr University in Seattle with her Master of Science in Nutrition (MSN). Come to find out, there were a few years that we simultaneously lived in Seattle. (And prior to moving to New York from Seattle, I'd hand-wrung over the idea of attending Bastyr's School of Naturopathic Medicine, but that's another story.)

As soon as I landed in Kansas City, I began sleuthing out anything I could find about the local and sustainable food and agriculture scene. My searches did not disappoint. Within a week, I was at a screening of two sustainable food and agriculture films—both hosted by the esteemed John Ikerd, Professor Emeritus of Agricultural and Applied Economics at the University of Missouri Columbia College of Agriculture, Food, and Natural Resources.

I asked Mr. Ikerd about organizations I could get involved with in the Kansas City area that support local and sustainable agriculture. The following week, I was at a meeting at Lisa's house, enjoying the bounty of summer with the Kansas City Food Circle, Kansas City's only organization that connected city residents to real, locally-grown food. I'd found my people.

This newcomer was enthusiastically inaugurated into the organization's steering committee, of which Lisa and her husband, Jim, were members, as were young farmers (and now friends) Rebecca Graff and Tom Ruggieri of Fair Share Farm and Pete Dulin, local writer and food enthusiast.

Out of the original organization came an offshoot group—the Kansas City 100-Mile Diet Group. You may remember the popular book by Alisa Smith and J.B. MacKinnon, *The 100-Mile Diet: A Year of Local Eating*. While we didn't seek to emulate Smith and MacKinnon's hardcore dedication to only eating what was grown within 100 miles of their home for a full year, we went on a collective mission to find any and all sources of any and all locally-produced foods in the area (nuts, fish, mushrooms, you name it!) that we could chronicle in Pete's new online magazine. As you can imagine, our monthly meetings were local food extravaganzas, sometimes in the fields of Rebecca and Tom's farm.

Our 100-Mile Diet column in Pete's publication was a raging success. We took turns researching and writing about various foods and after a year, had a veritable "handbook" of local foods available in the area. In fact, our little group gave a standing-room-only presentation at Kansas City's annual Eat Local & Organic Expo and received an exhilarating round of applause for our yearlong efforts.

To rewind, when Pete began talking about chronicling this food journey, I was stricken with serious fear. I didn't consider myself a "writer" and hadn't written anything substantive since college, mostly about things I wasn't that interested in. I graduated from architecture school, so most of my important "research papers" were "written" with a T-square.

Pete said it didn't matter—none of us were "writers" and that he'd copyedit as necessary. After my first submission (about tomatoes), Pete asked that in addition to our 100-Mile Diet pieces, I write a regular nutrition column for his magazine.

I discovered that I loved writing. My column for Pete's magazine turned into another writing gig, which turned into another and another, which turned into writing a few e-books and a feature article, Repair Your Thyroid, for the nationally-recognized magazine, Experience Life. And now, this book, with my beloved Lisa. In 2019, I'm writing my next book, *Reversing Alopecia*.

What excited Lisa the most about our 100-Mile Diet project was the opportunity to curate and create recipes featuring local foods to include in our resource guide. Looking back on it now, Lisa says that she has always had a deep passion and natural tendency towards being a "culinary translator." In the case of our 100-Mile Diet project, she helped translate seasonal, local food to the plate. And now with this cookbook, she sets out to help our readers translate healthy, thyroid-supportive recipes to their plates.

Were it not for Pete, I wouldn't have the library of health and nutrition articles under my belt that I do, nor would I have put myself out there as a health and nutrition writer as I have these last several years. And Lisa wouldn't have recognized her passion of turning simple food and nutrition recommendations into edible realities. We may not even have had the confidence to collaborate on this cookbook.

In 2007, I moved to Minneapolis and in 2012, Pete wrote *Last Bite: 100 Simple Recipes from Kansas City's Best Chefs and Cooks* and has since consulted with Lisa on the ins and outs of publishing a cookbook. Lisa and I are so grateful for Pete's friendship and guidance. His fingerprints are all over this cookbook.

Farm Huggers

In addition to being insatiably interested in the healing power of whole foods nutrition, Lisa and I are farm huggers. If I weren't a nutrition and hormone coach, I'd farm. (And maybe still will some day.)

I spent many idyllic summers on my grandparents' ranch in the rolling hills of the Ozarks. In addition to raising cattle, they had fruit trees, a massive garden, and a root cellar filled to the brim with my grandmother's canned fruits and vegetables. My other grandparents (in the same community) also had fruit trees and a massive garden. I was (mostly) raised on food they grew, butchered, canned, and froze. My memories of running around in the gardens, riding tractors and horses, chasing dogs and cats, picking strawberries and green beans, and playing in the barns are some of my very best childhood memories.

Fast forward many years; after moving to Minneapolis in 2007, I began working for Food Alliance, a nonprofit that certifies farms and ranches for sustainable agricultural practices. It has been my favorite job outside of my current career. Although I knew little about what it took to operate a farm, it was like sinking into an old familiar chair. In other words, the roots of my raisin' run deep.

Lisa didn't grow up on a farm and had never seen a vegetable or fruit growing in its natural habitat until she worked in an organic garden during graduate school. It was then that she forged a deeper relationship with food, learning more about the importance of what happens behind the scenes to get it from field to plate. As a nutritionist, but more importantly as someone who eats, Lisa began to believe wholeheartedly that it's in everyone's best interest to know and care about nutrition from the ground up.

She and I share a deep love for sustainable farming. Our standing-room-only presentation at Kansas City's annual Eat Local & Organic Expo in 2007 was one of the highlights of my post-nutrition school career.

We believe that food should be produced without the use of chemicals, pesticides, herbicides, fungicides, growth hormones, and subtherapeutic antibiotics. Sure, this may be a utopian vision, given today's culture of "bigger and faster" food production, but it's how food was grown prior to the introduction of farm chemicals.

The consolidation of our food system, which breeds plants and animals for the highest possible yields and profits over nutritional value, has resulted in environmental degradation, antibiotic resistance, large-scale contamination, food safety issues, and loss of food culture. Foods made from cheap, poor quality ingredients add "value" by providing volume and calories with no consideration for nutrient content, or lack thereof.

As a society, we've become accustomed to an industrial food system that prioritizes quantity over quality. The problems with this system are many, from rampant use of chemicals, including pesticides, hormones, and antibiotics, to degradation of soil quality, nutrient depletion, vulnerability to large-scale contamination and thus compromise of food safety, monoculture, genetically modified organisms (GMOs), and overall environmental degradation. This dysfunctional system also increases the distance that food travels from field to plate, which has its own set of environmental issues.

Large-scale conventional animal agriculture operations, often called CAFOs (confined animal feeding operations), generate enormous amounts of toxic waste, which can leach into groundwater and put nearby residents at risk. Extremely high concentrations of antibiotics have been found in dust in animal confinement houses.

Alternately, a more localized, organic/sustainable food system rejects these questionable practices and tends to promote biodiversity, not monoculture—monoculture is the cultivation of one crop, which, among other issues, lacks the diversity required for ecological balance, requires significantly more chemicals, and degrades soil. According to Michael Pollan, journalist, activist, and author of many books about people's relationship to the natural world, "I still feel that the great evil of American agriculture is monoculture."[1]

Biodiverse farming is also called polyculture. With increased biodiversity comes increased variety—not only of crops, but also soil organisms, which many claim makes for more nutrient-rich food, but the research is said to be tenuous.

The debate about whether organically grown, chemical-free food is more nutrient-dense rages on, but the established dangers of the use of pesticides is enough of a reason to eat foods raised without these chemicals. (For more information, see the subchapter within this chapter, *What This Means for You*.)

While some studies have shown that there's negligible difference in nutrient content, one key difference is antioxidant content.[2,3] Antioxidants fight free radical damage and are an important consideration in immune health.[4] Other studies have shown that crops grown organically/sustainably do contain higher levels of several nutrients, including Vitamin C, iron, magnesium, and phosphorus.[5]

Natural medicine pioneer, Dr. Joseph Mercola, states, "Healthy soils contain a huge diversity of microorganisms, and it is these organisms that are responsible for the plant's nutrient uptake, health, and the stability of the entire ecosystem. The wide-scale adoption of industrial agriculture practices has decimated soil microbes responsible for transferring these minerals to the plants.

"In 2009, the American Association for the Advancement of Science featured a presentation on soil health and its impact on food quality, concluding that healthy soil indeed leads to higher levels of nutrients in crops. Agricultural chemicals destroy the health of the soil by killing off its microbial inhabitants, which is one of the primary problems with modern farming, and the reason why the nutritional quality of conventionally-grown foods is deteriorating."

Lest we get bogged down in all of the reasons why an industrial food system is bad, let's talk about one of the benefits of soil diversity and nutrient content—taste. After all, isn't this where the enjoyment of eating comes from?

Dr. Mercola continues, "One of the primary reasons food doesn't taste as good as it used to is also related to the deterioration of mineral content. The minerals actually form the compounds that give the fruit or vegetable its flavor. All of these issues go back to the health of the soil in which the food is grown."[6]

The above statement is of particular concern to those with hypothyroidism, as minerals play a critical role in thyroid health. In the chapter, *The Nutritional Heavy Hitters* and the subsequent sections highlighting the key nutrients we've identified for this cookbook, you'll see that minerals get a spotlight; their role in thyroid health—and immune function—is outlined in detail.

According to Dr. Richard Shames, author of *Thyroid Power*, "More important than vitamins are minerals. These are absolutely crucial to thyroid function."[7] Naturopath and nutritionist, Dr. Carolyn Dean, states, "Minerals play a huge part in the rehabilitation of our hormones. In my experience, most low thyroid conditions are caused by mineral deficiency."[8]

Lastly, an analysis in March 2016 of the difference between conventional and organic meat showed that the nutrient quality was indeed different, with organic meat having more anti-inflammatory Omega-3 fatty acids.[9] This was corroborated by other researchers.[10]

In short, no matter what your health status, Lisa and I believe that food that's produced in a time-honored fashion and manner that's respectful to the earth is more health- and energy-giving than foods produced in a manner that goes against nature. Our views are an additional foundation upon which this cookbook was created.

Both/And: Organic and Sustainable Farming

Being the farm huggers and sustainable agriculture junkies that Lisa and I are, it's important for us to highlight the benefits of sustainable and organic farming and to also differentiate between "sustainable" and "organic"—a point of confusion for many.

Sustainable agriculture can be organic and organic agriculture can be sustainable, but there are some key differences that deserve an explanation. "Organic" typically means USDA organic certified. According to the USDA website, "Organic agriculture produces products using methods that preserve the environment and avoid most synthetic materials, such as pesticides and antibiotics." (Note the word, *most*.)

Up until about 15 years ago, conscious consumers had one primary label to check if they wanted to ensure the food they were buying was acceptable: organic. Until recently, USDA's organic certification has been considered the gold standard. It's the most recognizable and gleans much credibility, even if many consumers can't explicitly state what the label means. According to the National Organic Program, two thirds of Americans are confused about what organic really stands for.

Still, a food label could simply say "organically grown" versus "USDA certified organic." Not having the certification isn't necessarily a bad thing—many food producers grow food in a time-honored manner that's chemical-free and respectful to the laws of nature, but don't have the official USDA certification. These growers are often "beyond organic"—the criteria they set for themselves and their operations go beyond what USDA requires for organic certification.

Certification is a laborious, expensive process that many small- to medium-scale growers don't opt for or cannot afford. Additionally, some farmers who previously farmed conventionally and are now farming "organically" are in a three-year organic certification transition, in which case they often say, "organically grown." According to the Rodale Institute, "This 'transition effect' has been attributed to time required for necessary changes in chemical, physical, and biological properties of soil, which may take more than one year."[1]

"Sustainable" can be difficult to define and many say it's a moving target and a dynamic concept, as our world isn't static. When I worked at Food Alliance, we spent days—yes, days—at a work retreat crafting our unique definition of "sustainable agriculture."

The frequently quoted definition of sustainable is, "Development that meets the needs of the present without compromising the ability of future generations to meet their own needs." Another definition reflects many organizations' triple bottom line: "Sustainability is about actions that are ecologically sound, economically viable, and socially just and humane." In general, characteristics of "sustainable" are: holistic, place-based, long-term in focus, collaborative and inclusive, and practical and results-oriented.

Many feel that USDA organic standards aren't adequately inclusive or thorough enough and that sustainable farming practices are "beyond organic." For example, at Food Alliance, some of the criteria for meeting certification are:

- Provide safe and fair working conditions

- Treat animals humanely

- Practice integrated pest management (IPM) to minimize pesticide use and toxicity

- Conserve soil and water resources

- Protect biodiversity and wildlife habitat

- Reduce and recycle waste

- Show continual improvement practices

Today, the USDA organic certification program has come to adopt some of these same criteria, such as the preservation of natural resources and biodiversity and animal health and welfare.

According to George Mateljan, creator of The World's Healthiest Foods website, "Sustainable agriculture is a wider topic than organic farming. The way food is processed, packaged, and transported may pose a threat to the environment, even when the food was cultivated organically. For example, pretzels may be organic—meaning 95 percent of their ingredients are organically grown—but have been produced from highly refined flour processed using energy-wasting machinery, packaged in non-recyclable plastic, and shipped around the world using large amounts of fossil fuel. Growing foods organically is, therefore, only the first step in achieving sustainable agriculture. Most environmentalists and ecologists and many individuals involved in the production of organic foods believe that sustainable agriculture is necessary if we are to reach the long-term goals of personal health and ecological balance."[2]

"Sustainably-grown" is often considered "beyond organic" to many in the health/nutrition/farming profession and for this reason, Lisa and I feel that "sustainable" is a more powerful and inclusive descriptor. Still, it's imperative to ask questions about what "sustainable" really means to that farm or ranch—either by asking them directly or asking the purveyor of that product. Again, there isn't a single, go-to definition for "sustainable food" or "sustainably-grown."

Largely because of the criteria outlined above—criteria that go beyond simply the exclusion of pesticides and hormones—awareness of and interest in food issues is at an all time high. Consumers are deliberately searching for products that offer a safe and sound alternative to conventionally-raised and genetically modified foods, which may be undesirable from both a health and environmental standpoint, and they're also concerned about how farm workers and animals are treated, wildlife habitat, and how the farm or ranch conserves resources and recycles.

There's currently a big shift in consumer interest toward companies, brands, and products that embody value**s** vs. value. Value is often associated with conventionally-raised

> 66 Awareness of and interest in food issues is at an all time high."

food: price, taste, and convenience. Value**s**, on the other hand, represent how consumers feel about the product, but also how they want to feel about themselves. Value**s** include: community, stewardship, health, honesty, integrity, and authenticity. These value**s** are what make authentic eco-labeling meaningful.

With eco-labeling, the key is third party certification, where an independent, neutral, third party entity has exhaustively inspected the operation, based on predefined criteria. Some examples of authentic third party labels are: Non-GMO Project, American Grassfed Association, Animal Welfare Approved, Fair Trade Certified, Food Alliance Certified, Demeter Certified Biodynamic, Certified Humane, Bird Friendly, Marine Stewardship Council Certified, Rainforest Alliance Certified, Salmon-Safe, and USDA Certified Organic. (See Appendix D for an eco-label reading guide and resources for sustainable and organic foods.)

Lisa and I are abundantly aware that it's not feasible for everyone to eat all organic/sustainable all the time. But we're encouraged that organic/sustainable options are becoming more readily available every day as consumers demand better access to higher quality food. (See Appendix F for a guide on getting organic and sustainably-grown foods more affordably and how to prioritize foods based on their pesticide load.)

What This Means for You

The benefits of eating a chemical-free diet—whether it's "organic" or simply "sustainably-grown"—are vast and far-reaching; it's certainly beyond the scope of this book. But we'd like to take two of the points raised above—pesticide use/toxicity and personal health—and briefly highlight what they mean for the thyroid and immune system.

One of the primary reasons that environmental chemicals, including pesticides, are so impactful to our endocrine/hormonal system is that many of them interfere with thyroid hormone metabolism. According to thyroid expert, Dr. Richard Shames, "The number of hormone disruptors is astounding. Worldwide, this problem seems mainly due to pesticides (herbicides, fungicides, insecticides, nematicides) constantly being released into the environment."[1]

Internationally recognized leader, speaker, and educator, Dr. Mark Hyman, states, "One of the most important factors that lead to hypothyroidism is exposure to environmental toxins, such as pesticides, which act as hormone or endocrine disruptors and interfere with thyroid hormone metabolism and function. In fact, one study found that as people lost weight they released pesticides from their fat tissue. These pesticides then interfere with thyroid function and cause hypothyroidism."[2]

> 66 One of the primary reasons that environmental chemicals, including pesticides, are so impactful to our endocrine/ hormonal system is that many of them interfere with thyroid hormone metabolism."

He continues, ". . . as you lose weight, fat tissue releases stored toxins such as PCBs and pesticides (organochlorines). These toxins lower your T3 levels, consequently slowing your resting metabolic rate and inhibiting your fat-burning ability."[3]

The list of pesticides commonly administered to crops is dizzying, but methyl iodide, for example, is a known carcinogen and neurotoxin and the EPA sees no harm in using it, even though it's been associated with thyroid abnormalities.[4,5]

A study published in the American Journal of Epidemiology found that women exposed to the pesticides aldrin, DDT, and lindane were at much greater risk of developing thyroid disease.[6]

Pesticides also interfere with thyroid hormone conversion—they interrupt the body's ability to convert T4 into T3. (For more information, see the chapter, *Optimizing Thyroid Hormone Conversion*.) One of the issues with taking thyroid hormone replacement, while often warranted, is that some are unable to convert the T4 in those meds into T3, the active form of thyroid hormone. Dr. Hyman states, "Since 100 percent of us have pesticides stored in our bodies, we will all likely have some problem with [thyroid hormone replacement]."[3]

Pesticides are also considered xenoestrogens, which are synthetic compounds that mimic estrogen. Xeno means "foreign" or "outside the body." Among other things, exposure to xenoestrogens sets the stage for an increasingly common condition known as estrogen dominance. Estrogen dominance is a bit of a loose term and doesn't always mean that there's excess estrogen—for women, you can be estrogen dominant simply by virtue of having too little progesterone.

An important consideration is the link between excess estrogen and hypothyroidism.[7] Discussion of estrogen dominance is typically geared towards women, but men aren't unaffected and it often shows up as aggression, decreased sex drive, or male breasts.

Yet another significant source of pesticides, aside from food, is exposure from toxic lawn care chemicals, which are often tracked into homes from our shoes.

Additionally, pesticides contain bromine, a well-known endocrine disruptor. Bromine is a halide that competes for the same thyroid gland receptors that uptake iodine, which inhibits thyroid hormone production and can result in hypothyroidism.[8] (For more on iodine, see the *Minerals* subchapter in the chapter, *The Nutritional Heavy Hitters* and for a list of bromine sources, including suggestions for secreting bromines, see *The Essential Thyroid Cookbook Lifestyle Companion Guide*, which you can download for free on our website: www.thyroidcookbook.com/companion.)

While pesticides are clearly a concern for thyroid health, it's also important to consider the synthetic hormones and antibiotics administered to livestock, which we ingest when we eat the meat and dairy from these animals. For example, there's evidence that bovine growth hormone (rBGH) is specifically associated with thyroid cysts.[9] It's even mentioned on the U.S. Food and Drug Administration's website.[10]

In a general sense, it's not difficult to understand how these artificial hormones, including steroids, could have a far-reaching impact on our entire endocrine system, even though many conventional food production folks would like us to believe that they're perfectly safe. The vast majority of feedlot animals are given steroidal hormone implants to foster faster growth—they're the same androgens that athletes take. And we're supposed to believe that they have no affect on us?

Likewise, are we to believe that pesticides, synthetic hormones, and antibiotics have no affect on our immune system?

The link between pesticides and the immune system is solid. Remember, pesticides are xenoestrogens. Dr. Susan Blum, author of *The Immune System Recovery Plan*, states, "You need to know about [xenoestrogens] because they play a role in the development of autoimmune diseases. A group of researchers from the University of Milan conducted a review of all the studies looking at the role of environmental estrogens and autoimmunity. Over and over, they found a positive association between exposure to different agricultural chemical pesticides and [autoimmune diseases].[11]

"We know that estrogen affects the immune system, because all immune cells have estrogen receptors and these hormones also encourage your immune cells to begin to make too many antibodies. The role of estrogens in autoimmune diseases has been well studied."[12]

> 66 Consuming antibiotics in our diet is a specific concern for those with autoimmunity."

It's irrefutable that pesticides are chemicals. But there's a significant effort being put forth to convince us that they're not *harmful* chemicals. Lisa and I don't believe that every bite of food that passes your lips needs to be organic and as they say, "The dose makes the poison." But know that "a little here, a little there" can increase your toxic body burden.

Dr. Blum continues, ". . . every chemical you are exposed to adds to your toxic load. Having a high toxic load makes it harder for your liver to handle pesticides and environmental estrogens, toxins that we know will affect your immune system."[12]

One of the biggest concerns with subtherapeutic antibiotic use with feedlot animals is that it's contributing to antibiotic resistance—something we should all be worried about, as it's considered "a major public health threat."[13, 14] The CDC states, "Antibiotics must be used judiciously in humans and animals because both uses contribute to the emergence, persistence, and spread of resistant bacteria. Resistant bacteria in food-producing animals are of particular concern."[15]

Consuming antibiotics in our diet is also a specific concern for those with autoimmunity. While not the same dose or intensity as a 10-day round of antibiotics administered for an infection, ingestion of antibiotics in meat and dairy is a consideration for the health of our digestive tract because no matter how you get them, antibiotics take the good with the bad. Sure, they'll wipe out an infection, but they'll also wipe our your good bacteria—bacteria critical for a healthy digestive system. And when you consider that 70-80 percent of our immune system is in our digestive tract, it's difficult to ignore what antibiotics in our food supply may be doing to cause or exacerbate autoimmunity by way of disruption of our microbiome—our 100 trillion organism-strong "mini ecosystem."[16, 17]

Less is known about the link between synthetic hormones in conventional meat and dairy and the immune system, but research has suggested other possible negative health effects of these additives. Still, you are what you eat and you are what you eat eats. If animals are subjected to these chemicals, then so too are we if we eat their meat and dairy products. Any chemical circulating in your body is going to contribute to your overall toxic load and thus, affect your immune system. (See *The Essential Thyroid Cookbook Lifestyle Companion Guide* for tips on supporting liver function and reducing your toxic body burden. You can download it for free on our website: www.thyroidcookbook.com/companion.)

PART ONE:

Essential Thyroid Nutrition

ABOUT THE THYROID

The thyroid is a butterfly-shaped gland in your neck below your Adam's apple and is hailed as "the master gland" of our complex and interdependent endocrine (hormonal) system. It's the spoon that stirs our hormonal soup. It produces several hormones, with tri-iodothyronine (T3) and thyroxine (T4) being the most critical to our health.

Given that our endocrine system is responsible for growth, reproduction, energy, and repair and the thyroid is "the master gland" of this complex and interdependent system, an underfunctioning thyroid can have profound implications for the whole body.

Our Western/conventional medical model tends to isolate organs, glands, and body parts, when in fact, most of our body's systems are designed to work in harmony with one another. When the thyroid is under-functioning, many doctors are quick to prescribe thyroid hormone replacement or iodine supplementation without consideration for immune, adrenal, or estrogen status—all have implications for thyroid function. Concurrently, optimizing thyroid status can have a positive effect on these other systems.

The thyroid's job is to absorb iodine and combine it with the amino acid tyrosine. It then converts this iodine/tyrosine combination into T3 and T4. The thyroid produces some T3, the active form of thyroid hormone ("the big daddy"), but the majority is produced by the mostly inactive T4 ("the lame duck") by a process called T4/T3 conversion.

Simply put, T3 is the most *metabolically active* and has the greatest impact on our health and wellbeing. It's responsible for optimizing memory and brain function, keeping our bowels moving, hair growth, and keeping us thin and fertile, to name a few. Because the thyroid produces only about 7 percent T3, and T3 is how the body most benefits from what the thyroid should provide us, anything

> " The thyroid is the spoon that stirs our hormonal soup."

that inhibits the T4/T3 conversion should be examined. (Also see the chapter, *Optimizing Thyroid Hormone Conversion*.)

Thyroid hormones transport oxygen into your cells and are critical for energy production. Every cell in the body has receptors for thyroid hormone and the thyroid is a master toggle that flips on the genes that keep cells doing their jobs. It's the boss of our metabolism and an underactive thyroid can affect weight, mental health, and heart disease risk. Thyroid hormones affect our health systemically and directly act on the brain, gastrointestinal tract, cardiovascular system, bone metabolism, red blood cell metabolism, gallbladder and liver function, steroid hormone production, glucose metabolism, protein metabolism, neuromuscular function, digestion, and body temperature regulation.

In the U.S. alone, it's estimated that 53 million people have an autoimmune disease. According to Dr. Aviva Romm, 30 million women have Hashimoto's (autoimmune hypothyroidism—the most common form of autoimmunity). Experts in the functional medicine community claim that most with hypothyroidism are undiagnosed—it's estimated that there are 60 million with low thyroid function. It's also estimated that 97 percent of those with hypothyroidism have Hashimoto's, in which case we may be looking at 58 million with Hashimoto's. As you can see, this number is higher than the estimates for the total number of people with autoimmunity in the U.S.

*Hyper*thyroidism, or overactive thyroid, is much less common, although Graves' disease (autoimmune hyperthyroidism) is on the rise.

Symptoms of hypothyroidism include weight gain, the inability to lose weight despite your best efforts, brain fog, fatigue (including pronounced morning fatigue), constipation, dry and brittle fingernails, depression, low body temperature, low stamina, lack of motivation, sleep disturbances, difficulty concentrating, hoarseness upon waking, edema (fluid retention, including puffy face), hair loss (including thinning of outer eyebrows), infertility, irregular menstrual cycles, joint aches, poor ankle reflexes, high cholesterol, and light sensitivity. Lesser known symptoms include yellowing of palms and soles of the feet, hives, psoriasis, premature aging, premature greying of the hair, and muscle spasms.

Hypothyroidism is a grey area, but conventional/Western doctors tend to think in black and white—you have hypothyroidism or you don't, sort of like being pregnant. You can't be a little bit pregnant, but you can be a little bit hypothyroid, and it can have a significant impact on the quality of your life. Yet many doctors don't see it that way. This is why hypothyroidism and Hashimoto's have been called "the silent epidemic."

Too often, hypothyroid patients seeking answers from the conventional medical model continue to suffer with symptoms that aren't traced to a sluggish thyroid. If you're blue or feeling unmotivated, you may be prescribed an antidepressant. If you're constipated, you're told to take a laxative. If you're having difficulty sleeping, you're given a sleeping aid. If you're overweight and having trouble shedding pounds, you're instructed to work harder at the gym or consume fewer calories; both can exact a greater toll on this sensitive gland, including the adrenal glands, which play a significant role in thyroid function.

These myriad instructions may offer some relief, but if the root cause of these issues is an underactive thyroid and it remains undiagnosed, then symptoms, frustration, and feeling like you're not living up to your potential can persist indefinitely.

Hypothyroidism remains undiagnosed two ways:

1. Despite symptoms pointing to an under-functioning thyroid, the thyroid is never considered suspect.

2. Lab testing is limited.

The testing can be limited in two ways:

1. Doctors operate under the conventional medical conviction that hypothyroidism can be diagnosed via one blood test and one blood test only, thyroid stimulating hormone (TSH), a pituitary hormone that tells the thyroid to do its job.

2. Many doctors (endocrinologists included) utilize outdated blood lab reference ranges.

This type of thyroid "treatment" leaves many underdiagnosed. Dr. Mark Hyman states, "You may be told you have borderline thyroid problems or sub-clinical thyroid disease and your doctor will watch it. What will he or she watch for? For you to get really sick?"[1]

These archaic practices cast aside a vast group of people who have subclinical hypothyroidism that can trigger a bevy of symptoms, yet cause only slight changes in blood labs, primarily those tests that many doctors never run. The antibodies that show the presence of Hashimoto's, thyroid peroxidase antibody (TPOAb) and thyroglobulin antibody (TgAb), happen to be on the list of thyroid labs infrequently performed.

As the saying goes, "Don't guess, test." It's important to do the right tests and to evaluate your labs based on the *functional* reference ranges, not outdated ranges that often lead to misdiagnosis, mistreatment (like antidepressants or anti-anxiety drugs), and the passage of time with continued suffering.

Regarding the evaluation of TSH as a sole indicator of thyroid health, hormone expert, Dr. Aviva Romm states, "In a world where medical over-testing is rampant, I have to say, I find myself confounded by the fact that so many physicians are resistant to ordering anything but a TSH—or thyroid simulating test—as the first form of evaluation, when from a scientific and medical standpoint, that test can be normal and there can still be a low functioning thyroid. It's outdated medical dogma to order solely this test.

"Most of us, whether as doctors or patients, have been led to believe that medical guidelines and practices are pretty much set in stone, and are based on hard reliable facts. The former is definitely not true, in fact, in just the past five years or so, it's been found that many long-followed medical guidelines aren't correct. It has been found that sometimes, doing tests or interpreting them inappropriately can even lead to harm.

"On top of this, medical guidelines, while based on hard data, are only as good as the data they are based on, and on what's known at the time the guidelines are made. So for example, the TSH lab values for normal are based on TSH averages for most generally healthy Americans. But many Americans are under-diagnosed for thyroid disease. When we take an expanded view of thyroid health, and only include the TSH average of people with absolutely no hypothyroid symptoms, the number changes."[2]

A functional or integrative medicine doctor or naturopath will typically run the whole gamut of thyroid tests for you, without you having to cajole.

Below are what I feel are the most clinically relevant thyroid tests. Many in the functional medicine community, including Dr. Romm, recommend this set of labs:

Lab:	Functional reference range:
Free T3 (FT3) [a]	3.2 - 4.2 pg/mL
Free T4 (FT4)	1.1 - 1.8 ng/dL
Reverse T3 (RT3) [b]	90 - 350 pg/mL or < 10:1 ratio RT3:FT3
Thyroid stimulating hormone (TSH) [c]	0.9 - 2.0 mU/L
Thyroid peroxidase antibody (TPOAb) [d]	< 4 or negative
Thyroglobulin antibody (TgAb) [d]	< 4 or negative

[a] T3 is "the big daddy" of thyroid hormones and the most metabolically active, affecting almost every physiological process. The "free" in front of T3 (and T4) tells you what's available and unbound and therefore usable by the body.

[b] Reverse T3 is just that—the "reverse" of T3. It blocks thyroid receptors and can cause patients to be unresponsive or resistant to T3. When the body is in conservation mode due to stress, including fatigue, nutritional deficiencies, or infection, it will reroute thyroid hormones. You want RT3 low, and high RT3 is often brought about by intense or

prolonged periods of stress. RT3 is typically high in people with more advanced adrenal dysfunction (aka HPA (hypo-thalamic-pituitary-adrenal) axis dysfunction). Some in the medical community question the validity of this test, but I feel it's worthwhile, given that many functional medicine doctors continue to recommend it. You can see that there are two metrics in the chart above for RT3; while RT3 alone is an indicator of thyroid hormone resistance, calculating your RT3: FT3 ratio can also provide information on thyroid status. Go to www.stopthethyroidmadness.com/rt3-ratio/ to calculate your RT3:FT3 ratio.

[c] According to many in the functional medicine community, anyone with TSH over 2.0 is hypothyroid, although TSH is an overall poor marker of thyroid function and should always be taken in the context of other thyroid labs, especially given that TSH can be normal in the face of low thyroid hormone production, poor T4/T3 conversion, or cellular thyroid hormone resistance.

[d] It's estimated that a whopping 97 percent of people with hypothyroidism have autoimmune hypothyroidism (Hashimoto's). In 2008, when I began my journey, I learned that antibodies should be less than 30. Several experts I respect now say they should be less than 4, meaning anything greater than 4 indicates Hashimoto's.

Know that thyroid antibody tests aren't perfect. According to thyroid expert, Dr. Alan Christianson, "Over 40 percent [of those with] Hashimoto's may never have positive antibody tests. Negative antibody tests do not rule out Hashimoto's. In many cases, it only shows up on the ultrasound."[3] Conversely, often TSH, Free T3, and Free T4 are normal in the face of elevated antibodies.

Ultrasounds are often performed in the face of hypothyroid symptoms and low or negative antibodies labs. If you suspect Hashimoto's and your antibodies labs don't reveal Hashimoto's, test again in two to three months, or ask for an ultrasound.

Additionally, to keep tabs on yourself without getting labs done too frequently, you can opt for a simple, at-home basal body temperature test. While some experts feel this test isn't a true reflection of thyroid function, many I respect still recommend it. (See *The Essential Thyroid Cookbook Lifestyle Companion Guide* for instructions. You can download it for free on our website: www.thyroidcookbook.com/companion.)

What Causes Hypothyroidism?

There are many theories about the roots of hypothyroidism and Hashimoto's, all of which can contribute to the thyroid not functioning well and to the exacerbation of symptoms. In most cases, it's a combination of these influences.

Many doctors, both allopathic/Western and functional/integrative, claim that hypothyroidism is caused by iodine deficiency, but a lack of iodine tells a small part of the story. (For more on iodine, see the *Minerals* subchapter in the chapter, *The Nutritional Heavy Hitters*.)

Dr. Amy Myers, a respected leader in functional medicine, states, "Though thyroid disease is generally considered idiopathic (of unknown cause) by most conventional doctors, in functional medicine we believe that one or a combination of these factors are to blame: heavy metal (mercury) toxicity, iodine deficiency, and food sensitivities, particularly to gluten."[1] (See the chapter,

Elimination Provocation Diet Instructions for more on sleuthing out food sensitivities and the chapter, *Gluten and Your Thyroid* for more on the thyroid/gluten relationship.)

Other possible causes of hypothyroidism include (this is not an exhaustive list):

- Nutritional deficiencies

- Adrenal dysfunction/HPA axis dysfunction (See *The Essential Thyroid Cookbook Lifestyle Companion Guide* for our Restore Your Adrenals guide. You can download it for free on our website: www.thyroidcookbook.com/companion.)

- Exposure to environmental toxins such as pesticides and plastics

- Heavy metal toxicity—beyond mercury, lead, arsenic, and cadmium can also be problematic

- Unrelenting stress

- Other hormonal imbalances, such as estrogen dominance

- Genetic propensity (See the chapter, *The Basics of Mitigating the Autoimmune Response* for more on epigenetics, or how we can influence gene expression.)

- Pregnancy and delivery

- Leaky gut/irritable bowel syndrome

- A virus, like Epstein-Barr

- Oxidative stress

- Systemic, cellular inflammation

When you stack a few of these on top of one another, it's a recipe for hypothyroidism—and Hashimoto's. (See the chapter, *The Autoimmune Epidemic* for more information on factors leading to autoimmunity, of which many are mentioned in the list above.)

Hashimoto's thyroiditis is the most common autoimmune disorder in the U.S. Studies show that at least 90 percent of hypothyroid sufferers have impaired thyroid function due to autoimmune antibodies to their thyroid—Hashimoto's. Again, some claims are as high as 97 percent. But many with low thyroid function have never been tested for a possible autoimmune factor. Why? Because many doctors reckon, "If I can't write a prescription, why test for it?" Many will say, "If you have Hashimoto's, my treatment plan won't change."

This is not okay. Just because many doctors don't know how to treat autoimmune conditions doesn't mean that you

> " Many with low thyroid function have never been tested for a possible autoimmune factor."

don't deserve to know if you have one. Letting autoimmunity run rampant is inviting trouble. Any autoimmune condition that goes unaddressed can lead to other issues (MAS—multiple autoimmune syndrome) and thus, lower quality of life. Once you have one auto immune condition, other systems of the body are up for grabs. Studies have shown that those with autoimmune disease have a greater than 50 percent chance of developing another.[2]

It's not uncommon to experience an autoimmune cascade, such as Celiac, then Hashimoto's. Or alopecia, then Hashimoto's. Or Raynaud's, then MS, for example. I also see a lot of autoimmune skin conditions alongside Hashimoto's, like rosacea and psoriasis.

And here's a kicker—Hashimoto's and Graves' can exist concurrently (yes, autoimmune *hypo*thyroidism and autoimmune *hyper*thyroidism), both of which fall under the umbrella of autoimmune thyroid disease (AITD). In these cases, people present with Hashimoto's antibodies (TPOAb and/or TgAb) as well as Graves' antibodies (TSI). They typically fluctuate between the two conditions, in which case symptoms can be all over the map.

In other words, once one autoimmune condition has taken residence, the permutations can be far-reaching.

To manage autoimmune thyroid disease, or any autoimmune condition, it's imperative to get to the root issue—an overactive, hypervigilant immune system—not to simply suppress symptoms with medication. I'm not categorically against thyroid hormone replacement, but it's often a faulty strategy that allows the immune dysregulation and tissue damage to rage on. In the case of

> 66 Studies have shown that those with autoimmune disease have a greater than 50 percent chance of developing another."

Hashimoto's, it can further harm thyroid tissue. While you're replacing thyroid hormones, the immune response against the thyroid gland continues, in which case many get their thyroid drug doses increased repeatedly over time because they continue to be symptomatic—and symptoms often increase in intensity.

Many doctors, if they even know what Hashimoto's is and will test for it, will tell you it's a lifelong condition with no treatment options other than Synthroid, the most popular thyroid hormone replacement. I'm proof (as are many, including my clients and students) that Hashimoto's is manageable without thyroid drugs.

According to Chris Kresser, a globally recognized leader in the field of functional and integrative medicine, "The obvious shortcoming of [thyroid hormone replacement] is that it doesn't address the underlying cause of the problem, which is the immune system attacking the thyroid gland. And if the underlying cause isn't addressed,

> 66 Thyroid hormone replacement, of which there are many types, has its place. But it's not a cure for Hashimoto's."

the treatment isn't going to work very well—or for very long. If you're in a leaky rowboat, bailing water will only get you so far. If you want to stop the boat from sinking, you've got to plug the leaks. Extending this metaphor to Hashimoto's disease, thyroid hormones are like bailing water. They may be a necessary part of the treatment. But unless the immune dysregulation is addressed (plugging the leaks), whoever is in that boat will be fighting a losing battle to keep it from sinking."[3]

Thyroid hormone replacement, of which there are many types, has its place. But it's not a cure for Hashimoto's. If the underlying autoimmune component goes unattended to, you're barking up the wrong tree and could end up with years of frustration and all of the distress and fatigue associated with chasing symptoms.

But *don't change your dose or stop taking your prescription based on what you're reading here.* It's critical to work with your doctor on any changes to your prescriptions.

We Are the 3 Percent— Non-Autoimmune Hypothyroidism

What about the estimated 3 percent of those with non-autoimmune hypothyroidism—low thyroid function without the autoimmunity? According to Chris Kresser, respected functional medicine leader, "Non-autoimmune hypothyroidism is not an immune-mediated problem. It's a problem with the thyroid itself and is often caused by an iodine deficiency or excess bromine exposure. Bromine binds to iodine receptors and blocks the uptake and utilization of iodine. Even if you're getting enough iodine, which most of us aren't, you can't use it."[1] It's called the Bromine Dominance Theory.

Bromine is a toxic halogen found in brominated fire retardants (found in some carpet padding, mattresses, and electronics), pesticides and insecticides, soft drinks (especially Mountain Dew), and baked goods. Go organic, shop for non-brominated products (especially mattresses[2]—one of the worst offenders, given that we spend a third of our lives in bed), trade your soft drink for mineral water with a little fruit juice, and steer clear of commercial bakery products, which is easy when you're gluten-free. (See *The Essential Thyroid Cookbook Lifestyle Companion Guide* for a list of bromine sources, including suggestions for secreting bromines. You can download it for free on our website: www.thyroidcookbook.com/companion.)

This percentage of non-autoimmune hypothyroidism cases applies to the U.S.; worldwide, the most common cause of hypothyroidism is, in fact, iodine deficiency. Before the relatively recent findings that the majority of cases of hypothyroidism in the U.S. are Hashimoto's, it was common practice, and still is in many clinics, both allopathic and integrative/functional, to treat hypothyroidism with supplemental iodine. It was thought that anyone who has an underactive thyroid, Hashimoto's or not, is deficient in this trace mineral.

Yet many have complained that they don't tolerate supplemental iodine. Now we know why. Too much iodine is as bad as too little, as over-supplementation has been shown to over-stimulate the thyroid for some. (For more on iodine, see the *Minerals* subchapter in the chapter, *The Nutritional Heavy Hitters*.)

The Role of Nutrition in Thyroid Function

Eating carefully and mindfully is one of the best ways to support the thyroid. As we approach life's transitions, especially a period of prolonged or pronounced stress, pregnancy and delivery, or peri/menopause, it's critical to be intentional about how the foods we eat can help or hinder how our thyroid functions.

Focusing on whole foods should always be the initial step in managing hypothyroidism and Hashimoto's. These foods are minimally processed and contain naturally occurring vitamins, minerals, and phytonutrients that our bodies need for optimal health. A well-rounded, mostly organic/sustainably-raised, whole foods diet will support your whole endocrine system.

Whether you're on thyroid hormone replacement or not, addressing how and what you eat and also your lifestyle is critical to feeling better, regaining your energy,

firing up your metabolism, and promoting health and preventing disease. Often, a few changes can yield such significant results in a short time that people can't imagine going back to their old ways. The body is always looking for ways to balance and regulate itself and for the most part, is quick to respond to sound nutrition and being well cared for.

Thyroid expert, Dr. Mark Hyman, states, "The body requires certain raw materials to function optimally. This is certainly true in thyroid disease, where multiple nutrients are needed in various steps along the way, from the production of thyroid hormone and the conversion of the inactive form to the active form . . . to the action of thyroid hormone on the receptors on the nucleus of the cell, leading to gene transcription and increased metabolism."[1]

The standard American diet (SAD) that consists of what author Michael Pollan calls "edible foodlike substances"—processed foods, refined sugars, genetically modified foods, artificial additives and sweeteners,

> 66 Focusing on whole foods should always be the initial step in managing hypothyroidism and Hashimoto's."

" When you consider that every cell in the body has receptors for thyroid hormone and that the thyroid turns on the genes that keep cells doing their job, it's easy to understand how a nutrient-deficient diet can interrupt this cellular communication."

toxic vegetable oils, and antibiotic and hormone-laden animal products—cause oxidative stress and chronic systemic inflammation and affects how all of our cells communicate with one another.

When you consider that every cell in the body has receptors for thyroid hormone and that the thyroid turns on the genes that keep cells doing their job, it's easy to understand how a nutrient-deficient diet can interrupt this cellular communication.

The Thyroid/Digestion Connection

Most Americans need some level of gut repair. Digestive health is essential to thyroid health—an important step in taming Hashimoto's, or any autoimmunity, is to repair digestive function, especially considering that 70-80 percent of our immune system is housed in our gastrointestinal system.

The thyroid-gut association can be a negative feedback loop, as low thyroid function can cause impaired digestive health and poor

digestive health can exacerbate hypothyroidism and Hashimoto's. As long as you struggle with gut dysbiosis in the form of heartburn, bloating, indigestion, IBS (irritable bowel syndrome), leaky gut, gut infections like small intestine bacterial overgrowth (SIBO) or Helicobacter pylori (H. pylori), parasitic infections, or chronic constipation or diarrhea, it's unlikely (many experts say *impossible*) that you'll ever experience optimal thyroid function.

According to thyroid expert, Dr. Datis Kharrazian, "Studies show hypothyroidism can cause intestinal permeability, or 'leaky gut,' which allows undigested food into the bloodstream and instigates an immune attack."[1]

Dr. Mark Hyman states, "When the lining of the gut is inflamed, small fissures open between the tightly woven cells making up the gut walls. Known as leaky gut syndrome, these chinks in the gut's armor allow bacteria and partially digested food molecules to slip out into the bloodstream where they are considered foreign invaders. Once it spies a potential enemy, the body doesn't hold back. The immune system attacks full throttle."[2]

" The thyroid-gut association can be a negative feedback loop, as low thyroid function can cause impaired digestive health and poor digestive health can exacerbate hypothyroidism and Hashimoto's."

A whopping 20 percent of thyroid function depends on a sufficient supply of healthy gut bacteria to convert T4 to T3. (Also see the chapter, *Optimizing Thyroid Hormone Conversion*.)

Dr. Kharrazian continues, "When diets are poor and digestion falters, dysbiosis, an overabundance of bad bacteria, crowds out the beneficial bacteria, thus hampering the production of active thyroid hormone. Studies have also shown that bacterial gut infections reduce thyroid hormone levels, dull thyroid hormone receptor sites, increase the amount of inactive T3, decrease TSH, and promote autoimmune thyroid disorders."[1]

The starting place for digestive healing is an Elimination Provocation diet. (See the chapter, *Elimination Provocation Diet Instructions*.)

Gluten and Your Thyroid

What's the big deal about gluten and the thyroid? Many experts claim that none of us should be eating gluten and that you don't have to have Celiac disease for gluten to trigger digestive distress and autoimmune antibodies.

Celiac disease is an autoimmune condition that damages the lining of the small intestine and prevents it from absorbing parts of food, causing all kinds of unwanted symptoms, mostly digestive issues. For people with Celiac, eating gluten—which is the protein fraction of the grains wheat, barley, and rye, along with other less-popular grains like triticale and kamut—sets off an autoimmune reaction that causes damage to the small intestine.

It's not unusual to have more than one autoimmune condition (MAS—multiple

> 66 Hashimoto's sufferers have a distinct reason to completely abstain from gluten."

autoimmune syndrome) and studies have shown that many people who have Hashimoto's also have Celiac.[1] The treatment for Celiac? Complete abstinence from gluten.

Yet Hashimoto's sufferers also have a distinct reason to completely abstain from gluten. "Gluten shares a similar molecular structure to many of our own tissues, and this causes our body to mistakenly attack itself in a process known as molecular mimicry," notes autoimmunity expert, Dr. Amy Myers. "If you have a thyroid disorder I believe that by definition you also have a gluten sensitivity."[2]

Thyroid expert Chris Kresser concurs, stating, "Several studies show a strong link between [Hashimoto's] and gluten intolerance.[3, 4, 5] The link is so well-established that researchers suggest all people with [Hashimoto's] be screened for gluten intolerance, and vice versa.

"What explains the connection? It's a case of mistaken identity. The molecular structure of gliadin, the protein portion of gluten, closely resembles that of the thyroid gland. When gliadin breaches the protective barrier of the gut, and enters the bloodstream, the immune system tags it for destruction. These antibodies to gliadin also cause the body to attack thyroid tissue. This means if you have [Hashimoto's] and you eat foods containing gluten, your immune system will attack your thyroid."[6]

I tell my clients that I don't like a lot of black and white when it comes to food and nutrition. I don't take a hard line with many things, but this is one where I do. Moderation is not the key here because taking in even the smallest amount of gluten can fire up your thyroid antibodies. Most people feel remarkably better—often within a few days—by completely removing gluten from their diet.

Unfortunately, gluten is in many of our foods. You have to be vigilant about being gluten-free, as it's in many sauces, binders, additives, etc. By congressional directive, food labels now warn you what products contain ingredients to which you might be allergic or sensitive. Since 2004, Congress has insisted that the FDA require food manufacturers to state whether any ingredient in a packaged food comes from some of the most common foods that cause allergies or sensitivities, including dairy, eggs, nuts, wheat, and soybeans. When looking at an ingredient list, your eyes should go straight to the bottom of the list where it says, "Contains," to see if it says "wheat," knowing that there are other ingredients and less-common grains that have gluten in them, so you really have to be attentive.

To avoid cross-contamination, you also want to be careful of products that say that they were processed in the same facility with wheat and other gluten-containing grains. This is often listed on the packaging.

Going gluten-free can be a little overwhelming at first, but know that most of the time, you won't find gluten-containing additives in most foods at a health food store or a retail food co-op. Sure, they're going to have some foods that naturally contain wheat, rye, or barley but they do their due diligence and carry foods that don't contain cheap fillers and binders that you don't want. Additionally, the more you focus on whole, non-packaged foods, the less you have to worry about gluten hiding out.

More and more food companies and restaurants are becoming sensitive to those of us who don't eat gluten and it's much easier to be gluten-free now than it was even a couple of years ago. But still, a word of caution—many people are now gluten-free because they believe that gluten is bad or fattening or what have you and some in the restaurant industry have gotten lax about ensuring that what they're serving is, in fact, gluten-free. It's easy to assume that everyone who's asking doesn't really *need* to avoid gluten for their health, which can make eating out more difficult for people with Hashimoto's and Celiac. It's important to press the point with wait staff, making sure they know what foods were fried in the same fryers as gluten-containing foods or if the salad dressing truly is gluten-free.

In short, you'll never halt the destruction of your thyroid tissue if you continue to eat gluten. For Hashimoto's sufferers, it's vital to educate yourself on where gluten hides out and to become a label-reading sleuth. Eating gluten is never, ever a consideration for me because all I can think of is these little armed bandits launching an attack on my thyroid.

You can go to www.celiac.com for a complete list of gluten-containing foods, including surprising and hidden sources, but some of the common places that gluten hides out include: sauces, dressings, soups, and stews (thickened with flour); soy, teriyaki, and hoisin sauce (fermented with wheat); fried foods (cross-contaminated in the fryer); additives in processed and packaged foods; alcohol (beer, grain alcohol, malt beverages); and medications and supplements. You'll also want to read labels on your personal care products such as cosmetics, lotion, and shampoo. Other helpful websites include www.celiac.org, www.celiactravel.com, and www.ccliacsolution.com. (See the chapter, *Pantry Staples and Ingredients* for more on non-gluten grains and some of our favorite gluten-free products. You'll also find links to many of these products on our website: www.thyroidcookbook.com.)

Dairy and Your Thyroid

Many make the mistake of learning what I've outlined in the above section about gluten and think that going gluten-free will cure them. While some have managed their Hashimoto's simply by going gluten-free, these folks are the minority.

Many experts claim that some have a reaction to dairy (specifically the casein protein in dairy) similar to what those with Celiac experience when they eat gluten. It's said that dairy is a close second behind gluten as far as dietary triggers for Hashimoto's.

"There are several food proteins, such as casein in dairy, that have a similar molecular structure to gluten. Because of this molecular mimicry, when you eat dairy, your body can get confused and think you just ate a bowl of pasta and trigger an immune reaction," notes Dr. Amy Myers. "Fifty percent of people who are gluten intolerant are casein intolerant as well," she states.[1]

Many of my clients are dairy-sensitive. How do we know? I help walk thcm through "the gold standard" for identifying food sensitivities—an Elimination Provocation diet. (See the chapter, *Elimination Provocation Diet Instructions*.) But unlike gluten, I don't have a problem asking them to reintroduce dairy during their Provocation phase to see if there are any adverse symptoms. I believe that everyone with Hashimoto's should remain gluten-free in perpetuity, but I'm not so convinced that this should be the case with dairy, although I never recommend an overreliance on dairy, given the inflammatory nature of casein, and eat only minimal amounts myself.

I understand that one in two people may react to dairy similarly to gluten and that those are decent odds that dairy is a trouble-maker. But if you're one of the 50 percent that doesn't interpret dairy (casein) like gluten, then there's no reason to leave dairy out forever—it can likely be reintroduced and tolerated once again. I feel that if dairy shows up as a trigger during someone's Provocation phase, then yes, leave it out. But again, it's possible to heal that sensitivity for the half of the population that doesn't interpret casein like gluten.

If someone wants to remain gluten- and dairy-free for life, that's perfectly reasonable, even if it's a bit of a difficult row to hoe when not preparing your own food (social outings, when traveling, etc.). It's not impossible, and the ultimate goal with identifying food sensitivities is to heal them so that your diet isn't restrictive long-term.

Autoimmunity or no autoimmunity, dairy is one of the most prevalent food sensitivities, so Lisa and I have chosen to eliminate dairy products from this cookbook. (See the chapter, *Pantry Staples and Ingredients* for dairy alternatives and also see Lisa's homemade nut and seed milk recipes found in the *Nourishing Beverages* chapter.)

Optimizing Thyroid Hormone Conversion

If the body is to utilize thyroid hormones properly, the wheels that grease the T4 to T3 conversion need to be well oiled. Again, T4 is mostly inactive ("the lame duck") and is the forerunner to T3, the predominant and more active hormone ("the big daddy"). Conversion can become compromised due to:

- Mineral deficiencies, especially zinc, selenium, and iodine (For more on these minerals, see the *Minerals* subchapter in the chapter, *The Nutritional Heavy Hitters*.)

- Gut dysbiosis (An Elimination Provocation diet will largely address this; see the chapter, *Elimination Provocation Diet Instructions*.)

- Exposure to toxic halogens like fluoride, bromine, and chlorine *

- Inadequate beneficial gut bacteria—20 percent of T4/T3 conversion occurs in the presence of friendly gut bacteria (For more on probiotics, see the *Vitamins and Other Nutrients* subchapter in the chapter, *The Nutritional Heavy Hitters* and also Appendix B for our suggested supplements.)

- Impaired liver function—20 percent of conversion takes place in the liver *

- Yeast/candida *

- Heavy metal exposure, especially mercury *

- Radiation exposure

- Estrogen dominance

- The use of birth control pills

- Systemic inflammation (See the chapter, *The Basics of Mitigating the Autoimmune Response* for strategies for taming inflammation.)

- Low tyrosine, often due to inadequate protein intake (For more on tyrosine, see the *Vitamins and Other Nutrients* subchapter in the chapter, *The Nutritional Heavy Hitters*.)

- Certain pharmaceuticals

- High cortisol/adrenal dysfunction/HPA (hypothalamic-pituitary-adrenal) axis dysfunction *

*All of the factors in the list above should be considered for optimal thyroid hormone conversion and to go deeper, download *The Essential Thyroid Cookbook Lifestyle Companion Guide* for more information on:

- Bromine sources, including suggestions for secreting bromines

- The negative effects of fluoride on thyroid function

- Optimizing liver function

- Managing and cleansing systemic yeast/candida

- A holistic/biological dentistry guide

- Restoring optimal adrenal/HPA axis function

You can download the guide for free on our website: www.thyroidcookbook.com/companion.

WHY THIS IS NOT ANOTHER PALEO OR AIP COOKBOOK

If you've been tuned into the online communities related to thyroid health, Hashimoto's, and other autoimmune conditions, and perhaps read many of the same books and blogs that Lisa and I have, you've likely heard of—and likely tried—a Paleo (aka ancestral) or AIP (autoimmune protocol) diet. These diets help to heal the intestinal lining, which is critical for those with any manifestation of autoimmunity.

But we're guessing that at least some of you are beyond the initial diagnostic stage, have walked through immune modulation, and perhaps your Hashimoto's is managed. Maybe you've already embarked on a gut-healing program and diet and have identified your food sensitivities, which can cause the immune system to go rogue and create autoimmune antibodies. (The above is an oversimplification of immune modulation and doesn't necessarily include all of the approaches involved.) The point is, perhaps you simply need a cookbook to keep your thyroid and immune system supported for years to come.

While the entirety of this cookbook can't be all things to everyone, this cookbook is intended for . . . everyone—those just beginning their journey as well as seasoned veterans of autoimmunity management and digestive healing, and anyone in between.

Lisa and I have put a lot of thought into making this cookbook as appealing and helpful as possible. To that end, **many of our recipes are Paleo- and AIP-compliant or have Paleo and/or AIP adaptations**. But be sure to read this entire chapter to understand why we don't feel that a Paleo/AIP diet is the single solution for everyone, knowing that we fully understand its merits and effectiveness.

We created user-friendly icons to help you easily decipher which recipes will fit your needs at-a-glance and we provided sensible adaptations and modifications, where applicable, to fit the dietary practices of Paleo, AIP, and vegan and also recipes acceptable for an Elimination Provocation diet. In most cases, the adaptation may include simply omitting an ingredient or making a simple ingredient swap to make it compliant. You'll find our *Guide to the Essential Thyroid Recipes*, explaining each icon, at the beginning of Part Three.

One of the reasons that Lisa and I chose to be outliers is that there are currently more AIP cookbooks out there than you can shake a stick at, and for good reason. And in my work with hundreds of Hashimoto's clients and students, no one has ever said, "I want to be on the AIP diet for the rest of my life. I'm fine being on a restricted diet forever." Many people say that they'll "do what it takes" to get relief and to get their lives back, but getting Hashimoto's managed doesn't take years of dietary restrictions.

That level and duration of restriction isn't necessary. Even many AIP experts and proponents agree that AIP isn't a "forever diet."

In short, Lisa and I chose to take the *long view* with this cookbook—we want it to be a cookbook for the ages. We want it to be what you reach for no matter where you are in your journey and to feel confident that your thyroid and immune system will be well supported for a lifetime.

To further explain my position on Paleo/AIP:

- Most of the research on the benefits of a Paleo diet was done on men—it missed half the population.

- For those at the initial stages of their journey, I see merit in the Paleo and AIP diets right out the chute—in some circumstances. I explain below.

- I'm wholeheartedly skeptical of removing whole food groups from the diet.

Again, many of the recipes in this cookbook are Paleo- and AIP-compliant, but it wasn't our intention to make them so—we simply focused on the most dense thyroid- and immune-supportive nutrients and ingredients.

There are varying twists to these diets, but generally, with a Paleo diet, you're eating what is believed to be the foods that our ancient ancestors ate, as in, what they foraged for: meat (grass-based/pastured), fish, vegetables, fruits, nuts, seeds, herbs, spices, eggs, unrefined coconut and olive oil, and animal fats like ghee (butter oil), lard, and tallow. According to some Paleo proponents, fruits are off limits—others only support eating berries.

Foods not allowed include grains (including corn) and legumes

> " I see merit in the Paleo and AIP diets right out the chute—in some circumstances."

(including soy), dairy (although some allow grass-fed dairy), sugar, caffeine, and oils derived from seeds and grains, which can be high in inflammation-promoting Omega-6 fatty acids. Some claim no eggs and others say no starchy vegetables because they can't be eaten raw.

An AIP diet, for those with autoimmune conditions, is similar, but in addition to the above exclusions, altogether eschews nuts, seeds, eggs, dairy, nightshade vegetables, and generally, fruit.

Our inclusion of non-gluten grains, legumes, nuts, and seeds in this cookbook is thoughtful and intentional, based on personal and professional experience and a lot of research. I do have some "restrictions" around grains and legumes, which have remained unchanged, even going back to my pre-Hashimoto's days (both prior to my diagnosis and in my coaching practice):

- Largely limit (or eliminate) flour-based products and eat true whole (intact) non-gluten grains, in moderation, because it's true that a diet heavy in grains can be inflammatory and lead to weight gain and blood sugar imbalances. (See the chapter, *In Defense of Grains* and also the chapter, *Pantry Staples and Ingredients* for tips on soaking grains.)

- Legumes are a great source of plant-based protein, but I recommend not making legumes the sole protein of any meal, unless you can truly handle them without digestive distress. Even people who don't have autoimmune conditions can have a difficult time digesting too many legumes. (See the chapter, *In Defense of Legumes* and also the chapter, *Pantry Staples and Ingredients* for tips on enhancing digestibility of legumes.)

To provide context for our inclusions, Lisa and I were both diagnosed with Hashimoto's in early 2008. At that time, popularity of the Paleo diet hadn't crested. The AIP diet wasn't yet on the scene.

As I began my research into low thyroid function and autoimmunity/Hashimoto's, the importance of healing digestive function became abundantly clear, given that 70-80 percent of our immune system is in our digestive tract. I began to sleuth out the dietary triggers that were antagonizing my digestive lining and contributing to the leaky gut characteristic of autoimmune diseases.

In addition to going gluten-free, among other strategies, I did an Elimination Provocation diet—a version similar to the one I share with my clients today. You can find instructions for the diet in the chapter, *Elimination Provocation Diet Instructions* and as you'll see, *it's a temporary diet.* It excludes nuts—but not seeds, grains, or legumes, with the exception of peanuts (which are technically legumes) and soy. Our recipes that are compatible with an Elimination Provocation diet are designated with our EP icon.

At the onset of my journey, given that the research around how the phytic acids and lectins in grains and legumes (and supposedly nuts and seeds) contribute to leaky gut hadn't been popularized, I didn't know that I "should" remove these foods from my diet. And within a few months, my Hashimoto's was managed—without the use of thyroid hormone replacement. My

Hashimoto's antibodies were negligible, indicating reversal of the condition.

Along with my success in healing my autoimmunity came a significant shift in the thrust of my coaching practice—I began largely focusing on helping others with Hashimoto's (and adrenal dysfunction, which accompanies Hashimoto's in nearly every circumstance). Remember, by now, it's fall of 2008—the volume on Paleo and AIP hadn't yet been turned up. And over those next couple of years, prior to the popularization of the AIP diet, the vast majority of my clients had the same success that I did—plummeting antibodies and alleviation of their hypothyroid/Hashimoto's symptoms.

If I've learned anything in the decade I've been a nutrition and hormone coach, it's that we're all bio-individually unique. We all respond to foods differently—and have different trigger foods. While eggs may be the perfect food for you, they're an anti-nutrient for me. This left me in shock and awe when I did my first Elimination Provocation diet. I love eggs and had been eating them regularly for breakfast for some time. I had no idea that they were contributing to my Hashimoto's—and alopecia.

It's true that once food sensitivities are identified and the intestinal lining is healed, you can return to eating the offenders in moderation. (This is not the case with a true food *allergy*.) I'm in a bit of a unique situation, as eggs have been shown to continue to exacerbate my alopecia and I'd rather have hair than eat eggs. But given my digestive healing process, it's safe for me to eat eggs in moderation.

At the same time, for some, simply going gluten-free gets their Hashimoto's managed.

> ❝ Once food sensitivities are identified and the intestinal lining is healed, you can return to eating the offenders in moderation.❞

When you consider this, it's difficult, in my opinion, to rationalize an extreme diet, in all circumstances, for every single person with autoimmunity.

In fact, Laura Schoenfeld, Registered Dietitian and staff nutritionist for Chris Kresser, a long-time Paleo proponent, autoimmunity expert, and author of *The Paleo Cure*, says, "A strict Autoimmune Paleo Diet isn't necessary for many people with an autoimmune disease. In fact, there are few people with autoimmune diseases that would need to strictly and permanently avoid all the foods eliminated from the diet, as not everyone with autoimmunity is intolerant to all of these foods."[1] (To be clear, Kresser recommends the exclusion of grains and legumes for those with autoimmunity.)

Although our approaches differ somewhat, even Kresser's book outlines eliminations, followed by reintroductions/provocations, based on a *flexible* Paleo diet. And flexibility is key. Over half of the clients I've worked with have tried the Paleo and/or AIP diet. Here are the most frequent comments:

1. I could do it for a while, but couldn't hang on—I hit a wall. It was too restrictive.

2. I did it for several months and I actually feel worse. And my antibodies have gone up.

3. I wasn't given any additional instructions on how to heal my gut beyond the diet and didn't know how long to stay on it.

4. I travel for work and this diet is nearly impossible when I'm unable to prepare my own food.

I've proceeded to coach my clients in the same protocol I adopted—teaching them what I've learned by making myself a science experiment, during which I ate seeds and moderate amounts of non-gluten grains and legumes, with the exception of peanuts and soy. Again, nuts are excluded from the Elimination Provocation diet.

There's the saying, "If it ain't broke, don't fix it."

In years of this work, I haven't found the need to tell the majority of my clients to take on an even more restrictive diet than what's presented in the Elimination Provocation diet. Most people with Hashimoto's are already living with fatigue and overwhelm. And while many can embrace significant dietary restrictions with open arms and complete willingness, for many, being confronted with an inordinately restrictive diet can be met with a great deal of resistance and stress. It's my intent to explore how much progress we can make together while adding as little additional overwhelm as possible.

I like to see what can happen without asking people to resort to—simply meat and vegetables. And more meat and vegetables. I love meat and vegetables. And I would even say that I eat a "Paleo template." But to rely solely on these foods meal in, meal out, day in, day out can take the pleasure out of one of the most pleasurable acts we humans have—eating.

Today, it's prevailing theory that all people who have an autoimmune disease need to adopt an AIP diet, but I've continued to go against the grain (pun intended). I simply don't believe it's a one-size-fits-all approach and I guess you could call me a holdout—I'm still not convinced that it's required *for each and every person* with autoimmunity when, for most people, adopting that strict of a diet can be stressful. It can get old pretty quickly.

Some can thrive on the AIP diet and I'm not here to disregard its merits—that's not my point. But often, a super restrictive diet of any kind is a two-steps-forward-two-steps-back situation. The stress that ensues—at least for some people—isn't conducive to the healing that needs to take place.

If there's another way, I'd like to present it, especially when:

1. There's enough evidence showing that stress increases antibodies. It's even said to be a trigger for the onset of autoimmune diseases.[2] According to autoimmunity expert, Dr. Mark Hyman, "*Stress worsens the autoimmune response.*"[3] (My italics.)

2. AIP can require a lot of willpower to adhere to long-term. Willpower is a finite resource[4]—we need to be careful about how we expend our precious energy.

Many of my clients exhale audibly when I tell them that my approach includes small to moderate amounts of grains, legumes (with the exception of peanuts and soy), and seeds. This said, some have been clear that grains and/or legumes give them digestive distress. In these cases, I'm of course not going to tell them that they're fine to consume, but that after their gut-healing protocol, they can likely return to eating these foods (and the other foods they're currently sensitive to), to which I often hear, "Wow, really?"

While some may be directly affected by grains and legumes, others can get their autoimmunity managed while continuing to eat small amounts of these foods—as long as other dietary triggers are investigated. In most cases, it doesn't take months and years to tackle autoimmunity to the ground. In a healthy human, the intestinal epithelial cells regenerate every four to five days—one of the fastest rates of reproduction of any tissue in the body.[5] Given the right tools for healing, it's stunning what can happen in a matter of a few days and weeks—not months and years.

> **"** In most cases, it doesn't take months and years to tackle autoimmunity to the ground. Given the right tools for healing, it's stunning what can happen in a matter of a few days and weeks—not months and years."

But it isn't simply about diet and restriction of certain foods for a period of time. With immune modulation, there are other factors to consider, including:

- Addressing toxic body burden, including but not limited to toxins in skincare and cosmetics, food and water, home cleaning products, and exposure to endocrine/immune disruptors such as bisphenol-A (BPA), PCB, and heavy metals. The myriad ways in which we become exposed to environmental toxins is beyond the scope of this book, but going organic will significantly reduce your overall burden. (See *The Essential Thyroid Cookbook Lifestyle Companion Guide* for tips on reducing your toxic body burden. You can download it for free on our website: www.thyroidcookbook.com/companion.)

- Supplementation that's been shown to "heal and seal" the intestinal lining. (See Appendix B for our supplement recommendations, of which you can also find links to on our website: www.thyroidcookbook.com.)

- Possible bacterial infections such as small intestine bacterial overgrowth (SIBO) or Helicobacter pylori (H. pylori).

At the beginning of this chapter, I said that I see some merit in an AIP diet right out of the chute—in some circumstances. In addition to the foods listed in the Elimination Provocation diet instructions, I recommend the exclusion of grains, legumes, and seeds, in two circumstances:

1. When the symptoms of autoimmunity are so painful and distressing as to cause life-altering circumstances. A 49-year old client I worked with had psoriatic arthritis. What had been diagnosed 20 years prior as a fungal infection of her toenails was, in fact, autoimmune arthritis. (She went 20 years without a proper diagnosis!) The pain had become so intense that she could hardly walk, needed to ride in a cart at the grocery store, and, after finding the right doctor and diagnosis, found out that she had deformity in her joints. In these cases, I pull out all the stops and suggest an AIP diet.

2. When an Elimination Provocation diet hasn't proven successful. For clients who were dedicated to the process and don't find symptom relief and/or find that their antibodies have been unchanged or have increased, I recommend:

   a. Eliminating grains, legumes, and seeds

   b. Getting tested for heavy metal toxicity (this is a good idea anyway)

   c. In cases of continued and overt digestive distress, getting tested for a bacterial gut infection, like SIBO or H. pylori. (I typically suggest anti-bacterial supplementation anyway, given that many have SIBO, but treating H. pylori is more complicated than treating SIBO.)

The exclusion of grains, legumes, and seeds is much easier when the common digestive triggers have already been identified. In other words, once you've done an Elimination Provocation diet and know what you can and cannot tolerate, then the foods that you can tolerate are back on the table. Thus, the elimination of grains, legumes, and seeds isn't simultaneous to the elimination of several other foods, making the diet—and healing—much more feasible.

For example, you do an Elimination Provocation diet and find that of dairy, eggs, citrus, soy, nightshades, shellfish, corn, nuts, and peanuts, only dairy and nightshades prove to be trigger foods for you. (Gluten should be categorically avoided for everyone with Hashimoto's. See the chapter, *Gluten and Your Thyroid* for a full explanation.)

If you do find that grains, legumes, and seeds need to be avoided, you can remove them *while eating* eggs, citrus, soy, shellfish, corn, nuts, and peanuts and continuing with your supplemental digestive healing. You can then reintroduce them in a similar fashion to the reintroduction instructions in the Elimination Provocation diet.

Again, every situation is unique. But if you're still unconvinced that healing the gut and managing autoimmunity is possible eating small amounts of grains, legumes, and seeds, I can explain further.

In eight years of focusing on autoimmune hypothyroidism in my coaching practice, most of my Hashimoto's clients have seen a drastic reduction in their thyroid antibodies (and symptoms) and the majority of them have gotten the condition managed. Additionally, one of my areas of practice is alopecia—autoimmune hair loss. I've worked with alopecia clients from around the world and many have come to me saying, "I've tried everything." And "everything" often includes some iteration of an Elimination or restricted diet or autoimmune protocol.

With my approach to managing auto-immunity, each and every one of them has started to re-grow hair, including eyelashes, eyebrows, and even a full head of hair after being bald for several years. I don't expect that I'll always have this success rate, certainly. But I do so far, as of this writing, with one exception. One young girl started re-growing a significant amount of hair, only to lose it all again. It's heartbreaking.

Early on, based on some of her symptoms, I'd suspected mercury toxicity, which was later confirmed by her doctor. As of this writing, she's working to detox heavy metals from her system.

As explained, the Paleo and AIP diets differ, *but are similar enough* that I want to share this quote from nutrition and health expert, Sean Croxton, who said, "Let's face it, going 100 percent Paleo isn't for everyone. Even me. To the average person, despite its benefits, Paleo can seem intimidating, restrictive, and at times kinda annoying, to be honest."[6] Yes, and AIP is even more restrictive than Paleo.

According to respected autoimmunity expert, Chris Kresser, "The belief that 'everyone' will benefit from one particular dietary approach—no matter what it is—ignores the important differences that determine what is optimal for each person. These include variations in genes, gene expression, the microbiome, health status, activity levels, geography (e.g. latitude and climate), and more. When it comes to diet, there is no one-size-fits-all approach."[7]

According to integrative medicine pioneer, Dr. Andrew Weil, "There's no harm, and some potential benefit, in trying the Paleo diet, but I believe the diet is too restrictive for most people to stick with long-term. I think success is more likely for the majority if they regard it as healthy direction, rather than as a strict set of guidelines from which one can never deviate."[8]

Lastly, in his article, "Is There Anything New in Nutrition Worth Talking About," nutritional psychology consultant, Marc David, states, "I have watched too many friends, students, and clients get hooked on traditional systems that are old, wise, often brilliant, well thought out—and not always 100 percent applicable for humans of this day and age. In particular, many people embrace Ayurveda, Macrobiotics, or the concepts of the Paleolithic diet.

"Yes, these approaches bring tremendous insight and practical knowledge that we have long forgotten. I've benefited greatly from studying and practicing the principles of these diets. At the same time, the over-reliance on these systems often results in an intense fundamentalism, personal and nutritional isolation, and a waste of time in trying to follow in a precise and unwavering manner—principles that may have worked great eons ago, but don't necessarily translate fully into our world today.

"Every old and ancient system needs some updating. Macrobiotics is a great example. The principles in this worldview are powerful and far-reaching. The problem is, most people practice a form of macrobiotics that works fine if you're from Japan, but not so well let's say, if you're a white dude from Mississippi. The challenge is, *can you be bold and creative enough* to take what truly works from these approaches, and toss out what doesn't?"[9] (My italics.)

Spotlight: In Defense of Grains

Gluten-containing grains, including wheat (einkorn, durum, faro, graham, kamut, semolina, spelt), barley, rye, and triticale should be avoided for those with Hashimoto's and for some, going completely grain-free can be helpful for managing any form of autoimmunity. But Lisa and I don't believe that whole, gluten-free grains are categorically bad for everyone, especially after your Hashimoto's/autoimmunity is managed.

The argument against grains is that they contain the anti-nutrients phytic acid and lectin, along with enzyme-inhibitors that block mineral absorption and irritate the intestinal wall, which is clearly what you want to avoid when on an autoimmunity recovery program. Yet these anti-nutrients are also found in vegetables like beets and dark leafy greens, but that doesn't mean we shouldn't eat these foods.

Grains are naturally high in vitamins and minerals and the key is to properly prepare them to release these nutrients. It's only recently—the past century or so—that we've gotten away from the traditional practices of leavening/fermentation, soaking, and sprouting (germinating), which "pre-digests" grains. Additionally, Vitamin A inhibits the potentially negative effects of phytic acid. (For more on Vitamin A, see the *Vitamins and Other Nutrients* subchapter in the chapter, *The Nutritional Heavy Hitters.*)

When prepared traditionally, grains are much easier to digest, we're able to absorb their nutrition, and they help to produce serotonin, a neurotransmitter that brings about a sense of comfort, calm, and alertness. (The potential for serotonin production is enough right there to consider whether grains should be avoided.)

Additionally, when you consider that sprouted grains encourage the growth of friendly intestinal bacteria, help to keep the colon clean, and are high in antioxidants, we have to ask ourselves if moderate consumption of grains, along with a gut-healing protocol, is really such a bad idea.

Addressing the myth that our ancestors only ate meat and vegetables, globally recognized leader in natural health and Ayurvedic medicine, Dr. John Douillard, states, "According to the latest anthropological findings, much of the 'gathering' was harvesting grain from indigenous grasses. This contributed greatly to the starch that researchers believe made up some 35 percent of the hunter-gatherer diet." He continues, "The anti-grain sentiment that floods the media today has much to do with the fact that we have over-eaten grains. New studies suggest that we have microbes and specific enzymes specially designed to break down the hard-to-digest gluten protein—when eaten in season and in moderation."[1]

In sharing Dr. Douillard's quote, I'm *not* suggesting that anyone with Hashimoto's eat gluten. (See the chapter, *Gluten and Your Thyroid* for more on the specific thyroid/gluten relationship.) But I believe we can extrapolate his thinking about gluten to any grain mean-

> " When you consider that sprouted grains encourage the growth of friendly intestinal bacteria, help to keep the colon clean, and are high in antioxidants, we have to ask ourselves if moderate consumption of grains, along with a gut-healing protocol, is really such a bad idea."

ing, grains are likely tolerable by most people, in moderation.

Justin Sonnenburg, PhD and Associate Professor of Microbiology and Immunology at Stanford is the author of *The Good Gut*, co-authored by his wife, Erica Sonnenburg, PhD. They've been trailblazers in researching how the fiber in grains (and legumes) improves the health of our gut microbiome, our 100 trillion organism-strong "mini ecosystem" also known as "the forgotten organ."

The Sonnenburgs are considered some of today's preeminent experts in digestive health and Dr. Andrew Weil states in the foreword of *The Good Gut*, "I reject the notion that grains . . . are bad foods."[2] The Sonnenburgs state, "[A] diet . . . rich in complex carbohydrates from fruit, vegetables, legumes, and unrefined whole grains, . . . is designed to create and maintain diversity within the gut microbiota."[3]

Many experts also claim that grains improve digestive health by way of their prebiotic activity. Prebiotics promote the growth of good bacteria in our digestive system. Unlike probiotics, which are living organisms, prebiotics are a "functional food" and feed the good bacteria already present in the gut. (For more on probiotics, see the *Vitamins and Other Nutrients* subchapter in the chapter, *The Nutritional Heavy Hitters*.)

Spotlight: In Defense of Legumes

At the onset of the popularity of the Paleo/ancestral diet, it was widely reported that our ancestors didn't eat legumes/beans/pulses and therefore we shouldn't. But research has since found this to be incorrect—there is evidence that hunter-gatherer groups did, in fact, consume legumes.[1]

Similarly to grains, legumes contain the anti-nutrients phytic acid and lectin, which can compromise the integrity of the intestinal wall. But no one eats raw beans or legumes—and cooking has been shown to inactivate lectin.[2] Additionally, lectins are found in over 50 fruits and vegetables, so steering clear of them is impossible if you're eating a healthful, whole foods diet.

As for phytic acid, several foods are significantly higher in this anti-nutrient than legumes, including spinach, Swiss chard, sesame seeds, walnuts, and almonds. While a diet high in phytic acid can lead to mineral deficiencies, in the presence of healthy gut bacteria, we can break down phytic acid relatively easily, so I don't see a good reason to categorically remove these foods from the diet. (Just as with grains, soaking beans reduces a significant amount of the phytic acid.)

The nutritional benefits of legumes are too far-reaching to ignore. They're an affordable source of plant-based protein, they're loaded with antioxidants, they're an excellent source of energy-producing B vitamins that help to counter fatigue, they're loaded with satiating fiber that can help with weight and blood sugar

> " The nutritional benefits of legumes are too far-reaching to ignore."

management, and last but not least, they help to naturally lower cholesterol, commonly elevated in those with hypothyroidism.

Beans/legumes are a primary protein source for vegetarians and vegans. Those who don't eat meat, fish, or eggs have to get their protein some way, if for no other reason than to keep their blood sugar stable—balancing blood sugar and insulin is *critical* in balancing thyroid function. (For more information, I recommend my e-book, *Balance Your Blood Sugar,* available at www.healthfulelements.com/store.)

Without legumes, which includes soy (a popular protein source for many vegans/vegetarians and one that's not allowed on an Elimination Provocation diet), they're largely reliant on nuts (also not allowed on an Elimination Provocation diet). Consuming too many nuts can pose its own set of issues by way of digestive distress.

Many vegetarians eat eggs, which are a great source of protein, but they're also not allowed on an Elimination Provocation diet.

For these reasons and others, I'm not an advocate of not eating nutrient-dense animal proteins, but I'm also not anti-legume. Still, working with vegetarians and vegans who have autoimmunity is tricky territory, especially given that, again, protein is so stabilizing to blood sugar and that for those with hypothyroidism, limited protein in the diet can lead to limited T4/T3 conversion and inadequate tyrosine. (For more on tyrosine, see the *Vitamins and Other Nutrients* subchapter in the chapter, *The Nutritional Heavy Hitters*.)

For my meat-eating clients, I tell them to never make legumes the sole source of protein for any meal, but for vegetarians on an Elimination Provocation diet, it's the densest protein they're going to get. I still feel that legumes should be consumed in moderation, but it's difficult to be "moderate" and get adequate protein if you eschew animal proteins and you're on a gut-healing program.

Similarly to grains, I believe that being legume-free long-term may be challenging for many people, vegetarian or not. Although many will argue (and I agree) that being grain-free long-term would be more difficult than long-term avoidance of legumes.

Lisa and I are not alone in our belief that moderate amounts of gluten-free, whole grains and legumes/beans can be part of a healing diet for those with autoimmunity.

Dr. Susan Blum, author of *The Immune System Recovery Plan*, regularly mentions quinoa, amaranth, millet, teff, buckwheat, various types of rice, and legumes as part of her healing program and uses these foods in several of her recipes. She calls them "foods to include."

She recommends legumes as a quality plant-based protein and explains how beans are a good source of glutamine, ". . . an amino acid that's critical for healing leaky gut syndrome because it is the most important food for the cells that line the intestines."[3] Dr. Blum also claims that vegetarian protein in the form of lentils and beans is an important part of a "medically sound detox program."[4]

Similarly, Donna Jackson Nakazawa, author of *The Autoimmune Epidemic*, who healed from a paralyzing autoimmune disease, agrees that moderate amounts of non-gluten grains and beans help to "quiet down autoimmune activity" and espouses the powerful antioxidant activity of beans and legumes.[5]

Natural health expert, Dr. John Douillard, states, "Beans [have] been found to protect the brain from cognitive decline as we age and have repeatedly shown to be one of the most protective foods against blood sugar concerns. [They] provide an excellent source of protein, fiber, minerals, and vitamins. While fiber is linked to heart health, it is also critical for the protective health of the intestinal skin. If the intestinal skin breaks down, the beneficial gut microbes disappear."[6]

Like grains, many experts claim that legumes improve digestive health by way of their prebiotic or "functional food" activity because they promote the growth of good bacteria. The Sonnenburgs state, "Over the course of studying the microbiota our family has adjusted what we eat to maximize produce and legumes, largely for their prebiotic content."[7]

LOW-CARB: A DISASTER FOR THOSE WITH HASHIMOTO'S

I would be remiss in sidestepping the role of carbohydrates, especially given that many Paleo and AIP proponents are in favor of low-carb diets. But this isn't so much the case anymore. Many who've beaten the low-carb drum have softened their views on carb restriction, largely because of what I've known all along—a low-carb diet is an especially bad idea for those with hypothyroidism, Hashimoto's, and the adrenal dysfunction that almost always accompanies low thyroid function. To be clear, many Paleo proponents have clearly stated that Paleo isn't necessarily synonymous with low-carb.

Being overweight and weight loss resistant is one of the biggest complaints of hypothyroid sufferers. Perhaps many of you may have greatly restricted carbs in your efforts to lose those extra pounds, but I'm guessing your efforts backfired? Maybe it worked for a while and then you found yourself putting on weight once again?

There are three macronutrients—carbohydrates, fat, and protein. None of them should be vilified, as they're all critical for good health. (For more on the especially important role of healthful fats for health and hormone balance, see Appendix C.)

Back in the day, I watched with distant interest as the Paleo craze took hold. I read how Paleo proponents knocked carbs—but I wasn't buying it. I sat back in my chair, sure this would eventually blow over, knowing that this faulty advice was unfortunately going to backfire on those in the hypothyroid community.

Sure, it's not a good idea to overload our diet with grains and/or legumes, which I believe is true for everyone. But I had a particularly difficult time hearing the claim that starchy vegetables (sweet potatoes, yams, pumpkin, squash, parsnips, etc.) were off limits. I thought, "Here we go again, just as with 'goitrogenic' vegetables, we're denigrating perfectly healthful foods." (See the chapter, *The Myth of "Goitrogens."*)

One caveat with starchy vegetables is potatoes. They're in the nightshade family—nightshades can be inflammatory triggers for some with autoimmunity.

The role and benefit of carbs is fervently debated in the functional nutrition world and it's important to make the distinction between carbs from whole foods such as fruits, vegetables, tubers, and starches (gentle carbs) and carbs from sugar, grain flours, and highly processed and refined foods (junk carbs). Common sense tells us that foods in their whole state don't have a negative effect on the body like processed and refined junk does. One exception is fruit juice—I'm not anti-fruit, but concentrated fructose is a dense form of sugar.

It's true that some do well on a low-carb diet. In fact, it can be therapeutic for those with polycystic ovary syndrome (PCOS)—one of Healthful Elements' (my coaching business) practice areas. But a low-carb diet can be just that—a therapy, not meant to be adhered to long-term.

For those with hypothyroidism, carbohydrates are critical. I've seen too many people crash and burn on a low-carb diet. Or they've beaten themselves up because they "didn't have the willpower" to stick to primarily protein and fat.

According to naturopathic physician and women's health expert, Dr. Lara Briden, "A diet of only meat and non-starchy vegetables is great in theory, and great for many people. But it does not work for everyone. It does not work for the poor young women who tell me that they have valiantly avoided rice with dinner, only to collapse with tears and ice cream in the evening."[1]

I'm not advocating excessive carb intake. And if weight is an issue, you may want to consider a moderate-carb diet, but definitely not a carb-restricted diet.

Below are reasons why a low-carb diet is a bad idea. For each of these points, I'm of course referencing whole foods carb sources, not junk carbs from sugar, processed foods, and grain flours.

> " Common sense tells us that foods in their whole state don't have a negative effect on the body like processed and refined junk does."

> " For those with hypothyroidism, carbohydrates are critical."

- A low-carb diet can lower T3, your active thyroid hormone and increase Reverse T3 (RT3), which acts against thyroid hormone production.[2] Low-carb diets force the body to break down fat for energy. So yes, you can lose weight on a low-carb diet, until your RT3 increases and your weight loss efforts backfire.

- Caloric restriction incites a stress response (think famine), which is compounded when carb intake drops. More stress means higher RT3 production and decreased circulating thyroid hormones. See first bullet.

- Many with hypothyroidism have a difficult time with thermo-regulation—they're frequently cold. Carbs help with cold tolerance and better overall body temperature.

- The primary hormonal imbalance with adrenal dysfunction is overproduction of the stress hormone, cortisol. Low-carb diets can contribute to high cortisol.[3]

- For those prone to high stress, carbs help improve the cortisol response.[4]

- Adrenal dysfunction and a high protein diet often lead to low GABA—a calming neurotransmitter.[5] Carbs help to raise GABA.

- Insulin is generally low on a low-carb diet and insulin is required for T4 (inactive thyroid hormone) to T3 (active hormone) conversion.

- Low-carb diets are often lacking in potassium, a mineral that helps support the adrenals and nervous system and helps to support mood and energy.

- A carb-restricted diet is usually protein-heavy, which can cause brain fog and can leech calcium from the bones.

- Carbs are the primary fuel source for many of the body's vital organs, including the central nervous system, kidneys, heart, and brain. The brain is a glucose hog, and this is why many low-carb dieters become tired, angry, depressed, spaced out, and tense. Research has shown that carb-restrictive dieters tend to become depressed about two weeks into their diet, about the time their serotonin levels (a neurotransmitter and feel-good brain chemical that elevates mood, suppresses appetite, and has a calming effect) have dropped due to decreased carb intake.

- A low-carb diet can cause hair loss. Obviously, this is a double-whammy for those already losing hair due to low thyroid function and/or alopecia. The combination of caloric and nutritional restriction often present with a low-carb diet puts a significant amount of stress on the body, which can cause telogen effluvium—stress-induced, diffuse hair loss.

Fiber: The Other Low-Carb Casualty

We can't discuss the important role of carbohydrates and not consider fiber. Most Americans are deficient in fiber and some experts in the functional medicine community claim that it's is the most clinically important deficiency in our diet.

A low-carb diet, with its overreliance on fat and protein and under-reliance on grains, legumes, and starchy vegetables, tends to be low-fiber. Fiber not only helps reduce the risk of heart disease and diabetes, but also helps with weight loss. According to Monica Reinagle, licensed nutritionist, "Trying to lose weight on a low-fiber diet is like parallel parking without power steering."[1]

The importance of fiber in the diet is indisputable and has a profound impact on our digestive health and microbiome, our 100 trillion organism-strong "mini ecosystem." An equally important consideration for those with autoimmunity and the concomitant digestive concerns is our gut microbiome—"the forgotten organ."

Justin and Erica Sonnenburg, PhDs, are experts in the science of the fibers found in grains, beans, and vegetables and their role in providing an important fuel source for the microbiome. In a recent interview, Justin said, "You have to ask the question of what it means when we're consuming 15 grams of dietary fiber per day instead of 150—a 10-fold decrease in the foods that feed our gut microbe."[2]

In their book, *The Good Gut*, the Sonnenburgs state, "Increasing dietary fiber is essential to cultivating diversity in the microbiota. Microbes in the gut thrive on the complex carbohydrates that dietary fiber is primarily composed of. But rather than 'dietary fiber,' we prefer 'microbiota accessible carbohydrates,' or MACs. MACs are the components within dietary fiber that gut microbes feed on. Eating more MACs can provide more nourishment to the microbiota, help gut microbes thrive, and improve the diversity of this community. Our family eats what we jokingly refer to as a 'Big MAC diet.' This diet is rich in complex carbohydrates from fruit, vegetables, legumes, and unrefined whole grains, and is designed to create and maintain diversity within the gut microbiota."[3]

Fiber is also important for healthy estrogen levels, which can improve thyroid function, as there's an important relationship between estrogen and thyroid hormones.[4]

> 66 The importance of fiber in the diet is indisputable and has a profound impact on our digestive health and microbiome, our 100 trillion organism-strong 'mini ecosystem.'"

OUR SPRINGBOARD

In preparation for our choices of foods and ingredients for these recipes, Lisa and I created a nutritional "springboard" that is the foundation of this cookbook. We spent weeks (think late nights and hair-splitting research) weeding wide-eyed through the subjective nature of nutrition and sleuthing out the most supportive nutrients for the thyroid and immune system and then researching the foods that are *dense sources* of these nutrients—not simply moderate or mediocre sources, but concentrated sources.

You can find a pretty version of our findings at www.thyroidcookbook.com/nutrition_guide.

In other words, you can rest assured that the foods we've chosen to highlight in this cookbook are an excellent bang for your buck—each one possesses a broad and substantive thyroid- and immune-supportive spectrum. Get a variety of these foods regularly, and you'll be feeding your thyroid and immune system well.

Despite this insane amount of dissection, we don't necessarily subscribe to "nutritionism," a term popularized by author and activist Michael Pollan. We wanted to avoid getting too granular with our research and thus, losing people (and ourselves) with our nerdy and too-scientific approach.

In his *New York Times* article, "Unhappy Meals," Pollan states, "The first thing to understand about nutritionism is that it is not quite the same as nutrition. As the 'ism' suggests, it is not a scientific subject but an ideology. In the case of nutritionism, the widely shared but unexamined assumption is that the key to understanding food is indeed the nutrient.

". . . the whole point of eating is to maintain and promote bodily health. Hippocrates's famous injunction to 'let food be thy medicine' is ritually invoked to support this notion. I'll leave the premise alone for now, except to point out that it is not shared by all cultures and that the experience of these other cultures suggests that, paradoxically, viewing food as being about things other than bodily health—like pleasure, say, or socializing—makes people no less healthy;

indeed, there's some reason to believe that it may make them more healthy. This is what we usually have in mind when we speak of the 'French paradox'—the fact that a population that eats all sorts of unhealthful nutrients is in many ways healthier than we Americans are. So there is at least a question as to whether nutritionism is actually any good for you."[1]

Put simply, nutritionism refers to the "parts" (in this case, vitamins, minerals, amino acids, etc.) in the saying, "The whole is greater than the sum of its parts."

Lisa and I believe that indeed, when it comes to food and nutrition, the whole is certainly greater than the sum of its parts. But it didn't stop us from doing what we felt was the critical, nitty-gritty research needed to make this cookbook the best that we could make it—and the most beneficial for you.

So while we perhaps strayed into a bit of "nutritionism" in creating these recipes, we did the necessary foundational work to prevent this cookbook from being "just another cookbook." We certainly aren't reductionists; we're generalists. But sometimes it takes analyzing the details in order to zoom out to the 30,000 foot level and paint the broad brush strokes that keep our readers (and us) from glazing over from too much analysis and science. Had we succumbed to analysis paralysis, this book would have never come to fruition.

The nutrient information in this cookbook is substantive. Again, it's the foundation upon which it was built. You may choose to skim it, which is okay. We don't blame you for diving right into the recipes.

Additionally, Lisa and I felt it was important to complement the nutrient information

> " When it comes to food and nutrition, the whole is certainly greater than the sum of its parts."

with some basic hypothyroid and Hashimoto's education, which you'll find in the chapter, *About the Thyroid*. If you'd like to go deeper, be sure to read *The Essential Thyroid Cookbook Lifestyle Companion Guide* that addresses several thyroid- and immune-supportive topics that we couldn't fit into this cookbook. It's a free download at:

www.thyroidcookbook.com/companion.

Disclaimer:

The information below is based on our best thinking and research and we believe its contents are accurate, effective, and sound. It's not intended to diagnose, treat, cure, or prevent any disease or condition. The information provided herein is not medical advice or instruction. It has not been evaluated by the FDA and it does not replace any advice you may receive from your medical practitioner. No action should be taken solely based on this information. We, the Authors, are not responsible for any errors or omissions, inadvertent or not, that may be found in these nutrient lists, and we assume no liability whatsoever on behalf of any user of this information. Please consult your primary care physician or other appropriate health professionals before beginning any nutrition program.

Below are the thyroid- and immune-supportive heavy hitters we identified, including the nutrient symbols we incorporated into each recipe, as appropriate. In the chapter, *The Nutritional Heavy Hitters*, we show you how and why these nutrients are so beneficial.

Nutrients supportive to *both* thyroid and immune function:

Vitamin A (as beta-carotene)	A(beta)
Vitamin A (as retinol)	A(ret)
Vitamin B_1[a]	B_1
Vitamin B_2	B_2
Vitamin B_6	B_6
Vitamin B_{12}	B_{12}
Vitamin C	C
Vitamin D[b]	D
Vitamin E	E
Calcium	Ca
Copper	Cu
Iron	Fe
Magnesium	Mg
Selenium	Se
Zinc	Zn
Omega-3 fatty acids	O3

Additional nutrients supportive to thyroid function:

Iodine	I
Manganese	Mn
Tyrosine	Ty

Additional nutrients supportive to immune function:

EGCG	Eg
Glutathione [c]	Gl
Lycopene	Ly
Probiotics	Pr
Resveratrol	Rv

[a] *Generally, the whole gamut of B vitamins is supportive to the thyroid and immune system; we've highlighted what we feel are the most important.*

[b] *It's impossible to get adequate Vitamin D from food sources alone. While we've highlighted some foods, such as eggs and seafood, it's critical to supplement with Vitamin D and get safe sun exposure for proper hormonal pathway function and immune modulation. (For more on Vitamin D, see the* Vitamins and Other Nutrients *subchapter in the chapter,* The Nutritional Heavy Hitters.*)*

[c] *Foods don't inherently contain glutathione, but some foods help your body produce glutathione, a critical antioxidant in the fight against Hashimoto's. Adequate dietary Vitamin C, Vitamin E, and selenium help the body recycle glutathione. (For more on glutathione, see the* Vitamins and Other Nutrients *subchapter in the chapter,* The Nutritional Heavy Hitters.*)*

OUR METHODOLOGY

B efore reading the list of foods that we've chosen to highlight, it's important to explain more about the method behind our madness.

After studying the most thyroid- and immune-supportive nutrients from various reliable sources, we embarked on the nitty-gritty research on whole foods sources of those nutrients that ultimately determined what foods we would highlight in this cookbook. Our research came from the USDA National Nutrient Database for Standard Reference, The World's Healthiest Foods nutrient rating database, and the Linus Pauling Institute Micronutrient Information Center.

It's important to know that there are oodles of online sources—and books—that claim that this or that food is high in such and such nutrient. For example, we found several seemingly reputable sources that reported that their research came from the USDA National Nutrient Database. Yet when we did our due diligence and cross-referenced that information with the USDA, it often didn't corroborate. Therefore, we stuck with the above three resources for the foundation of this cookbook.

When in doubt as to whether a food should be included and highlighted, we looked at the RDA—Recommended Dietary Allowance—and created a 30 percent threshold. If the food in question offered more than 30 percent RDA per serving, we included it.

Although there are other whole foods, aside from the ones listed below—and of which there are plenty in this cookbook—that contain at least some of the nutrients we identified, for the sake of simplicity and effectiveness, we created a comprehensive ranking system and chose to shine the spotlight on foods that are "excellent" or "very good" sources of at least four of these nutrients. Again, not simply moderate or mediocre sources, but *dense sources of at least four of these nutrients*.

In other words, each food/ingredient "made the cut" by getting a high score. Again, they're an excellent bang for your buck—each one possesses a broad and substantive thyroid- and immune-supportive spectrum and you'll see that each food/ingredient listed in the following chapter, *The Nutritional Heavy Hitters*, has at least four nutrient symbols associated with it.

Additionally, each recipe—including suggested combinations of recipes, such as a side paired with a main dish—contains at least five ingredients rich in one of these key nutrients, with the exception of our healing beverages, which would likely be consumed as part of a meal anyway.

You'll see that the vast majority of our recipes have a legend displaying at least five of our nutrient symbols. The ones that don't are beverages or the recipes that can be paired (side plus main dish, for example) to round out the spectrum to meet our criteria.

This cookbook isn't comprised of only these ingredients—they're simply the dense nutritional sources that each recipe or recipe combination contains at least five of.

For example, fruits, such as berries and citrus, are some ingredients that didn't rank high in our analyses—they weren't "excellent" or "very good" sources of at least four thyroid- and immune-supportive nutrients. But they're important and will be included in some of our recipes because they're an excellent source of Vitamin C, a powerful antioxidant that's important for glutathione production and recycling. Glutathione is one of the pillars in fighting Hashimoto's. (For more on glutathione, see the *Vitamins and Other Nutrients* subchapter in the chapter, *The Nutritional Heavy Hitters*.)

Below is a visual that will make things clear. Many of you will be surprised to know that Brazil nuts, popular for their selenium content, didn't rank high on our analyses. Again, that doesn't mean that they're not included in some of our recipes. Yes, they're one of the best sources of selenium, but they didn't offer a broad enough nutritional spectrum to qualify as a "biggie."

As you can see, sunflower seeds scored a 7, whereas Brazil nuts a 3.

> **4**
> The number of thyroid- and immune-supportive nutrients each food needed in order to be highlighted.

> **5**
> The number of featured ingredients that each recipe or recipe combination (e.g. side + main dish) contains.

	Thyroid-supportive nutrients	Thyroid- and immune-supportive nutrients																	Immune-supportive nutrients				
	Iodine	Manganese	Tyrosine	Vitamin A (as beta-carotene)	Vitamin A (as retinol)	Vitamin B1	Vitamin B2	Vitamin B6	Vitamin B12	Vitamin C	Vitamin D	Vitamin E	Calcium	Copper	Iron	Magnesium	Selenium	Zinc	Omega-3 fatty acids	EGCG	Glutathione	Lycopene	Probiotics	Resveratrol
Sunflower seeds		•				•		•				•		•		•	•							
Brazil nuts														•		•	•							

If you'd like to view our entire Essential Hypothyroidism and Hashimoto's Nutrition Guide in an easy-to-read chart, you can find it at www.thyroidcookbook.com/nutrition_guide. Know that the information is also presented in the next chapter, simply in a different format.

It's because of the nature of our springboard and methodology and the research that went into each that we specifically chose not to include recipe nutrition facts. These whole food, nutrient-dense recipes highlight foods that are supportive to thyroid and immune function and you won't find caloric content, fat grams, carbohydrate grams, fiber content, or a list of the Recommended Dietary Allowance (RDA) of any nutrient in this cookbook. Lisa and I believe that for most people on a healthful, whole foods diet, this information is irrelevant and unnecessary—and fuels "nutritionism." (One exception is that carb-counting is important for some diabetics, for example.)

THE NUTRITIONAL
HEAVY HITTERS

Below are the thyroid- and immune-supportive foods we've chosen to highlight. Again, you'll see that each food has at least four thyroid- and immune-supportive nutrient symbols associated with it. The exception is green tea, which is the only source of immune-supportive EGCG.

This cookbook is gluten-free and dairy-free; all gluten-containing grains and milk products have been omitted.

Each food is listed in order of nutrient density versus alphabetically. You'll find nearly each of these ingredients in at least one recipe.

Remember, what's outlined below **does not represent the full nutritional spectrum of these foods.** The nutrients associated with each ingredient are the ones that are particularly thyroid- and immune-supportive, based on our research.

Leafy Greens	
Spinach	A(beta), B_1, B_2, B_6, C, E, Fe, Ca, Cu, Mg, Mn, Zn, Gl
Swiss chard	A(beta), B_2, B_6, C, E, Ca, Cu, Fe, Mg, Mn
Turnip greens	A(beta), B_2, B_6, C, E, Ca, Cu, Fe, Mg, Mn
Mustard greens	A(beta), B_2, B_6, C, E, Ca, Cu, Fe, Mg, Mn
Collard greens	A(beta), B_2, B_6, C, Ca, Fe, Mg, Mn, Gl

Kale	A(beta), B_6, C, Ca, Cu, Mn, Gl
Romaine lettuce	B_1, C, Fe, Mn
Other vegetables	
Asparagus	B_1, B_2, B_6, C, E, Cu, Fe, Mn, Gl, Ly
Sea vegetables[1]	B_2, B_6, Ca, Cu, Fe, I, Mg, Mn, Zn
Broccoli	B_2, B_6, C, E, Ca, Mn, Gl
Mushrooms, crimini	B_1, B_2, D, Cu, Mn, Se, Zn
Cabbage, red	B_6, C, Ca, Fe, Mg, Mn, Ly
Green beans	B_1, B_2, B_6, C, Ca, Mg, Mn
Mushrooms, shiitake	B_2, B_6, Cu, Mn, Se, Zn
Squash, winter	A(beta), B_6, C, E, Mn, Gl
Squash, summer	B_2, B_6, C, Mn, Gl
Cauliflower, orange	A(beta), B_6, C, Mn, Gl
Bell peppers	B_6, C, E, Ly
Brussels sprouts	B_1, B_6, C, Mn
Cabbage	C, Ca, Mn, Gl
Carrots	A(beta), C, E, Ly
Cauliflower, white	B_6, C, Mn, Gl
Leeks	B_6, C, Fe, Mn
Potato, skin on	B_6, C, Fe, I
Fruits[2]	
Avocado	B_6, E, Mg, Gl
Tomatoes	B_6, C, Mn, Ly
Protein: Meat and Eggs	
Liver (grass-fed)	A(ret), B_{12}, D, Ca, Cu, Fe, Mg, Zn, O3, Ty
Beef (grass-fed)	B_2, B_6, B_{12}, Fe, Se, Zn, O3, Ty
Eggs (pastured, with yolk)	A(ret), B_2, B_{12}, D, I, Se, Ty
Chicken, dark meat	B_2, B_{12}, Fe, Se, Zn, Ty

Chicken, white meat	B_2, B_6, B_{12}, Se, Ty
Lamb	B_{12}, Fe, Se, Zn, Ty
Turkey, white meat	B_6, B_{12}, I, Se, Ty
Turkey, dark meat	B_6, B_{12}, Se, Zn, Ty
Pork	B_6, Se, Zn, Ty
Protein: Seafood	
Oysters	A(ret), D, Cu, Fe, Mn, Se, Zn, O3, Ty
Salmon	A(ret), B_2, B_6, B_{12}, D, Se, O3, Ty
Halibut	B_2, B_6, B_{12}, Mg, Se, O3, Ty
Sardines	A(ret), B_{12}, D, Ca, Se, O3, Ty
Crab	A(ret), B_{12}, Cu, Se, Zn, O3, Ty
Shrimp	A(ret), B_{12}, E, Fe, I, Se, Ty
Tuna	B_6, B_{12}, Fe, Se, O3, Ty
Clams	A(ret), B_{12}, Cu, Fe, Mn, Ty
Cod	B_6, B_{12}, I, Se, Ty
Mussels	A(ret), B_{12}, Fe, Mn, Ty
Scallops	A(ret), B_{12}, Se, Zn, Ty
Lobster	B_{12}, Cu, Zn, Ty
Trout	B_2, E, O3, Ty
Protein: Legumes[3]	
Tempeh[4] (*see also*: Fermented)	B_2, B_{12}, E, Ca, Cu, Fe, Mg, Mn, Ty, Pr
Natto[4] (*see also*: Fermented)	B_2, C, Ca, Cu, Fe, Mg, Mn, Se, Zn, Pr
Peanuts	B_6, E, Cu, Fe, Mg, Mn, Zn, Rv
Miso[4] (GF) (*see also*: Fermented)	B_2, B_6, C, Ca, Fe, Mg, Mn, Pr
Beans, adzuki	Cu, Fe, Mg, Mn, Zn
Beans, garbanzo (chick peas)	B_6, Cu, Fe, Mn, Zn
Beans, lima	Cu, Fe, Mg, Mn
Lentils	Cu, Fe, Mg, Mn

Fermented Foods	
Tempeh[4] (*see also*: Legumes)	B_2, B_{12}, E, Ca, Cu, Fe, Mg, Mn, Ty, Pr
Natto[4] (*see also*: Legumes)	B_2, C, Ca, Cu, Fe, Mg, Mn, Se, Zn, Pr
Kefir (coconut milk-derived)	C, E, Cu, Fe, Mg, Mn, Se, Zn, Pr
Yogurt (coconut milk-derived)	C, E, Cu, Fe, Mg, Mn, Se, Zn, Pr
Miso[4] (GF) (*see also*: Legumes)	B_2, B_6, C, Ca, Fe, Mg, Mn, Pr
Sauerkraut	C, Ca, Cu, Fe, Mg, Mn, Pr
Kimchi	A(beta), C, Ca, Fe, Pr
Kombucha tea (*see also*: Beverages)	B_2, B_6, B_{12}, C, Pr
Nuts and Seeds	
Sesame seeds (includes tahini)	B_2, B_6, Ca, Cu, Fe, Mg, Mn, Se, Zn
Almonds	B_2, E, Ca, Cu, Fe, Mg, Mn, Zn
Sunflower seeds	B_1, B_6, E, Cu, Mg, Mn, Se
Hazelnuts	B_6, E, Cu, Fe, Mg, Mn
Pumpkin seeds	Cu, Fe, Mg, Mn, Zn
Walnuts	B_6, Mn, Se, O3, Gl
Flaxseeds, ground	B_1, Cu, Mg, Mn, O3
Cashews	Cu, Fe, Mg, Zn
Chia seeds	Ca, Mg, Mn, O3
Whole Grains[3]	
Amaranth	B_2, B_6, Ca, Cu, Fe, Mg, Mn, Se, Zn
Buckwheat	B_2, B_6, Cu, Fe, Mg, Mn, Se, Zn
Millet	B_6, Ca, Fe, Mg, Mn, Zn
Oats (GF)	Cu, Fe, Mg, Mn, Zn
Brown rice	B_6, Mg, Mn, Se
Quinoa[5]	B_6, Fe, Mg, Mn
Herbs[6], Spices, and Flavoring Agents	
Chili powder	B_2, B_6, C, E, Ca, Cu, Fe, Mg, Mn, Se, Zn

Garlic	B_6, C, Ca, Cu, Mg, Mn, Se, Gl
Chocolate (dark)	Cu, Fe, Mg, Mn, Zn, Pr
Basil	A(beta), Ca, Fe, Ly
Oregano	E, Ca, Fe, Mn
Thyme	C, Ca, Fe, Mn
Beverages	
Kombucha tea (*see also*: Fermented)	B_2, B_6, B_{12}, C, Pr
Green tea	Eg
Sweeteners	
Blackstrap molasses	B_6, Ca, Cu, Fe, Mg, Mn

[1] *Sea vegetables include kelp, dulse, hijiki, nori, arame, wakame, and kombu.*

[2] *Most fruit didn't rank high in our analyses, but fruits like berries and citrus are excellent sources of antioxidants, particularly Vitamin C, which are critical for glutathione production and recycling. Therefore, these fruits are featured in our recipes.*

[3] *We understand that for those with Hashimoto's (and other autoimmune conditions), a diet free of grains and legumes, among other foods, is often recommended. We've found that, while these diets can be extremely helpful for many, they're not categorically necessary for everyone with Hashimoto's. (For our full explanation, see the chapter,* Why This Is Not Another Paleo or AIP Cookbook.*)*

[4] *We're not fans of highly processed soy products, but in our opinion, tempeh, natto, gluten-free tamari, and miso are fine in moderation, as the soybeans are fermented and whole. (See the chapter,* A Word About Soy *for more information.)*

[5] *Quinoa is a seed but unlike most nuts and seeds, it needs to be cooked before consumption. We're therefore designating it as a whole grain. (Technically all whole grains are seeds.)*

[6] *Herbs should be fresh vs. dried and used in sufficient quantities for maximum nutrient benefit. (Chili powder is obviously not fresh.)*

Thyroid- and Immune-Supportive Nutrients: How They Work

Again, at the risk of straying into nutritionism, it's important for us to provide explanations of why the vitamins, minerals, and nutrients found in the ingredients in our recipes boost thyroid function and help mitigate the autoimmune response.

It's important to remember that we're taking each nutrient out of the context of the whole food. When you strive to eat in a balanced way as demonstrated through the recipes in this cookbook, you'll find it easier to obtain the nourishment your body needs to function optimally.

Minerals

- Calcium
- Copper
- Iodine
- Iron
- Magnesium
- Manganese
- Selenium
- Zinc

Perhaps the word "minerals" conjures memories of the rocks you studied in your seventh grade science class. I do remember examining them in awe, thinking, "Wow, this is far from boring. Look at all of these beautiful colors!"

I now know that our bodies are comprised largely of the same minerals that the earth is made from. Minerals are little engines that make our bodies run optimally. They keep our immune system running well, give us strong bones, have powerful antioxidant properties, and are critical for cell generation.

Often times, when people think of "nutrients," they only think of vitamins. I'm often asked, "What's the best multi-vitamin to take?" But it's important to know that the thyroid is particularly mineral-dependent and that minerals work in concert with vitamins. (And yes, most good multi-vitamins contain a spectrum of minerals.)

According to expert Dr. Richard Shames, author of *Thyroid Power*, "More important than vitamins are minerals. These are absolutely crucial to thyroid function."[1] Naturopath and nutritionist, Dr. Carolyn Dean, states, "Minerals play a huge part in the rehabilitation of our hormones. In my experience, most low thyroid conditions are caused by mineral deficiency."[2]

Causes of mineral deficiencies include a nutrient-poor diet, inadequate absorption from low stomach acid (which is common for those with autoimmunity), dehydration, kidney issues, and congestive heart failure. (See Appendix G for instructions on how to restore stomach acid with a hydrochloric acid challenge.)

Let's break them down.

Calcium

Calcium is the most abundant mineral in the human body. And according to Dr. Shames, calcium is "absolutely essential" for proper thyroid function. In his book, *Thyroid Power*, he states that calcium deficiency is a "related condition" to low thyroid function.[1]

> " More important than vitamins are minerals. These are absolutely crucial to thyroid function."
> —Dr. Richard Shames

Additional things to know about the thyroid/calcium relationship:

- Proper thyroid function helps to regulate blood calcium levels.[2]
- Hypothyroidism can inhibit calcium metabolism.[3]

In addition to supporting bone health, adequate calcium helps to regulate our acid/alkaline balance and supports muscle and nerve function. It also supports adequate immune response for healing damaged tissue,[2] aids Vitamin D in its important role as an immune system regulator,[4] and serves as "second messenger" in immune system cells.[5]

We've been browbeaten into believing that dairy is the best food source of calcium, but this is simply untrue. Rich food sources of calcium include: sardines, collard greens, spinach, turnip greens, mustard greens, beet greens, bok choy, Swiss chard, kale, broccoli, cabbage, green beans, sauerkraut, kimchi, sesame seeds, almonds, chia, amaranth, millet, blackstrap molasses, cinnamon, garlic, basil, oregano, thyme, sea vegetables, tofu, tempeh, natto, miso, and yogurt. (We're not a fan of tofu, as it's not fermented.)

> " We've been browbeaten into believing that dairy is the best food source of calcium, but this is simply untrue."

The above list highlights foods that are rich sources of calcium, regardless of whether they ranked high in our analyses or not. As explained in the Our Methodology *chapter, there are other whole foods, aside from the ones we've chosen to highlight in this cookbook per our thoughtful ranking system, that are rich in the nutrients we identified as being especially thyroid- and immune-supportive. In other words, there are foods listed above that aren't included in this cookbook because our ultimate goal is to expand perceptions of healthy eating and health-supportive foods.*

Again, my general stance on supplementation is that less is more, but know there's quite a bit of controversy around calcium supplementation specifically. Firstly, given my mom's history with advanced osteoporosis, I learned many years ago that supplemental calcium needs carriers—magnesium and Vitamin D. Aside from Vitamin D being a carrier for calcium, adequate levels of D will also help with calcium absorption.

I don't recommend calcium supplementation outside of a food-based multi-mineral. This may surprise you, given that thyroid hormone replacement is said to lead to bone loss. It's also known that low thyroid function is a leading cause of osteoporosis. So you'd think I'd be recommending calcium supplementation left and right.

Supplemental calcium, especially without the carriers Vitamin D and magnesium, can do bad things—it can settle into your joints and soft tissues such as your heart and arteries. Any deposits into the joints can cause arthritis. It also incites a false sense of security, as in, "I'm taking my calcium, so I don't have to worry about osteopenia or osteoporosis." But you do need to take care of your bones beyond popping a pill. Supplemental calcium isn't a panacea.

If you're still unconvinced, I recommend the book *Death by Calcium* by Dr. Thomas Levy.

If you're unable to get what you need from the above list of food sources and you feel that supplementation is warranted:

- Take a food-based magnesium as a carrier for calcium. (See Appendix B for our supplement recommendations.)

- If you're taking thyroid hormone replacement, be sure to allow at least six hours after taking your meds before taking any calcium supplementation.

- The dose for calcium most commonly recommended is 1200-1500 milligrams/day. But Dr. Levy states, "If you're over 36 years old, you only need 200 to 300 milligrams of calcium per day. Not the 1300 milligrams the government recommends." (This is clearly less than the above-mentioned "500 milligrams at a time.")[6]

Copper

In Dr. Richard Shames' claim that minerals are "absolutely crucial to thyroid function," he singles out copper, zinc, and selenium.[1]

Copper is a powerful antioxidant and essential trace mineral that's needed for neurological, cardiovascular, bone, and skin health and also connective tissue and lipid metabolism.

While it's important to ensure that you're getting adequate copper from your diet, it's also important to know that many with thyroid issues experience copper overload or copper toxicity (copperiedus). When we think of "heavy metals" and heavy metal toxicity, the metals that often come to mind are mercury, lead, and cadmium. But copper overload is one of the most common heavy metal toxicity conditions, can exacerbate autoimmune conditions,[2] and can lead to poor immune function.[3]

We can become copper-heavy through environmental exposure from water from copper pipes, copper cookware, fungicide- and pesticide-laden foods, and a copper IUD (ParaGard).

According to nutritionist, Ann Louise Gittleman, "Copper and zinc tend to work in a seesaw relationship with each other. When the levels of one of these minerals rise in the blood and tissues, the levels of its counterpart tend to fall. Ideally, copper and zinc should be in a 1:8 ratio in favor of zinc. But stress, overexposure to copper, or a low intake of zinc can throw the critical copper-zinc balance off, upsetting normal body functioning."[4]

This imbalance can slow thyroid function. Dr. Gittleman goes on to say that a copper-zinc imbalance can not only keep us weight loss resistant, but can also thwart that important T4/T3 conversion.

When the thyroid is underactive, it can inhibit your digestive system from absorbing those above-mentioned, "critical" thyroid minerals—copper, zinc, and selenium. This is a classic negative feedback loop. You need these minerals for proper thyroid function, but low thyroid function can keep you from absorbing them.

A copper/zinc imbalance can also lead to compromised immune function, sun sensitivity, general skin sensitivities, depression, anxiety, panic attacks, acne, psoriasis, migraines, eczema, attention deficit, white spots on fingernails, severe PMS, and extreme fatigue.[5]

Interestingly, not only are copper and zinc minerals, but they're also considered neurotransmitters—chemical messengers that keep our brain cells communicating with one another. Our diet heavily influences the type and amount of neurotransmitters in our system and the right minerals and vitamins are critical to the production of these "happy chemicals." This is why so many behavioral and mood issues are often a result of a copper/zinc imbalance.

To bring your copper/zinc ratio into balance, it's better to focus on replenishing zinc than reducing copper.

Rich food sources of copper include: spinach, Swiss chard, turnip greens, mustard greens, beet greens, kale, asparagus, sauerkraut and cabbage, mushrooms, sweet potatoes, peas, Brussels sprouts, beets, tomatoes, romaine lettuce, broccoli, eggplant, fennel, leeks, parsley, basil, sea vegetables, oysters, crab, shrimp, clams, lobster, tempeh, natto, peanuts, adzuki beans, garbanzo beans, lima beans, kidney beans, lentils, kefir, yogurt, sesame seeds, sunflower seeds, flaxseeds, pumpkin seeds, cashews, almonds, hazelnuts, walnuts, amaranth, buckwheat, oats, garlic, chili powder, blackstrap molasses, olives, pineapple, raspberries, kiwi, and dark chocolate.

The above list highlights foods that are rich sources of copper, regardless of whether they ranked high in our analyses or not. As explained in the Our Methodology *chapter, there are other whole foods, aside from the ones we've chosen to highlight in this cookbook per our thoughtful ranking system, that are rich in the nutrients we identified as being especially thyroid- and immune-supportive. In other words, there are foods listed above that aren't included in this cookbook because our ultimate goal is to expand perceptions of healthy eating and health-supportive foods.*

If you're deficient in copper, in addition to eating the above-mentioned copper-rich foods, Dr. Shames suggests 1-2 milligrams of copper per day (this is the dose commonly found in multi-vitamins).

Iodine

Ah, iodine. "The big daddy." There's no doubt that it's a critical mineral—and not just for the thyroid.

Sea vegetables are the highest source of iodine, with saltwater fish a close second. We've provided dietary sources of iodine in this cookbook, of course, but believe that it's also important to break down the controversy around iodine supplementation, given that iodine is a critical thyroid mineral, that sea vegetables aren't that popular in Western culture, and that many of us aren't getting the fish intake that we should. You'd be hard-pressed to get your iodine needs from potato skins and eggs.

Nary have I found a more widely-challenged and widely-supported health topic than whether those with hypothyroidism and Hashimoto's should supplement with iodine.

I'll begin by saying that some of the doctors and professionals I respect most are in different

> **" The thyroid has the only cells capable of uptaking iodine."**

camps on the iodine controversy. The confusion is, without a doubt, one of the things I'm most often asked to provide clarity on. *But I don't have the final word on iodine.* I'm simply going to do my best to provide both sides of this hotly-contested story.

The thyroid has the only cells capable of uptaking iodine and many who have Hashimoto's are deficient in this important mineral, but the iodine deficiency isn't the cause of their low thyroid function.

The thyroid's job is to absorb iodine and combine it with the amino acid tyrosine. It then converts this iodine/tyrosine combination into T3 and T4. The thyroid produces some T3, the active hormone, but the majority is produced by the mostly inactive T4 by a process called T4/T3 conversion. (Also see the chapter, *Optimizing Thyroid Hormone Conversion.*)

After all of the research, studies, reports, and examination that make it clear that upwards of 90 percent of hypothyroidism cases are a result of Hashimoto's, many doctors will still claim that hypothyroidism is an iodine deficiency and will suggest iodine supplementation.

The percentage of non-autoimmune hypothyroidism (it's really more like 3 percent versus 10 percent) applies to the U.S.; worldwide, the most common cause of hypothyroidism is, in fact, iodine deficiency, although Hashimoto's is on the rise all over the globe.

According to Chris Kresser, a globally recognized leader in the field functional and integrative medicine, (from my interview of him in 2012), "Non-autoimmune hypothyroidism is not an immune-mediated problem. It's a problem with the thyroid itself and is often caused by an iodine deficiency or excess bromine exposure."[1] (See *The Essential Thyroid Cookbook Lifestyle Companion Guide* for a list of bromine sources, including suggestions for secreting bromines. You can download it for free on our website: www.thyroidcookbook.com/companion.)

Maintaining adequate levels of iodine is critically important. Without it, your thyroid simply can't do its job. But iodine—from food or supplementation—isn't going to cure your Hashimoto's. If only it were that easy. Still, some controversial doctors claim the contrary—that it will cure. Later, I'll explain why I feel this is questionable and short-sighted.

> **" Without iodine, your thyroid simply can't do its job."**

According to the World Health Organization (WHO), 72 percent of the global population is affected by some manifestation of iodine deficiency. Iodine insufficiency can result from:

- Lack of iodine-rich foods in the diet, like seaweed and seafood

- Removal of iodized salt from the diet, either through overall reduction in salt intake or switching to sea salt, which contains trace minerals but no iodine

- Iodine-deficient soil—iodine concentration in soil varies considerably by region, but it's plentiful in the ocean; coastal regions tend to have higher soil iodine concentration due to absorption from the atmosphere

- Fluoride in drinking water (See *The Essential Thyroid Cookbook Lifestyle Companion Guide* on our website for more information on the negative effects of fluoride on thyroid function.)

- Discontinued use of iodine to disinfect machinery in the dairy and meat industry

Again, worldwide, iodine deficiency is the leading cause of hypothyroidism but low thyroid function can also result from a goiter, which is an inflammatory enlargement of the thyroid gland. In parts of the world where iodine deficiency is prevalent, goiters are common. It's less common to see iodine deficiency in the U.S., given that iodized salt is readily available in salt shakers at home and when eating out. But note that in most cases, salt added to canned and processed foods is not iodized.

Thyroid expert, Dr. Richard Shames, says that deficiency in the U.S. is "hardly the case."[2] Prior to the fortification of salt with iodine, iodine insufficiency was quite present. (You've likely heard of the "goiter belt"—the inland region of the U.S. that includes the Midwest, Great Lakes, and intermountain regions, where goiters were once common because many foods were grown in iodine-deficient soil.)

You may think, "Wait, above, you said that hypothyroidism is a result of either Hashimoto's or iodine deficiency. Or, as Kresser said, bromine exposure. And now you're saying that it can result from a goiter." This is all true. Hypothyroidism can also be triggered by stress, pregnancy, environmental toxins, Vitamin D deficiency, and your genetic propensity. And when you consider that in the initial stages, Hashimoto's can be symptomless (usually before diagnosis), any one of these other triggers can tip the scales.

Speaking of goiters, some claim that excessive intake of "goitrogenic" vegetables interferes with iodine uptake. Lisa and I are very pro-"goitrogenic" vegetables (quotation marks intentional). (See the chapter, *The Myth of "Goitrogens"* for our full explanation.)

In early 2010, author Dr. Datis Kharrazian, a leading expert in thyroid health and autoimmunity, claimed that supplementing with iodine was "like throwing gas on a fire"—that iodine supplementation would fan the flames (pun intended) of Hashimoto's and increase antibody levels. His best-selling book spread like wildfire (pun intended) through the integrative/holistic healthcare community.

Many well-respected and well-researched practitioners followed suit: writing, blogging, and educating about the dangers of iodine supplementation for those with Hashimoto's. I too followed suit. As I told my clients, "There aren't many things I take a black and white approach to, but this is one of them. Don't supplement with iodine—even kelp supplementation."

I've certainly had many clients who've felt truly awful on iodine supplementation. So they were relieved to hear that I asked them to stop (if they hadn't already) and after explaining the "fire" analogy, they then understood why they felt horribly on iodine. The reason for this phenomenon is that, in theory, iodine supplementation increases thyroid antibodies. Anytime antibodies increase in a sudden or substantive way, the thyroid can temporarily dump thyroid hormones into the bloodstream and cause hyper symptoms. So yes, there can be a diagnosis of hypothyroidism/Hashimoto's, but people can periodically swing into a hyper state that can include

> " I don't like black and white when it comes to food, nutrition, and supplementation. Sure, I want to tell all of my clients, 'Do this, don't do that,' but it's rarely that straightforward."

heightened anxiety, heart palpitations, sleeplessness, sweating, and shortness of breath.

Dr. Shames states, "How does excess iodine harm the thyroid? A high amount of iodine in the body becomes concentrated in the thyroid gland, in the hormone precursor protein called thyroglobulin. A high amount of iodinated thyroglobulin triggers an auto-immune response."[3]

Fast forward a couple of years. I had a cluster of Hashimoto's clients, all taking iodine supplementation, who claimed that it was a non-negotiable for them, that it helped them feel remarkably better and that if they didn't take it, all bets were off—they'd feel terribly. Some had tried not taking iodine based on the well-publicized concerns, only to resort to taking it again and feeling more like themselves, with much more energy and focus. The placebo effect? I don't think so.

The claims couldn't be ignored because these clients weren't being thrown into a state of hyperactivity and feeling like they wanted to crawl out of their skin. That was undisputed. And for many, their thyroid antibodies decreased significantly after starting iodine supplementation. As they say, what's one person's remedy is another's poison.

Although I knew I was in for much more research around iodine, I was somewhat relieved. I don't like black and white when it comes to food, nutrition, and supplementation. Sure, I want to tell all of my clients, "Do this, don't do that," but it's rarely that straightforward.

So what differentiates those who can tolerate iodine from those who can't? We're all bio-individually unique, to be sure. There's no one-size-fits-all solution. But one well-publicized discovery was that if you have an excess or deficiency in selenium, you're likely to be intolerant of iodine supplementation.

Mario Renato Iwakura is a Brazilian engineer and Hashimoto's patient who is thoroughly well-versed in Hashimoto's literature. In Part 2 of Renato Iwakura's well-documented report, "Iodine and Hashimoto's Thyroiditis," he states, "A survey of the literature suggests that Hashimoto's is largely unaffected by iodine intake. However, the literature may be distorted by three circumstances under which iodine increases may harm, and iodine restriction help, Hashimoto's patients:

- Selenium deficiency causes an intolerance of high iodine;

- Iodine intake via seaweed is accompanied by thyrotoxic metals and halides;

- Sudden increases in iodine can induce reactive hypothyroidism."

Halides are chemical components of halogens—iodine is part of the halogen family that includes bromine, chlorine, and fluorine. Functional medicine pioneer, Dr. Amy Myers, states, "Fluorine, chlorine, and bromine are similar enough to iodine that your thyroid will suck them up and store them in place of iodine, effectively 'displacing' iodine."[4] It's referred to as the Bromine Dominance Theory.

Renato Iwakura continues, "All three of these negatives can be avoided by supplementing selenium along with iodine, using potassium iodide rather than seaweed as the source of iodine, and increasing iodine intake gradually. It's plausible that if iodine were supplemented in this way, then Hashimoto's patients would experience benefits with little risk of harm. Anecdotally, a number have reported benefits from supplemental iodine. Other evidence emphasizes the need for balance between iodine and selenium. Just as iodine without selenium can cause hypothyroidism, so too can selenium without iodine. Both are needed for good health."[5]

Thyroid expert Chris Kresser, who at one time strongly warned against iodine supplementation, later softened his view, stating, "A lot of studies show that selenium can protect against the potentially negative impacts of iodine supplementation for people who have autoimmune thyroid disease. So, if you do have Hashimoto's or Graves' . . . and you're considering taking iodine, you want to make sure that you're getting at least 200 micrograms of selenium combined from food and supplements each day."[6]

In June of 2013, The American Thyroid Association (ATA) published a statement warning about the risks of iodine overconsumption, especially from iodine, potassium iodide, and kelp supplements. They advised against taking more than 500 micrograms (note that this is micrograms, not milligrams) of iodine daily and stated that ingesting more than 1100 micrograms per day could cause thyroid dysfunction.

A study from *The American Journal of Clinical Nutrition* showed that taking relatively higher doses of iodine—400 micrograms daily or more—ironically lead to hypothyroidism.

> **" Iodine is a double-edged sword for thyroid sufferers."**
> **—Dr. Richard Shames**

"Iodine is a double-edged sword for thyroid sufferers. More than adequate amounts may further irritate and inflame an already ailing thyroid gland," says Dr. Shames.[7]

Naturopathic doctor and thyroid expert, Dr. Alan Christianson states, "Adequate iodine is especially important, but it is essential not to take too much. Iodine is one of the nutrients you can get too little or too much of, both impacting proper thyroid function. Most iodine supplements have too high of a dosage and can throw off thyroid balance. Patients who are on thyroid replacement have no need for iodine in excess of what is naturally occurring in their thyroid medication."[8]

If supplementing with iodine, some experts claim that it's important to start with a low dose and build up over time, as going too quickly can provoke or exacerbate an autoimmune thyroid response, especially in the presence of inadequate selenium.

Additionally, excess iodine intake can cause the thyroid to decrease productivity, temporarily, to protect against a hyperactive thyroid—it's a self-preservation mechanism called the Wolff-Chaikoff effect.

But here's a kicker. Iodine experts Dr. Guy Abraham and Dr. David Brownstein have had "great success" in treating those with Hashimoto's with high doses of iodine. Really high doses.

In Dr. Abraham's epic article on the topic,[9] he states that he administered his thyroid patients 50 milligrams (that's milligrams, not micrograms—so we're talkin' 50,000 micrograms!) of iodine/iodide solution daily, with "fantastic" results. These doctors claim that in Japan, where iodine intake is high, the population has low incidence of disease, including Hashimoto's. But it's also been found that Hashimoto's cases are similar in Japan and the U.S.

They've also claimed that animal studies have proven that high dosing doesn't fire up Hashimoto's unless the supplementation is paired with "goitrogenic" foods. (The "goitrogen" topic is a non sequitur. Again, see the chapter, *The Myth of "Goitrogens"* for a full explanation.)

But Dr. Christianson states, "I see all the unfortunate cases where high-dose iodine goes wrong." He calls iodine "the Goldilocks

> **" I see all the unfortunate cases where high-dose iodine goes wrong."**
> **—Dr. Alan Christianson**

mineral," stating, "Remember how Goldilocks wanted her porridge not too hot, but not too cold, and her bed not too hard, but not too soft? Iodine is like this. It is the Goldilocks mineral: too little is not good, and too much is not good. As vital as it is for your health, iodine can become toxic by as little as a few hundred extra *micrograms*. (My italics.)

"The tricky thing about iodine is that if you have too little, there's not enough to meet the nutritional requirements, but if you have too much, you blow the fuse and your thyroid quits working. Iodine in doses above nutritional requirements is the single best-documented environmental toxin capable of inducing autoimmune thyroid disease."[10]

Although I've followed Dr. Brownstein for a while and love his sassy, no-nonsense approach to everything from statins to diabetes to thyroid health, I've never taken him up on his suggestion to flood my body with iodine. And I have a real problem with Dr. Abraham's claim that it's "obvious" that iodine deficiency, not excess, is the cause of Hashimoto's.

It's far from obvious! Iodine deficiency is not the cause of Hashimoto's. I know plenty of other professionals who agree with me on this.

I haven't read Dr. Brownstein's claims and dosing recommendations in great detail, but I know that at one point, even he said that excessive iodine intake can aggravate Hashimoto's.

Dr. Christianson says that the risks of high-dose iodine are "irrefutable" and he's been vocal about how many have come to him for thyroid treatment after high doses of iodine. But he says, "To be clear, not all patients who take high-dose iodine will get thyroid disease, just like not all smokers get lung cancer."[11]

Here are the considerations:

- Whether or not to supplement with iodine to begin with?
- If so, with what—are sea vegetables and seafood enough?
- Are you taking thyroid hormone replacement, a source of iodine?
- Whether to use the sledgehammer approach, as suggested by Abraham and Brownstein, or the "tapping the nail into the wall" approach, as suggested by many others in the functional medicine community?

Dr. Christianson suggests 100-300 micrograms daily. And many doctors and professionals I respect recommend something in this range. Remember, if you're on thyroid hormone replacement, you need to take this into consideration. Dr. Christianson states, "If you have thyroid disease or others in your family do, you may be more at risk of the danger of too much. If you are on thyroid medications, you already receive substantial amounts of iodine."[10]

Many iodine and "thyroid support" supplements use kelp (aka kombu). And many people are drawn to kelp because they consider it a "natural" form of iodine. (Many iodine supplements are potassium iodide.) But it's just as risky to get too much iodine in the form of kelp supplementation as it is any other form of iodine.

Here are my general suggestions, whether you choose to supplement or not:

- Consider minimal use of iodized salt; perhaps use sea salt and iodized salt interchangeably.

- Eat sea vegetables 1-2 times per week (dulse, wakame, nori, etc.).

- Eat fish and seafood twice weekly: scallops, cod, and shrimp are said to be the best sources, but salmon, sardines, and small tuna species are also good choices. Make sure it's sustainably-sourced vs. farmed. (See Appendix E for locating sustainably-sourced seafood.)

- Based on the dangers of bromine, chlorine, and fluoride (they can displace iodine): filter your water to reduce chlorine and fluoride exposure, avoid bromines as much as possible, and swim in salt water to avoid absorbing chlorine through your skin.

- Avoid added fluoride in toothpaste, dental treatments, and some teas and medications.

- Eat organic as often as possible. Insecticides contain chlorine and bromine.

- Be mindful of iodine levels in your multi-vitamin, including prenatals.

- Cook more at home, where you can control the type of salt and how much you use.

- Eat other foods rich in iodine: potatoes with skin on, egg yolks, turkey, and believe it or not, strawberries.

See *The Essential Thyroid Cookbook Lifestyle Companion Guide* for a list of bromine sources and more information on how fluoride affects thyroid function, including our Biological Dentistry guide. You can download it for free on our website: www.thyroidcookbook.com/companion.

I'll leave you with this. As one doctor in my nutrition education program stated, "Nutrition is the only science in the world where diametrically opposed theories can be proven right because we're all bio-individually unique."

The above list highlights foods that are rich sources of iodine, regardless of whether they ranked high in our analyses or not. As explained in the Our Methodology *chapter, there are other whole foods, aside from the ones we've chosen to highlight in this cookbook per our thoughtful ranking system, that are rich in the nutrients we identified as being especially thyroid- and immune-supportive. In other words, there are foods listed above that aren't included in this cookbook because our ultimate goal is to expand perceptions of healthy eating and health-supportive foods.*

Iron

Iron's job is to transport oxygen through the body and to promote cellular growth. It's common for those with hypothyroidism to become low in iron. Women are especially prone to deficiency because during childbearing years, we require a great deal more iron than men.

Many of the symptoms of hypothyroidism and low iron overlap and can exacerbate one another: fatigue, breathlessness, heart palpitations, muscle pain/achiness, low libido, brain fog, and hair loss.

If you're low in iron, it can[1]:

- Inhibit the ability to produce adequate thyroid hormones

- Interfere with thyroid hormone metabolism

- Impair the production of your thyroid peroxidase enzyme—an iron-dependent enzyme that catalyzes thyroid hormone production

Insufficient iron can inhibit the proliferation of immune cells and autoimmune diseases are frequently characterized by anemia (low iron).[2] The most common cause of anemia is iron-deficient anemia. Dr. Richard Shames, thyroid expert, states, "[When anemia and hypothyroidism are present together], the low thyroid can be partially, or totally, causing the anemia, due to sluggish production of red blood cells and sluggish absorption of iron from the intestine."[3]

Iron needs an acid for proper absorption. Therefore, antacids (and calcium supplements) taken with meals can inhibit iron uptake. When testing, it's important to not only test serum iron levels, but also:

> 66 Insufficient iron can inhibit the proliferation of immune cells and autoimmune diseases are frequently characterized by anemia (low iron)."

- Hemoglobin

- Serum ferritin (a measure of iron stores)

- Total iron binding capacity (TIBC)

Having a picture of your total iron status is important, especially if you're hypothyroid and have difficulty thermo-regulating (you're frequently cold).

It's often assumed that if hemoglobin (red blood cell quantity and quality) is normal, iron is normal. But this isn't always true. Ferritin is particularly important for the body's ability to use T3, the active form of thyroid hormone. This is why I always ask my clients to get their ferritin

> 66 Ferritin is particularly important for the body's ability to use T3, the active form of thyroid hormone."

tested along with their thyroid hormones and Hashimoto's antibodies.

Low ferritin is also a primary factor in hair loss, which many with hypothyroidism and Hashimoto's suffer from. While low thyroid function alone can cause thinning, so can low ferritin—a double whammy. While the causes of hair shedding can be multifactorial, assessing iron levels is a first step in remedying the problem and several of my clients have said that iron supplementation "literally stopped" their hair loss.

While eating iron-rich foods is important, it's often necessary to supplement, especially in the face of low ferritin. Supplement until ferritin (iron storage) is replenished, not simply until your serum iron level normalizes. This can take some time. But know that the sledgehammer approach isn't a good idea, as it's possible to overdose on iron—it can cause liver issues. So it's best to work closely with your doctor for the right dosing.

Iron supplementation, even in reasonable doses, is known for causing constipation and sometimes nausea. Two things that can help with constipation are magnesium and probiotics, but you can also opt for a gentle form of iron such as Ferrasorb or Ferrochel (iron bisglycinate). (See Appendix B for our supplement recommendations, of which you can also find links to on our website: www.thyroidcookbook.com.)

Rich food sources of iron include: spinach, Swiss chard, turnip greens, collard greens, mustard greens, beet greens, romaine lettuce, asparagus, bok choy, leeks, potatoes (skin on), sea vegetables, sauerkraut, kimchi, organ meats, beef, chicken (dark meat), lamb, oysters, tuna, shrimp, clams, mussels, tempeh, natto, miso, peanuts, adzuki beans, garbanzo beans, lima beans, lentils, yogurt, kefir, cumin, parsley, turmeric, basil, oregano, thyme, sesame seeds, pumpkin seeds, almonds, hazelnuts, cashews, amaranth, buckwheat, millet, oats, quinoa, chili peppers, chili powder, blackstrap molasses, and dark chocolate.

The above list highlights foods that are rich sources of iron, regardless of whether they ranked high in our analyses or not. As explained in the Our Methodology *chapter, there are other whole foods, aside from the ones we've chosen to highlight in this cookbook per our thoughtful ranking system, that are rich in the nutrients we identified as being especially thyroid- and immune-supportive. In other words, there are foods listed above that aren't included in this cookbook because our ultimate goal is to expand perceptions of healthy eating and health-supportive foods.*

Other considerations:

- Adequate Vitamin C helps with iron absorption. Squeezing lime juice on your beans, lemon juice on kale, or marinating meat with citrus are all great ways to promote this synergy.

- If you're taking thyroid hormone replacement, allow at least four hours before taking any iron supplementation.

- Coffee and tea inhibit iron uptake and should be consumed an hour away from iron-rich foods and/or iron supplementation.

- Cooking with cast iron is a good way to get iron into your food.

Magnesium

Magnesium has been nicknamed "the miracle mineral." It's even been called a panacea.

Many are deficient (the estimates are as high as 70 percent of the population) due to excessive exposure to nitrogen (largely from fertilizers), phosphorus (largely from soft drinks), copper (largely from water pipes), and iron (largely from excessive red meat and/or supplements). Deficiency can also be a result of taking too much supplemental calcium.

There are many foods that are considered rich in magnesium, but given that we don't have the mineral-rich soils of yore, we're not getting as much of this important mineral (including other minerals) from our food.

Dr. Carolyn Dean, an outspoken, sassy voice of reason in the functional medicine community, has been a magnesium "activist" for years. She's the author of *The Magnesium Miracle* and has written extensively about the dangers of magnesium deficiency.

She says, "Magnesium is responsible for the function of 325 enzymes; is an absolute requirement for calcium to be incorporated into bone; keeps toxic chemicals out of the brain; dances with calcium to create nerve impulses and muscle impulses; keeps muscles relaxed, including the heart and blood vessels; and triggers dozens of health conditions if it is deficient."[1]

Some of those deficiency conditions include anxiety, sleep issues, fatigue, palpitations, PMS, bloating, migraines, restless leg syndrome, muscle cramping/spasms, increased inflammation, compromised pathways of detoxification, depression, Syndrome X (aka metabolic syndrome), kidney disease, constipation, sluggish heart function, twitching, irritability, osteoporosis, and diabetes.

> " Magnesium promotes a robust immune system and is a proven immune modulator for those with autoimmune conditions."

Magnesium promotes a robust immune system[2] and is a proven immune modulator for those with autoimmune conditions.[3]

Every organ in the body, including the thyroid, needs adequate magnesium. It's not so much that a magnesium deficiency is a direct trigger of hypothyroidism or Hashimoto's, it's that the deficiency acts in a sneaky, back-of-the-barn way. As you can see from the list above, many of the symptoms of magnesium deficiency and low thyroid function overlap. So insufficient magnesium levels can slow symptom alleviation for those on a thyroid-healing journey.

Earlier, we talked about how magnesium is a carrier for calcium and discussed these checks and balances relationships with minerals (copper/zinc and iodine/selenium). The same goes for calcium and magnesium—a balance of these two minerals is important for a healthy thyroid. When calcium levels are high in the blood, often due—at least in part—to magnesium and Vitamin D deficiencies, the thyroid makes a hormone called calcitonin that helps to regulate calcium and reduce blood calcium levels.

According to nutritional consultant, Dr. Lawrence Wilson, "The higher the level of hair calcium, in general, the lower the effective activity of the thyroid gland. This occurs because one of the effects of [the thyroid hormones] T3 and T4 is to lower calcium levels in the tissues and at times, in the blood.

"Once released into the blood, T4 must be absorbed into our cells. For this to occur, the cell membranes must function properly. Too little or too much cell membrane permeability will affect the uptake of T4. Problems with cell permeability can be due to accumulation of biounavailable calcium and magnesium in the cell membranes. This excessively stabilizes the cell membranes and reduces cell permeability. Deficient calcium and magnesium cause excessive cell permeability.

"Once inside the cells, thyroxine [T4] must be converted to T3 or triiodothyronine, the more active form of the hormone. This conversion requires selenium, magnesium and other nutrients." He sums things up by saying, "As you can see, calcium is crucial for proper thyroid health, but for calcium to properly function it must have its friend, magnesium."[4]

Rich food sources of magnesium include: spinach, Swiss chard, turnip greens, mustard greens, collard greens, beet greens, green beans, summer squash, pumpkin seeds, almonds, brown rice, sea vegetables, lentils, lima beans, tempeh, natto, miso, and tofu. (We're not a fan of tofu, as it's not fermented.)

The list below highlights foods that are rich sources of magnesium, regardless of whether they ranked high in our analyses or not. As explained in the Our Methodology *chapter, there are other whole foods, aside from the ones we've chosen to highlight in this cookbook per our thoughtful ranking system, that are rich in the nutrients we identified as being especially thyroid- and immune-supportive. In other words, there are foods listed above that aren't included in this cookbook because our ultimate goal is to expand perceptions of healthy eating and health-supportive foods.*

Summary:

- Adequate magnesium levels make you less prone to excess calcium.

- Without excess calcium, your thyroid works better.

- For calcium to work for you versus against you, you need adequate magnesium.

Other considerations:

- Vitamin C competes with magnesium—make sure you're not taking excessive C supplementation.

- If supplementing with magnesium while on thyroid hormone replacement, take the magnesium four hours from your thyroid meds.

- Magnesium supplementation can cause loose stools. Gradually increase to tolerable dose.

Dr. Dean states, "The Recommended Dietary Allowance (RDA) for magnesium is between 350 and 400 milligrams per day, which is just enough to ward off outright deficiency. But for optimal health and for the twenty-two conditions that are triggered by magnesium deficiency, perhaps twice as much magnesium is needed. Because we probably don't get nearly enough magnesium from our diet, we have to investigate magnesium supplements."[1]

There are several types of magnesium and I'm often asked what type of supplementation to take. My answer is, "It depends." The short of it is that people respond differently to the various types—and by "respond," I'm referring to bowel tolerance in the form of possible loose stools.

According to respected natural health expert, Dr. John Douillard, the best forms of supplemental magnesium are magnesium malate, magnesium glycinate, and magnesium citrate. He says to avoid magnesium oxide.[5]

Dr. Dean concurs. She says, "I stopped using magnesium oxide in 2005 when I read a study that showed only 4 percent of the oxide form of magnesium is absorbed. That's why magnesium oxide is a great laxative but if you want to stock up on magnesium, you need to use other forms."[1]

Applying magnesium oil to the skin is a good way to get this important mineral if you have digestive issues or if taking an oral supplement gives you bowel troubles. Many in the functional medicine community suggest magnesium citrate. Another effective way to increase magnesium levels without taking it orally is by taking epsom salt baths. For relaxing muscle spasms or soreness, magnesium oil can be massaged and absorbed directly into the skin.

Manganese

Manganese. You just don't hear a lot about it. And maybe, when you've seen the word, you thought that the writer didn't know how to spell "magnesium."

The term is derived from the Greek word for "magic" and indeed, the ancient Greeks regarded manganese as having magical powers. It's a mineral, but it's also a powerful antioxidant (free radical scavenger) that helps to prevent cell damage.

Manganese deficiency can lead to low cholesterol (manganese is needed for cholesterol synthesis), fat accumulation in the liver, asthma, osteoporosis, joint pain, selenium deficiency, pancreatic dysfunction (including elevated insulin), reduced immune function, hair loss, tremors, muscle cramping, and mitochondrial abnormalities.

Speaking of mitrochondria, manganese is required for the production of superoxide dismutase (MnSOD)—MnSOD is an anti-inflammatory and has a calming effect on the immune system. It's also important for our mitochondrial antioxidant "security system."[1] These mitochondrial engines help us to produce heat and energy, which is especially important for those with hypothyroidism, given that fatigue and difficulty thermo-regulating (being frequently cold) are hallmark symptoms of low thyroid function.

Manganese is involved in thyroid hormone synthesis—it's important for the production of T4. As you may know, much of our T4 needs to be converted into T3 and this T4/T3 conversion largely takes place in the liver. MnSOD helps to facilitate this activity. Selenium increases liver MnSOD expression.

Other benefits of manganese include

> " Manganese is involved in thyroid hormone synthesis—it's important for the production of T4."

aiding in the absorption of magnesium, boosting the effectiveness of calcium, and supporting the utilization of B, C, and E vitamins—all of which are important for thyroid and immune function.

Because so many with hypothyroidism and Hashimoto's suffer from hair loss, it's important to understand the role of manganese. As I tell my clients, when it comes to nutrition for hair loss, among other things, focus on minerals, minerals, minerals—primarily iron (including ferritin, our iron storage protein), zinc, and manganese.

According to functional medicine physician, Dr. Jeremy Kaslow, "Trace Minerals International of Colorado examined the mineral metabolism of 19 patients with alopecia (hair loss). The spectrophotometric analysis showed manganese deficiency in all 19."[2] Alopecia is autoimmune hair loss, which I've had, off and on (mostly off), for over 30 years.

While rare, manganese excess, mostly from overexposure to industrial pollution; overconsumption of coffee, tea, and chocolate; and excess supplementation can reduce

T4 and T3 thyroid hormone levels, which shows that both deficiency and excess of manganese can impact thyroid function.

Other considerations:

- Calcium supplementation can interfere with manganese absorption.

- If you have anemia (low iron), the body will try to absorb as much manganese as possible, so even minimal supplementation can lead to manganese excess.

- Manganese and zinc therapy can reduce copper levels and therefore manganese and/or zinc may be of therapeutic value in the treatment of symptoms linked to excess copper.[2]

Rich food sources of manganese include: collard greens, beet greens, Swiss chard, spinach, kale, turnip greens, mustard greens, sea vegetables, summer squash, sweet potato, winter squash, green peas, beets, green beans, Brussels sprouts, cabbage, broccoli, asparagus, leeks, tomatoes, crimini mushrooms, cauliflower, romaine lettuce, celery, garlic, basil, bok choy, garbanzo beans, lentils, lima beans, navy beans, pineapple, raspberries, strawberries, blueberries, cranberries, barley, quinoa, oats, brown rice, buckwheat, rye, cloves, cinnamon, walnuts, almonds, flaxseeds, pumpkin seeds, sesame seeds, fennel, turmeric, cumin, oregano, mustard seeds, tempeh, miso, and tofu. (We're not a fan of tofu, as it's not fermented.)

The above list highlights foods that are rich sources of manganese, regardless of whether they ranked high in our analyses or not. As explained in the Our Methodology *chapter, there are other whole foods, aside from the ones we've chosen to highlight in this cookbook per our thoughtful ranking system, that are rich in the nutrients we identified as being especially thyroid- and immune-supportive. In other words, there are foods listed above that aren't included in this cookbook because our ultimate goal is to expand perceptions of healthy eating and health-supportive foods.*

Selenium

If iodine is "the big daddy" thyroid mineral, then selenium is "the big mama." When it comes to a healthy thyroid, the importance of selenium simply can't be underestimated. As such, I've nicknamed selenium "the thyroid triple play" because it:

- Supports healthy thyroid hormone metabolism[1]

- Helps the body convert T4 (the inactive form of thyroid hormone) into T3 (the active form)[2]

- Helps to reduce Hashimoto's antibodies[3]

> 66 When it comes to a healthy thyroid, the importance of selenium simply can't be underestimated."

According to Dr. Bruce Ames (per Dr. Andrew Weil), "Even modest selenium deficiency appears to be associated with age-related diseases and conditions such as cancer, heart disease and immune dysfunction."[4]

Many with hypothyroidism and Hashimoto's are privy to the benefits of selenium specifically. A common question I hear is, "How much selenium should I take?" Perhaps none, especially if your Hashimoto's is managed. But selenium supplementation is sometimes warranted, especially considering that studies have shown that taking selenium reduces thyroid antibodies.[5] The recommended dose is 200 micrograms.

According to thyroid health leader, Chris Kresser, "Several research studies have demonstrated the benefits of selenium supplementation in treating autoimmune thyroid conditions. One study found that selenium supplementation had a significant impact on inflammatory activity in thyroid-specific autoimmune disease and reducing inflammation may limit damage to thyroid tissue. Another study followed patients for nine months and found that selenium supplementation reduced thyroid peroxidase antibody levels in the blood, even in selenium sufficient patients."[6]

Dr. David Brownstein states, "Selenium has been shown to slow the progression of autoimmune thyroid disorders."[7]

It's generally thought that a little selenium goes a long way, which is why I've been historically reluctant to recommend supplementation. Selenium supplementation may not be a good idea for those already eating a selenium-rich diet, but considering that our soils aren't as rich as they were in the past century and because soil quality varies, we may not be getting the selenium (or other nutrients) we think we are.

Too many read about the benefits of selenium and say, "I'm going to get myself a bottle of that!" and go gangbusters. More isn't more. I've seen too many people fall prey to "too much of a good thing" with selenium and experience anxiety, anxiousness, monkey mind, irritability, sleep issues, and heart palpitations. So really, the concern is over-supplementation. The 200 micrograms recommended for the reduction of thyroid antibodies isn't likely to give people the jitters.

Still, there's another factor that can contribute to overstimulation. Let's harken back to iodine—in the *Iodine* subchapter, I shared that one well-publicized discovery was that if you have an excess or deficiency in selenium (the big mama), you're likely to be intolerant of iodine supplementation (the big daddy). That "intolerance" of iodine can lead to the same hyper-like symptoms I list above.

Mama and daddy need to be in balance. Given that iodine and selenium are the two thyroid-supportive minerals that get the most airtime, often, people are supplementing with

> 66 Selenium has been shown to slow the progression of autoimmune thyroid disorders."
> —Dr. David Brownstein

both. Maybe it's in the same "thyroid support" supplement. (I'm generally leery of "thyroid support" supplements.) Or they're taking iodine and selenium separately. Regardless, here's another situation where there's a checks and balances with mineral intake.

Adequate selenium supports efficient thyroid hormone synthesis and metabolism and protects the thyroid from damage due to excessive iodine.[8]

In the *Iodine* subchapter, I quote Mario Renato Iwakura, a Brazilian engineer and Hashimoto's patient well-versed in Hashimoto's literature, who states, ". . . evidence emphasizes the need for balance between iodine and selenium. Just as iodine without selenium can cause hypothyroidism, so too can selenium without iodine. Both are needed for good health."[9]

Likewise, Kresser states, "If you do have Hashimoto's or Graves' . . . and you're considering taking iodine, you want to make sure that you're getting at least 200 micrograms of selenium combined from food and supplements each day. Adequate selenium nutrition supports efficient thyroid hormone synthesis and metabolism and protects the thyroid gland from damage from excessive iodine exposure."[10]

Another critical role of selenium is that it helps with glutathione recycling. Glutathione is a superpower antioxidant that significantly strengthens the immune system and is considered by many functional medicine doctors to be one of the pillars of fighting Hashimoto's. (For more on glutathione, see the *Vitamins and Other Nutrients* subchapter in the chapter, *The Nutritional Heavy Hitters*.)

I would be remiss in concluding this section without mentioning selenium's relationship to mercury. Mercury has been shown to bind to thyroid tissue and inhibit proper thyroid function, including T4/T3 conversion. According to Dr. Brownstein, "Because mercury binds so tightly to our tissues and enzymes, the body has a very difficult time disposing of mercury. Selenium is one of the most potent chelators (binders) of mercury."[11]

Here's the Catch-22. Mercury can displace selenium. So even if you're getting adequate selenium, the mercury may be displacing it. So then the selenium doesn't have the capacity to act as a mercury chelator.

My suggestion? Remove your mercury dental fillings—stat. Many have reported significant improvement in their hypothyroidism and Hashimoto's by removing their mercury/amalgam fillings. Ensure that you work with a dentist who knows what they're doing. Firstly, they need to guide you on how to prepare your body for the removal,

> " Adequate selenium supports efficient thyroid hormone synthesis and metabolism and protects the thyroid from damage due to excessive iodine."

which usually lasts a week prior to the procedure. Secondly, they should use a throat dam so that the mercury vapors aren't inhaled during the removal process. (See *The Essential Thyroid Cookbook Lifestyle Companion Guide* for our Biological Dentistry guide. You can download it for free on our website: www.thyroidcookbook.com/companion.)

The second most prevalent source of mercury is fish, especially larger species of tuna. You'll see that several of our recipes include fish, so we recommend being careful about how you source it. (See Appendix E for safe seafood resources.)

Other considerations:

- Although it's easy to get too much selenium, selenium toxicity is rare.
- Vitamin E helps to facilitate selenium absorption.
- Selenium up-regulates MnSOD expression; if you remember from the manganese section, MnSOD is an anti-inflammatory and has a calming effect on the immune system.

Rich food sources of selenium include: tuna, shrimp, sardines, salmon, cod, scallops, turkey, chicken, lamb, beef, barley, eggs, mushrooms (crimini and shiitake), asparagus, mustard seeds, and tofu. (We're not a fan of tofu, as it's not fermented.)

The above list highlights foods that are rich sources of selenium, regardless of whether they ranked high in our analyses or not. As explained in the Our Methodology *chapter, there are other whole foods, aside from the ones we've chosen to highlight in this cookbook per our thoughtful ranking system, that are rich in the nutrients we identified as being especially thyroid- and immune-supportive. In other words, there are foods listed above that aren't included in this cookbook because our ultimate goal is to expand perceptions of healthy eating and health-supportive foods.*

Zinc

I dubbed selenium "the thyroid triple play" and zinc is deserving of the title "the thyroid quad play." Adequate zinc levels help to[1]:

- Increase Free T3, the unbound, available form of the active thyroid hormone, T3
- Lower RT3, the "anti-T3 hormone"
- Normalize TSH
- Convert T4 to T3

Many with hypothyroidism are zinc-deficient, which can also compromise immune function.[2]

According to Dr. David Brownstein, "The serum levels of zinc are positively correlated with the levels of the active thyroid hormone, T3. My experience has clearly shown a decrease in the conversion of T4 into T3 in zinc-deficient individuals."[3]

In the copper section, I referenced zinc, given that there is such an important relationship between these two minerals. To review, copper and zinc have a seesaw relationship whereby when one rises, the other falls. Our ideal copper to zinc ratio should be 1:8 in favor of zinc. If we veer too far from this ratio, it can slow thyroid function by thwarting that important T4/T3 conversion.

While hair loss, a hallmark symptom of low thyroid function, is often multifactorial, a zinc deficiency is a primary consideration. When it comes to minerals, low ferritin (your iron storage protein) and low manganese can also be culprits.

According to pharmacist Suzy Cohen, "When you run out of zinc, you may gain weight, develop hypothyroidism, experience chronic diarrhea, or lose interest in sex. You may also get sick more frequently. That's because zinc plays an important role in immune function, and without enough of it, you lose your defense system, most notably some of your T-helper cells and natural killer cells. Ultimately, this means that you are less able to defend yourself from pathogens in your environment.

"Zinc is involved in the creation of thyroid hormone. You need it to activate your hormone T4, which is a precursor to the active, useful form called T3; and you need this T3 to enter the cell, where it wakes you up. With low zinc, you may develop hypothyroidism."[4]

Zinc (and manganese) may interfere with iron absorption. So while zinc and iron are both important, this is another "not too much, not too little" situation where over-supplementation with zinc could lead to malabsorption of iron.

Rich food sources of zinc include: spinach, asparagus, sea vegetables, mushrooms, beef, chicken (dark meat), turkey (dark meat), lamb, pork, oysters, crab, lobster, scallops, natto, peanuts, sesame seeds, pumpkin seeds, almonds, cashews, amaranth, buckwheat, millet, oats, adzuki beans, garbanzo beans, kefir, yogurt, chili powder, and dark chocolate.

> **" Many with hypothyroidism are zinc-deficient, which can also compromise immune function."**

The above list highlights foods that are rich sources of zinc, regardless of whether they ranked high in our analyses or not. As explained in the Our Methodology *chapter, there are other whole foods, aside from the ones we've chosen to highlight in this cookbook per our thoughtful ranking system, that are rich in the nutrients we identified as being especially thyroid- and immune-supportive. In other words, there are foods listed above that aren't included in this cookbook because our ultimate goal is to expand perceptions of healthy eating and health-supportive foods.*

Red meat is said to be the best of the best sources of zinc. Therefore, vegetarians are much more prone to zinc deficiency and often need supplementation—about 50 percent higher doses.

Vitamins and Other Nutrients

- Vitamin A
- B Vitamins
  - Vitamin B_1
  - Vitamin B_2
  - Vitamin B_6
  - Vitamin B_{12}
- Vitamin C
- Vitamin D
- Vitamin E
- Omega-3 Fatty Acids
- Tyrosine
- Epigallocatechin gallate (EGCG)
- Glutathione
- Lycopene
- Probiotics
- Resveratrol

Vitamin A

The term "Vitamin A" refers to a broad group of related nutrients including retinoids such as retinol, and carotenoids such as beta-carotene, astaxanthin, and lutein, which are inactive forms of Vitamin A that are ideally converted into retinol, the bioactive form.

Vitamin A plays a critical role in immunity and those with Hashimoto's are often deficient.[1] It's an essential fat-soluble vitamin that reduces systemic inflammation; inflammation and autoimmunity are kissing cousins, so strategies that tame inflammation are critical for those with any form of autoimmunity.

It's also a powerful antioxidant that protects the body from disease-causing pathogens and infections, which is of particular importance, given that infections, including stealth infections such as Epstein-Barr, can trigger autoimmune conditions. Vitamin A also inhibits the potentially negative effects of phytic acid found in grains. (See the chapter, *In Defense of Grains*.)

According to functional medicine expert, Dr. Mark Hyman, "Vitamin A is critical for activation of the thyroid receptor and making your thyroid hormone turn on the genes that

> **❝ Vitamin A plays a critical role in immunity and those with Hashimoto's are often deficient.❞**

improve your metabolism. It combines with the active hormone T3, which allows the hormone to 'dock' on its receptor or landing spot on the cell."[2]

The thyroid requires more Vitamin A than other glands[3] and a deficiency can inhibit T4/T3 conversion. Conversely, thyroid hormones play a significant role in the conversion of beta-carotene to retinol, also known as "true Vitamin A." Thus when hypothyroidism is present, Vitamin A deficiency may result. What we have here is a conversion negative feedback loop.

Low thyroid function somewhat explains why so many have trouble converting beta-carotene to Vitamin A. Ideally, the body can convert beta-carotene into retinol, or "true Vitamin A," but only a measly 3 percent gets converted in a healthy adult.[4] Many don't convert at all.

The conversion of beta-carotene to retinol takes place in the presence of sufficient bile salts and fat-splitting enzymes, which many with digestive dysfunction are deficient in.

Other reasons for non-conversion include but aren't limited to: digestive issues (rampant for those with autoimmunity), bacterial imbalances in the digestive tract (also prevalent), elevated exposure to toxic chemicals including pesticides, stress, excessive alcohol use, certain medications, a low-fat diet, diabetes, intestinal parasites, and Celiac disease.

According to Sarah Pope, passionate nutrition educator and creator of the popular website, The Healthy Home Economist, "The biological conditions under which [conversion] occurs must be optimal meaning the person must be in excellent health with a highly efficient digestive system. Who today has excellent digestive health? Not many."[5]

Nutrition researcher, Dr. Michelle Kmiec, states, "If you have zero digestive issues, are in perfect health, eat at least twelve full servings of fruits and vegetables a day, allow yourself to eat 'real' fat, never eat processed or fast foods, and have no stress in your life, then congratulations! You may have an excellent shot at getting sufficient amounts of Vitamin A (retinol) from beta-carotene."[6]

Lisa and I had a good discussion about whether we wanted to highlight beta-carotene in our recipe ingredients at all. Beta-carotene is found in plant foods and is often

> **❝ The thyroid requires more Vitamin A than other glands and a deficiency can inhibit T4/T3 conversion.❞**

> 66 Both beta-carotene and retinol are important. If someone has issues with fat malabsorption, that's problematic—they likely will convert little to nothing. But I don't want to completely rule out carotenoids. I think there's something beautifully important about our body being able to bio-regulate conversion of beta-carotene to active Vitamin A based on need."
> —Lisa Markley, MS, RDN

associated with orange vegetables—the best sources are sweet potatoes, carrots, pumpkin, winter squash, and also dark green leafy vegetables such as spinach and kale. It's important to eat these vegetables of course, but we understand that you cannot rely solely on these foods for adequate Vitamin A and that given the importance of "true Vitamin A" (retinols), it's wise to get Vitamin A in a form that's readily available to the body—no conversion required. Retinoids are found in pastured butter, ghee, cream, egg yolks, organ meat (especially liver), cod liver oil, shellfish (especially shrimp), wild salmon, and sardines. (This cookbook is dairy-free, but if you can tolerate dairy, you have more sources of Vitamin A available to you.)

Lisa said, "Both beta-carotene and retinol are important. If someone has issues with fat malabsorption, that's problematic—they likely will convert little to nothing. But I don't want to completely rule out carotenoids. I think there's something beautifully important about our body being able to bio-regulate conversion of beta-carotene to active Vitamin A based on need."

Lisa and I are pro-orange veggies because it's possible to become a better beta-carotene to retinol converter by way of:

- Optimizing thyroid function, which we hope to help you achieve with this cookbook

- Immune modulation, achieved largely by healing the digestive system

- Addressing toxic body burden and reducing exposure to chemicals and toxins (eating organic will get you a long way)

- Optimizing gallbladder function, which helps us produce the bile acids and enzymes required to break down carotene and convert it to Vitamin A

Additionally, we should be eating sweet potatoes, carrots, pumpkin, winter squash, and dark green leafy vegetables such as spinach and kale anyway. The beta-carotene in these foods provides other nutritional value beyond its potential—even if limited—to convert to retinol.

It's important to understand that Vitamin A is one of the few supplements that's toxic at high doses—more than 10,000 IU per day has been associated with toxicity that can cause night blindness, irritability, hair loss, and blurred vision.

Rich food sources of Vitamin A as retinol include: pastured butter, ghee, cream, egg yolks, organ meat (especially liver), cod liver oil, shellfish (especially shrimp), wild salmon, and sardines.

Rich food sources of Vitamin A as beta-carotene include: sweet potatoes, carrots, pumpkin, winter squash, and dark green leafy vegetables such as spinach and kale.

The above list highlights foods that are rich sources of Vitamin A as beta-carotene and Vitamin A as retinol, regardless of whether they ranked high in our analyses or not. As explained in the Our Methodology *chapter, there are other whole foods, aside from the ones we've chosen to highlight in this cookbook per our thoughtful ranking system, that are rich in the nutrients we identified as being especially thyroid- and immune-supportive. In other words, there are foods listed above that aren't included in this cookbook because our ultimate goal is to expand perceptions of healthy eating and health-supportive foods.*

B Vitamins

Below, we highlight four of the B vitamins, but nearly all are supportive to the entire body. They help to make us more metabolically efficient and have been nicknamed "the anti-stress vitamins." Stress and anxiety are common in the hypothyroid community due to not only the fatigue that's often present with the condition, but also the concomitant adrenal dysfunction/HPA axis dysfunction. Our adrenals make our stress hormones, adrenaline and cortisol, and adrenal dysfunction often leads to an overproduction of these hormones. (See *The Essential Thyroid Cookbook Lifestyle Companion Guide* for our Restore Your Adrenals guide. You can download it for free on our website: www.thyroidcookbook.com/companion.)

Additionally, B vitamins work in tandem with bioflavonoids—brightly-colored chemicals in fruits and vegetables that act as protective antioxidants and also quell inflammation, which is significant for anyone with an autoimmune condition. Overall, the Bs help to reduce stress-induced damage, increase our natural resiliency, and strengthen the immune system.

When it comes to thyroid health, the only exception is Vitamin B_3 (niacin). There's some evidence that *supplemental* niacin disrupts some, but not all, thyroid hormone production. The study was done on people with no hypothyroid symptoms who maintained a euthyroid (healthy thyroid) state during and after treatment.[1] Again, this is only a potential concern for those supplementing with niacin—niacin is often used as a cholesterol-lowering mechanism. There's no reason to believe that eating foods that contain niacin or taking a multi-vitamin with niacin will negatively affect thyroid function.

Vitamin B_1 (thiamine)

Vitamin B_1 has been shown to help with the fatigue associated with hypothyroidism.[1] According to physician and clinical nutritionist, Dr. Josh Axe, "Vitamin B_{12} and thiamine [B_1] are important for neurologic function and hormonal balance. Research shows that supplementing with thiamine can help combat symptoms of autoimmune disease, including chronic fatigue."[2]

> " Vitamin B_1 has been shown to help with the fatigue associated with hypothyroidism."

Additionally, thyroid expert, Dr. Alan Christianson states, "There is current data showing [that] thiamine is beneficial for both the antibodies of Hashimoto's and hormone conversion." [3]

Thiamine's primary job is to convert carbohydrates into energy; it also helps with the digestion of proteins and fats. Many with autoimmunity have an enzymatic dysfunction that inhibits the metabolism of thiamine and it's not uncommon for those with hypothyroidism and Hashimoto's to be deficient, given that digestive malabsorption is a known cause of thiamine deficiency.

Rich food sources of Vitamin B_1 include: asparagus, green peas, crimini mushrooms, Brussels sprouts, beet greens, spinach, eggplant, cabbage, romaine lettuce, sunflower seeds, flaxseeds, pistachios, navy beans, black beans, and barley.

The above list highlights foods that are rich sources of B_1, regardless of whether they ranked high in our analyses or not. As explained in the Our Methodology *chapter, there are other whole foods, aside from the ones we've chosen to highlight in this cookbook per our thoughtful ranking system, that are rich in the nutrients we identified as being especially thyroid- and immune-supportive. In other words, there are foods listed above that aren't included in this cookbook because our ultimate goal is to expand perceptions of healthy eating and health-supportive foods.*

Vitamin B_2 *(riboflavin)*

According to thyroid expert, Dr. Sara Gottfried, we need Vitamin B_2 for our neuroendocrine system to work properly.[1] Thyroid hormone helps to regulate the enzymatic conversion of Vitamin B_2 to its active form.[2]

Adrenal status plays a significant role in thyroid status and a lack of B_2 suppresses thyroid function and can also affect adrenal hormone production.

Vitamin B_2 also plays a significant role in maintaining glutathione status, which is critical for a properly functioning immune system; a deficiency in B_2 can lead to immune response abnormalities.[3] (For more on glutathione, see the *Vitamins and Other Nutrients* subchapter in the chapter, *The Nutritional Heavy Hitters.*)

Rich food sources of Vitamin B_2 include: asparagus, collard greens, spinach, beet greens, bok choy, turnip greens, kale, mustard greens, Swiss chard, green beans, bell peppers, broccoli, crimini mushrooms, shiitake mushrooms, sea vegetables, tempeh, and eggs.

The above list highlights foods that are rich sources of B_2, regardless of whether they ranked high in our analyses or not. As explained in the Our Methodology *chapter, there are other whole foods, aside from the ones we've chosen to highlight in this cookbook per our thoughtful ranking system, that are rich in the nutrients we identified as being especially thyroid- and immune-supportive. In other words, there are foods listed above that aren't included in this cookbook because our ultimate goal is to expand perceptions of healthy eating and health-supportive foods.*

Vitamin B_6 (pyridoxine)

Vitamin B_6 helps convert iodine into thyroid hormone, reduces bloating associated with digestive dysfunction, helps to make serotonin (a feel-good neurotransmitter), and helps relieve anxiety. It also helps our neuro-endocrine system to work properly.[1]

> 66 Unrelenting stress can deplete B_6 and a deficiency can cause an increase in the antibodies associated with Hashimoto's."

Unrelenting stress can deplete B_6 and a deficiency can cause an increase in the antibodies associated with Hashimoto's. Vitamin B_6 also plays a significant role in maintaining glutathione status, which is critical for a properly functioning immune system; a deficiency in B_6 can lead to immune response abnormalities.[2] (For more on glutathione, see the *Vitamins and Other Nutrients* subchapter in the chapter, *The Nutritional Heavy Hitters*.)

Rich food sources of Vitamin B_6 include: beet greens, spinach, turnip greens, kale, Swiss chard, mustard greens, collard greens, cabbage, winter squash, broccoli, Brussels sprouts, bok choy, bell peppers, asparagus, cauliflower, carrots, tomatoes, leeks, summer squash, sweet potatoes, potatoes, chili peppers, bananas, garlic, tuna, turkey, beef, chicken, and salmon.

The above list highlights foods that are rich sources of B_6, regardless of whether they ranked high in our analyses or not. As explained in the Our Methodology *chapter, there are other whole foods, aside from the ones we've chosen to highlight in this cookbook per our thoughtful ranking system, that are rich in the nutrients we identified as being especially thyroid- and immune-supportive. In other words, there are foods listed above that aren't included in this cookbook because our ultimate goal is to expand perceptions of healthy eating and health-supportive foods.*

Vitamin B_{12} (cobalamin)

According to thyroid expert, Dr. David Brownstein, "It's impossible to have a properly functioning thyroid gland without adequate Vitamin B_{12} in the body."[1]

Vitamin B_{12} is essential for energy, the health of our red blood cells, and our nervous system and many with hypothyroidism have difficulty absorbing B_{12}. It's critical for immune function and low levels have been shown to lead to stunted growth of villi (tiny

> 66 It's impossible to have a properly functioning thyroid gland without adequate Vitamin B_{12} in the body."
> —Dr. David Brownstein

protrusions in the digestive system that absorb nutrients), digestive dysfunction, and inflammation—inflammation and autoimmunity lead a coexistent relationship. An insufficiency is also associated with anemia and a serious form of B_{12} deficiency is pernicious anemia, an autoimmune condition that's not uncommon for those with Hashimoto's.

B_{12} is released for absorption by the activity of hydrochloric acid (HCl) and protease, an enzyme in the stomach. But low HCl stores are common for those with Hashimoto's, which in turn puts people at risk for B_{12} deficiency. Generally, low HCl and B_{12} deficiency go hand-in-hand.

Dr. Brownstein states that B_{12} is a helpful nutrient for autoimmune thyroid disorders and continues, "When cattle were fed a diet that resulted in a Vitamin B_{12} deficiency, the result was a significant reduction in the conversion of T4 to T3. I believe B_{12} deficiency to be one of the most common nutrient deficiencies in the U.S. today because of inadequate levels in food and poor absorption. Furthermore, B_{12} levels are lowered in those [who] take acid-blocking medications."[2]

The cosmic joke here is that the symptoms of low stomach acid are the same as the symptoms of an overproduction of acid—heartburn, acid reflux, etc. In other words, many are on acid-blockers who are, in fact, *deficient* in stomach acid. The last thing these folks need is anything suppressing stomach acid production; they need to do a simple and straightforward hydrochloric acid challenge. (See Appendix G for instructions how to address low stomach acid.)

Unrelenting stress can deplete B_{12} and adequate levels help to quell anxiety. Sufficient B_{12} also helps to support the production of beneficial estrogens—there's an important relationship between estrogen and thyroid function.[3]

When supplementing, the preferred form of B_{12} is methyl B_{12}, which is well-absorbed orally.

Rich food sources of Vitamin B_{12} include: sardines, salmon, tuna, cod, lamb, scallops, shrimp, beef, yogurt, and eggs.

The above list highlights foods that are rich sources of B_{12}, regardless of whether they ranked high in our analyses or not. As explained in the Our Methodology *chapter, there are other whole foods, aside from the ones we've chosen to highlight in this cookbook per our thoughtful ranking system, that are rich in the nutrients we identified as being especially thyroid- and immune-supportive. In other words, there are foods listed above that aren't included in this cookbook because our ultimate goal is to expand perceptions of healthy eating and health-supportive foods.*

Vitamin C

According to Dr. Richard Shames, author of *Thyroid Power*, "There are whole books written about the benefits of Vitamin C. Suffice it to say that its antioxidant properties alone make it an excellent addition for thyroid sufferers."[1]

Vitamin C helps with the conversion of T4 to T3. According to thyroid expert, Dr. David Brownstein, "When heavy metals, such as cadmium, have interfered with the conversion of T4 into T3, Vitamin C was shown to normalize this conversion."[2]

It also supports the immune system in functioning optimally, reduces the damage caused by stress (including regulating cortisol production), supports detoxification, and increases our natural resistance. It has powerful antioxidant properties, aids in iron absorption, and supports glutathione recycling, which is critical for those with Hashimoto's. (For more on glutathione, see the *Vitamins and Other Nutrients* subchapter in the chapter, *The Nutritional Heavy Hitters*.) Additionally, Vitamin C helps to raise resting metabolism, making you a hotter metabolic burner, even when you're not exercising.

According to functional medicine leader, Dr. Sara Gottfried, "[Vitamin C] helps prevent cancer and stroke, keeps your eyes working well, boosts immunity, and increases longevity. Because it's water soluble, any excess Vitamin C is excreted in your urine. It's a win/win situation."[3]

There's some evidence that thyroid hormone replacement is better absorbed when taken with C.[4] But as with many things, more isn't more—you don't want to over-supplement with Vitamin C, as it can cause diarrhea, loose stools, or cramping.

As with many nutrients, unrelenting stress can deplete Vitamin C.

Rich food sources of Vitamin C include: bell peppers, broccoli, Brussels sprouts, cauliflower, kale, cabbage, bok choy, turnip greens, romaine lettuce, beet greens, mustard greens, collard greens, Swiss chard, spinach, asparagus, sea vegetables, tomatoes, sweet potatoes, winter squash, green peas, green beans, summer squash, carrots, plums, papaya, strawberries, pineapple, oranges, kiwi, cantaloupe, grapefruit, raspberries, lemons, limes, blueberries, cranberries, watermelon, parsley, fennel, thyme, garlic, basil, and dill.

The above list highlights foods that are rich sources of Vitamin C, regardless of whether they ranked high in our analyses or not. As explained in the Our Methodology *chapter, there are other whole foods, aside from the ones we've chosen to highlight in this cookbook per our thoughtful ranking system, that are rich in the nutrients we identified as being especially thyroid- and immune-supportive. In other words, there are foods listed above that aren't included in this cookbook because our ultimate goal is to expand perceptions of healthy eating and health-supportive foods.*

Vitamin D

An adequate level of Vitamin D is essential for those with hypothyroidism and Hashimoto's. Vitamin D is critical for immune function—it's one of the most potent immune modulators we have.

Despite its name, Vitamin D is not a vitamin or a nutrient. It's a hormone produced via photolytic reaction when we receive direct sunlight on our skin—something many of us gasp at the thought of because of the potential risk of skin cancer. Because the body cannot produce any vitamin on its own, Vitamin D is considered a hormone because it's made within the body via photosynthesis.

Since Vitamin D is a hormone, it can fluctuate. Add to this the dearth of direct sunlight in colder months, especially for those in Northern latitudes (north of Texas, surprisingly), and we can find ourselves deficient. With many of our modern activities taking place indoors (office jobs, time on the computer), we're simply not getting the sunlight we need to maintain adequate levels of this warrior hormone.

According to Dr. Frank Lipman, an internationally recognized expert in integrative and functional medicine who has written extensively on Vitamin D, "Vitamin D is involved in making hundreds of enzymes and proteins, which are crucial for preserving health and preventing disease. It has the ability to interact and affect more than 2,000 genes in the body. It enhances muscle strength and builds bone. It has anti-inflammatory effects and bolsters the immune system. It helps the action of insulin and has anti-cancer activity. This is why Vitamin D deficiency has been linked with so many of the diseases of modern society."[1]

Vitamin D supports thyroid function by:

- Making Free T3, the unbound, active form of thyroid hormone
- Transporting thyroid hormone into cells
- Helping the pituitary gland make TSH
- Helping with T4 to T3 conversion

According to Dr. Mark Hyman, "Vitamin D is critical for activation of the thyroid receptor and making your thyroid hormone turn on the genes that improve your metabolism. It combines with the active hormone T3, which allows the hormone to 'dock' on its receptor or landing spot on the cell. It's a critical factor in thyroid function as it helps T3 bind to the receptor on the nucleus that controls gene function and our overall metabolism."[2]

A deficiency in Vitamin D has been linked to insufficient immune function and many autoimmune disorders[3]—in part because it influences T-regulatory cells that help to balance the immune system. Vitamin D is a powerful immune modulator and studies have shown its ability to reduce thyroid autoimmune antibodies.[4]

The further from the equator you live, the more prone you may be to an autoimmune condition. In fact, there's an Italian saying that goes, "Where the sun does not go the doctor does."

For some time, the standard acceptable Vitamin D levels have been 32-100 ng/mL—this is still the acceptable range according to many doctors. Indeed, anything below 32 can contribute to hormone pathway disruption.

Many in the functional medicine community state that Vitamin D levels should be between

> " A deficiency in Vitamin D has been linked to insufficient immune function and many autoimmune disorders."

50-80 ng/mL. But according to internist and integrative medicine physician, Dr. Gregory Plotnikoff, "Vitamin D is crucial for health and far too many people are (unknowingly) deficient in this hormone. This is a true public health concern; Vitamin D replenishment is the single most cost effective thing we can do in modern medicine. But while we want more people to have higher levels, there's no evidence that more and more Vitamin D is even better. In fact, there's some evidence suggesting that for large populations, the higher the levels, the greater risk of morbidity and mortality. Such observations are often based on just one measurement in time, so they're very far from definitive. But the Vitamin D story is likely to be like that of other hormones—more estrogen isn't better; more testosterone isn't better. There's an upper limit to the benefit. At this time, the best data supports a blood level of at least 30 ng/mL with a level of 40-60 ng/mL likely to be ideal.

"The Vitamin D dose doesn't matter. What matters, and what's a big deal, is your blood level. And that can only be measured through a blood test. Like with cholesterol levels, you cannot look at somebody and know their numbers."

It's best to get our nutrition from foods, but we only receive about 10 percent of our Vitamin D requirement from our diet because there are so few foods that contain Vitamin D. This is why dairy and other products are fortified with it.

Even 20 minutes in mid-day direct sunlight, sans sunscreen, increases our Vitamin D levels. The more sunlight we're exposed to in the warmer months, the less supplementation we need in winter because our bodies store Vitamin D in our fat cells. Dr. Plotnikoff continues, "We know that Vitamin D is free from the sun. A general guide is that you can make Vitamin D from sun exposure if your shadow is shorter than you are tall. Vitamin D cannot be made through glass, clothing, or through sunscreens SPF-8 or higher."[5]

Dr. Hyman states, "For those who do not fear the sun, judiciously expose as much skin as possible to direct midday sunlight for

> " Vitamin D replenishment is the single most cost effective thing we can do in modern medicine."
> —Dr. Gregory Plotnikoff

> 66 We know that Vitamin D is free from the sun. A general guide is that you can make Vitamin D from sun exposure if your shadow is shorter than you are tall."
> —Dr. Gregory Plotnikoff

one quarter of the time it takes for one's skin to turn red during those months when the proper ultraviolet light occurs at one's latitude (usually late spring, summer, and early fall). Vitamin D production is already maximized before your skin turns pink and further exposure does not increase levels of Vitamin D but may increase your risk of skin cancer."[6]

In months where you can't get Vitamin D from the sun, it's important to supplement with Vitamin D3, (cholecalciferol), the active form of Vitamin D, versus Vitamin D2 (ergocalciferol), which does not raise our levels as well. Vitamin D is fat-soluble, so to optimize absorption, it should be taken with foods rich in fat. Doses of 5000 to 10,000 IUs per day may be required to adequately increase levels.

Given that inadequate Vitamin D inhibits our body's ability to produce and regulate thyroid hormones and modulate the immune system, testing for Vitamin D should go right alongside thyroid hormone and antibody testing.

The importance of Vitamin D simply cannot be underestimated, especially considering that insufficient levels have been linked to nearly every degenerative disease in the book. If you're deficient, supplementation and smart sun exposure may make a tremendous difference in your health.

Rich food sources of Vitamin D include: egg yolks, fatty wild fish (salmon, mackerel, tuna, herring, halibut, and sardines), fortified foods (milk, yogurt, some cereals, and orange juice) and shiitake mushrooms.

The above list highlights foods that are rich sources of Vitamin D, regardless of whether they ranked high in our analyses or not. As explained in the Our Methodology *chapter, there are other whole foods, aside from the ones we've chosen to highlight in this cookbook per our thoughtful ranking system, that are rich in the nutrients we identified as being especially thyroid- and immune-supportive. In other words, there are foods listed above that aren't included in this cookbook because our ultimate goal is to expand perceptions of healthy eating and health-supportive foods.*

Vitamin E

Vitamin E is often low for those with hypothyroidism. It bolsters the immune system by increasing our natural resistance, reduces the damage caused by stress, and works synergistically with key thyroid minerals including manganese and selenium.

According to thyroid expert, Dr. Richard Shames, Vitamin E is a "potent antioxidant"[1] and helps with T4/T3 conversion. It also aids in glutathione recycling, which is critical for those with any type of autoimmunity. (For more on glutathione, see the *Vitamins and*

Other Nutrients subchapter in the chapter, *The Nutritional Heavy Hitters*.)

Vitamin E has also been shown to ameliorate the effects of over-supplementation with iodine.[2] (For more on the iodine supplementation controversy, see the *Minerals* subchapter in the chapter, *The Nutritional Heavy Hitters*.)

If you have low ferritin (iron storage capacity) and are using ferrous sulfate to raise your levels (ferritin is commonly low for those with hypothyroidism), it's important to supplement with Vitamin E, as ferrous sulfate can deplete Vitamin E. Many experts recommend the natural form of Vitamin E—d-alpha-tocopherol.

Rich food sources of Vitamin E include: spinach, Swiss chard, turnip greens, beet greens, mustard greens, kale, broccoli, bell peppers, asparagus, tomatoes, chili peppers, almonds, and sunflower seeds.

The above list highlights foods that are rich sources of Vitamin E, regardless of whether they ranked high in our analyses or not. As explained in the Our Methodology *chapter, there are other whole foods, aside from the ones we've chosen to highlight in this cookbook per our thoughtful ranking system, that are rich in the nutrients we identified as being especially thyroid- and immune-supportive. In other words, there are foods listed above that aren't included in this cookbook because our ultimate goal is to expand perceptions of healthy eating and health-supportive foods.*

Omega-3 Fatty Acids

Omega-3 fatty acids are essential fatty acids (EFAs) and are some of the most potent anti-inflammatory compounds known. Given that autoimmunity and inflammation are so intertwined, anything that reduces systemic, cellular inflammation is critical for those with an autoimmune condition.

Many of our body's systems rely on EFAs; these important fatty acids produce prostaglandins, which regulate our immune, central nervous, digestive, cardiovascular, endocrine, and reproductive systems. EFAs make hormone-like eicosanoids that not only control the inflammatory response, but also the immune response, thus reducing autoimmune damage. They help to promote lean body mass, foster healthy cholesterol levels, and reduce insulin resistance, blood pressure, and inflammation in muscles and joints.

> " Essential fatty acids make hormone-like eicosanoids that not only control the inflammatory response, but also the immune response, thus reducing autoimmune damage."

Every cell in the body has receptors for thyroid hormone and the thyroid turns on the genes that keep cells doing their job. Omega-3 fatty acids are required for the integrity of every membrane of every cell in the body, increase energy at the cellular level, improve the body's ability to respond to thyroid hormones, and can help protect against hypothyroidism-induced cognitive impairment.[1]

According to Dr. Susan Blum, autoimmunity expert and author of *The Immune System*

Recovery Plan, "There are two primary ways that fats influence your immune system. Your cell membranes are made of fatty acids. If you eat a lot of Omega-3 fats, the cell membranes will be loose and fluid, which is the way they work best."[2]

Omega-3s are a class of essential fatty acids (EFAs) that the body cannot make on its own—we only get Omega-3s through diet and supplementation. If supplementing with Omega-3s in the form of fish oil, make sure to get a third-party tested, molecularly-distilled supplement free of mercury. The International Fish Oil Standards (IFOS) assesses purity and contaminants in fish oil, including mercury, and provides a directory of fish oil supplements and their levels of toxins. (See Appendix B for our fish oil recommendation.)

Rich food sources of Omega-3 fatty acids include: flaxseeds, hemp seeds, chia seeds, algae, pumpkin seed oil, mustard seeds, walnuts, sardines, salmon, grass-fed beef and dairy, Brussels sprouts, and cauliflower.

The above list highlights foods that are rich sources of Omega-3 fatty acids, regardless of whether they ranked high in our analyses or not. As explained in the Our Methodology *chapter, there are other whole foods, aside from the ones we've chosen to highlight in this cookbook per our thoughtful ranking system, that are rich in the nutrients we identified as being especially thyroid- and immune-supportive. In other words, there are foods listed above that aren't included in this cookbook because our ultimate goal is to expand perceptions of healthy eating and health-supportive foods.*

Tyrosine

Tyrosine is an amino acid that's required for thyroid hormone production. The thyroid has the only cells capable of absorbing iodine, which, along with tyrosine, converts into T3 and T4.

It's easy to get adequate tyrosine from a non-vegetarian diet given that meat, fish, and eggs are plentiful in this critical amino acid. "Tyrosine is the basis for both kinds of thyroid hormone. It is so abundant that a lack of it cannot be causing the widespread low thyroid epidemic seen in industrialized nations," says Dr. Richard Shames.[1]

I generally don't recommend supplementing with tyrosine, especially for non-vegetarians. Because tyrosine is a precursor to thyroid hormone, supplementation can lead to an abundance of circulating thyroid hormones and thus, overstimulation. There's a double whammy that's common with tyrosine supplementation—the extra thyroid hormones can also lead to overstimulation of the adrenals, which itself can cause overstimulation via overproduction of adrenaline and cortisol.

As with many nutrients, unrelenting stress can deplete tyrosine, which is also a precursor to neurotransmitters that are often depleted by chronic stress.

Rich food sources of tyrosine include: all animal protein including dairy, eggs, and seafood; tempeh; peanuts; and pumpkin seeds.

The above list highlights foods that are rich sources of tyrosine, regardless of whether they ranked high in our analyses or not. As explained in the Our Methodology *chapter, there are other whole foods, aside from the ones we've chosen to highlight in this cookbook per our thoughtful ranking system, that are rich in the nutrients we identified as being especially thyroid- and immune-supportive. In other words, there are foods listed above that aren't included in this cookbook because our ultimate goal is to expand perceptions of healthy eating and health-supportive foods.*

EGCG

Epigallocatechin gallate (EGCG), found in green tea, has powerful immune-supportive benefits, including immune modulation for those with autoimmunity.[1] It can turn on the body's defense system against the proteins and molecules involved in systemic inflammation and may even help to prevent autoimmune diseases.[2]

According to Emily Ho, a principal investigator at the Linus Pauling Institute and associate professor in the Oregon State University Department of Nutrition and Exercise Sciences, "[EGCG] appears to be a natural, plant-derived compound that can affect the number of regulatory T cells, and in the process improve immune function."[3]

Dr. Susan Blum echoes, "[EGCG] has been shown to be beneficial in treating and preventing cancer, cardiovascular disease, weight loss, neurodegenerative diseases, and more. Now a recent study from Oregon State University has shown that EGCG has a powerful effect in increasing T regulator cells, which are critical for the maintenance of tolerance and prevention of autoimmunity."[4]

Even with its astounding health benefits, including its anti-cancer properties, I don't recommend overuse of green tea, which contains caffeine. I'm not anti-caffeine necessarily, but for those with more advanced fatigue and adrenal dysfunction (often associated with hypothyroidism), consuming too much caffeine can exacerbate these imbalances. Green tea is a more health-giving substitute for coffee, although again, I'm not anti-coffee. I don't recommend more than one cup of caffeine per day—and it's a good idea to make it organic and fair trade.

Glutathione

Glutathione is a powerful antioxidant that modulates, regulates, and strengthens the immune system. It's considered by many in the functional medicine community to be one of the pillars of fighting Hashimoto's. It also fights cancer, viruses, and bacterial infections and protects against inflammation and allergies. It's a critical component of our body's detoxification system.

It's considered "the master antioxidant" and autoimmunity expert, Dr. Mark Hyman, states that it's one of the most important molecules in the body. He calls it "the maestro of your immune system."[1]

It also helps to balance the Th1 and Th2 pathway. A full explanation of the Th1/Th2 pathway is beyond the scope of this book, but know that T-helper cells, of which Th1 and Th2 are subgroups, are a critical component of the immune system. They're types of white blood cells that recognize unfamiliar pathogens. With autoimmune disease, the "pathogen" is normal tissue.

In a well-functioning immune system, the Th1 and Th2 helper cells work cooperatively to balance the immune system. But in some people with autoimmunity, dominance of either the Th1 or Th2 pathway can occur. For a full explanation, I recommend Dr. Datis Kharrazian's book, *Why Do I Still Have Thyroid Symptoms When My Lab Tests are Normal?*[2]

Glutathione dampens autoimmune flare-ups and protects and heals thyroid tissue. When free radicals begin to destroy your body's tissue, glutathione will absorb the attack, sparing tissue and minimizing destruction. It then gets recycled so it's

> ❝ Glutathione dampens autoimmune flare-ups and protects and heals thyroid tissue.❞

ready for action again. The nutrients Vitamin C, Vitamin E, and selenium help to recycle and maintain adequate levels of glutathione.

According to functional medicine leader, Dr. Susan Blum, "[Selenium] is a required element for the enzymes that make thyroid hormone and for the glutathione peroxidase enzyme, which plays a critical antioxidant role and prevents damage to the thyroid follicles."[3]

Dr. Kharrazian states, "The overall effect [of glutathione recycling] is to dampen both the autoimmune reaction and damage to body tissue. It also helps body tissue and the intestinal tract regenerate and recover. Glutathione is like the bodyguard or Secret Service agent whose loyalty is so deep that she will jump in front of a bullet to save the life of the one she protects. When there is enough of the proper form of glutathione in the body to 'take the bullet,' no inflammatory response occurs. However when glutathione becomes depleted it triggers a destructive inflammatory process."[4]

In the *What Causes Hypothyroidism?*, *Optimizing Thyroid Hormone Conversion,* and *The Autoimmune Epidemic* chapters, we

discuss how heavy metal exposure can be a cause of low thyroid function, how it hinders T4/T3 conversion, and how it's often a component in the toxic body burden that can bring about and exacerbate autoimmune diseases. Glutathione can help remove heavy metals from the body.

Dr. Blum continues, "Glutathione is the most important antioxidant. It's in every cell in your body, but it's found in highest concentrations in the liver. Not only does glutathione clean up heavy metals such as mercury, cadmium, and arsenic, but it also aids in protecting the body from pesticides, solvents, and plastic residues such as BPA. It has a natural role in mopping up the everyday end products of your body's metabolism, called free radicals. With so much work to do, glutathione is always getting used up and constantly has to be made by the body. If you have environmental exposures to heavy metals, solvents, and pesticides, the glutathione levels in your body can get depleted."[5]

She continues, "The first and most important way that mercury is removed from your body is by glutathione. The bottom line: if you don't have enough glutathione, you can have trouble removing mercury, which can build up, harm your cells, and cause autoimmune diseases."[6]

Our glutathione stores can also become depleted from some of the same factors that contribute to hypothyroidism and Hashimoto's—oxidative stress, food sensitivities/leaky gut, and adrenal dysfunction.

The sulfurs in cruciferous vegetables (broccoli, kale, collard greens, cabbage, cauliflower) and garlic and onions are particularly boosting to glutathione levels. (Several of these foods are

> **❝ If you don't have enough glutathione, you can have trouble removing mercury, which can build up, harm your cells, and cause autoimmune diseases."**
> —Dr. Susan Blum

so-called "goitrogens," but see the chapter, *The Myth of "Goitrogens"* for the reasons why you don't need to fear these foods.)

Given glutathione's superhero properties and that it's easily depleted, this is one supplement that Lisa and I can get behind. While we take a "food first" approach in supporting the body's ability to regenerate glutathione, there may be some cases of deficiency where therapeutic glutathione supplementation can be supportive. It can be taken orally as liposomal glutathione, and can also be administered by a functional medicine doctor via an IV. (See Appendix B for our supplement recommendations, of which you can also find links to on our website: www.thyroidcookbook.com.)

Foods that help the body make glutathione are: spinach, kale, collard greens, watercress, asparagus, broccoli, cabbage, cauliflower, squash, avocado, grapefruit, peaches, garlic, onions, and raw eggs. Again, foods rich in Vitamin C, Vitamin E, and selenium help to recycle and maintain adequate levels of glutathione.

The above list highlights foods that help the body produce glutathione, regardless of whether they ranked high in our analyses or not. As explained in the Our Methodology *chapter, there are other whole foods, aside from the ones we've chosen to highlight in this cookbook per our thoughtful ranking system, that are rich in the nutrients we identified as being especially thyroid- and immune-supportive. In other words, there are foods listed above that aren't included in this cookbook because our ultimate goal is to expand perceptions of healthy eating and health-supportive foods.*

Lycopene

Lycopene is an important antioxidant carotenoid that helps give vegetables and fruits their reddish color. It has been shown to reduce damage to the thyroid caused by insecticide ingestion.[1]

Lycopene has an anti-diabetic effect and has strong antioxidant properties critical for proper thyroid and immune function. Its protective cellular properties help to guard against thyroid damage.[2]

Low thyroid function is often met with high cholesterol because the body doesn't break down and eliminate LDL cholesterol as efficiently as it should and yet another well-researched benefit of lycopene is that it can prevent the oxidation of LDL cholesterol.

Th1 and Th2 are subgroups of our T-helper cells that work in conjunction to help keep our immune system homeostatic; lycopene helps to balance these Th1/Th2 cells, which can become imbalanced in those with autoimmunity.

Rich food sources of lycopene include: tomatoes, red cabbage, red peppers, red carrots, asparagus, basil, chili powder, watermelon, mango, papaya, red grapefruit, and guava.

The above list highlights foods that are rich sources of lycopene, regardless of whether they ranked high in our analyses or not. As explained in the Our Methodology *chapter, there are other whole foods, aside from the ones we've chosen to highlight in this cookbook per our thoughtful ranking system, that are rich in the nutrients we identified as being especially thyroid- and immune-supportive. In other words, there are foods listed above that aren't included in this cookbook because our ultimate goal is to expand perceptions of healthy eating and health-supportive foods.*

Probiotics

Probiotics are "friendly bacteria" that promote healthy digestive flora, which is crucial for proper digestive function. They populate the intestines with beneficial bacteria, which is critical to the breakdown and absorption of nutrients, and also crowd out the less-than-friendly flora, essentially having an antibiotic effect.

When digestion isn't optimized, an over-abundance of bad bacteria crowds out beneficial bacteria. This has significant implications for thyroid hormone production, given that much of our T4 to T3 conversion takes place in our digestive tract.

The science around the critical importance of a healthy microbiome, our 100 trillion organism-strong "mini ecosystem," has exploded in recent years, thanks largely to David A. Relman's The Human Microbiome Project. You can't shake a stick without encountering a book, article, post, expert interview, or TED Talk espousing the role that the microbiome plays in everything from immune function to brain health to prenatal development.

Entire books have been devoted to optimizing digestive function and promoting a healthy microbiome and ensuring that your gut is properly populated with friendly bacteria is a critical factor in a healthy immune system. Experts claim that 70-80 percent of our immune system is housed in our gut, so a well-functioning digestive system is a non-negotiable for proper immune function.

According to digestive health expert, Dr. Susan Blum, "The good bacteria that live in your intestines have the most important influence on the function of the T cells that are located there. It is believed that imbalances in gut flora are a big part of the problem [with the epidemic of autoimmune diseases], causing both autoimmunity and making your symptoms and antibodies worse if you already have a diagnosed autoimmune disease."[1]

A question I often get is whether fermented foods provide enough beneficial bacteria. Fermentation is a chemical change brought on by the action of beneficial yeast and bacteria and eating fermented foods is

> 66 When digestion isn't optimized, an overabundance of bad bacteria crowds out beneficial bacteria. This has significant implications for thyroid hormone production, given that much of our T4 to T3 conversion takes place in our digestive tract."

ideal for optimal digestion. While it's true that foods like yogurt, kefir, pickles, tempeh, miso, sauerkraut, and kombucha help to populate the gut with friendly flora and are an essential component of a healthful, whole foods diet, for those with autoimmunity and the adjacent digestive concerns, it's not enough—it's important to also supplement. In fact, I feel that a good probiotic is one of the supplements that all of us can benefit from in perpetuity.

It's generally best to ensure that your probiotic contains a variety of bacteria from each of the three main types of probiotics: Lactobacillus, Bifidobacterium, and a soil-based organism (SBO).

Soil-based organisms are particularly important for those with autoimmunity. Nutrition expert Dr. Natasha Campbell-McBride MD, author of *Gut and Psychology Syndrome* and creator of the Gut and Psychology Syndrome diet (GAPS), claims that the specific SBO strain Bacillus subtilis is a critical component of gut-healing journey and especially effective for those suffering from allergies and autoimmune conditions.

According to Sarah Pope, writer and creator of the informative The Healthy Home Economist website, "Soil based probiotics are not endemic to humans and as such are resistant to stomach acid, most antibiotics, temperature changes and other degrading factors that can affect lactic acid based organisms. Soil based microbes are used in the waste management industry because they have an incredible ability to break down putrefying matter and suppress pathogenic microbes. Use of soil based probiotics has been found to be particularly effective for those suffering from allergies and other autoimmune diseases."[2]

Natto happens to be particularly plentiful in Bacillus subtilis, but you can't get enough from this food alone. You can find Bacillus subtilis in Campbell-McBride's brand of probiotics, BioKult. (See Appendix B for our supplement recommendations, of which you can also find links to on our website: www.thyroidcookbook.com.)

Additionally, probiotics have been shown to prevent absorption of bisphenol A (BPA) the synthetic, estrogen-like chemical in polycarbonate plastic found in the lining of many food and drink cans, baby bottles and sippy cups, microwave ovenware, eating utensils, food storage containers, hard-plastic drinking bottles, 5-gallon water jugs, and plastic wraps, to name a few. BPA easily leaches into food and liquids and hundreds of studies have linked it to harmful endocrine-disrupting effects, causing reproductive, developmental, behavioral, and neurological harm. (See the chapter, *Pantry Staples and Ingredients* that includes a list of companies that make BPA-free food and drink can liners.)

Foods rich in probiotics include: raw cheese and all fermented foods—sauerkraut, kimchi, miso, natto, tempeh, pickles, yogurt, kefir, and kombucha tea.

The above list highlights foods that are rich sources of probiotics, regardless of whether they ranked high in our analyses or not. As explained in the Our Methodology *chapter, there are other whole foods, aside from the ones we've chosen to highlight in this cookbook per our thoughtful ranking system, that are rich in the nutrients we identified as being especially thyroid- and immune-supportive. In other words, there are foods listed above that aren't included in this cookbook because our ultimate goal is to expand perceptions of healthy eating and health-supportive foods.*

Resveratrol

Resveratrol is a phytonutrient that helps give vegetables and fruits their color. You may be familiar with it because red wine is rich in resveratrol.

Remember, every cell in the body has receptors for thyroid hormone and the thyroid turns on the genes that keep cells doing their job. Resveratrol helps to improve this cellular communication. According to Dr. Susan Blum, "Deep within every cell in your body is a complete book of your life, your complete genetic code. Each cell has all your genes in it. The genes that code for those cells are activated and direct all the activity of that cell so that it is doing its job properly. Some of these chapters [of your book] are fixed on or off when you're a baby developing in your mother's uterus. But throughout life there are many chapters that are not fixed, so

> 66 *Food is information—* it can have a powerful effect on activating your immune system in a way that makes it work better or in a way that promotes autoimmune diseases."
> —Dr. Susan Blum

they can be opened and read, or closed and ignored. A great example is how your cells respond to resveratrol. Studies have shown that when you eat food such as red grapes or drink red wine, the resveratrol from these foods travels into the cells in your body and straight to the nucleus of the cell, where it turns on what has been called the 'longevity gene,' because it makes enzymes that help the cell live longer.

"This is why we say *food is information*—it can have a powerful effect on activating your immune system in a way that makes it work better or in a way that promotes autoimmune diseases."[1]

According to autoimmunity expert, Dr. Amy Myers, resveratrol helps to "... quell inflammation, regulate the malfunctioning immune response, and protect against cancer."[2]

Like glutathione and lycopene, it also helps to balance our Th1 and Th2 cells, which are components of our T-helper cells. When things are functioning as they should, our Th1 and Th2 cells work together to balance our immune system. But in some with autoimmunity, dominance of either the Th1 or Th2 pathway can occur.

A full explanation of Th1 and Th2 is beyond the scope of this book, but generally, T-helper cells are white blood cells that recognize unfamiliar pathogens. With autoimmune disease, the "pathogen" is normal tissue, such as the thyroid gland in the case of Hashimoto's. For a full explanation, I recommend Dr. Datis Kharrazian's book, *Why Do I Still Have Thyroid Symptoms When My Lab Tests are Normal?*[3]

Rich food sources of resveratrol include: red grapes, red wine, blueberries, cranberries, peanuts, pistachios, cocoa, and dark chocolate.

The above list highlights foods that are rich sources of resveratrol, regardless of whether they ranked high in our analyses or not. As explained in the Our Methodology *chapter, there are other whole foods, aside from the ones we've chosen to highlight in this cookbook per our thoughtful ranking system, that are rich in the nutrients we identified as being especially thyroid- and immune-supportive. In other words, there are foods listed above that aren't included in this cookbook because our ultimate goal is to expand perceptions of healthy eating and health-supportive foods.*

THE MYTH OF "GOITROGENS"

Without question, leafy greens and cruciferous vegetables are some of the most health-giving, antioxidant-rich, cancer-fighting foods on the planet. Unfortunately, some steer clear of them due to the claims that these foods (and others) are "goitrogenic"—they reportedly cause a goiter and slow thyroid function.

I like using quotation marks around the words "goitrogen" and "goitrogenic" because these terms are so misleading. The root word of "goitrogen" and "goitrogenic" is goiter, an enlargement or swelling of the thyroid. So it's difficult to extricate these words from something that many with hypothyroidism have and fear—a goiter. As one functional medicine doctor said, and I paraphrase, "We need to come up with a different term for these compounds because if we continue to call them 'goitrogens,' people will naturally fear getting a goiter, when these foods haven't been shown to cause thyroid enlargement."

(I'll refrain from using quotation marks for the rest of this chapter—even though I really want to.)

According to Dr. Datis Kharrazian, "I know [that the myth that goitrogens cause a goiter] is widely believed in the natural medicine community, but anyone who tells you this does not know how to read the scientific literature."

Additionally, many who believe or have been told that they have a goiter don't, in fact, have a goiter. They have what's called painless thyroiditis swelling from the autoimmune antibody attack on their thyroid (Hashimoto's). Dr. Kharrazian continues, "Many people with Hashimoto's are misdiagnosed with goiter when in fact they have swelling from autoimmune thyroiditis."[1]

The way to differentiate is if the swelling comes and goes or stays constant. If the swelling is painless and fluctuates, that's associated with Hashimoto's. If the swelling stays constant and diffuse and even causes some pain, that's more often associated with a goiter and can also result from swelling from a virus or infection.

So what are goitrogens? Reportedly, goitrogens are naturally-occurring compounds found in many whole foods, to varying degrees. Some research—*on animals*[2]—has suggested that they may suppress thyroid function by interfering with iodine uptake, in essence, slowing the thyroid's absorption of iodine, which is important for thyroid hormone synthesis. This, in turn, could cause a goiter, or so it's claimed. It's also reported that goitrogens may inhibit the production of thyroid hormone.

Goitrogenic foods include: bok choy, broccoli, broccolini, Brussels sprouts, cabbage, canola, cauliflower, Chinese cabbage, choy sum, collard greens, horseradish, kai-lan (Chinese broccoli), kale, kohlrabi, mizuna, mustard greens, radishes, rapeseed (yu choy), rapini, rutabagas (swedes), tatsoi, turnips, tempeh, tofu, and edamame and to a lesser extent, arugula, watercress, peanuts, strawberries, flax, peaches, millet, sweet potatoes, pears, spinach, pine nuts, and bamboo shoots.

Because these foods simply contain too many beneficial nutrients and are far too beneficial to the immune system (beneficial to those *with Hashimoto's*) to eliminate them from our diets, many leaders in the functional medicine community caution against throwing the baby out with the bathwater.

Of this list, one food to watch out for is soy (primarily, tofu). Soy can have an estrogenic effect in the body, and many are prone to estrogen dominance. Lisa and I aren't

> 66 [The myth that goitrogens cause a goiter] is widely believed in the natural medicine community, but anyone who tells you this does not know how to read the scientific literature."
> —Dr. Datis Kharrazian

categorically against soy and you'll see some fermented soy ingredients in our recipes. We feel that as long as the soybeans are whole and fermented, soy products such as tempeh, natto, gluten-free tamari, and miso are fine in moderation. (For more information about soy, see the next chapter, *A Word About Soy*.)

Author, physician, and nutrition researcher, Dr. Joel Fuhrman clarified the research on goitrogens saying, "Concerns about potential effects of cruciferous vegetables on thyroid function arose from animal studies, followed by findings suggesting that certain breakdown products of glucosinolates could interfere with thyroid hormone synthesis or compete with iodine for uptake by the thyroid. However, this is only a hypothetical issue. The scientific consensus is that cruciferous vegetables could only be detrimental to thyroid function in cases of iodine deficiency or insufficient iodine intake."[3]

Dr. Amy Myers concurs, "Human trials

have found that the consumption of cruciferous vegetables has little to no effect on the thyroid, unless a person is deficient in iodine.”[4]

What's more, according to Dr. Fuhrman—and this is a biggie, “*No human study* has demonstrated a deficiency in thyroid function from consuming cruciferous vegetables.”[3] (My italics.)

Dr. Alan Christianson agrees. He argues that if an individual's hypothyroidism is not caused by iodine deficiency—which is the case for well over 90 percent of hypothyroid sufferers—there's no need to worry about the potential for slower iodine absorption.

Thyroid expert Chris Kresser reports that in countries where iodine has been added to table salt, the incidence of autoimmune thyroid disease has increased. He says, “Increased iodine intake, especially in supplement form, increases the autoimmune attack on the thyroid.”[5] If this holds true, mild inhibition of iodine absorption may prove beneficial for Hashimoto's patients.

Furthermore, if there's potential risk to thyroid function by consuming cruciferous vegetables, it may be outweighed by the benefits those same vegetables can provide. Many foods containing so-called goitrogens help the body produce glutathione, a powerful antioxidant (“the master antioxidant”) that's one of the pillars of fighting Hashimoto's. Glutathione modulates and regulates the immune system, dampens autoimmune flare-ups, protects and heals thyroid tissue, and detoxifies the liver. Cruciferous vegetables also help protect against thyroid cancer. (For more on glutathione, see the *Vitamins and Other Nutrients* subchapter in the chapter, *The Nutritional Heavy Hitters*.)

As Dr. Fuhrman says, “Eating cruciferous vegetables is not optional.”[3]

He continues, “The fear [circulating the internet by some authors] of eating cruciferous vegetables or that those with hypothyroidism should reduce or avoid the consumption of kale or other cruciferous vegetables is unfounded and does a disservice to the community. Whether you have normal thyroid function or hypothyroidism, there is no benefit for you to avoid or restrict your intake of cruciferous vegetables.”[3]

If you're still concerned and your low thyroid function is a result of iodine deficiency (non-autoimmune hypothyroidism, which again, is rarely the case), not Hashimoto's, keep a couple of things in mind.

First, cooking reportedly inactivates goitrogenic compounds. Any potential harm to your thyroid exists only when the foods are eaten raw. So roast, steam, sauté, or blanch these foods. If you love to add raw greens to your morning smoothies, try blanching the greens and then freezing them in single-serving portions, like in an ice cube tray. They'll be as easy to add to the blender as your frozen fruit.

But know that Dr. Fuhrman says, "A person would have to consume an insane amount of raw cruciferous vegetables to have a negative effect on thyroid function."[3]

Second, make sure you're getting adequate iodine intake. Third, avoid juicing so-called goitrogenic fruits and vegetables, which concentrates the chemical components.

A WORD ABOUT SOY

S oy is one of the most controversial foods out there. Many doctors I respect are in different camps as to whether soy is health-giving or wreaks hormonal havoc. In fact, Dr. Mark Hyman wrote an article titled, "How Soy Can Kill You and Save Your Life."[1]

Most soy foods in the Standard American Diet are highly processed forms made from soy protein isolates and poor quality soybean oil. Lisa and I don't believe that soy is fit to consume unless it's fermented and then only in moderation.

Fermented soybeans are a staple in many Asian cultures, but in the U.S., we've mass-produced the soybean without the fermentation process. Fermentation is a chemical change brought on by the action of beneficial yeast and bacteria and eating fermented foods is ideal for optimal digestion. This process activates enzymes and helps to break down or "pre-digest" many of the anti-nutrients found in soy, thereby making it easier to assimilate.

According to Dr. Richard Shames, "A compound found in soy, called genistein, apparently blocks the action of iodine and tyrosine in the production of thyroid hormone. This effect is dose-related. In other words, if the amount you eat of this otherwise healthy food is modest, then your thyroid will not be bothered."[2]

We believe that unfermented soy products such as soy milk, soy ice cream, soy nuts, and most tofu, are endocrine/hormonal disrupters and mimic hormones, specifically estrogen, in your body. There's a big difference between *replacing* hormones and *mimicking* hormones. Many believe that it's good to eat soy if you're low in estrogen or going through peri/menopause, but there are wildly differing opinions about whether this is the case. We certainly don't have the last word on soy and we don't know who does.

THE AUTOIMMUNE EPIDEMIC

The title of this chapter mimics the title of a powerful book by Donna Jackson Nakazawa, *The Autoimmune Epidemic*.[1] You'd do well to get this critically-acclaimed book for a full explanation of the stark rise in autoimmunity. (I have Donna's permission to use her book title for this chapter.)

Following her own crippling autoimmune health crisis, Jackson Nakazawa thoroughly researched the origins of autoimmunity and in her book, explains how environmental triggers have tripled the rate of disease in the last 30 years and how we can limit our exposure to toxins that could cause an overactive immune response. Her guidelines are rooted in research and cutting-edge medical science and I was comforted to see that much of her guidance mimics what I'd already been sharing with my autoimmunity clients.

As you likely know, the foods many Americans eat today bear little resemblance to what was on our plates 100 years ago. We've transitioned from a diet of food we personally grew and animals we personally raised to a diet of factory-made, chemically-laden, processed foods. When we do manage healthier choices, our produce and meat is often loaded with pesticides, fungicides, hormones, antibiotics, and chemical dyes.

In her book, Jackson Nakazawa describes the food manufacturing process as, ". . . taking a food from nature, removing everything natural from it, then adding preservatives, dyes, bleaches, flavors, emulsifiers, and stabilizers to make it taste, look, feel, and smell like what it was originally supposed to be, but no longer is."

Processed foods are not healthy for anyone. But for those of

> 66 The foods many Americans eat today bear little resemblance to what was on our plates 100 years ago."

us with a predisposition to autoimmunity, the risks of such a diet increase dramatically. Our immune system is challenged with the job of parsing out the good from the bad. The "bad," known as antigens, are toxins and foreign substances that induce an immune response in the body. The more antigens we ingest, the greater the potential for our immune system to turn against our bodies as it struggles to deal with the toxins.

According to Moises Velasquez-Manoff, author of *An Epidemic of Absence, a New Way of Understanding Allergies and Autoimmune Disease*, "Ideally, your immune system should operate like an enlightened action hero, meting out inflammation precisely, accurately and with deadly force when necessary, but then quickly returning to a Zen-like calm."[2]

With autoimmunity, the immune system doesn't return to its Zen-like calm. The system has gone awry and the body imposes an inappropriate assault on itself. Normal tissue is confused with a pathogen and a rogue immune response launches a seek-and-destroy mission on otherwise healthy tissue—it's unable to differentiate between self and non-self.

In the U.S. alone, it's estimated that 53 million people have an autoimmune disease and of these, an estimated 30 million have Hashimoto's, although estimates are as high as 60 million. Aside from Hashimoto's, which is the most prevent form of autoimmunity in the U.S., other examples of the 90-plus autoimmune conditions include rheumatoid arthritis, scleroderma, multiple sclerosis (MS), lupus, Celiac disease, and psoriasis, to name a few.

Experts in the functional medicine community claim that most with hypothyroidism are undiagnosed—it's estimated that there are 60 million with low thyroid function. It's also estimated that 97% of those with hypothyroidism have Hashimoto's, in which case we may be looking at 58 million with Hashimoto's. As you can see, this number is higher than the estimates for the total number of people with autoimmunity in the U.S.

With autoimmunity cases tripling in recent decades and so many now affected (mostly women), the pervasiveness of autoimmune diseases is cause for serious concern. Many people are scrambling to uncover the why. "Why did I get an autoimmune disease? What did I do wrong?"

There's no "wrongdoing" associated with autoimmunity. There are many factors that we're only beginning to realize contribute to the prevalence of the disease. Integrative medicine practitioner, Dr. Bob Rountree states, "I would put pharmaceuticals up there pretty high as triggers for autoimmunity.

> 66 Ideally, your immune system should operate like an enlightened action hero, meting out inflammation precisely, accurately and with deadly force when necessary, but then quickly returning to a Zen-like calm."
> —Moises Velasquez-Manoff

Lithium and high dose iodine are well known triggers for autoimmune thyroiditis. (For more on the iodine controversy, see the *Minerals* subchapter in the chapter, *The Nutritional Heavy Hitters*.) Certain bacteria and gluten can trigger a wide range of autoimmune diseases. Additionally, I suspect that a number of environmental toxins may act as triggers. For example, several studies have shown that cigarette smoking, which involves a potent mix of airborne toxicants, significantly increases the risk of rheumatoid arthritis, systemic lupus, and many other autoimmune diseases. Asbestos has been linked to an increase in autoimmune antibodies. Heavy metals including mercury, cadmium, and gold have been linked to autoimmune glomerulonephritis (kidney disease). This said, many of these exposures can occur years before the onset of disease, so it can be difficult to prove that they're causative factors. I'll be honest, it can be like chasing ghosts."[3]

Our modern lifestyle is contributing to the proliferation of our bodies turning against themselves. The spike in autoimmunity

> " The spike in autoimmunity parallels the production of modern, can't-live-without-them products that we haven't been exposed to for millions of years—*and these are factors we can control*."

parallels the production of modern, can't-live-without-them products made from plastics, chemicals, dyes, flame retardants, and personal care products like chemical-laden skincare and cosmetics products and cleaning supplies. Eighty percent of autoimmune sufferers are women because of the prevalence of immune- and hormone-disrupting chemicals in body care products. We haven't been exposed to these chemicals and compounds for millions of years—*and these are factors we can control*.

While it's important to address all of the factors that have been shown to tip the scales, worrying about pinpointing the exact origin(s) can cause people to chase their tails, especially when addressing all of these factors leads to overall better health, less toxic body burden, optimized digestion, and decreased cellular inflammation. *Everyone can benefit*, whether they have autoimmunity or not.

It's often reported in the functional medicine community that the "three legged stool" of autoimmunity is genetic propensity, leaky gut/irritable bowel syndrome, and body burden from exposure to environmental toxins. There's often a stealth infection in the mix, such as Epstein-Barr.

Many are under the misguided belief that our genetic propensity is the strongest leg of this stool. Too often, we assume that our genes will determine what diseases we may develop or how long we may live. We also assume we have very little control over the outcome. While our family history and genetic code certainly play a role, we can affect how our genes are expressed. The science of epigenetics shows us that our genes may not be our destiny.

> " While our family history and genetic code certainly play a role, we can affect how our genes are expressed. The science of epigenetics shows us that our genes may not be our destiny."

thoughts), will turn the genes for health on and the 'disease' genes off."[4]

I love the saying, "Genetics loads the gun and environment pulls the trigger." Again, we can control many of the factors that lead to the onset of autoimmune diseases and once autoimmunity has set in, addressing these factors can put you on the road to recovery. The healthier your lifestyle choices, the healthier your genes.

> " We can't change the hardwiring of our genetic code, but epigenetic factors such as lifestyle and diet can radically change what our genes do. It means that you have a lot more control over your health than you think."
> —Dr. Frank Lipman

According to respected functional medicine physician, Dr. Frank Lipman, "Epigenetics is the study of molecular mechanisms by which the environment controls gene activity. It is a new scientific field and it shows that DNA blueprints passed down through genes are not set in stone at birth. Each of us inherits our own unique variation of the genetic code. We can't change the hardwiring of our genetic code, but epigenetic factors such as lifestyle and diet can radically change what our genes do. It means that you have a lot more control over your health than you think.

"Several studies have shown that changing lifestyle causes changes in gene expression. Stress, diet, behavior, toxins, and other factors activate chemical switches that turn genes on and off and regulate gene expression. Bathing your genes in the right environment (good nutrients, food, love and

The Basics of Mitigating the Autoimmune Response

The information here isn't intended to "cure" any autoimmune condition. Like the title of this chapter says, these are "basics." Whole books have been devoted to helping people mitigate the autoimmune response [1, 2, 3] and I work with clients for months to help them address all of the factors in managing autoimmunity. A full explanation of autoimmunity management is beyond the scope of this book.

To start, address your digestive system, including sleuthing out your food sensitivities. I feel, as do many in the functional medicine and functional nutrition communities, that cleaning up the gut and restoring digestive function is the *single most important factor* in taming autoimmunity. Many claim that autoimmunity is usually (many say *always*) preceded by some level of gut dysbiosis.

Given that 70-80 percent of our immune system is housed in our gut,[4] it's imperative to clean up your digestive environment to calm down the immune response. According to autoimmunity expert, Donna Jackson Nakazawa, "A healthy intestine allows only digested nutrients to pass into the bloodstream. In patients with immune and inflammatory-based illnesses, the body's intestinal lining often becomes impaired, thus permitting larger molecules, such as bacteria and undigested foods, to slip through. In the bloodstream, these foreign items can trigger an immune reaction, making the body think that it's under attack and promoting the body's immune system to lash out to battle those foreign pathogens."[5]

Much has been said about the inflammation/autoimmunity connection. I call them kissing cousins. Systemic/cellular inflammation fans the flames of autoimmunity and vice versa.

Fortunately, anything you do to address inflammation will help reduce your autoimmune antibodies and what you do to lower your antibodies will help to tame your inflammation. Instead of writing an Inflammation chapter, I've opted to outline the following 26 factors that can help to address both—inflammation and the autoimmune response.

Factors to address:

1. An Elimination Provocation diet is the place to start. It's nothing short of life-changing. It's one of the single best ways to quell systemic/cellular inflammation. (See the chapter, *Elimination Provocation Diet Instructions*.)

2. Go completely gluten-free. Not sort of gluten-free, but completely. (For more on the thyroid/gluten relationship, see the chapter, *Gluten and Your Thyroid*.)

3. Eat whole, unprocessed, non-GMO (genetically modified) foods, from the earth. This cookbook is a great place to start. Eliminate packaged, refined foods and eliminate or greatly reduce sugar, processed grain flours, and artificial sweeteners. Choose organic/sustainably-raised foods as often as your pocketbook will allow. These foods are free of synthetic hormones, antibiotics, pesticides, herbicides, and fungicides. (The chapter, *Pantry Staples and Ingredients* lists many of our favorite products. You'll also find links to many of these items on our website: www.thyroidcookbook.com.)

4. Supplement wisely. FDA regulations cannot be trusted to guard against all manufacturing errors, changes, or unethical practices that could compromise

otherwise safe supplements. Do your research, choose products from respected and reputable producers, and consult with experts.

For the supplements listed below, please see Appendix B for our recommendations. You can also find links to all of these products at our website: www.thyroidcookbook.com. Please use supplements under the supervision of a qualified healthcare provider.

5. Boost your glutathione stores, "the master antioxidant" and "pillar of fighting Hashimoto's." (For more on glutathione, see the *Vitamins and Other Nutrients* subchapter in the chapter, *The Nutritional Heavy Hitters*.)

6. Address yeast/candida. Candida albicans is a naturally occurring, relatively harmless yeast strain in our digestive system that becomes problematic when it proliferates. In the presence of a weak intestinal barrier, it can wander out of the intestinal lining, further interfering with digestion, feeding inflammation, and contributing to hormonal imbalance. The immune system soon identifies the yeast particles as foreign, attacking them like any other pathogen.

   Yeast only thrives in your digestive system because of the current environment and when you change the environment, you can cleanse this toxin from your body. Candida/yeast is not often recognized in the conventional/Western medical community.*

7. Take Vitamin D, one of the most powerful immune modulators known. (For more on Vitamin D, see the *Vitamins and Other Nutrients* subchapter in the chapter, *The Nutritional Heavy Hitters*.)

8. Take turmeric, one of the most powerful anti-inflammatory immune modulators on the planet. Turmeric is best absorbed along with piper nigrum (black pepper).

9. Take glutamine, an effective amino acid that helps to quickly turn over the epithelial cells of the digestive lining and heal intestinal permeability.

10. Get collagen/gelatin in the form of homemade bone broth (see Lisa's recipe in the *Soups and Stews* chapter) or take a collagen/gelatin supplement. Like glutamine, collagen/gelatin helps to turn over the epithelial cells of the digestive lining and heal intestinal permeability.

11. Take a quality, multi-strain probiotic with a soil-based organism (SBO) like Bacillus subtilis. (For more on probiotics, see the *Vitamins and Other Nutrients* subchapter in the chapter, *The Nutritional Heavy Hitters*.)

12. Take a quality, Omega-3 essential fatty acid (EFA) in the form of mercury-free fish oil. EFAs help to quell systemic inflammation. (For more on Omega-3s, see the *Vitamins and Other Nutrients* subchapter in the chapter, *The Nutritional Heavy Hitters*.)

13. Consider a digestive enzyme, which can help break down your macronutrients: carbohydrates, fat, and protein.

14. Consider black seed oil, an antioxidant-rich immune modulator that has been used in alternative HIV protocols for years and it's often recommended for varying types of autoimmunity. It's helpful in improving allergies, digestion, systemic yeast, and H. pylori, among other conditions. It's been said that black seed oil is "a cure for everything but death."

15. Support your liver to optimize your pathways of detoxification. Three of the best ways I know to do this are to drink warm lemon water first thing in the morning (simply squeeze the juice of half a lemon into a mug of warm water), get plenty of fiber (you may want to consider a powdered fiber for about 30 days, like triphala or psyllium), and to take an herbal liver-supportive tincture. (See Appendix B for our favorite liver support supplements.)*

16. Hydrate, hydrate, hydrate. Consider filtering your water to remove impurities like metals, fluoride, and chlorine. (You can find the water filters we recommend on our website: www.thyroidcookbook.com.)

17. Balance your blood sugar. The importance of this simply cannot be underestimated. If you're prone to dysglycemia and blood sugar dysregulation, *all bets are off* in regulating other hormones, mitigating the stress response, and managing autoimmunity. All roads lead back to blood sugar. (For more information, I recommend my e-book, *Balance Your Blood Sugar,* available at www.healthfulelements.com/store.)

18. Get plenty of fermented foods in your diet. Fermentation is a chemical change brought on by the action of beneficial yeast and bacteria and eating fermented foods is ideal for optimal digestion. This cookbook contains several recipes with fermented foods, which should be a staple for anyone looking to heal gut imbalances. These foods include kefir, kombucha, kimchi, miso, natto, gluten-free soy sauce (tamari), tempeh, yogurt (can be non-dairy, like coconut or nut milk), and sauerkraut.

19. If digestive distress is acute, consider getting tested for digestive infections such as small intestine bacterial overgrowth (SIBO) and Helicobacter pylori (H. pylori).

20. Get tested for MTHFR gene polymorphism, as there's an association between MTHFR and autoimmunity. [6]

21. Address adrenal health, including the stressors in your life. When we're under stress, our immune system knows it and this is of particular concern for those of us with autoimmune disease or who are at risk for autoimmunity.

    When we're stressed (whether it's because we're in physical danger, because our job is demanding, because we're caring for a sick loved one, or any other physical, mental, or emotional strain), our adrenals produce stress hormones that impact body temperature, respiration, hunger, sleep cycles, and numerous other functions.

    Cortisol, in particular, is responsible for putting our immune system on high alert—and it's been shown to contribute to damage to the intestinal lining. Prolonged periods of stress thus increase the likelihood that our immune system will become overactive and confused, causing autoantibodies to attack the body.

    Learn to say no to any obligations that don't serve your wellbeing, whether that's a relationship, a job, or tasks that you can outsource. Lighten your load, even if it's for a few months, as your body heals.

    I don't have the "magic bullet" for slaying stress, but if I had to name one, it would be breathwork/meditation. Autoimmunity expert, Donna Jackson Nakazawa, states, "Redirecting our thoughts through meditation literally rewires the brain and drastically decreases the level of stress hormones and chemical secretions that can be so damaging to our bodies." [3]*

22. Get dirty. A relatively new theory that holds my fascination is the hygiene hypothesis. Think hand sanitizers, antibacterial soaps, and our general aversion to anything "dirty," an obsessive fear that's working against us.

    According to Mary Ruebush, PhD, an award-winning professor of immunology and microbiology, "Because of some common misunderstandings about how illness works, we've begun to mistake any and all microbes for public enemy No. 1. But if bacteria itself were the problem, we'd all be long gone by now."

    She continues, "... the modern obsession with cleanliness, along with an increasing tendency to stay indoors in germ- and parasite-free environments, [is] leading to weaker immune

> " Because of some common misunderstandings about how illness works, we've begun to mistake any and all microbes for public enemy No. 1. But if bacteria itself were the problem, we'd all be long gone by now."
> —Mary Ruebush, PhD

systems and an increase in autoimmune disorders. The immune system is like an athlete: to become strong and adept, it needs training and practice. Hyper-sanitized environments deny it that opportunity and keep it sedentary and out of shape."[7]

You can stop worrying about dirt that won't harm you. Use good ol' soap and water. Germs and bacteria are our friends. This is why a probiotic in the form of a soil-based organism is a good idea.

23. Sleep. Sleep like it's your job, even if this means nine, ten, or more hours. The body heals when we sleep. Among other problems, lack of sleep fires up our adrenal stress hormones, leading to further hormonal and immune imbalances.

24. Assess whether the pharmaceuticals you're on are worth it, given that many have side effects and can do harm to the intestinal lining. *I'm not suggesting that you quit taking any of your drugs*—always consult with your doctor about changes to your medications.

25. Be compassionate with yourself. With autoimmune disease, we're often told our bodies have turned against us and are no longer our friends, but are now enemies. This is untrue. Our body's job is to help us maintain health and homeostasis. Dis-ease is our body's way of communicating that something is out of balance and autoimmunity is a miscommunication within the body, not a deliberate internal battle. When we get upset and blame, condemn, and hate our bodies, it often leads to poor choices. We're hating on ourselves, which itself can fire up autoimmune antibodies.

26. Reduce your toxic body burden. This is a significant and far-reaching topic that I can only scratch the surface on in this book.

Our bodies face a barrage of chemicals and toxins on a daily, hourly, minute-by-minute basis. It's impossible to completely eliminate our exposure to these antigens, but there are steps we can take to mitigate the risks. Some of the pillars of addressing toxic body burden are using nontoxic skincare and cosmetics; safe kitchen tools, gadgets, and utensils; and home cleaning supplies.

Our skin is our largest organ of the body. Any chemicals or toxins you slather on it are going to be absorbed by your pores and will go straight to your bloodstream, profoundly affecting your immune system. The importance of getting toxins out of our body care products cannot be underestimated. This is the starting place, as you move toward a cleaner and greener home, body, and environment.

Avoid cosmetics or personal hygiene products that contain parabens, phthalates, sodium laureth/sodium laurel sulfate, butyl/ethyl acetate, petrolatum, cocmide DEA/lauramide DEA, diazolidinyl urea, propylene glycol, toluene, synthetic colors and fragrances, and triethanolamine, to name a few. Utilize the Environmental Working Group's Skin Deep Database to rate your products at www.ewg.org/skindeep.

It's also imperative to use nontoxic cleaning supplies in the home. There are some ridiculously simple and cheap recipes on the web for making your own, if you're so inclined. However you do it, ditch the cleaners you get at most conventional supermarkets and drugstores; they're loaded with toxins and chemicals that become airborne and we absorb them through inhalation and skin contact. The chemicals in conventional cleaning products help to make the air inside our homes and offices five times more polluted than the air outdoors.*

*All of the factors in the list above should be considered for reducing inflammation and mitigating the autoimmune response and to go deeper, download *The Essential Thyroid Cookbook Lifestyle Companion Guide* for more specific information.

- Managing and cleansing systemic yeast/candida

- Optimizing liver function

- Restoring optimal adrenal/HPA axis function

- Addressing toxic body burden

You can download the guide for free on our website: www.thyroidcookbook.com/companion.

Elimination Provocation Diet Instructions

Food sensitivities are best determined with an Elimination Provocation diet. This experiment is *life-changing*—it's the foundation for any health-improvement program. It can be one of the most important things you do for your wellbeing.

If the thought of going on a restricted diet strikes fear, know that an Elimination Provocation diet is *temporary*. As one presenter at the Food as Medicine Conference that I attended in the summer of 2015 put it, "Focus on the 'in' when doing an ElimINation diet."

There are many more foods that you can eat than you can't. In fact, many of the recipes in this cookbook are compatible with the Elimination Provocation diet and are designated as such with our EP icon. We also provide simple adaptations, where applicable, for making some of our recipes fit an EP diet.

While sometimes it's good to take baby steps on your healing journey, in my work with clients, we take out several potential dietary triggers all at once, then reintroduce to see if there's a reaction.

Most say that the diet is very doable and given that most people start to see results within a matter of days, I'm not so keen on the "baby steps" approach, like simply removing eggs, for instance, and *then* wondering about other possible sensitivities.

It's important to know that food sensitivities are different than food allergies. Food allergies (the IgE immune response) are much less common than food sensitivities (the IgG immune response) and often result in an immediate reaction like anaphylactic shock. A food sensitivity, on the other hand, is a reaction to a food with no antigen-antibody response. IgG antibodies have a much longer half-life than IgE antibodies.

> 66 Food sensitivities can be subtle and many people live with them for years, if not their whole lives."

Food sensitivities can be subtle and many people live with them for years, if not their whole lives. They can trigger systemic, cellular inflammation that can wreak havoc on metabolism, make us hold on to extra weight, cause joint pain, feed autoimmune antibodies, and can contribute to all of the major degenerative diseases. The Elimination Provocation diet is a key factor in snuffing out this fire.

Several doctors in the functional medicine community claim that this experiment is "the gold standard" for uncovering food sensitivities. Many of the blood and skin tests have proven largely inconclusive, although the blood testing from Cyrex and US BioTek is reportedly the best. But neither test is perfect and some claim that any blood testing for food sensitivities can be inconclusive.

In a healthy human, the epithelial cells of the intestinal lining turn over every few days. But many don't experience this cellular turnover because they're eating foods that are irritating the lining of their intestines. The intestinal wall needs to be a wall—not a fishnet (intestinal permeability). The cellular junctions of the digestive lining need to be "tight and right" so that undigested food, pathogens, and bacteria don't escape into the bloodstream and fan the flames of autoimmunity, among other problems.

> 66 The cellular junctions of the digestive lining need to be 'tight and right' so that undigested food, pathogens, and bacteria don't escape into the bloodstream and fan the flames of autoimmunity."

Symptoms include, but aren't limited to: fatigue, drowsiness after eating, brain fog, poor memory and concentration, agitation, mood swings, intense cravings (especially for sugar, refined carbs, and starch), abdominal cramping, weight gain and weight loss resistance, depression, restlessness, irritability, headaches (including migraines), swollen and painful joints, muscle pain and stiffness, shortness of breath, bloating, flatulence/gas, heartburn, constipation, loose stools, blurry vision, broken sleep, skin issues (eczema, etc.), recurring sinusitis, and repetitive throat clearing.

The most common foods that people can have sensitivities to include:

- Eggs

- Dairy (including goat and sheep milk)

- Wheat/gluten (including einkorn, durum, faro, graham, kamut, semolina, spelt, barley, triticale, and rye)

- Soy

- Corn

- Nuts

- Peanuts (which are legumes)

- Shellfish

- Citrus

- Nightshades

Nightshades include: Ashwagandha (an Ayurvedic adaptogenic herb), all peppers (sweet, hot, bell, chili (including paprika), jalapeno, habanero, cayenne, pimento) potatoes (but not sweet potatoes), tomatoes, cape gooseberries, tobacco, cocona, eggplant, garden huckleberries, goji berries, kutjera, naranjilla, pepino, tamarillo, and tomatillos.

Books have been devoted to this experiment[1], but below is the straightforward protocol I've used with clients for years, with great success.

- Eliminate the above foods 100 percent for three weeks. Don't allow even small amounts into your diet. After three weeks, reintroduce each food or food group one at a time, eating **4-5 servings** of that food or food group on your **one provocation day**. Provocations entail one day per food/food group, as long as you get 4-5 servings. If you have Hashimoto's or any autoimmune condition, gluten should be categorically avoided, 100 percent and *not reintroduced*.

- During your reintroductions, for the food groups, you can eat any or all of those foods. I'm referring to citrus, nightshades, dairy, shellfish, and nuts. In other words, when you reintroduce nightshades, it's not necessary to break out tomatoes, potatoes, peppers, etc. and reintroduce them separately. The same goes for the other food groups.

- Monitor symptoms for up to 72 hours. Don't rush your next provocation/reintroduction. With food sensitivities, reactions can take 2-3 days. Allow your body enough time to respond before the next reintroduction.

- If you have a reaction, continue eliminating that particular food and re-challenge three months later. For foods that you don't have a reaction to, continue eating.

- Incorporate some smart supplementation. Details below.

Much to many of my clients' and readers' surprise, grains and legumes aren't on the list of foods that you'll temporarily omit during this diet. In fact, this causes outright shock for some people. (See the chapters, *In Defense of Grains* and *In Defense of Legumes*.)

Even the prestigious Institute for Functional Medicine doesn't exclude grains and legumes from their comprehensive Elimination Diet. If you were to omit these foods in addition to the foods identified as common triggers in these Elimination Provocation diet instructions, your diet would be very close to an Autoimmune Protocol (AIP) diet, which I'm not necessarily against. I explain more in the chapter, *Why This is Not Another Paleo or AIP Cookbook* about why I take a different approach and feel that *moderate amounts* of these foods are acceptable, including when I feel that removing grains and legumes is warranted.

If, after completing this experiment, digestive symptoms haven't improved significantly and/or antibodies haven't decreased, consider getting tested for a gut infection such as small intestine bacterial overgrowth (SIBO) and Helicobacter pylori (H. pylori).

Recommendations and tips:

- Read all food labels—the food industry can be tricky with naming ingredients.

- Many prepared foods have hidden additives and fillers that contain wheat and egg byproducts.

- Avoid packaged, canned, and convenience foods during this diet.

Reactions during the Provocation phase will look differently for different people. Frequently, a reoccurrence or worsening of symptoms previously experienced (your weak links) is what shows up. But see the full symptoms list mentioned earlier in this chapter for what to watch out for. Keeping a journal of reactions during this experiment can be helpful.

Many clients come to me having previously done some iteration of an Elimination Provocation diet but didn't experience the results they'd hoped for. When I ask if they were taking some critical gut-healing supplements during the diet, most say, "no." They complete this version, along with the supplement recommendations below, and get fantastic results.

There are three supplements that will fast-track your healing. The diet itself is therapeutic and detoxifying, but by itself, likely won't give you the cellular regeneration and turnover that the lining of your intestinal wall needs to tame a hypervigilant immune system. With consistency, these supplements will offer you a smoother Provocation phase and you'll be able to reintroduce any inflammatory triggers sooner than if you were on the diet alone.

It's important to take the following during your Elimination phase, your Provocation phase, and during the three months that follow your Provocation phase (and possibly longer), as you're healing from your proven triggers. (See Appendix B for our supplement suggestions. You can also find links to all of these at our website: www.thyroidcookbook.com.)

1. Collagen/gelatin, either via bone broth or a supplement: Collagen and gelatin help to heal intestinal permeability (leaky gut) and restore the mucosal layer.

   I recommend making your own bone broth. You can find our recipe in the *Soups and Stews* chapter of this cookbook. In lieu of broth, you can take a collagen/gelatin supplement. Daily dose: Two to three cups of broth or two to three servings of collagen/gelatin. You can also use these interchangeably and alternate between the two.

2. Glutamine: Glutamine is an amino acid that supports the integrity and optimal function of the gastrointestinal lining and promotes optimal gut mucosal integrity. Daily dose: Powdered glutamine, 3-4 grams, mixed into anything (smoothie, water, soup, even your broth). More is not more with glutamine, as it can convert to glutamate in the brain and cause overstimulation.

   Note: Children should take a low-dose glutamine.

3. Probiotic with a soil-based strain: Probiotics are "friendly bacteria" that promote healthy digestive flora, which is crucial for proper digestive function. They populate the intestines with beneficial bacteria, which is critical to the breakdown and absorption of nutrients, and also crowd out the less-than-friendly flora. (For more on probiotics, see the *Vitamins and Other Nutrients* subchapter in the chapter, *The Nutritional Heavy Hitters*.)

   There are many good brands out there, but I prefer a broad-spectrum probiotic that contains a soil-based organism (SBO) like BioKult, Prescript-Assist, or MegaSporeBiotic. Daily dose: One with each meal. With the MegaSporeBiotic, start slowly, one per day, and work up. (See Appendix B for our supplement recommendations, of which you can also find links to on our website: www.thyroidcookbook.com.)

This is a very cleansing and detoxifying experiment and most people feel amazing during this diet—lighter and brighter, more energetic and positive, and most report losing a few pounds within a mere week. But please know that during the initial Elimination phase, you may experience withdrawal symptoms, such as fatigue, headache, malaise, irritability, or possibly a mild skin reaction. It's called the Herxheimer reaction or "herxing." These should subside shortly, so don't despair. For many, taking activated charcoal capsules can alleviate symptoms quickly.

Lastly, I'm frequently asked about the validity of blood testing for food sensitivities. As I mention above, there are now better tests on the market than there were a few years ago, but I'm not convinced they're conclusive—they often result in false negatives.

Integrative medicine pioneer, Dr. Andrew Weil, states, "I discussed the issue of testing for food intolerances with Randy Horwitz, MD, PhD, medical director of the Program in Integrative Medicine at the University of Arizona, who specializes in immunology. We agree that the only reliable approach to determining food intolerances or sensitivities is to use avoidance and provocative testing—in other words, an elimination diet followed by a 'challenge' to see whether a suspect food really does set off a reaction. Dr. Horwitz notes that when food sensitivities—not true allergies—are a problem, traditional allergy tests such as the IgE RAST blood tests or skin prick tests often yield negative results. He says that in his practice, he has not seen uniformly good results with IgG anti-food blood tests, applied kinesiology (muscle strength testing), or 'live blood' microscopic analysis, all of which have been advocated by some practitioners as ways of determining food intolerances. Dr. Horwitz said that results 'go all the way from questionable to downright useless.'"[2]

CONCLUSION

It has been a joy for Lisa and me to create this first-of-its kind cookbook. We enjoyed geeking out on the research, creating our nitty-gritty nutritional springboard, writing the exhaustively researched educational component, and developing and testing these original, nutrient-dense thyroid- and immune-supportive recipes. Our sincere hope is that you use this cookbook (and our other, yet-to-be-published cookbooks) for years to come.

Managing hypothyroidism and Hashimoto's is an exercise in becoming the CEO of your health. This cookbook is a great place to start—and will help keep your thyroid nourished throughout your life, even after your hypothyroidism/Hashimoto's is under control.

Remember, the body is always seeking ways to balance and regulate itself and for the most part, is quick to respond to sound nutrition and being well cared for.

It's imperative that the relationship you have with your healthcare provider is open and accepting. As integrative medicine pioneer, Dr. Aviva Romm, states, "You should be able to have mutually respectful conversations with your care provider, to get the answers you are seeking, and to be able to explore your concerns."[1]

Don't allow your doctor to use outdated lab reference ranges or to neglect testing for the antibodies that could reveal Hashimoto's. It's important to continue to monitor these values to know whether you're recovering from Hashimoto's. Reject the notion that TSH alone determines your thyroid status.

Don't tolerate intimidation or condescension from your doctor—something I know is commonplace because I hear it from my clients frequently. Dr. Romm says, "For many women, the lab tests that doctors currently use, and the way those tests are interpreted, leads many women to be told that they don't have a thyroid problem, and in fact, they are just fine. This translates as, 'This is all in your head because I, with my medical degree, cannot find a darned thing wrong with you, Lady.' And this often results in an antidepressant prescription." (Our intention in sharing this quote is not to be dismissive of the many men who have Hashimoto's!)

Being a recipient of the go-to thyroid drugs, with no conversation about immune modulation, nutritional and lifestyle changes, or drug alternatives may get you minimally treated at best. Dr. Romm states, "As a doctor, I can tell you that in medical school we are taught that doctors know best. But this is often not the case. You are your body's best expert."[1]

There's no one-size-fits all protocol for hypothyroidism and addressing the condition in an integrative manner will make all the difference in your health and wellbeing.

A well-rounded, mostly organic/sustainably-raised, whole foods diet will help to support your thyroid gland. A poor-quality diet causes oxidative stress and chronic systemic inflammation and affects how all of our cells communicate with one another.

> 66 Being a recipient of the go-to thyroid drugs, with no conversation about immune modulation, nutritional and lifestyle changes, or drug alternatives may get you minimally treated at best."

When you consider that every cell in the body has receptors for thyroid hormone and that the thyroid turns on the genes that keep cells doing their job, it makes it easier to understand how a nutrient-deficient diet can interrupt this cellular communication. Again, this cookbook is a great place to start.

Whether you're on thyroid hormone replacement or not, addressing your diet and lifestyle is critical to getting back on track—feeling like yourself again, regaining your vitality, and firing up your metabolism.

Don't forget to download our free resource, *The Essential Thyroid Cookbook Lifestyle Companion Guide,* where I address factors associated with hypothyroidism and Hashimoto's beyond what we could fit into this cookbook. You can download it for free on our website:

www.thyroidcookbook.com/companion.

Lisa and I wish you a lifetime of vibrant health.

PART TWO:

Essential Thyroid Kitchen

PANTRY STAPLES AND INGREDIENTS

When adopting a healthier diet and lifestyle, making changes can often feel overwhelming, especially if the foods and ingredients you're being asked to eat are foreign to you. While this section is not intended to fully encompass every healthful ingredient you could possibly use in your kitchen, we've provided a great starting point for understanding key ingredients used in Part Three: Essential Thyroid Recipes. The information in these pages will inspire and empower you to successfully create a well-stocked kitchen.

Begin by adding a few ingredients you think you'll use most often. Over time, as you learn about and experiment with new items, your cooking repertoire and culinary confidence will grow, naturally. As you build your pantry with healthful ingredients, start discarding any unhealthy, processed, and outdated items. This may include poor quality processed oils, expired condiments, old spices, processed breakfast cereals, and junk foods.

To discover brands and products we love, including sources for many of the items in this section, visit our website (www.thyroidcookbook.com). We'll expand and update our list as we discover new products that may be of benefit to you.

Non-Gluten Grains

For a full explanation of why we feel that gluten-free grains are acceptable in moderation, see the chapters, *In Defense of Grains* and *Why This is Not Another Paleo or AIP Cookbook.*

Non-gluten grains are a fiber-rich pantry staple that can build a foundation for a healthful meal. We're in favor of *true whole grains*, which take longer to digest and are considered complex carbohydrates. Alternately, grains that have been pulverized into flour and made into pastries, bagels, cookies, pasta, and cakes (even the gluten-free variety, aka gluten-free junk food) and many of today's processed, prepackaged foods are simple carbohydrates.

While not categorically horrible, simple carbohydrates shouldn't be a dietary staple because the body treats them like sugar. Eaten alone or without adequate fat and protein to slow the release of sugar, the sugar breaks down rapidly and heads straight to your bloodstream (like rocket fuel), causing blood sugar to spike (hyperglycemia) and then plummet (hypoglycemia).

A diet high in these refined, simple carbs is a recipe for insulin resistance, metabolic syndrome, and pre-diabetes/diabetes. To help avert these conditions, we recommend opting for grains in their whole, intact form, whenever possible.

As Jill explained in the chapter, *Gluten and Your Thyroid,* gluten should be avoided on a thyroid-supportive diet. The following grains and their products contain gluten:

- Wheat (einkorn, durum, farro, graham, kamut, semolina, spelt)
- Rye
- Barley
- Triticale

You can go to www.celiac.com for a complete list of gluten-containing foods, including surprising and hidden sources, but some of the common places that gluten hides out include:

- Sauces, dressings, soups, and stews (thickened with flour)
- Soy, teriyaki, and hoisin sauce (fermented with wheat)
- Fried foods (cross-contamination in the fryer)
- Additives in processed and packaged foods
- Alcohol (beer, grain alcohol, malt beverages)
- Medications and supplements

You'll also want to read labels on your personal care products such as cosmetics, lotion, and shampoo. Other helpful websites include www.celiac.org, www.celiactravel.com, and www.celiacsolution.com.

The following grains are gluten-free. Not all of the grains listed below are featured in this cookbook. See the *Our Methodology* chapter for a detailed explanation of our thoughtful ranking system that helped us choose the ingredients featured in our recipes.

Amaranth is a tiny grain rich in protein, calcium, and iron. It can be easily stirred into soups or can be mixed with other grains like quinoa and oats to make a hearty breakfast cereal. Amaranth takes 20 minutes to cook. Use 2½-3 cups water per 1 cup grain.

Brown rice comes in a variety of options from slightly chewier short-grain to aromatic long-grain options like jasmine or basmati. You can also find many styles of gluten-free noodles made from brown rice flour. Brown rice takes 45 minutes to cook. Use 2 cups water per 1 cup grain.

Buckwheat is a heart-shaped seed related to rhubarb. You may find it in stores as raw groats or in a toasted form, called kasha. The raw groats are milder in flavor, but the toasted groats have a nice nutty flavor. Used in its whole form, buckwheat can be made into a savory pilaf or mixed with other grains to make a filling breakfast cereal. As flour, it's great for pancakes, crepes, and waffles. Buckwheat kasha takes 15-20 minutes to cook, while raw buckwheat takes 20-30 minutes. Use 2 cups water per 1 cup grain for either variety.

Forbidden rice is an unusual black rice that gets its unique color from a rich source of the anti-oxidant pigment, anthocyanin, making it the most nutrient-dense of all of the rices. Forbidden rice has a slighty nutty flavor and chewy texture. It takes about 35-40 minutes to cook. Use 2 cups water per 1 cup grain.

Job's tears is a grass that produces ivory, bead-like seeds that have a high protein to carbohydrate ratio. Although it's often labeled as "Chinese barley," it's a gluten-free grain unrelated to barley. It's often found in Asian grocery stores and well-stocked natural food stores. Although it has a significant list of health benefits, Job's Tears isn't recommended for pregnant or nursing women or for diabetics, because of its reported ability to lower blood sugar. It takes 60 minutes to cook. Use 2 cups water per 1 cup grain.

Millet is a small, round, yellow seed similar in shape and size to quinoa. It can be combined with vegetables and herbs to make a warm and savory pilaf or blended with other gluten-free grains for a nutritious hot breakfast cereal. Millet takes 25 minutes to cook. Use 2 cups water per 1 cup grain. For a more porridge-like consistency, increase water to 3 cups.

Oats (certified gluten-free) come in three main forms: steel cut, rolled (or old-fashioned), and quick. We recommend foregoing quick oats and opting for steel cut or rolled because they're less processed and better for digestion and blood sugar regulation. It's important to ensure the oats and oat products are *certified* gluten-free to reduce potential for cross-contamination from gluten-containing grains. Rolled oats take 5-10 minutes to cook. Use 2 cups water per 1 cup grain. Steel cut oats take 25 minutes to cook. Use 3 cups water per 1 cup grain.

Polenta is a quick and easy pantry staple made from coarsely ground corn kernels. It can serve as a base to a meal by topping it with your protein of choice, sautéed vegetables, and marinara sauce. Polenta takes 30 minutes to cook; stir frequently. Use 3 cups water per 1 cup grain.

Popcorn kernels are nice to keep on hand for making a simple, yet healthful snack. Heirloom kernels come in a variety of colors and have great flavor. Popcorn is easy to cook on your stovetop in less than 5 minutes using a high heat oil like refined coconut oil or avocado oil.

Quinoa is cooked like a whole grain, but is a seed from the same plant family as spinach and Swiss chard. It's a nutrient-dense option because it contains a broad assortment of minerals, plus it's a unique plant-based source of all nine essential amino acids, the building blocks of protein. Quinoa is easy to make into a chilled grain salad or can be simply stirred into soups, stews, and chili. You can also find gluten-free noodles made from quinoa flour. Quinoa takes 15-20 minutes to cook. Use 2 cups water per 1 cup grain.

Sorghum is a whole grain that is most often utilized in flour form, but can also be enjoyed intact as a pilaf or grain salad. When ground, it most closely resembles the texture and flavor of wheat flour, but doesn't contain gluten, so it's best used as part of a gluten-free flour blend. Intact sorghum takes 50-60 minutes to cook. Use 3 cups water per 1 cup grain.

Teff is most commonly found as dark red or brown, but also comes in white. It's a tiny but mighty grain native to Africa, where it's commonly prepared as a breakfast porridge or made into a fermented flatbread called injera. It can easily be mixed into hot cereal recipes, preferably with other gluten-free whole grains, to add a sweet, robust flavor. Teff takes 20 minutes to cook. Use 3 cups water per 1 cup grain.

Wild rice is an aquatic grass plant grown in North America that's great for making pilafs and stuffings. It has a complex nutty and sweet flavor and is rich in protein, minerals, and B vitamins. Wild rice takes 45-60 minutes to cook. Use 4 cups water per 1 cup grain.

Grains are fairly easy to prepare using the following basic steps:

1. **Pre-soak (recommended):** Grains can be challenging to digest for some, therefore we suggest soaking prior to cooking to help break down phytic acid. Soak grains (with the exception of amaranth and teff) in their measured amount of water in a glass measuring cup for 12-24 hours on your kitchen counter. Add 1 tablespoon of raw apple cider vinegar, if desired. When ready to cook, note the water level of the soaked grain, drain off the soaking water, add fresh water to the measure you noted, and simmer on

stove with a pinch of salt for recommended cooking time. Note that soaking some grains reduces their overall cooking time by a few minutes, but the cooking time for pre-soaked steel cut or rolled oats is reduced by about half.

2. **Toast (optional):** Lightly toasting grains deepens their flavor and adds a delicious nuttiness. To toast grains, pour measured amount evenly into a dry skillet and cook over medium heat for 3-5 minutes, stirring regularly, until they smell nutty. Remove from heat before they get too brown, then proceed with normal cooking instructions.

3. **Rinse:** Certain grains should be rinsed before cooking to remove dust or other debris and to yield the best flavor. These include millet, quinoa, and rice. Quinoa has a bitter coating on the outside called saponin that will negatively impact flavor if not rinsed. Rinse the grains by placing in a fine mesh strainer and rinsing with warm water.

4. **Cook:** Place measured grain with water or stock and a pinch of sea salt in a pot, cover with a tight fitting lid, and bring to a boil. A 1-quart pot is best for cooking 1 cup of grain, a 2-quart pot for 2 cups of grain, and so on. Reduce heat and simmer for suggested cooking time, which will vary depending on grain, so refer to our individual grains information for guidance. Refrain from stirring the pot while the grains are cooking; this will disrupt the steam pockets that allow the top layer to cook as evenly as the bottom and cause some not to fully cook. To check if all of the water has been absorbed, simply tilt the pot to the side to see if there's still water pooling at the bottom; if water is still present, continue to cook for a few additional minutes until it has all been absorbed.

Gluten-Free Flours

There are many options when it comes to gluten-free flours. We've listed a few we find to be good staples.

Almond flour is made from blanched, raw almonds that have been ground to a fine consistency. It's mildly sweet and can be used to make pancakes, muffins, cookies, cakes, breads, and more. We don't recommended swapping out cup for cup in a recipe that calls for gluten-containing flours, like all-purpose flour. For best results, we recommend using the recipes in this book or seeking out grain-free recipe sources (e.g. Paleo) that regularly use almond flour.

We recommend nut flour/nut meal in moderation. Many have difficulty digesting nuts and one cup of almond flour contains about 90 almonds. While we understand that this quantity will be reduced due to serving size, it's still an inordinate amount of nuts in one sitting.

Arrowroot flour (also known as arrowroot starch) is a starch that's extracted from the rhizome of the arrowroot plant grown in the rainforest. It's commonly blended with other gluten-free flours to create a softer consistency. It can also be used as a one-to-one substitute in place of cornstarch to thicken sauces, soups, and gravies. Simply mix the arrowroot flour with a small amount of cold water to create a slurry before stirring into a sauce or gravy.

Buckwheat flour is made from ground, toasted buckwheat groats and has a robust flavor. It's commonly used in soba noodles and pancakes, but read labels because it's blended with wheat flour in most products and recipes.

Coconut flour is a high-fiber flour made from dried coconut meat that has had the oil removed. It's highly absorbent, making it somewhat tricky to bake with; a small amount goes a long way. It cannot be swapped out cup for cup in a recipe calling for a gluten-containing flour, like all-purpose flour.

Legumes/Beans

For a full explanation of why we feel that legumes/beans are acceptable in moderation, see the chapters, *In Defense of Legumes* and *Why This is Not Another Paleo or AIP Cookbook*.

Beans come in a variety of shapes and colors, providing satisfying texture to a meal. They also supply more fiber than any other food group. Beans are an important source of phytonutrients that can help prevent cancer cells from multiplying and the resistant starch found in these nutritional powerhouses is vital for nourishing the health of beneficial microbes in our gut.

Cooking beans from scratch (using dried beans) can be an economical way to prepare this hearty, nutrient-dense plant protein. Dried beans are often available in the bulk department of most natural food stores. Shop for beans where there's good turnover to ensure you're not purchasing old, stale beans that won't cook properly. Older beans will be faded and lusterless versus shiny and rich in color. Dried beans can be stored for approximately 6-9 months. In a pinch, canned organic beans in BPA-free cans are a convenient alternative. See the *Our "Go-To" Canned and Packaged Foods* chapter for more on BPA.

General cooking instructions for dry legumes/beans:

1. Clean beans by sorting out any debris like stones or shriveled pieces. This is easiest done on a cutting board or white plate.

2. To help improve digestibility, soak beans (except red lentils) overnight by placing in a large bowl and covering with twice as much water. After 8 hours, drain and rinse away soaking water.

3. Add 3 cups fresh water for every 1 cup of dried beans that you started with. Bring to a boil, then lower heat and simmer until beans are fully cooked and can easily be mashed on the roof of your mouth. Refer to appropriate cooking times for each individual bean, as this will vary.

4. Add herbs, spices, and/or kombu while cooking. It's best to wait to season with salt until beans are fully cooked because salt can toughen the outer layer of the bean and slow the cooking process.

Cook's tip: Consider investing in a pressure cooker to shorten the cooking time of dried beans. See our website for our suggested pressure cooker (www.thyroidcookbook.com).

Not all of the legumes/beans listed below are present in this cookbook. See the *Our Methodology* chapter for a detailed explanation of our thoughtful ranking system that helped us choose ingredients to highlight for our recipes.

Small Beans

Aduki (adzuki beans) are small red beans that are easy to digest and assimilate. They take approximately 45-60 minutes to cook.

Green/brown/black lentils are flat disc-shaped legumes that hold their shape and have a toothsome bite when added to soups or made into chilled salads. Lentils have a fairly neutral flavor, making them an incredibly versatile ingredient that will readily take on the flavor of any seasonings you choose. Lentils cook in about 45 minutes.

Mung beans are small, green, oval-shaped beans that are often sprouted into mung bean sprouts. Alternately, they can be cooked into soups and stews and are especially delicious when seasoned with curry. They cook in about 30-45 minutes.

Red lentils are split lentils and have the quickest cooking time, about 25-30 minutes. Once cooked, they have a comforting, creamy, mushy texture. They are best in soups and stews, especially in an Indian-style soup called dal.

Split peas have a thick, creamy texture. They're delicious when made into a soothing bowl of soup and take about 35-45 minutes to cook.

Large Beans

Black beans are a favorite for using in a variety of ways from soups, stews, chili, and salads. They're delicious when seasoned with Mexican spices, lime juice, and fresh herbs. Black beans take 60-90 minutes to cook.

Black-eyed peas are a popular bean for cooking with Cajun spices and collard greens in Hoppin' John stew. They're also delicious dressed with vinaigrette and tossed into a cold bean salad. They take 60 minutes to cook.

Cannellini beans are creamy, white beans that taste great in Italian soups like minestrone. They take 60-90 minutes to cook.

Chickpeas (garbanzo beans) have a round shape and pleasing texture. They're a staple ingredient for making hummus and other Middle Eastern and Moroccan dishes. They take about 90 minutes to cook.

Kidney beans are large red beans that are essential for making chili or tri-color bean salads. They take 90 minutes to cook.

Lima beans (butter beans) are a larger, light green bean with a creamy, buttery texture. They're delicious tossed in cold salads, like succotash. They take 60 minutes to cook.

Navy beans are a classic for baked bean recipes, but can also be added to tomato-based soups or pureed into a protein-rich dip. They take about 60-90 minutes to cook.

Pinto beans are familiar brown beans common in Mexican cuisine. They're great mashed into refried beans or added to chili or soup. They take 60-90 minutes to cook.

Improving Digestibility of Legumes/Beans

Many are familiar with the intestinal discomfort and flatulence that beans can cause. This is due in part to the action of complex undigested sugars. Using the following methods will help to improve digestibility and reduce flatulence:

- If beans are new to your diet, be sure to work them in slowly, allowing your body time to adjust.

- Experiment with your level of digestibility. Aduki beans, lentils, mung beans, and peas digest most easily. Pinto, kidney, navy, garbanzo, lima, black beans, and black-eyed peas are more challenging to digest and should be eaten occasionally.

- Chew beans thoroughly.

- With canned beans, draining and rinsing prior to cooking can help reduce some of the indigestible sugars. Select beans that are free of preservatives and added salt.

- Use spices like cumin, epazote (a Mexican herb), fennel, or ginger to help tenderize beans and improve digestibility.

- Add a piece of the sea vegetables kombu or kelp to the cooking water to help tenderize the beans. This not only improves flavor but also adds important minerals like iodine to your dish.

- Pour a splash of apple cider vinegar, brown rice vinegar, or white wine vinegar into the water in the last stages of cooking. This softens the beans and breaks down protein chains and indigestible compounds. You can also dress cooked beans with a vinaigrette made from lemon juice, apple cider vinegar, or brown rice vinegar.

- Legumes/beans combine best with green or non-starchy vegetables and seaweeds.

- Season with unrefined sea salt or miso near the end of cooking because if added at the beginning, the beans will not cook completely. Salt is a digestive aid when used correctly.

- If you try these methods and beans still give you trouble, consider using a digestive enzyme. (See Appendix B for our enzyme recommendation.)

Nuts and Seeds

Nuts and seeds provide a healthful combination of essential fats, protein, and fiber all contained in a nutrient-dense package. They can be enjoyed in their whole form, as a flavorful nut or seed butter, or in some cases, used in their flour form for baked goods.

Individually, nuts and seeds vary in key nutrients. To obtain a broad spectrum of essential nutrients, be sure to eat a variety of nuts, seeds, or nut butters in their raw, soaked, or gently toasted forms.

In general, nuts, seeds, and their products can be found in most grocery stores (especially natural food stores) in their raw form free of excess salt, sugar, and added oils. You can find links to many of our favorite products and brands on our website (www.thyroidcookbook.com).

Nuts, seeds, nut/seed butters, and their flours all contain fragile oils that are sensitive to light, heat, and oxygen. Check for signs of rancidity when buying. To keep them from quickly turning rancid, it's best to store them in a tightly sealed container at 50°F or below. In general, they'll stay fresh for up to six months stored in the refrigerator and for up to one year stored in the freezer. Whenever possible, it's best to purchase nuts and seeds in their whole form and chop or grind yourself.

Not all of the nuts and seeds listed below are present in this cookbook. See the *Our Methodology* chapter for a detailed explanation of our thoughtful ranking system that helped us choose ingredients to highlight for our recipes.

Nut/Seed	Nutritional Benefits
Almonds	Almonds provide a great plant-based source of calcium, heart healthy monounsaturated fats, cholesterol lowering plant sterols, and energy producing manganese, copper, and Vitamin B_2, Almond flour and almond butter can be used in gluten-free baking.[a]
Brazil nuts	Brazil nuts offer a unique source of the trace mineral, selenium. The thyroid gland has more selenium content per gram of tissue than any other organ in your body and selenium is a key component of the molecules that are necessary for your body to create and use thyroid hormones.
Cashews	Raw cashews have a bland or neutral flavor, making them a blank canvas for infusing flavors into them. Their velvety, smooth, creamy texture helps add nice body when pureed into soups and sauces, which makes them a great replacement for cream. Homemade cashew milk is an easy to make favorite. (See my Chocolate Cashew Milk recipe.) Cashews provide a great source of Vitamin B_1, Vitamin B_5, Vitamin B_6, and the minerals iron, copper, manganese, and magnesium.
Cashew butter	Cashew butter is a rich, creamy spread made from grinding raw or roasted cashews. It has a milder flavor, but can be used interchangeably with almond butter, peanut butter, or sunflower seed butter in most recipes.
Chia seeds	Chia is a tiny, power-packed seed loaded with calcium, iron, magnesium, and Omega-3s. The soluble fiber in chia seeds promotes a feeling of satiety. Unlike flaxseeds, they don't need to be ground for us to access/absorb the Omega-3s.
Coconut flakes	Botanically speaking, coconut is a drupe, not a nut, and is therefore safe for most people with tree nut allergies. We chose to include it in this category because it shares many similar characteristics to nuts and seeds—it can be soaked and blended into homemade plant-based milk or sprinkled on hot cereal, smoothies, and desserts. Coconut contains a great source of fiber, as well as an important saturated fatty acid called lauric acid.

Coconut butter (manna)	Creamed coconut/coconut butter/coconut manna are three names for essentially the same thing: 100 percent coconut meat that has simply been ground into a butter-like consistency much in the same way peanuts are ground to make peanut butter. This novel ingredient can be found at most natural food stores in one of two places: in a small rectangular cardboard package in the baking aisle by the brand Let's Do Organic or in a jar in the peanut butter aisle by the brands Artisana or Nutiva. It imparts a smooth, silky texture when incorporated into smoothies, sauces, and desserts. Whole coconut products provide an excellent source of trace minerals including manganese, molybdenum, zinc, and copper. It's also a unique source of selenium, an essential mineral for thyroid and immune health.
Flaxseeds (ground)	Flax is a source of anti-inflammatory Omega-3s and cholesterol lowering soluble fiber and lignans. Store in a tightly sealed container in the fridge or freezer to prevent rancidity. It can be used to substitute an egg in a recipe; to make a "flax egg," soak 1 tablespoon of ground flaxseeds in 3 tablespoons warm water and let stand for 10 minutes, until it becomes viscous and gel-like. You can use this 1:1 in a recipe, but we would not recommend subbing more than 1 egg using this method because it won't have the same leavening effect that eggs do.
Hazelnuts	Hazelnuts provide a rich source of the antioxidant Vitamin E and the energy producing nutrients Vitamin B_1, Vitamin B_6, copper, and manganese. They have a distinctly delicious flavor with a subtle sweetness. Hazelnut flour can be swapped out cup for cup with almond flour.[a]
Hemp seeds	Hemp seeds are a small, nutty tasting seed that provide an excellent source of essential Omega-3 and Omega-6 fats that can support hormone balance. They're also a rare plant-based food that contains all nine essential amino acids (the building blocks of protein). They're delicious sprinkled on salads, dips, and smoothies or made into homemade hemp milk.
Macadamia nuts	Macadamia nuts are a rich tasting nut with a sweet flavor. They're an oilier nut, but the healthful oils come primarily from cardio-protective monounsaturated fats. They also provide a great source of Vitamin B_1, manganese, and copper.
Pecans	Pecans have a natural buttery sweetness and pleasing crunch, whether enjoyed toasted or raw. They're loaded in Vitamin E, which protects cells from oxidative stress and free radical damage. They also provide an excellent source of manganese, copper, zinc, and iron.
Pine nuts	Pine nuts are small slender creamy white kernels with a delicate buttery, sweet flavor. They're among the richest source of dietary manganese, an important mineral that supports the body's antioxidant enzyme, superoxide dismutase, that protects against free radical damage. They're also a great source of copper, iron, magnesium, and zinc.

Pistachios	Pistachios have a distinctly sweet flavor and a vibrant green color that comes from the presence of chlorophyll, an important nutrient that makes these nuts unique. Pistachios are also loaded in Vitamin B_6, Vitamin E, and copper.
Pumpkin seeds (pepitas)	Hulled pumpkin seeds are an excellent source of the amino acids tryptophan and glutamate, which are converted into the beneficial neurotransmitters serotonin and GABA, respectively. Pumpkin seeds also boast ample protein, balanced essential fats, and high concentrations of the minerals copper, iron, magnesium, and zinc. They have a deliciously satisfying crunch when eaten lightly toasted.
Sesame seeds	These tiny seeds add an exceptional nutty flavor and delicate crunch to any dish. They're also an excellent source of beneficial fibers called lignans that have been shown to help lower cholesterol. Their rich copper content may be helpful in reducing inflammation.
Sesame tahini	Tahini is a nutty paste made from ground sesame seeds. Sesame seeds are chock full of multiple thyroid- and immune-supportive nutrients, especially Vitamin B_2, Vitamin B_6, copper, manganese, iron, calcium, magnesium, zinc, and selenium. Tahini can be found in the international foods section or near the peanut butter at any natural foods store.
Sunflower seeds	Sunflower seeds offer a mild, nutty flavor and a rich source of Vitamin E, copper, and Vitamin B_1. They're an inexpensive source of plant protein and a great substitute for those with peanut and tree nut allergies.
Sunflower seed butter	Sunflower seed butter is a rich, creamy spread made from grinding raw or roasted sunflower seeds. It's a nutrient-dense substitute for people with peanut and tree nut allergies.
Walnuts	Walnuts provide a great source of anti-inflammatory Omega-3 fats and also contain more antioxidant polyphenols than any other nut or seed. They're also a good source of copper, manganese, Vitamin B_6, and Vitamin E. It's recommended that they're eaten primarily in raw form due to fragile Omega-3s.

[a] *We recommend nut flour/nut meal in moderation. It's the "darling" of Paleo and grain-free baking, but it's important to know that one cup of almond flour contains about 90 almonds. We can extrapolate a similar number for other nuts. And many nut flour recipes call for more than one cup. While we understand that this quantity will be reduced due to serving size, it's still an inordinate amount of nuts.*

How to Soak Nuts and Seeds

Some may find nuts and seeds difficult to digest and may benefit from soaking prior to eating. Soaking also helps to remove some of the phytic acid, which may aid in the bioavailability of the minerals found in nuts and seeds.

1. Place nuts or seeds in a glass or ceramic bowl with ¼ - ½ teaspoon sea salt. Cover with water, and soak for time indicated below. Gently drape a light towel over the bowl and keep out on counter or place in fridge.

2. Discard any nuts or seeds that float to the top. Drain and rinse.

3. They can be eaten right away or used to make homemade nut or seed milks.

4. Keep for 2-3 days in the refrigerator or dehydrate at the lowest temperature setting on your oven for 12-24 hours, until crisp. Dehydrating until fully dry will prevent mold growth and enable nuts and seeds to be stored longer.

Nuts/Seeds	Soaking time (hours)
Almonds	8-12
Brazil nuts	3
Cashews	2-4
Hazelnuts	8
Macadamia nuts	0-2
Pecans	6-8
Pine nuts	8
Pistachios	8
Pepitas (shelled pumpkin seeds)	6-8
Sunflower seeds	6-8
Walnuts	6-8

How to Toast Nuts and Seeds

Gently toasting nuts or seeds can significantly enhance their flavor while also helping to break down phytic acid. The key is to use a lower heat (300°F to 350°F) to prevent burning. Nuts and seeds contain relatively high levels of monounsaturated and saturated fats that support the overall stability of the nutrients. According to The World's Healthiest Foods website (www.whfoods.com), research studies do not show significant nutrient changes when roasting at temperatures 300°F and below.

Easy Oven-Toasted Nuts

Makes 1 cup

Ingredients:
1 cup of any raw nut (almonds, cashews, hazelnuts, walnuts, pecans, etc.)

Preparation:

1. Preheat oven to 300°F.

2. Spread nuts out evenly on a baking sheet and place sheet on middle rack in the oven. Toast nuts for 10-12 minutes. Be sure to set a timer to avoid burning.

3. Remove from oven and set aside to cool. Once cool, transfer to a tightly sealed container and store in the fridge until ready to use.

Easy Pan-Toasted Seeds

Makes ¾ cup

Ingredients:
¾ cup raw sesame, sunflower, or pumpkin seeds

Preparation:

1. Toast seeds by placing them in a dry skillet over low-medium heat. Stir the seeds continuously with a wooden spoon for 2-3 minutes, taking care to adjust heat if necessary to avoid burning. Seeds are ready when they begin to emit a nutty aroma. Note: pumpkin seeds will puff up when they are ready.

2. Remove seeds from skillet and set aside to cool. Once cool, store in a tightly sealed container in the fridge until ready to use.

3. Enjoy sprinkled on salads, soups, hot cereal, avocado toast, etc.

Plant-Based Milks

Homemade plant milks are delicious and can easily be made in a blender from nuts, seeds, grains, or coconut (see recipes in the *Nourishing Beverages* chapter). They offer the full versatility of cow's milk without the potentially inflammatory protein (casein) or bothersome lactose. They provide a blank slate for pleasing flavors like vanilla or chocolate and can be sweetened naturally, as desired.

In recent years, the market has become flooded with non-dairy, plant-based milk options, which can serve as a convenient "go-to." Most store-bought varieties have stabilizers and emulsifiers added to keep the ingredients from separating; select one that has the shortest ingredient list and doesn't contain carrageenan. Plant-based milks will differ in the amount of protein they contain when compared to cow's milk, but many have also been enriched with Vitamins A and D, calcium, and Vitamin B_{12}.

We recommend the unsweetened versions of the following plant-based milks:

- Almond milk

- Cashew milk

- Coconut milk

- Hemp milk

- Oat milk (certified gluten-free)

- Quinoa milk

Making substitutions: any plant-based milk can be substituted cup for cup with cow's milk in a recipe.

Cooking Oils

When it comes to cooking oils, there are many options, but sadly, the oils that are most ubiquitous on our grocery shelves, present in most processed food products, and used almost exclusively in restaurants are highly processed industrial oils (e.g. soybean, corn, canola, safflower, sunflower, or vegetable oil blends) that can oxidize, are prone to rancidity, and are considered major contributors to cellular inflammation.

Processing and Smoke Point

Cooking oils are extracted from nuts and seeds through a process of mechanical crushing and pressing. Cold-pressed, raw, or virgin oils are a result of the first pressing of the oil and the heat applied is tightly controlled to prevent oxidation of nutrients and flavor compounds. These oils have a stronger, more characteristic flavor and many of the antioxidant polyphenols are retained. But virgin oils are more fragile and have a lower smoke point; these oils are typically best suited for use in salad dressings, lower temperature cooking, or drizzling as a finishing oil to add flavor.

To produce an oil with a high smoke point, manufacturers use refinement processes like bleaching, filtering, and high-temperature heating to extract and eliminate compounds that may cause the oil to react with heat or rancidify faster. What you're left with is a neutral-flavored oil with a longer shelf life and a higher smoke point.

Smoke point is not defined as the moment when a heated oil first begins to smoke, but as the moment when a heated oil begins to smoke continuously. When an oil is heated past its smoke point, it begins to break down, releasing free radicals and a substance called acrolein. When consumed, these compounds can cause oxidative stress and cellular damage. That's why selecting the right cooking oil for the right cooking temperature and keeping a close eye on how high you heat your pan is very important.

Here's how to make some healthier choices:

Avocado oil is pressed from the fleshy pulp of an avocado and has a mild, neutral taste. Avocado oil is fairly versatile in that the refined form can be used for higher heat cooking, up to 400°F. Unrefined avocado oil is better suited for lower-heat cooking or without heat, as in salad dressings. Both refined and unrefined avocado oils are great sources of heart-healthy monounsaturated fats.

Coconut oil is a flavorful, traditional cooking oil extracted from the meat of a mature coconut. The high percentage of saturated fat found in coconut allows the oil to be more shelf-stable and less likely to become rancid compared to other cooking oils. Virgin coconut oil has a stronger coconut flavor and more phytonutrients because it's less processed. But its smoke point is lower (280°F), so you have to watch the heat. Refined coconut oil has a higher smoke point (365°F) and a bland, neutral flavor. Coconut oil can be used for sautéing and is also great in baked goods, but needs to be melted before measuring for recipes. Along with ghee, coconut oil is said to be one of the most thyroid-supportive cooking oils.

Extra virgin olive oil (EVOO) is a flavorful, unrefined oil made from the first pressing of olives. It's high in heart-healthy monounsaturated fats and is best used as a finishing oil in dips, dressings, and sauces, but can also be used in lower heat cooking. EVOO's smoke point is 325°F and should not be used in high-heat cooking. Note: I find it's okay to oven roast items like vegetables in olive oil at 400°F or less because oven heat is radiant, indirect heat and the food item will not reach olive oil's smoke point of 325°F. Make sure that you're purchasing high quality, unadulterated EVOO, as there are many fraudulent oils on the market that have had processed vegetable oils and other questionable ingredients added. You can read Dr. Frank Lipman's guide on choosing a quality oil at bit.ly/2duZR5f and also visit our website for a list of the oils we recommend (www.thyroidcookbook.com).

Ghee (clarified butter) is an excellent cooking fat because it has a higher smoke point (450-485°F) than most other cooking oils. It imparts a delicious buttery flavor without the added concerns of lactose (milk sugar) or casein (milk protein) found in whole butter. The clarification and straining process removes nearly all lactose and casein from the product, making it acceptable to use on a dairy-free diet. Along with coconut oil, ghee is said to be one of the most thyroid-supportive cooking oils.

Toasted sesame oil is a delicious finishing oil that can be used to make Asian-inspired salad dressings or drizzled over sautéed vegetables like dark greens. It has a low smoke-point (350°F), so if using to sauté, do so over low heat only.

Storage

Cooking oils are best when used within 4-6 months of opening. Store away from light and heat in a tightly sealed bottle. Keep any oils that aren't used often stored in the refrigerator. If you purchase any of these oils in a larger, value sized container, transfer a smaller one-month supply to a smaller glass jar (preferably opaque) that can be kept in the cupboard and refrigerate the rest until ready to refill. Note that olive oil will partially solidify when refrigerated, but will return to liquid at room temperature.

Herbs, Spices, and Flavor Builders

Herbs and spices are aromatic, colorful, and rich with pleasurable flavors and inspire creativity in the kitchen. These gateways to flavor can also amp up the nutrition and health benefits of a meal and get your digestive juices flowing.

Herbs come from green leafy plants. Some examples include basil, rosemary, oregano, tarragon, thyme, sage, parsley, and cilantro. In contrast, spices come from the seed, root, bud, or other part of the plant. Common spices include black pepper, cumin, chili powder, cinnamon, turmeric, ginger, cloves, and nutmeg.

Health-supportive phytochemicals found in herbs and spices are what give them their color, distinct flavors, and aromas. Several herbs and spices like caraway, dill, fennel, peppermint, thyme, basil, and cinnamon contain the gas-relieving chemicals camphor, carvone, eugenol, menthol, and thymol that can calm the digestive tract and reduce gas and bloating.

The green leafy herbs, such as parsley, cilantro, basil, and oregano, provide a great source of chlorophyll that acts as a natural deodorizer and detoxifier. The yellow roots, ginger and turmeric, contain phytochemicals with powerful anti-inflammatory properties. Many herbs and spices also promote detoxification of the liver, aiding in the removal of harmful substances from the body.

Unless you're an active cook, buy small amounts at a time for maximum freshness because dried herbs and spices can become stale or rancid over time. If your spices are older than one year, throw them out and start fresh for optimum flavor and nutritional potency. My favorite place to buy dried herbs and spices is in the organic bulk spice department at my local natural foods store.

Buying in bulk allows you to get more product for your money and the fresher the dried herb or spice the less you'll need – a little goes a long way.

When possible, buy whole spices and grind them yourself to yield the freshest quality and best flavor. This can easily be done using a mortar and pestle or a coffee grinder designated solely for grinding spices. With whole spices, you know exactly what you're getting and they'll also keep longer. Try it – you'll definitely taste the difference.

Select fresh herbs and spices over dried when possible and choose organic to avoid pesticides, fungicides, and irradiated products. Keep dried herbs and spices away from heat and moisture. Store in airtight containers. To preserve freshness, they can be stored in the refrigerator or freezer. When cooking with herbs and spices, avoid pouring from the bottle directly into a steaming hot skillet or pot. The steam can enter the bottle and the condensation can cause the herb or spice to spoil more rapidly. Measure out what's needed first into small bowls and then pour into pot.

When purchasing fresh herbs like parsley, basil, mint, or cilantro, choose herbs that are not yellowing or wilted. Fresh leafy herbs are best kept in the refrigerator in a glass of water or herb keeper; they can be loosely covered with a plastic bag. Use them in pesto, salads, soups, pilafs, and even smoothies.

Vinegars

Vinegar is an essential flavor builder that adds a delightful zip and zing to a dish and comes in a bevy of interesting flavors. It's made through the bacterial fermentation of liquids such as wine or fruit juices; its taste and acidity will vary depending on what it was made from. Acetic acid, the compound that gives vinegar its characteristic sour taste, has some amazing health benefits. Incorporating vinegar in your diet can aid in digestion, regulate blood sugar metabolism, and fight infections.

Here are a few favorite vinegars that are featured in the recipes in this cookbook:

Apple cider vinegar is made from apples and has a sweet, tangy flavor. Opt for raw, unpasteurized apple cider vinegar to add friendly bacteria to your dish.

Balsamic vinegar is made from grapes and aged in wooden barrels. It has a rich, sweet taste.

Champagne vinegar is made from champagne grapes. It has a crisp, light flavor.

Rice vinegar is the sweetest tasting vinegar and has a delicate flavor that's not as strong or acidic as other vinegars.

Wine vinegar may be red or white and has a muted winy flavor.

Storage: Vinegar will store indefinitely, unopened; once opened it's best used within a year.

Citrus (lemons, limes, oranges, grapefruit)

Citrus juice provides mouthwatering brightness to a dish. The citric acid helps to tenderize ingredients and supports your body in absorbing minerals in the food. If you've gone too far, bring back the balance by rounding out flavor with the addition of sweetness or fat.

Citrus zest provides deeper, zingier flavor than its juice and can be used to perk up dishes, especially where using too much juice may oversaturate. The zest of citrus fruits contains a higher concentration of vitamins and minerals than the juice. Flavonoids found in the zest possess anti-oxidant and anti-cancer properties.

Salts

Salt and salty seasonings like tamari soy sauce, coconut aminos, and miso are indispensable flavor enhancers.

Unrefined sea salt is salt that hasn't been subjected to conventional salt production methods of using heat processing and chemical additives. I keep three main types in my cupboard:

- Redmond Real Salt, a light pink salt with flecks of minerals that's mined from an ancient sea bed in Utah

- Himalayan sea salt, a pink salt mined from ancient sea beds in Pakistan

- Celtic sea salt, a grey salt harvested off the shores of France

Tamari soy sauce is a traditional Japanese style of soy sauce that's often made without wheat and therefore may be gluten-free (check the label!). Regular soy sauce tends to contain 40-60 percent wheat; we like organic reduced sodium San-J Tamari gluten-free soy sauce that's made with 100 percent organic soybeans, no wheat, and is brewed for up to six months, creating a deep, rich flavor. Generally, we're not a fan of soy products, unless they're fermented, as in tempeh, natto, and tamari.

Coconut aminos are a raw, gluten-free, soy-free alternative to soy sauce made from the enzymatically active coconut sap collected from coconut blossoms. The sap is aged to create a savory umami flavor like soy sauce, but is milder and slightly sweeter. It provides 17 important amino acids and is significantly lower in sodium. Coconut aminos can be used interchangeably with soy sauce in salad dressings, stir-fries, marinades, and sauces. We like Coconut Secret brand coconut aminos.

Miso is a unique way to add salty, savory, umami flavor to food while also providing a source of beneficial probiotic bacteria. It's a bean paste the consistency of peanut butter that's made from fermenting soybean or chickpeas with a culture called koji. Lighter colored miso is milder in flavor than the darker versions, which are often aged longer. While it's typically used to make a flavorful soup base, miso can also be added to salad dressings and dips. It's easily digested and loaded with B vitamins and protein. Miso can be stored in the refrigerator indefinitely. Not all miso is gluten-free, so be sure to check the label.

While soy is considered to be an estrogen mimicker, miso is considered anti-estrogenic. The thyroid is particularly sensitive to radiation and miso also contains radio-protective benefits and can help to reduce damage from radiation exposure.[1]

Other Nutritious Seasonings

Gomasio is a delicious and nutty Japanese condiment containing sesame seeds, sea salt, and sea veggies that's great on steamed veggies. You can find it store-bought, or make your own using a simple recipe called Sesame Seaweed Sprinkle found in this cookbook.

Kelp and dulse are two nutrient-dense sea vegetables that can be easily incorporated as a condiment sprinkled on food. They're an exceptional source of the thyroid-supportive trace mineral, iodine. It's important to add sea vegetables to your diet for thyroid health, especially when reducing or eliminating iodized salt.

Nutritional yeast (also known as nooch) is an inactive form of the yeast strain known as Saccharomyces cerevisiae. This is the same strain of yeast bakers use to leaven bread, except it has been pasteurized to dry out the yeast in order to access its nutritional benefits – it's loaded with energy-supportive B vitamins. Dubbed "nature's Cheeto dust," it can be added to foods to create a savory, cheesy flavor.

Natural Sweeteners

There's no one perfect sweetener and most are relatively equivalent in the grams per teaspoon of sugar. For example, natural sweeteners like coconut sugar and Sucanat contain 4 grams of sugar/teaspoon, which is the same as white sugar.

While it's generally a good idea to reduce your overall intake of added sweeteners, natural or not, there are some key differences between processed and unrefined sweeteners. Natural sweeteners tend to be more flavorful than highly processed sweeteners like white sugar; depending on the sweetener, a little can go a long way.

Some retain their mineral content, giving them their characteristic brownish color. But ultimately, it's how these sweeteners are combined with other ingredients that will determine the overall effect on your blood sugar levels. When a sweetener is used in small to moderate amounts in combination with other less processed ingredients like nuts, seeds, and whole grains that provide a balanced source of fiber, protein, and healthy fat, the release of carbohydrates from the sugar into your bloodstream will be much slower. This ideal balance is less likely to cause a drastic spike (and subsequent crash) in your blood sugar levels.

Here are the natural sweeteners featured in the recipes in this cookbook:

Blackstrap molasses is a concentrated, mineral-rich syrup that's created as a byproduct of making refined sugar. It has a deep, robust flavor and provides an exceptional source of iron. Opt for the unsulphured version and stir it into hot cereal, bake into cookies or muffins, or puree into smoothies.

Coconut sugar (also known as coconut palm sugar) is a sugar made from dehydrated sap of a coconut palm tree. It has a golden brown color with a consistency close to brown sugar. It imparts a delicious caramel flavor and is relatively low on the glycemic index, making it blood sugar friendly, in moderation. It can be swapped out cup for cup with other granulated sugars.

Dates are a great whole food ingredient for providing natural sweetness in desserts and smoothies. Their mildly sweet flavor tastes like a combination of honey and brown sugar with hints of caramel. We recommend Medjool dates because of their higher moisture content. Date sugar provides a good source of fiber and potassium, copper, and magnesium and while quite sweet, will not impart a sugary taste to cooked dishes, but it's good for baking. Because of the high fiber content, it doesn't dissolve in warm drinks.

Honey is a flavorful, viscous sweetener made by bees from flower nectar. Its flavor and texture vary with the type of flower the nectar was sourced from. Clover, alfalfa, orange blossom, and wildflower are common varieties of honey. The darker the color of the honey, the deeper the flavor and higher the level of antioxidants. Raw honey is a great choice because it's not heated to high temperatures and therefore retains more antioxidant polyphenols and enzymes than pasteurized honey. Store at room temperature. Honey is stickier and more viscous than maple syrup, but can be used fairly interchangeably in most recipes that call for maple syrup or other liquid sweeteners. Honey and maple syrup have different flavor profiles.

Maple sugar is a fine granulated sweetener that's made from the dried sap of a maple tree. It has a more delicate maple flavor than maple syrup. Maple sugar can be swapped out cup for cup with other granulated sugars.

Pure maple syrup is simply the boiled tree sap from a maple tree. Did you know it takes three months to collect 40 gallons of sap to make one gallon of syrup? Maple syrup is an excellent source of the trace mineral manganese and also provides a good source zinc. Maple syrup is less viscous than honey, but can be used fairly interchangeably in most recipes that call for honey or other liquid sweeteners. Honey and maple syrup have different flavor profiles. Once opened, syrup can be stored in the refrigerator for 3-6 months.

Sucanat (unrefined cane sugar) stands for "sugar cane natural." True sucanat is the least refined of the granulated sweeteners derived from sugarcane. It's pure, dried cane juice that hasn't been stripped or bleached, so it's darker in color and richer in flavor than other cane sugars. It can be swapped out cup for cup with other granulated sugars.

Our "Go-To" Canned and Packaged Foods

We all know that fresh whole food, especially foods eaten within 24-48 hours of harvest, is at its peak of flavor and nutrition. But we also live in the real world, where fresh food isn't always available due to changes in the growing season, nor is it always realistic to prepare because of our busy lifestyles. It's okay and often necessary to take savvy shortcuts by supplementing with conscientiously selected canned and packaged options.

No matter how healthy a product sounds, never ever believe the health claims loudly proclaimed on the package. Dig deeper and learn to read the labels to understand what you're putting in your body. If you'd like to learn how to become a label-reading sleuth, you can find a link to Jill's *Understanding Nutrition Labeling on Our Food* class on our website (www.thyroidcookbook.com). It's an audio transcript of a class that she taught at the University of Minnesota's College of LearningLife.

When selecting packaged products, keep these tips in mind:

- Find products that contain only whole food ingredients that are as close to nature as possible. Note: if you need a PhD in chemistry to understand the ingredients list, it's likely loaded with chemical additives and preservatives that we simply don't need to be consuming. Oftentimes there are preservative-free versions of your favorite pantry staples. Just keep looking. Or shop online from websites like Barefoot Provisions or Thrive. You can find many of our favorite products on our website (www.thyroidcookbook.com).

- Read labels to minimize added sugars. Hidden sugar may be listed as sugar, corn syrup, molasses, brown rice syrup, honey, agave nectar, maple syrup, evaporated cane juice, malt syrup, corn sweetener, beet sugar, fruit juice concentrate, glucose, lactose, fructose, dextrose, or maltose. On an ingredient list, the higher up the sugar is listed, the more sugar there will be in the product. Keep in mind that every 4 grams of added sugar indicated on the Nutrition Facts

Panel equals 1 teaspoon of sugar. The American Heart Association (AHA) recommends the *upper* limit of added sugars for women to be no more than about 6 teaspoons of sugar or 24 grams. For men, it's 9 teaspoons or 36 grams.

- Avoid products that contain highly processed poor quality oils like corn, soybean, safflower, sunflower, canola, and vegetable oil blends.

- Most sodium in the diet comes from packaged, processed foods. Read labels and select packaged foods that contain close to or less than 5% of the Daily Value for sodium as indicated on the Nutrition Facts Panel.

- Opt for sustainably produced, certified organic, and Non-GMO Project verified products, whenever possible. (See Appendix D for information on how to make sustainable choices.)

- When looking for non-perishables, items that are packaged in glass are typically better than those in tin cans because glass is naturally BPA-free. The downside, however, is that they tend to be slightly more expensive than comparable options in metal cans. Be sure to reuse or recycle.

- Items packaged in paperboard Tetra-paks are also a good alternative to tin cans because they're BPA-free. I also find their contents often taste fresher than items that come out of a metal can. Products packaged in these aseptic cartons are also lighter, requiring less energy to transport. The downside is that they're not easily recyclable. Examples of some common items typically packaged in Tetra-paks include: soup broths, plant-based milks, and juices.

- When opting for canned items, read the package to see if it's BPA-free. BPA is a synthetic estrogen found in the epoxy coatings of food cans and has been linked to many hormonal and other health problems.[2] Keep in mind that many canned items that are BPA-free are not always labeled as such. Don't hesitate to visit product websites or call customer service to help determine if the product is BPA-free. You can also visit the Environmental Working Group's website to read research on this topic (www.ewg.org/research/bpa-canned-food).

What's in Our Pantries?

While this is not an exhaustive list of everything that may be available in your market, we've attempted to provide a fairly comprehensive list of common staples that meet the criteria that we've listed after each food category below. Visit our website for ongoing updates to our list (www.thyroidcookbook.com).

Tomato Products

- Tomato sauce
- Diced tomatoes
- Tomato paste
- Fire-roasted tomatoes

Watch out for added salt, sugar, and poor quality oils. Muir Glen, Jovial, Bionaturae, and 365 Everyday Value brands have BPA-free canned tomato options.

Canned Beans

- Black beans
- Garbanzo beans
- Pinto beans
- Kidney beans
- Cannellini beans
- Butter beans (baby lima)

Watch out for added salt and preservatives. Eden Organic, 365 Everyday Value, and Westbrae Naturals have BPA-free and salt/preservative-free options.

Canned Fish

- Tuna*
- Wild salmon
- Crabmeat
- Sardines
- Anchovies

Watch out for added salt, preservatives, and poor quality oils. Wild Planet, Crown Prince Seafood, and 365 Everyday Value brands are great for canned seafood.

Tuna can be high in mercury, but know that it's typically the larger, more predatory species that tend to be a problem. Smaller species like skipjack, aka chunk light tuna, are safer. See Appendix E for our Sustainably-Sourced Seafood Guide.

Canned Pumpkin, Sweet Potatoes, and Squash

Watch out for added preservatives. Farmer's Market brand is a good choice for all three and 365 Everyday Value is great for canned pumpkin.

Gluten-Free Broths

- Low-sodium vegetable broth
- Low-sodium chicken broth
- Chicken bone broth
- Turkey bone broth
- Lamb bone broth
- Beef bone broth

Watch out for added salt and preservatives. Pacific Foods is a great brand for flavorful, gluten-free broths.

Coconut Products*

- Canned full-fat coconut milk
- Dried coconut flakes
- Coconut butter or coconut manna

Watch out for added preservatives and sugar. Native Forest and 365 Everyday Value are great brands for coconut milk. Let's Do Organic has high quality coconut flakes. Artisana and Nutiva make wonderful coconut butter/manna.

See Cooking Oils section for more on coconut oil.

Whole Grain Gluten-Free Crackers

Watch out for highly refined flours, poor quality oils, and excess salt. Mary's Gone Crackers and Lundberg Organic Thin Stackers (red rice or quinoa puffed grain) are good choices.

Gluten-Free Pasta

Tinkyada, Ancient Harvest, and DeLallo make pastas from gluten-free grains like brown rice and quinoa.

Sea Vegetables

- Arame
- Wakame
- Nori
- Kombu
- Kelp Granules
- Dulse Flakes

Maine Coast Sea Vegetables, Eden, and SeaSnax brands are the best options for sea vegetables.

Gelatin

Great Lakes or Vital Proteins gelatin are good choices.

Perishable Items

- Kite Hill Artisanal and Punk Rawk Labs (dairy-free cheeses)
- CoYo unsweetened coconut milk yogurt
- Happy Campers gluten-free breads
- Canyon Bakehouse gluten-free breads
- Little Northern Bakehouse gluten-free breads
- Capello's handmade almond flour pastas
- Fermented vegetables: Ozuke and Bubbies kimchi and sauerkraut
- Primal Kitchen avocado oil mayonnaise

Visit our website for ongoing updates to our pantry staples list (www.thyroidcookbook.com).

KITCHEN TOOLS AND GADGETS

Once you've got your pantry stocked and you're ready to venture into trying new recipes, you'll want to learn about essential kitchen equipment and tools. Having the proper cooking equipment can help cut down on prep time and will ultimately make cooking easier and more fun. Start with the basics like a good chef's knife and cutting board, then build from there, one item at a time.

I've honed this list of essential kitchen cooking equipment and tools based on years of teaching cooking classes and experimenting in my own kitchen. I promise that having some of these tools on hand will make the time spent in your kitchen more efficient and enjoyable. I include several pro tips on the hows and whys of selecting and using these items.

Please see our website for links to many of these products (www.thyroidcookbook.com).

Sharp knives: Invest in a high quality knife. When well cared for, it will last a lifetime. Some reliable brands include Wüsthof, Henckels, and Global. It's important to keep your knives sharpened and honed. I do this regularly with a sharpening steel and every few months, I take my knives in to be professionally sharpened. I can accomplish most tasks with just these three types of knives:

- **Chef's knife:** A good chef's knife that feels comfortable in your hand is essential. The weight of the knife should feel balanced. Knives can range in length from 6-14 inches, but most people do well with an 8- to 10-inch knife. My personal preference for cutting most vegetables and some meat is a Santoku style chef's knife. If you want your spouse or partner to help with meal prep, make sure you both have your own knife that you love.

- **Paring knife:** A paring knife allows for more controlled, detailed cutting. It's great for peeling fruits and vegetables, slicing and mincing single garlic cloves or shallots, and delicately removing the ribs from a jalapeno or core of an apple.
- **Serrated knife:** I have a small 5-inch serrated knife that's my go-to knife for slicing through foods with tough resistant skins, such as citrus and tomatoes. When cutting a large pineapple, I also rely on my larger 8- to 10-inch serrated knife.

Spacious wood or bamboo cutting board: I recommend at a minimum, an 18x12 board for cutting produce comfortably. I prefer the texture and feel of a wood or bamboo cutting board because they hold up well and have natural antimicrobial properties. Boos brand is among the best. I also prefer to keep a separate board for cutting garlic and onions and to prevent fruit and other milder tasting foods from absorbing pungent flavors.

Microplane grater: I use my microplane daily to help disperse bursts of flavor into many dishes. It has several tiny sharp teeth that allow me to zest oranges, lemons, and limes very easily. I also use it for grating ginger for tea and stir-fries, grating whole nutmeg for my oatmeal, and finely grating dark chocolate over desserts.

Box grater: Box graters are typically used for grating cheese, which you won't find in our dairy-free cookbook. But I find that having one is essential for grating vegetables like zucchini, carrots, and beets.

Y-shaped vegetable peeler: A Y-shaped vegetable peeler is more user friendly than a straight, swivel peeler for peeling broader vegetables like butternut squash and sweet potatoes, but is versatile enough to easily peel slender vegetables like carrots. It's also fun to use for making broad zucchini noodles or thin asparagus ribbons. If I could only pick one peeler to have on hand, it would be a Y-shaped peeler.

Julienne slicer: Julienne cut is an essential knife skill method where you cut vegetables into small matchstick pieces. If you haven't mastered how to julienne or are looking for a quick, easy way to do so, this inexpensive tool is your shortcut. It easily peels veggies into strips that are great for salads, stir-fries, and garnishes.

Spiralizer: A spiralizer is great for the gluten-free cook who may want to turn dense veggies like zucchini, butternut squash, carrots, and beets into grain-free "noodles" for pasta dishes. Spiralized veggies are also a fun way to get people who don't usually like vegetables to try them. I have the Paderno 4-blade spiralizer that I love, but if you're in search of a less expensive option, check out several of the hand-held versions.

Kitchen shears: These are high quality kitchen scissors that won't rust. They come in handy for neatly cutting into food packages and are even handier for clipping fresh herbs, trimming meats, and cutting dried fruits into smaller pieces.

Electric Equipment

High-powered blender: My personal preference is a Vitamix because of its power and versatility. A good blender can be used regularly to make smoothies, salad dressings, nut butters, sauces, velvety soups, and desserts in just minutes. If a Vitamix is out of your price range, there are still many things that a regular kitchen blender can do to help reduce time in the kitchen.

Food processor: I can't live without my food processor. It makes bean dips (like hummus), raw date and nut crusts for desserts, and homemade nut flours like almond meal and hazelnut meal. I also love the attachment that shreds veggies and I use it to stock my fridge with shredded carrots, beets, or zucchini for salads and sautés. I recommend a 10-14 cup food processor; anything smaller becomes too crammed when making most recipes.

Hand-held immersion blender: This handy little tool is great for quickly pureeing soups or blending salad dressings. For durability, I would recommend getting one made out of stainless steel instead of plastic; plastic will also leach harmful chemicals.

Cooking Vessels: Pots, Pans, and Baking Dishes

Stainless steel pots and pans: Select 18/10 stainless steel pots and pans for the best durability and find products that feature aluminum or copper cores in both the base and side walls of each pan. This helps your food cook more evenly and helps the pan retain heat when you add more food. Make sure they have sturdy handles and glass lids for easy viewing. I recommend one of each of these: 2- to 3-quart saucepan with a lid, a 10-inch straight-sided sauté pan with a lid, and a large 4-quart pot with a lid.

Cast iron pots and pans: Cast iron heats evenly and quickly and is naturally non-stick[a] when seasoned and maintained properly. They come in all shapes and sizes for various uses. I rely on my cast iron skillets in assorted sizes on a daily basis, but also love my cast-iron wok, griddle, and grill pan.

Glass baking pans: Pyrex baking dishes are my go-to for roasting veggies, whole chickens, fish, or for baking. They come in a variety of sizes. A 9x13 pan is a mainstay in my kitchen, but I also use a few smaller 8x8 pans, plus circular glass pie pans.

Stainless steel or bamboo steaming basket: These are useful for inserting into a pot to steam veggies within just minutes.

Sheet pans: It's good to have two to three stainless steel sheet pans on hand. Choose pans that don't have a non-stick[a] coating. My favorites measure 18x13 and have a 1-inch lip around the edges. A quality pan won't warp at high temperatures. Be comfortable with the pan becoming stained over time and never getting it as clean and shiny as the day you bought it. Lining your pan with parchment paper will make for easier clean up.

[a] *Non-stick cookware should be thoroughly avoided, especially for those with a thyroid condition. The fluoride-containing chemical that makes products non-stick is perfluorooctanoic acid (PFOA, made by DOW Chemical) and is part of a group of problematic chemicals that fall into the perfluorinated compounds (PFCs) class. PFOA exposure is associated with thyroid dysfunction.*[3, 4]

In addition to non-stick cookware, you'll also find non-stick chemicals in some dental flosses, raincoats, pizza boxes, fast food containers, microwave popcorn bags, furniture, carpeting, paper plates, shampoo, and most products with a "stain-guard" claim. (See The Essential Thyroid Cookbook Lifestyle Companion Guide *for more information on the negative effects of fluoride on thyroid function. You can download it for free on our website: www.thyroidcookbook.com/companion.)*

Other Useful Tools

Mortar and pestle: Be a sensory inspired cook. Using a mortar and pestle is one of the best ways to engage all of the senses when cooking and is a great tool for getting kids involved. I use my mortar and pestle for grinding whole spices and herbs into powders to contain more potent flavors and nutrients.

Wooden and metal spoons and cooking utensils: It's important to replace plastic with something that's more durable, less likely to melt, and eliminates exposure to the chemicals that leach out of plastic counterparts. I have a set of bamboo cooking utensils that were very inexpensive and have lasted me several years.

Stainless steel tongs: A good pair of tongs can help you get a handle on turning meat or veggies, scooping pasta, and serving salad greens.

Citrus reamer: This gadget helps squeeze every last drop of flavorful juice from lemons, limes, or oranges. Citrus is a delicious way to brighten and amplify the flavors in any dish.

Salad spinner: A salad spinner makes washing, preparing, and storing greens a breeze. If you plan to wash greens ahead of time to cut down on prep, it's essential to make sure they're thoroughly dried before storing, as soggy greens will spoil rapidly.

Metal colander: I have replaced my plastic colander with a much more durable stainless steel variety to prevent the leaching of plastic into hot foods like pasta and blanched veggies.

Scale: A scale is great for weighing precise amounts when baking.

Fine mesh strainer: A mesh strainer is essential for rinsing and straining whole grains like quinoa, millet, and brown rice and also for rinsing dried beans before soaking and cooking.

Nut milk strainer: Rawsome Creations makes a mesh bag made from nylon that can be used to strain pulp from homemade nut and seed milks. Alternately, you easily could use a French press to finely strain homemade milks.

Glass storage containers: Several years ago I replaced all of my plastic storage containers with glass containers with lids. I also use wide mouth mason jars for storing sauces and dressings. You can buy a BPA-free plastic top for these jars that won't rust like the canning lids and will last longer. Having a variety of sizes will make food prep and storage a breeze.

Stainless steel measuring cups and spoons: I have two sets of each.

Glass measuring cups (2- and 4-cup): These provide accuracy for measurement of liquid ingredients.

Digital thermometer: A digital thermometer equipped with a probe and timer allows you to monitor the exact temperatures of meat, poultry, or any food. Most are magnetic and can be mounted to the outside of the oven, allowing you to set an alarm when the food reaches its ideal cooking temperature. It can also be used for checking temps on grilled meats and other items. I love that this gadget takes the guesswork out of doneness and is the best way to prevent over- or under-cooking.

Small cooler: These are handy for packing lunches, meals, and snacks when on the go.

Reusable and insulated shopping bags: I've found that the insulated bags cue the grocery bagger to keep cold items separate from non-perishables.

Silicone oil brush: I use an oil brush for helping to spread just the right amount of oil in the bottom of a pan.

PART THREE:

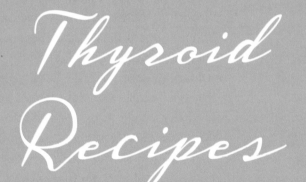

GUIDE TO THE ESSENTIAL THYROID RECIPES

While this cookbook is targeted specifically towards those who want to nourish their thyroid through optimal nutrition, the recipes were thoughtfully created to appeal to all palates, no matter what your health condition.

They've been crafted from the most health-supportive, whole food ingredients and are full of color, flavor, and texture. Each recipe is free of gluten, dairy, and highly processed ingredients. (For more information on why gluten and dairy are not recommended for those with Hashimoto's, see the chapters *Gluten and Your Thyroid* and *Dairy and Your Thyroid* in Part One.)

There's no one-size-fits-all way to make these recipes work for everyone, so we made every effort to provide sensible adaptations to modify them to fit the dietary practices listed, whenever possible. Jill and I recognize there are varying therapeutic dietary approaches in the functional and integrative nutrition communities that support thyroid health, so we created user-friendly icons to help you easily decipher the recipes that will fit your individual needs at-a-glance.

In most cases, the adaptation may include simply omitting an ingredient or making a simple ingredient swap to make it compliant. If you're curious to know more about certain ingredients or kitchen tools that may be mentioned, be sure to peruse Part Two: Essential Thyroid Kitchen for additional guidance.

We hope you find these recipes incredibly delicious and nourishing, no matter where you are on your dietary path.

Vegan. These recipes are free of all animal products (meat, dairy, fish, and eggs). They feature 100 percent plant-based ingredients such as fruits, vegetables, whole grains, beans/legumes, and nuts and seeds. Some of our recipes include honey although many vegans may choose to omit it.

Paleo. These recipes are free of grains, beans/legumes, dairy, refined sugars, and highly processed oils. They may include fish, grass-fed and pasture-raised meats and eggs, vegetables (including starchy vegetables), fruit, nuts and seeds, and healthful oils.

Autoimmune Protocol. These recipes are free of grains, beans/legumes, dairy, eggs, nuts and seeds, refined sugars, highly processed oils, nightshades (peppers, potatoes, eggplant, tomatoes), spices derived from nightshades (e.g. cayenne, paprika, chili-based spices), and spices derived from seeds (e.g. cumin, nutmeg, fennel, mustard, caraway). Black pepper is not a nightshade so it was not eliminated from our AIP adaptations. Additionally, ghee (clarified butter) may be tolerable for some, but may cause issues for those with known dairy reactions. If you're on an AIP diet, we recommend you're mildly cautious with both.

Elimination Provocation Diet. These recipes are safe to eat during a targeted, temporary Elimination Provocation diet, also known as "the gold standard" for sleuthing out food sensitivities. They're free of gluten, dairy, eggs, soy, corn, nightshades, nuts, peanuts (a legume), shellfish, citrus, and refined sugars. When considering ghee (clarified butter), it may be tolerable for some, but may cause issues for those with known dairy reactions. See the chapter, *Elimination Provocation Diet Instructions* in Part One for additional information.

30 Minutes or Less. These recipes take a total of 30 minutes or less to prepare.

Nutrient Legend

As mentioned in the *Our Springboard* chapter, it was important to Jill and me to do the hard grafting and necessary foundational nutrient research to keep this cookbook from being "just another cookbook" and to make it the most beneficial for you. We spent a great deal of time weeding through the subjective nature of nutrition and sleuthing out the most supportive nutrients for the thyroid and immune system and then researching the foods that are *dense sources* of these nutrients. This research is the heart and soul of this cookbook. You can find a pretty version of our findings at www.thyroidcookbook.com/nutrition_guide.

Thus, the foods we've chosen to highlight in these recipes possess a broad and substantive thyroid- and immune-supportive spectrum. You can find a legend at the bottom of most of the following recipes—the only ones missing a legend are some of the Nourishing Beverages, of which many can be used to complement a meal or be consumed as an after-meal treat.

Below are the thyroid- and immune-supportive nutrients we identified, including the symbols we incorporated into each recipe, as appropriate. In the chapter, *The Nutritional Heavy Hitters*, we show you how and why these nutrients are so beneficial.

Nutrients supportive to both thyroid and immune function:

Vitamin A (as beta-carotene)	A(beta)
Vitamin A (as retinol)	A(ret)
Vitamin B_1	B_1
Vitamin B_2	B_2
Vitamin B_6	B_6
Vitamin B_{12}	B_{12}
Vitamin C	C
Vitamin D	D
Vitamin E	E
Calcium	Ca
Copper	Cu
Iron	Fe
Magnesium	Mg
Selenium	Se
Zinc	Zn
Omega-3 fatty acids	O3

Additional nutrients supportive to thyroid function:

Iodine	I
Manganese	Mn
Tyrosine	Ty

Additional nutrients supportive to immune function:

EGCG	Eg
Glutathione	Gl
Lycopene	Ly
Probiotics	Pr
Resveratrol	Rv

NOURISHING BEVERAGES

TROPICAL GREEN SMOOTHIE

This tropical treat is a refreshing go-to green smoothie. The invigorating zip and zing of the citrus and the mild kick from the pepper will get your circulation flowing. It's great to start the day with or it can be enjoyed as an energizing afternoon snack.

Serves 2

Ingredients

1 cup filtered water

½ medium cucumber, peeled and chopped

1 small lemon or lime, peeled and seeded

1½ cups fresh or frozen pineapple

1 fresh or frozen banana

1 cup packed fresh spinach or kale

2 tablespoons chia seeds

1 tablespoon chopped jalapeño or pinch of cayenne (optional)

1-2 cups ice (optional)

Preparation

1. Place all ingredients into a high-speed blender in the order listed, secure lid, and blend on high for 45-60 seconds until smooth. Add ice if not using frozen fruit and thin with additional water, if needed, to reach your desired consistency.

2. Pour into individual glasses and enjoy.

Cook's notes: Make a double batch and pour leftovers into popsicle molds. Freeze for 4-6 hours before eating.

For a richer variation, substitute full-fat coconut milk for water.

AIP adaptation: Omit chia seeds and jalapeno/cayenne.

Elimination/Provocation Diet adaptation: Omit citrus and jalapeno/cayenne.

Nutrients: A(BETA), B₁, B₆, C, CA, CU, MN, O3, GL

BLUEBERRY SUNRISE SMOOTHIE

This full-bodied smoothie is great for helping get the day off to a sunny start. Avocado is the secret ingredient that provides a rich, creamy texture plus a sustainable source of energy. Adding ground flaxseeds offers a healthful boost of Omega-3 fatty acids.

Serves 2

Ingredients

- 1-2 cups unsweetened coconut, cashew, almond, or hemp milk or plain unsweetened coconut milk yogurt
- 1 whole orange, peeled, segmented and seeded
- 1½ cups fresh or frozen blueberries
- 1 banana
- ½ avocado
- 1 tablespoon local honey
- 1 tablespoon ground flaxseeds
- ¼ teaspoon ground cinnamon
- 1-2 cups ice (optional)

Preparation

1. Place all ingredients into a high-speed blender in the order listed, secure lid, and blend on high for 45-60 seconds until smooth. Add ice if not using frozen berries and thin with additional milk, if needed, to reach your desired consistency.

2. Pour into individual glasses and enjoy.

Cook's notes: Make a double batch and pour leftovers into popsicle molds. Freeze for 4-6 hours before eating.

AIP adaptation: Use coconut milk and omit flaxseeds.

Elimination/Provocation Diet adaptation: Use coconut milk and omit orange. Increase blueberries to 2½ cups.

Nutrients: B$_6$, C, E, M$_G$, G$_L$, O3

COCONUT BANANA MATCHA SMOOTHIE

Matcha green tea is made from green tea leaves that are finely ground into a powder, making it a concentrated source of antioxidant-rich polyphenols that provide 10-15 times more antioxidants when compared to traditional green, black, white, rooibos, and yerba mate teas. This recipe is especially delicious when made with my Homemade Coconut Milk recipe also found in this chapter.

Serves 2

Ingredients

- 1 cup unsweetened coconut milk
- 1 fresh or frozen banana
- ¼ avocado
- 2-3 teaspoons matcha green tea powder
- ½ cup baby spinach leaves
- 1 tablespoon pure maple syrup or local honey
- 1 teaspoon vanilla extract (optional)
- 1-1½ cups ice (optional)

Preparation

1. Place all ingredients into a high-speed blender in the order listed, secure lid, and blend on high for 45-60 seconds until smooth. Add ice if not using frozen banana and thin with additional milk or water, if needed, to reach your desired consistency.

2. Pour into individual glasses and enjoy.

Cook's notes: Matcha can be a pricey product, but keep in mind that you only need 1-2 teaspoons per serving, so it should last quite awhile. Store in the refrigerator.

AIP adaptation: Omit vanilla extract and reduce sweetener.

Nutrients: A(BETA), B₁, B₂, B₆, C, E, Cᴀ, Cᴜ, Fᴇ, Mɢ, Mɴ, Zɴ, Gʟ, Eɢ

CHOCOLATE ALMOND BUTTER BANANA MILKSHAKE

This healthful and balanced vegan milkshake can be enjoyed with breakfast, as a snack, or as a guilt-free dessert.

Serves 2

Ingredients

2 cups unsweetened coconut, cashew, almond, or hemp milk

1 cup baby spinach

2 chopped frozen bananas

3-4 tablespoons unsweetened cocoa powder

3-4 tablespoons almond butter

1 tablespoon ground flaxseeds (optional)

2-3 dates, pitted and softened in warm, filtered water 5-10 minutes

1-2 cups ice (optional)

Preparation

1. Place all ingredients into a high-speed blender in the order listed, secure lid, and blend on high for 45-60 seconds until smooth. Add ice as needed, especially if bananas are not frozen.

2. Pour into individual glasses and enjoy.

Cook's notes: Frozen ripe bananas are great to keep on hand. As soon as you notice your bananas starting to turn, peel and chop them before placing in an airtight food storage bag and freezing. If you'd like to transform this smoothie into popsicles, double the batch and pour leftovers into popsicle molds. Freeze for 4-6 hours before eating.

Nutrients: A(BETA), B$_1$, B$_2$, B$_6$, C, E, CA, CU, FE, MG, MN, ZN, GL, PR

COCONUT MANGO LASSI SMOOTHIE

A lassi is a traditional Indian smoothie made with yogurt that's often served after a spicy meal to help cool things down. Anytime you're in need of a tummy-soothing treat, try this dairy-free version that features probiotic-rich coconut milk yogurt. Rose water or orange water add sweet, fragrant notes.

Serves 2

Ingredients

¾ cup unsweetened coconut milk

½ cup plain unsweetened coconut milk yogurt

1½ cups frozen mango

2 teaspoons local honey

½ teaspoon ground cardamom

¼ teaspoon rose or orange water (optional)

Fresh mint or strawberry

Preparation

1. Place all ingredients except mint/strawberry into a high-speed blender in the order listed, secure lid, and blend on high for 45-60 seconds until smooth.

2. Pour into individual glasses and garnish with mint or strawberry.

3. Store any extra in the refrigerator and enjoy within a day or two.

Cook's notes: If you'd like to transform this smoothie into popsicles, double the batch and pour leftovers into popsicle molds. Freeze for 4-6 hours before eating.

AIP adaptation: Omit cardamom. Reduce or eliminate honey.

Nutrients: C, E, Cu, Fe, Mg, Mn, Se, Zn, Pr

PUMPKIN GINGERBREAD CHIA SMOOTHIE

This energizing, immune-boosting smoothie is loaded with beta-carotene from the pumpkin and iron from the sesame seeds and blackstrap molasses.

Serves 2

Ingredients

2 cups unsweetened coconut, cashew, almond, or hemp milk

1 cup pumpkin puree

2 chopped frozen bananas

2 tablespoons blackstrap molasses

2 teaspoons freshly grated ginger or ½ teaspoon ground ginger

½ teaspoon ground cinnamon

¼ teaspoon ground nutmeg

1-2 cups ice (optional)

1 tablespoon chia seeds

Preparation

1. Place all ingredients except chia seeds into a high-speed blender, secure lid, and blend on high for 45-60 seconds until smooth. Add ice as needed, especially if bananas are not frozen.

2. Pour into glasses and stir in chia seeds.

Cook's notes: Frozen ripe bananas are great to keep on hand at all times. As soon as you notice your bananas starting to turn, peel and chop them before placing in an air-tight food storage bag and freezing.

If you don't have blackstrap molasses, you can substitute pure maple syrup, local honey, or two softened pitted dates.

If you have leftover pumpkin puree, use an ice cube tray to freeze into cubes for future smoothies.

AIP adaptation: Use coconut milk. Omit chia seeds and nutmeg.

Elimination/Provocation Diet adaptation: Use coconut milk or hemp milk.

Nutrients: A(BETA), B$_6$, C, E, CA, Cu, Fe, MG, MN, GL, O3

REFRESHING GINGER TURMERIC LIMEADE

Fresh squeezed lime juice is swirled together with anti-inflammatory turmeric and ginger in this vibrant and refreshing elixir.

Serves 1

Ingredients

2 limes, juiced (approximately ¼ cup)

1½-2 tablespoons pure maple syrup

1 teaspoon freshly grated ginger

½ teaspoon dried ground turmeric or
    1 teaspoon freshly grated turmeric

1 pinch of sea salt

Pinch of cayenne pepper (optional)

10-12 ounces filtered water

Preparation

1. Place all ingredients in a tall glass and top off with water, allowing room for ice cubes, if desired. Stir well, add ice, and enjoy.

Cook's notes: Triple or quadruple the batch and refrigerate for up to 5 days. Shake or stir well before drinking. Can substitute sparkling water, if desired.

AIP adaptation: Omit cayenne pepper.

WARMING ANTI-INFLAMMATORY GOLDEN TURMERIC MILK

Creamy and rich, this satisfyingly soothing beverage warms the body while it calms inflammation. This recipe is sure to become your favorite go-to for a healthful cold weather fix. For additional flavor, steep a bag of chai green tea in the spiced milk.

Serves 2

Ingredients

- 2 cups unsweetened coconut, cashew, almond, or hemp milk
- 1 tablespoon local honey or pure maple syrup
- 1 teaspoon ground turmeric
- 1 teaspoon ground cinnamon
- 1 teaspoon freshly grated ginger or ¼-½ teaspoon dried ground ginger
- Dash of black pepper
- 2 organic chai green tea bags (optional)

Preparation

1. Pour all ingredients except for tea bags into a small saucepan. Bring to a gentle boil while whisking until spices are well incorporated. Reduce heat and simmer for 5 minutes to allow flavors to blend. Whisk again and serve or steep with chai green tea bags for 2-3 minutes, if desired.

Cook's notes: Double or triple the batch and store in a glass container in the refrigerator for 3-4 days. Gently reheat leftovers on the stovetop or shake well and serve chilled.

AIP adaptation: Use coconut milk. Omit chai green tea bags.

Elimination/Provocation Diet adaptation: Use coconut milk.

RELAXING CHAMOMILE LEMON GINGER TEA

Chamomile is a flower that's very soothing to the nervous and gastrointestinal systems. This is a great "anytime tea" — when you need help relaxing or a little digestive support. For a calming ritual for restful sleep, brew a cup before bedtime or a nap.

Serves 1

Ingredients

12-16 ounces filtered water

1 chamomile tea bag

1 teaspoon freshly grated ginger

1 teaspoon local honey

1 wedge of lemon

Preparation

1. Bring water to a rolling boil.

2. Pour water over tea and grated ginger. Steep for 5-7 minutes. Strain grated ginger away, if desired, and discard tea bag.

3. Stir in honey and a squeeze of lemon juice.

Cook's notes: This can also be enjoyed as a cold, refreshing beverage on warmer days. Brew a triple or quadruple batch and refrigerate for up to 7 days.

Elimination/Provocation Diet adaptation: Omit lemon.

HAPPY TUMMY GREEN TEA

Ginger, cardamom, and fennel are potent culinary spices that help to combat common tummy troubles. Sip on this tea and find relief from gas, bloating, and constipation. This can be enjoyed hot or cold.

Serves 1

Ingredients

- 12-16 ounces filtered water
- 1 teaspoon freshly grated ginger
- 1 teaspoon fennel seeds
- 3 cardamom pods, slightly crushed (or ¼ teaspoon ground cardamom)
- 1 organic green tea bag
- 1 teaspoon local honey

Preparation

1. Place water, ginger, fennel seeds, and crushed cardamom in a medium-sized saucepan. Bring to a gentle boil then turn off heat. Allow spices to steep for 5 minutes.

2. Using a fine mesh strainer, strain away solids and pour liquid into a large mug. Add green tea bag to mug and steep for 2-3 minutes before discarding.

3. Sweeten with honey and serve.

Cook's notes: This can also be enjoyed as a cold, refreshing beverage on warmer days. Brew a double or triple batch and refrigerate for up to 7 days.

COOLING PEPPERMINT NETTLE INFUSION

Stinging nettles are a mineral-rich green leafy plant available dried as loose leaf or in tea bags that can be used to make a tonifying infusion. Nettle infusion is wonderfully nourishing and helps combat fatigue. This tea is best enjoyed cold.

Makes 1 quart

Ingredients

1 quart filtered water

1 cup dried loose leaf nettle or 8-10 nettle tea bags

1 tablespoon dried loose leaf peppermint or 2 peppermint tea bags

1 tablespoon local honey (optional)

Preparation

1. Bring water to a boil.

2. Place loose tea leaves or tea bags in a 1-quart mason jar and fill with boiling water. Add honey, if using, then stir and allow tea leaves to steep for 8-12 hours or overnight on a countertop.

3. Strain away tea leaves using a fine mesh strainer, or remove tea bags. Enjoy the quart of infusion served cold. Drink over the course of 2-3 days.

Cook's notes: If you cannot find dried loose leaf nettle in the bulk herb or tea section of your natural foods store, check the boxed tea section for Alvita or Traditional Medicinals brands of nettle tea bags.

SUNNY HEMP MILK

It's easy to make a nourishing, protein-packed plant-based milk using a blend of hemp and sunflower seeds. You may want to pre-soak the seeds for 3-4 hours beforehand to ensure easy blending. This milk has a nutty flavor and the nutrient-dense seeds provide essential Omega-3 fatty acids, protein, and calcium.

Makes 1 quart

Ingredients

½ cup raw sunflower seeds

½ cup hulled hemp seeds (aka hemp hearts)

4 cups filtered water

Pinch of sea salt

1¼ teaspoons sunflower lecithin (optional)

½ teaspoon vanilla extract (optional)

1 tablespoon pure maple syrup, or more to taste (optional)

Preparation

1. Place all ingredients into a high-speed blender, including optional sunflower lecithin to help emulsify and vanilla and maple syrup for additional flavor, if desired. Blend on high until smooth, approximate 60 seconds.

2. Strain milk. If a smoother, silkier texture is desired, use a filtration bag (aka nut milk bag) to strain pulp. Place bag over a pitcher or other container and slowly pour milk into bag. Twist the bag closed and gently squeeze, allowing milk to pass through.

3. Store in the refrigerator and use within 2-3 days. Separation is natural, especially if you don't use the sunflower lecithin. Shake well before serving.

Cook's notes: Sunflower lecithin is an emulsifier that can be added to help prevent milk from separating.

Nutrients: B$_1$, B$_2$, B$_6$, E, Ca, Cu, Fe, Mg, Mn, Se, Zn, O3

HOMEMADE COCONUT MILK

It's surprisingly easy and inexpensive to make your own coconut milk using dried coconut. My favorite way to enjoy this tasty plant-based milk is in smoothies, but it also works great as a creamy cooking liquid for hot cereal, a base for Thai-inspired sauces, or a tasty snack enjoyed cold in a tall glass.

Makes 1 quart

Ingredients

- 2 cups shredded unsweetened dried coconut flakes
- 4 cups filtered water
- 1 tablespoon pure maple syrup
- ½ teaspoon vanilla extract (optional)

Preparation

1. Place ingredients into a high-powered blender container and allow dried coconut to soak for 30 minutes.

2. Blend on high for 60-90 seconds.

3. Strain pulp from mixture by draping a nut milk bag or fine mesh strainer over a large pitcher to collect the milk. Squeeze the nut milk bag or press the milk into the strainer using a wooden spoon to extract as much milk from the coconut pulp as possible.

4. Store in refrigerator and use within 2-3 days. Separation is natural – shake well before serving.

Cook's notes: For a toasty variation, use toasted coconut flakes. Spread coconut flakes evenly on a sheet pan and toast in oven at 325°F for 5-7 minutes, until flakes are light golden brown. Be careful not to burn.

AIP adaptation: Omit optional vanilla extract.

CHOCOLATE CASHEW MILK

For refreshing chocolaty decadence in a glass, make this recipe! Enjoy chilled or gently heat over the stove on low for a delightful plant-based variation of hot cocoa. For a basic cashew milk recipe, simply omit the cocoa.

Makes about 5 cups

Ingredients

1 cup raw cashews, soaked 4-6 hours

4 cups filtered water

¼ cup unsweetened cocoa powder

Pinch of sea salt

1¼ teaspoons sunflower lecithin (optional)

2 tablespoons pure maple syrup or coconut sugar (optional)

1 teaspoon vanilla extract (optional)

Preparation

1. Drain and rinse soaked cashews and place in a high-speed blender. Add water and other remaining ingredients, including optional sunflower lecithin to help emulsify and sweetener and vanilla for additional flavor, if desired. Blend on high until completely smooth, approximate 60 seconds.

Cook's notes: Sunflower lecithin is an emulsifier that can be added to help prevent milk from separating.

To make plain cashew milk, omit cocoa powder.

Nutrients: Cu, Fe, Mg, Mn, Zn, Pr

BREAKFASTS

AVOCADO TOAST WITH OVER EASY EGG AND SESAME SEAWEED SPRINKLE

This is a simple, healthful breakfast redefined. Swap out regular toast with a whole grain gluten-free option and amplify your intake of healthy fats with the satisfyingly creamy avocado spread. Garnish this dish with the Sesame Seaweed Sprinkle recipe from the Condiments, Sauces, and Seasonings *chapter to add mineral density and some flavorful flair.*

Serves 1-2

Ingredients

2 slices of gluten-free bread

1-2 eggs

1 tablespoon ghee, refined coconut oil, or avocado oil

½ or 1 avocado, pitted and mashed

2 teaspoons Sesame Seaweed Sprinkle from the *Condiments, Sauces, and Seasonings* chapter.

Sea salt and black pepper to taste

Preparation

1. Place bread in toaster while egg(s) cook.

2. Gently crack 1-2 eggs into a small bowl or ramekin.

3. Heat a medium-sized skillet over low heat and add ghee or oil; brush oil around the bottom of pan to ensure it's evenly coated.

4. Holding the handle, tilt the pan slightly while gently pouring egg(s) from the bowl into the pan; keeping the pan tilted will prevent the egg's thin, runny whites from spreading all over the bottom of the pan. Keep tilted for about 20-30 seconds before lowering the pan back flat. Season with salt and pepper and let cook until whites become opaque. Using a spatula, gently flip the egg(s); they'll be ready to flip when the whites are set, but not hard. Let cook for another 20-30 seconds.

Nutrients: A(ʀᴇᴛ), B₂, B₆, B₁₂, D, E, Cᴀ, Cᴜ, Fᴇ, I, Mɢ, Mɴ, Sᴇ, Zɴ, Tʏ, Gʟ

5. Meanwhile, remove toast and spread with mashed avocado.

6. Remove egg(s) from heat and place on top of avocado toast. Sprinkle with Sesame Seaweed Sprinkle.

Cook's notes: For gluten-free bread options, we like Canyon Bakehouse 7-Grain, Little Northern Bakehouse, and Happy Campers. For a gluten- and grain-free option, try Julian Paleo Bread.

Paleo adaptation: Serve on grain-free Paleo bread or omit bread completely and serve egg and avocado on a bed of spinach or arugula.

TOMATO, KALE, AND LEEK FRITTATA

This delicious frittata is a crust-free alternative to quiche that can easily be served for brunch or batch cooked for a quick breakfast to get you through the week. Feel free to substitute 1 cup of chopped onions for the leek or another green like spinach, chard, or collards for the kale. If you don't have a cast iron skillet, read cook's notes below.

Serves 4

Ingredients

8 large eggs

¼ cup plain unsweetened coconut, cashew, almond, or hemp milk

½ teaspoon sea salt

¼ teaspoon black pepper

2 teaspoons refined coconut oil, avocado oil, or ghee

1 cup chopped leeks (light green and white parts only)

1 cup chopped tomatoes

1 cup chopped and packed kale leaves (or other greens)

Suggested toppings

Arugula

Brazil Nut "Parmesan" from the *Condiments, Sauces, and Seasonings* chapter

Preparation

1. Preheat oven to 350°F.

2. Whisk eggs, milk, salt, and pepper in a medium-sized bowl, just enough to blend the whites and yolk. Overbeating may cause the frittata to puff up while baking. Set aside.

3. Heat oil or ghee over medium heat in a 10-inch oven-proof pan (cast iron is preferred). Add leeks and sauté for 3-4 minutes, stirring frequently until softened. Add tomatoes and sauté for an additional 3 minutes. Add kale and sauté for 1-2 minutes, just until it begins to wilt and becomes more vibrant in color. Evenly distribute vegetable mixture across the bottom of pan.

4. Gently pour in eggs and ensure they evenly cover the whole pan. Turn heat down to low and let mixture sit on burner until edges begin to set. This may take up to 60-90 seconds, depending on your pan. Once set, carefully transfer oven-proof pan to preheated oven and cook for 14-16 minutes until eggs are set

Nutrients: A(BETA), A(RET), B₁, B₂, B₆, B₁₂, C, D, CA, CU, FE, I, MN, SE, GL, LY, TY

throughout. The center will be slightly soft. It's not unusual for the eggs to puff up in the pan; they'll deflate once removed from oven.

5. Remove from oven, cut into wedges, and serve. Sprinkle with Brazil Nut "Parmesan" if desired.

Cook's notes: If you don't have a pan that can easily be transferred to the oven, simply cook the vegetable mixture as directed then transfer to a greased 9-inch pie pan, cover with whisked eggs, and place in oven. It may take a few minutes longer to cook this way since the edges of the eggs were not allowed time to pre-set in the pan on the stovetop.

GOLDEN SWEET POTATO AND BRUSSELS SPROUT HASH

This savory hash doubles as a wonderful breakfast side dish and great dinner addition served with chicken, pork, or fish. For a delicious breakfast, serve it with eggs or the Fresh Breakfast Sausage Patties found in this chapter and a side of lacto-fermented vegetables like kimchi or kraut.

Serves 4-6

Ingredients

- 2 medium sweet potatoes, cut into ½-inch cubes
- 10-12 large Brussels sprouts, trimmed and halved
- 1 small yellow onion, chopped
- 3 large cloves garlic, chopped
- 3-4 tablespoons olive oil, coconut oil, or melted ghee
- 1½ teaspoons sea salt
- ½ teaspoon black pepper
- 1 tablespoon dried rosemary or thyme
- ½ cup coarsely chopped fresh parsley (optional)

Preparation

1. Preheat oven to 425°F. Line a baking sheet with parchment paper.

2. Toss all ingredients (except for parsley) together in a large bowl until evenly coated with oil or ghee.

3. Spread evenly on baking sheet, ensuring vegetables aren't crowded. Roast for 25-30 minutes, flipping once with a spatula halfway through, until sweet potatoes and Brussels sprouts are tender throughout. Brussels sprouts may become a little crispy on the outside.

4. Serve garnished with fresh parsley.

Vegan, AIP and Elimination/Provocation Diet adaptations: Use coconut or olive oil in place of ghee.

Nutrients: A(ret), B₁, B₆, C, Ca, Cu, Mg, Mn, Se, Gl

SAVORY TEMPEH, MUSHROOM, AND EGG HASH

This dish makes a filling plant-based breakfast that's full of protein and flavor. Tempeh is a traditional fermented whole soy food that has been enjoyed in Asian cultures for thousands of years. Fermenting the soybeans with a probiotic culture makes the beans easier to digest. If you don't have a cast iron skillet, read cook's notes below.

Serves 4-6

Ingredients

2 tablespoons ghee, coconut oil, or avocado oil

1 onion, chopped

3 cloves garlic, minced

1 (8-ounce) package of tempeh, crumbled into small pieces

8 ounces crimini mushrooms, sliced thinly

¼ cup reduced sodium tamari soy sauce or coconut aminos

2 teaspoons garlic powder

2 teaspoons onion powder

2 teaspoons smoked paprika

2 cups chopped spinach or kale

4 eggs

Sea salt and black pepper to taste

Preparation

1. Preheat oven to 400°F.

2. Warm ghee or oil in a medium-sized oven-proof skillet, like cast iron, and add onion and garlic. Cook for 4-5 minutes over medium heat until onions become translucent.

3. Add tempeh and mushrooms to pan and sauté for an additional 6-7 minutes, allowing tempeh to brown and mushrooms to soften. If bits begin to stick, deglaze pan with a few tablespoons of water as often as needed. Halfway into cook time, stir in tamari or coconut aminos, and spices. Season with salt and pepper.

4. Remove sauté pan from heat and make four small wells in the hash. Crack eggs and fill each well with an egg. Transfer pan to the oven and cook for 10-12 minutes or until eggs reach your desired level of doneness.

Nutrients: A(BETA), A(RET), B₁, B₂, B₆, B₁₂, C, D, E, Ca, Cu, Fe, I, Mg, Mn, Se, Zn, Gl, Pr, Ty

Cook's notes: A cast iron skillet is perfect for this recipe. If you don't have one or another oven-proof sauté pan, simply transfer tempeh mixture to an oiled medium-sized baking dish, form the wells, add the eggs, and place in the oven. Note that the cooking time in the oven may take a few minutes longer in a baking dish.

Substitute portobello, shiitake, or white button mushrooms for crimini mushrooms, if desired.

Vegan Adaptation: Use coconut or avocado oil in place of ghee. Omit eggs.

FRESH BREAKFAST SAUSAGE PATTIES

Here's a simple recipe for making your own breakfast sausage that can be prepared ahead of time and used throughout the week or frozen to be enjoyed later. The ground pork is incredibly flavorful, but if a leaner version is desired, feel free to use equal parts ground chicken breast to chicken thigh.

Makes 8 (2-inch) patties

Ingredients

- ½ pound ground pork
- ½ pound ground chicken breast or thigh
- 1 teaspoon dried thyme
- 1 teaspoon sea salt
- ¼ teaspoon dried sage
- ¼ teaspoon dried rosemary
- ¼ teaspoon fennel seed
- ¼ teaspoon ground nutmeg
- ¼ teaspoon black pepper
- 1-2 tablespoons ghee, coconut oil, or avocado oil

Preparation

1. Combine ground pork and chicken in a medium-sized bowl with seasonings. If time allows, chill in refrigerator for 30-60 minutes to allow time for flavors to meld.

2. Remove sausage from refrigerator and form into well-packed 2-inch rounds. Heat ghee or oil in a large pan over medium heat. Pan fry patties for 4-5 minutes on each side until sausages are brown and cooked through to an internal temperature of 165°F.

3. Set cooked sausage on a plate lined with paper towels to absorb oils.

Cook's notes: You can use parchment paper to separate individual uncooked patties and store in an airtight food storage bag in the refrigerator for up to 3 days or freezer up to 3 months. Frozen patties don't need to be thawed before cooking, but will take longer to cook thoroughly.

AIP Adaptation: Omit fennel seed and nutmeg. Cook in coconut oil.

Nutrients: B$_2$, B$_6$, B$_{12}$, C, D, Ca, Fe, Mn, Se, Zn, Ty

GRAIN-FREE COCONUT BANANA WAFFLES

These grain-free waffles are made with coconut flour, a naturally gluten-free flour alternative that's made from ground and dried coconut meat. Loaded with fiber, protein, and healthful fats, these waffles are sure to fuel you with energy and keep you satiated for a busy day ahead.

Makes 4 waffles

Ingredients

2 bananas

4 eggs

1 tablespoon pure maple syrup or local honey

1 teaspoon vanilla extract

½ cup coconut flour

½ teaspoon baking soda

¼ teaspoon sea salt

Coconut oil spray for greasing waffle iron

Suggested toppings

Maple Almond Drizzle from the *Condiments, Sauces, and Seasonings* chapter.

Raspberry Orange Chia Jam from the *Condiments, Sauces, and Seasonings* chapter.

Preparation

1. Preheat waffle iron.

2. Mash bananas in medium-sized bowl. Add eggs, maple syrup or honey, and vanilla extract and whisk together until well incorporated.

3. Add coconut flour, baking soda, and salt. Stir until well mixed, working out any lumps from the flour. Batter will be thick.

4. Spray heated waffle iron with coconut oil spray or brush oil on with a silicone brush.

5. Add batter to heated, oiled waffle iron and spread evenly with a spatula.

6. Cook according to waffle iron instructions. Waffles will be slightly golden and easily release with a fork when done.

Cook's notes: Waffle iron capacity may vary, but most waffle irons should be able to yield 4 waffles. Double the recipe and refrigerate or freeze any extra waffles. Can be stored in the refrigerator for 3-4 days or up to 3 months in the freezer. Reheat in a toaster oven.

Nutrients: A(RET), B_2, B_6, B_{12}, D, I, SE, TY

WHOLE GRAIN CORNMEAL AND OAT WAFFLES

These satisfyingly filling waffles are made with oat flour to provide wholesome fiber and delicious cornmeal for a subtle crispiness. They're super tasty when topped with my Raspberry Orange Chia Jam from the Condiments, Sauces, and Seasonings *chapter.*

Makes 4 waffles

Ingredients

Dry Ingredients

1 cup certified gluten-free oat flour

½ cup organic cornmeal

½ teaspoon baking powder

½ teaspoon sea salt

Wet Ingredients

2 eggs

⅔ cup unsweetened coconut, cashew, almond, or hemp milk

½ cup applesauce, pumpkin puree, or mashed bananas (approximately 2)

2 tablespoons avocado oil or melted coconut oil

2 tablespoons pure maple syrup

1 teaspoon vanilla extract

Coconut oil spray for greasing waffle iron

Preparation

1. Preheat waffle iron.

2. Whisk dry ingredients together in a large mixing bowl.

3. Whisk wet ingredients together in a medium-sized mixing bowl.

4. Combine wet ingredients with dry ingredients and mix together.

5. Spray heated waffle iron with coconut oil spray or brush oil on with a silicone brush.

6. Add batter to heated, oiled waffle iron and gently spread evenly with a spatula. (Whole grain batters are usually thicker than standard waffle batters.)

7. Cook according to the instructions that came with your waffle iron. Waffles will be slightly golden and easily release with a fork when done.

Cook's notes: Waffle iron capacity may vary, but most waffle irons should be able to yield 4 waffles. Double the recipe and refrigerate or freeze any extra waffles. Can be stored in the refrigerator for 3-4 days or up to 3 months in the freezer. Reheat in a toaster oven.

Nutrients: A(RET), B$_2$, B$_{12}$, D, Cu, Fe, I, Mg, Mn, Se, Zn, Ty

WHOLESOME 3-GRAIN PANCAKES

These pancakes are made from intact whole grains that are soaked first, which improves their overall digestibility. This recipe was inspired by "Ben's Friday Pancakes" by my culinary instructor, Cynthia Lair. Make egg-free by substituting the egg with a flax "egg," if desired.

Makes 6 pancakes

Ingredients

⅓ cup gluten-free steel cut oats

⅓ cup raw buckwheat groats

⅓ cup quinoa, rinsed

1¼ cups unsweetened coconut, cashew, almond, or hemp milk

2 teaspoons apple cider vinegar

1 large egg (or flax "egg" – see cook's notes)

¾ teaspoon baking powder

¼ teaspoon sea salt

½ teaspoon ground nutmeg

1 teaspoon ground cinnamon

1½ tablespoons coconut palm sugar, Sucanat, or maple sugar

Coconut oil, ghee, or avocado oil

Suggested toppings

Maple Almond Drizzle from the *Condiments, Sauces, and Seasonings* chapter

Raspberry Orange Chia Jam from the *Condiments, Sauces, and Seasonings* chapter

Preparation

1. Combine steel cut oats, buckwheat groats, quinoa, milk, and vinegar in a blender container. Cover with lid and let grains soak overnight or 6-8 hours in the refrigerator.

2. After soaking, place blender container on base. Add egg or flax "egg" substitute, along with baking powder, salt, nutmeg, cinnamon, and sweetener to grain mixture. Blend until smooth.

3. Preheat an oiled griddle or skillet to medium-low heat. Once surface of pan is hot enough that a drop of water sizzles on it, pour ⅓ cup batter onto griddle and cook for approximately 2 minutes on each side. Transfer finished pancakes to warm oven (170-190°F) to hold while you finish using all the batter.

4. Serve drizzled with Maple Almond Syrup or Raspberry Orange Chia Jam.

Nutrients: B₂, B₆, Cu, Fe, I, Mg, Mn, Se, Zn, Ty

Cook's notes: To substitute egg with flax "egg," soak 1 tablespoon of ground flaxseeds in warm water for 10 minutes until it becomes viscous.

Double the batch and freeze extras for a quick, easy breakfast that you can reheat in a toaster oven. To freeze, cool pancakes completely, place parchment paper between pancakes, and seal in a food storage bag before placing in the freezer.

Vegan adaptation: Use flax "egg" substitute.

Elimination/Provocation Diet adaptation: Use coconut or hemp milk and flax "egg" substitute.

TOASTED STEEL CUT OATMEAL WITH CHAI SPICES AND CARAMELIZED APPLES

Toasting oats is an incredibly simple method that can really bring out their delicious flavor. The warming chai spices paired with the fiber from the oats aid digestion and ease the elimination of toxins. Peaches or pears can be substituted for apples, if desired.

Serves 3-4

Ingredients

Oatmeal

- 2 teaspoons coconut oil or ghee
- 1 cup certified gluten-free steel cut oats
- 2½ cups filtered water
- 1 cup unsweetened coconut, cashew, almond, or hemp milk
- 1 teaspoon vanilla extract
- ¾ teaspoon ground cinnamon
- ¼ teaspoon ground cardamom
- ¼ teaspoon ground nutmeg
- ¼ teaspoon sea salt
- ⅛ teaspoon black pepper
- 2 tablespoons local honey or pure maple syrup

Caramelized Apples

- 2 tablespoons coconut oil or ghee
- 1 tablespoon coconut sugar or Sucanat
- 2 apples, sliced thinly

Suggested topping

Pecans

Nutrients: Cu, Fe, Mg, Mn, Zn

Preparation

1. To make the oatmeal, melt the oil or ghee over medium-low heat in the bottom of a medium-sized saucepan. Add the oats and cook for about 2-3 minutes while stirring frequently to toast. Oats will become lightly golden and fragrant when toasted.

2. Reduce heat to low and carefully pour in the water and milk. Add vanilla and spices. Increase heat until mixture begins to simmer. Reduce heat to low, cover, and simmer gently for 20-25 minutes, stirring occasionally. Oats will thicken as liquid is absorbed.

3. To caramelize the apples, melt oil or ghee in a large skillet over medium heat. Stir in coconut sugar or Sucanat and continue to stir until sugar begins to melt, about 1 minute. Add sliced apples and sauté until brown and tender, about 10 minutes.

4. Remove oatmeal from heat, sweeten with honey or maple syrup, and top with caramelized apples and pecans. Allow any extra oatmeal to cool completely before covering and refrigerating leftovers.

Cook's notes: Expedite cooking time by toasting oats in the evening and soaking the toasted oats overnight. Resume step 2 in the morning, but simply cook the oats for 15 minutes.

Vegan adaptation: Use coconut oil instead of ghee.

Elimination/Provocation Diet adaptation: Use coconut oil in place of ghee. Substitute sunflower seeds for pecans, if desired.

SIMPLE MORNING MUESLI

This recipe makes a large jar of muesli that is wonderful to keep on hand for a versatile, power-packed breakfast. Muesli is traditionally served cold with your choice of milk but you can heat, if desired. It's also delicious mixed with unsweetened coconut milk yogurt. And of course, don't forget to top it with fresh berries or other seasonal fruit.

Makes 16 (½ cup) servings

Ingredients

½ cup raw or toasted nuts (almonds, cashews, walnuts, pecans, hazelnuts, Brazil nuts)

½ cup raw or toasted seeds (pumpkin, sunflower, pine nuts)

4 cups certified gluten-free rolled oats

1 cup unsweetened, shredded coconut

1 cup currants or raisins

½ cup dried Turkish apricots, dried apples, or prunes, chopped

½ cup unsweetened cacao nibs

⅓ cup chia or hemp seeds

1 tablespoon ground cinnamon

1 teaspoon ground nutmeg

½ teaspoon sea salt

Suggested toppings

Unsweetened coconut, cashew, almond, or hemp milk

Unsweetened coconut milk yogurt

Fresh berries

Local honey

Preparation

1. Preheat oven to 350°F. Spread nuts out on a sheet pan and toast in the oven for 6-8 minutes. Be careful not to burn. Remove from heat and set aside.

2. Toast seeds in a dry skillet over medium heat for 3-4 minutes while stirring frequently. Be careful not to burn. Remove from heat and set aside.

3. Combine all ingredients in a large bowl and mix well. Pour into a sealed, airtight container like a mason jar until ready to serve.

4. To serve, measure out approximately ½ cup and top with plant-based milk of your choice or coconut milk yogurt and fresh berries. Sweeten with a small amount of honey, if desired.

Elimination/Provocation Diet adaptation: Omit nuts and cacao nibs. Serve with coconut or hemp milk or coconut milk yogurt.

Nutrients: B$_6$, Ca, Cu, Fe, Mg, Mn, Se, Zn, O3

WARMING MULTIGRAIN BREAKFAST BOWL

This nourishing bowl is a surefire way to easily incorporate the nutrient-dense ancient grains quinoa, millet, and amaranth into your diet. If you don't have amaranth on hand, simply double the quinoa or millet.

Serves 3-4

Ingredients

¼ cup quinoa or millet

½ cup certified gluten-free steel cut oats

¼ cup amaranth

1 cup unsweetened coconut, cashew, almond, or hemp milk

1½ cups filtered water

1 teaspoon ground cinnamon

¼ teaspoon ground nutmeg

¼ teaspoon sea salt

2 tablespoons pure maple syrup or local honey

Suggested toppings

Chopped nuts or seeds

Toasted coconut flakes and banana

Diced apple or pear

Fresh berries

½ cup pumpkin puree

Preparation

1. Rinse and drain quinoa or millet in a fine mesh strainer to wash away bitter compounds on the outside of the grains.

2. Place grains, milk, water, salt, and spices in a medium-sized saucepan over medium heat. Using a whisk, stir spices in thoroughly and bring mixture to a boil. Lower heat and simmer for 20 minutes until grains are thoroughly cooked.

3. Sweeten to taste with maple syrup or honey. Add toppings, as desired.

Cooks notes: If you measure out and soak the grains overnight in your cooking liquid it will improve their digestibility and cut the cooking time down by about half.

Elimination/Provocation Diet adaptation: Use coconut milk. Use seeds in place of nuts as a topping.

Nutrients: B$_2$, B$_6$, Ca, Cu, Fe, Mg, Mn, Se, Zn

APPETIZERS AND SNACKS

CUCUMBER MANGO RADISH SALSA

This zippy, cooling salsa provides a uniquely delicious way to use antioxidant-rich radishes. The creaminess of the mango contrasts well with the crunchiness of the radishes and cucumbers. Serve as a condiment for fish tacos or as a dip for organic corn chips.

Makes 2½ cups

Ingredients

4 radishes, diced

1 mango, diced

½ cucumber, peeled, seeded, and diced

1 jalapeno, seeded and minced

¼ cup chopped fresh cilantro

2 tablespoons chopped fresh mint

1 tablespoon fresh lime juice

1 teaspoon local honey

¼ teaspoon chili powder

¼ teaspoon sea salt

Preparation

1. Toss all ingredients together in a medium-sized bowl. Taste and adjust seasonings as desired.

2. Serve immediately or store in refrigerator for up to 4 days. Flavors will build the longer ingredients marinate together.

AIP adaptation: Omit jalapeño and chili powder.

Elimination/Provocation Diet adaptation: Omit lime juice, jalapeño, and chili powder.

Nutrients: B$_2$, B$_6$, C, E, C$_A$, C$_U$, F$_E$, M$_G$, M$_N$, S$_E$, Z$_N$

PINEAPPLE RAINBOW SALSA

This colorful salsa provides the perfect balance of sweet and spicy without being too fiery hot. With every color of the rainbow represented, this salsa boasts a wide variety of important health-supportive nutrients. It's especially delicious served over chicken or fish.

Makes approximately 2 cups

Ingredients

1-1½ cups diced fresh pineapple

1 medium tomato, diced

1 red, yellow, or orange bell pepper, diced

1 jalapeño or serrano pepper, seeded and diced

2 cloves garlic, minced

¼ cup minced red onion

¼ cup chopped fresh cilantro or parsley

3 tablespoons fresh lime juice

½ teaspoon sea salt

¼ teaspoon chili powder (optional)

Preparation

1. Toss all ingredients together in a medium-sized bowl. Add additional lime juice to taste.

2. Serve immediately or store in refrigerator for up to 4 days. Flavors will build the longer the ingredients marinate.

AIP adaptation: Omit tomato, bell pepper, jalapeño, and chili powder. Add in 1 medium peeled and diced cucumber.

Nutrients: B₆, C, Ca, Cu, Mg, Mn, Se, Gl, Ly

FESTIVE KALE POMEGRANATE GUACAMOLE

Guacamole is an all-time favorite that's easy to make and this variation offers a fun twist on a classic. The addition of finely chopped kale amplifies its nutrient density and no one will notice it's there. The antioxidant-rich pomegranate arils pack a juicy burst of flavor into each bite.

Serves 4-6

Ingredients

2 large ripe avocados, pitted and diced

1 medium lime, juiced (approximately 2 tablespoons)

3 tablespoons red onion, finely chopped

1 jalapeño, seeded and finely chopped

¼ teaspoon sea salt

⅛ teaspoon black pepper

1-2 large kale leaves, finely chopped

½ cup pomegranate arils

¼ cup fresh cilantro, chopped

Preparation

1. Scoop avocados into a medium-sized bowl. Add lime juice, onion, jalapeño, salt, and pepper and mash ingredients together using a potato masher or a fork, until well combined.

2. Fold in kale, pomegranate arils, and cilantro.

3. Enjoy immediately or pack tightly in a sealed container and store in refrigerator.

Cook's notes: Pomegranate arils are the juicy seeds of the pomegranate, enmeshed in a white membrane inside the fruit. The easiest way to release the arils from this membrane is to cut the pomegranate in half horizontally, then while holding each half over a large bowl, whack the back of the rind with a wooden spoon until all of the arils have been released.

AIP adaptation: Omit jalapeño.

Elimination/Provocation Diet adaptation: Omit jalapeño and lime juice.

Nutrients: A(beta), B₁, B₆, C, E, Ca, Cu, Mg, Mn, Gl

CURRIED SWEET POTATO HUMMUS

This recipe provides a contemporary twist on traditional hummus. The complex carbohydrates and fiber present in both beans and sweet potatoes have been shown to help stabilize blood sugar levels, crucial for thyroid and adrenal health. Plus, hummus is an amazing medium for getting more raw veggies in your diet, so go crazy dipping!

Serves 6-8

Ingredients

1 (15-ounce) can garbanzo beans, drained and rinsed

1 cup cooked sweet potato (roasted or steamed)

1 lemon, juiced (approximately 2 tablespoons)

1-2 cloves garlic

¼ cup extra virgin olive oil, plus a few tablespoons more as desired

2 tablespoons sesame tahini

1 tablespoon curry powder

¾ teaspoon sea salt

¼ teaspoon black pepper

Filtered water

Serving suggestions

Sliced cucumbers, bell peppers, carrots, celery, radishes, or zucchini to dip

Gluten-free crackers for dipping

Spread on gluten-free rice cakes or gluten-free bread/wraps

Preparation

1. Place all ingredients in a food processor and puree until smooth and creamy.

2. Add a few tablespoons of water or additional olive oil a little at a time, until you reach desired consistency.

3. Store in the refrigerator for up to 7 days.

Cook's notes: This is a great recipe to use up leftover roasted sweet potatoes. If you don't have roasted sweet potatoes on hand, simply cut a sweet potato into ½-inch pieces and place in a steaming basket for 7-8 minutes until fork tender.

Nutrients: B$_2$, B$_6$, C, Ca, Cu, Fe, Mg, Mn, Se, Zn, Gl

SUNFLOWER SEED HUMMUS

This hummus is a Paleo-friendly, bean-free variation that utilizes sunflower seeds, an inexpensive yet rich source of protein, healthful fats, and Vitamin E. Sumac is a beautiful red spice derived from a berry that has a tart, lemony flavor – if you can track it down in the spice aisle of your grocery store, it's sure to create a very authentic tasting hummus.

Serves 6-8

Ingredients

1 cup raw sunflower seeds, pre-soaked 4-6 hours in 1 cup filtered water

¼ cup extra virgin olive oil

3 tablespoons fresh lemon juice

2 tablespoons sesame tahini

1-2 cloves garlic

2-4 tablespoons filtered water (or more to achieve desired consistency)

1 teaspoon ground sumac (optional), divided

Sea salt and black pepper to taste

Serving suggestions

Sliced cucumbers, bell peppers, carrots, celery, radishes, or zucchini to dip

Gluten-free crackers for dipping

Spread on gluten-free rice cakes or gluten-free bread/wraps

Preparation

1. To soak, place sunflower seeds in a container and cover with water. Soak for 4-6 hours.

2. Drain and rinse seeds, then place in a food processor with oil, lemon juice, tahini, garlic, water, salt, and ¾ teaspoon of sumac. Blend until smooth, adding a tablespoon of water or additional olive oil a little at a time, until you reach desired consistency. Season with salt and pepper.

3. Place in a bowl and garnish with ¼ teaspoon of sumac. Serve immediately or store in an airtight container in refrigerator for up to 7 days.

Cook's notes: Double batch and enjoy as a dip or spread on sandwiches and wraps.

Nutrients: B_1, B_2, B_6, C, E, Ca, Cu, Fe, Mg, Mn, Se, Zn

STUFFED CRIMINI MUSHROOMS WITH KALE AND SAUSAGE

This savory, crowd-pleasing appetizer offers a healthier twist on traditional stuffed mushrooms — and they're easy to make. Mushrooms and kale contain a spectrum of important minerals, as well detoxifying antioxidants and energizing B vitamins that support the thyroid and immune health.

Makes 20 mushrooms

Ingredients

20 medium crimini mushrooms

3-4 tablespoons avocado oil or melted coconut oil or ghee, divided

1 medium onion, diced small

3 cloves garlic, minced

1 pound gluten-free chicken sausage (without casing)

1 red bell pepper, diced small

1½ cups chopped kale leaves

⅔ cup almond meal

½ teaspoon sea salt

¼ teaspoon black pepper

Preparation

1. Prehcat oven to 350°F.

2. Rinse and dry mushrooms. Remove stems. Reserve stems for making vegetable broth, if desired; place in a food storage bag and freeze.

3. Toss mushroom caps in a bowl with 1-2 tablespoons oil or ghee. Set aside.

4. Heat 2 tablespoons of oil or ghee in a large skillet over medium heat. Add onion and garlic and sauté for 3 minutes to allow onion to soften. Add sausage and break apart with a spoon or spatula into very small pieces. Cook for 4-5 minutes to allow sausage to cook most of the way through. Add bell pepper and kale and sauté for 2-3 more minutes, just long enough to allow kale to wilt.

5. Remove skillet from heat and add almond meal, salt, and pepper. Stir until well combined.

6. Spread mushroom caps out evenly on a sheet pan and using a scoop or a spoon, stuff each one with a generous amount of the kale and sausage mixture, packed tightly into a mound. Place in the oven for 25 minutes. You may want to cover mushrooms with foil after the first 15 minutes to prevent overbrowning.

Nutrients: A(BETA), B$_1$, B$_2$, B$_6$, B$_{12}$, C, D, E, CA, CU, FE, MG, MN, SE, ZN, GL, LY, TY

MEDITERRANEAN LAMB SLIDERS WITH COCONUT YOGURT TZATZIKI

These Mediterranean-inspired lamb sliders are seasoned with antioxidant-rich Za'Atar spices and finished with a delicious dairy-free tzatziki. Your taste buds will thoroughly enjoy being taken on an exotic culinary journey with this flavorful dish.

Serves 4-6

Ingredients

Sliders

1 pound grass-fed ground lamb

2 cloves garlic, minced

2 tablespoons chopped fresh parsley and/ or mint

1 teaspoon sumac

1 teaspoon sesame seeds

1 teaspoon ground cumin

1 teaspoon sea salt

1 teaspoon black pepper

½ teaspoon dried oregano

½ teaspoon smoked paprika (optional)

Zest of one lemon

1 head butter or romaine lettuce

Coconut Yogurt Tzatziki
(makes 1½ cups)

1 cup unsweetened coconut milk yogurt

½ cup cucumber, peeled, seeded, and diced

2-3 tablespoons fresh mint

1 tablespoon fresh lemon juice

½ teaspoon ground cumin

¼ teaspoon sea salt

Nutrients: B₁₂, C, E, Cu, Fe, Mg, Mn, Se, Zn, Pr, Ty

Preparation

1. Preheat oven to 400°F. Line a large baking sheet with parchment paper.

2. In a large bowl, mix the lamb slider ingredients except for the lettuce until well combined. Shape into approximately 8 patties that are 2½ inches in diameter and ½-inch thick. Transfer to baking sheet.

3. Place in oven for 12-15 minutes until thoroughly cooked and golden brown, flipping halfway through. Sliders are done when they reach an internal temperature of 160°F.

4. While sliders are cooking, mix all of the Coconut Yogurt Tzatziki ingredients together in a small bowl. Chill in the refrigerator until ready to serve.

5. Serve sliders atop a bed of lettuce and finish with a dollop of tzatziki.

Cook's notes: For an entrée-sized portion, make four larger patties. These can also be cooked on the grill or in a skillet over medium-high heat until they're cooked to desired level of doneness.

Elimination/Provocation Diet adaptation: Omit lemon zest and smoked paprika from the sliders and lemon juice from the tzatziki.

GOLDEN FLAX BREAD

This nourishing bread recipe comes from my friend and nutrition colleague, Leigh Wagner, PhD, RD, of GoodKarme.com. Its soft, comforting texture makes it the perfect accompaniment to a warming bowl of soup. It's also divine with a drizzle of good local honey.

Makes 12-16 pieces

Ingredients

2 cups golden flax meal

1 teaspoon baking soda

¾ teaspoon sea salt

5 eggs

½ cup filtered water

⅓ cup olive oil

2 tablespoons local honey or pure maple syrup

2 teaspoons lemon juice

Preparation

1. Preheat oven to 350°F. Grease an 8-inch square baking dish or pan.

2. In a large bowl, combine flax meal, baking soda, and salt.

3. In a smaller bowl, whisk together eggs with water, oil, sweetener, and lemon juice.

4. Stir wet ingredients into dry, mix well, and let stand for 2-3 minutes to allow batter to thicken.

5. Pour batter into greased baking dish and bake for 30-35 minutes. Test for doneness by inserting a toothpick or knife in the center; if it comes out clean, it's ready.

6. Remove from oven and allow to cool. Cut into 12-16 pieces.

Cook's notes: Flax meal is made from ground flaxseeds. I recommend using flax meal from golden flaxseeds because it results in a much more appealing color. Dark brown flaxseeds turn the bread much darker.

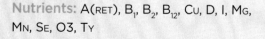

Nutrients: A(RET), B₁, B₂, B₁₂, Cu, D, I, Mg, Mn, Se, O3, Ty

(P)

BASIL, AVOCADO, AND HEMP SEED DIP

Creamy, cooling, and fresh, this flavorful dip makes eating raw vegetables much more enjoyable. This can also be enjoyed as a spread on gluten-free toast, dolloped on fish, or thinned out and drizzled over gluten-free pasta or zucchini noodles.

Serves 4-6

Ingredients

2 cups packed fresh basil

2 ripe avocados

½ cup hemp seeds

2 tablespoons fresh lemon or lime juice

2 cloves garlic

1 tablespoon chickpea miso

½ teaspoon sea salt

⅓ cup extra virgin olive oil

Black pepper to taste

Filtered water to thin to desired consistency

Preparation

1. De-stem basil leaves and add to a food processor along with avocados, hemp seeds, lemon juice, garlic, miso, and salt. Pulse until finely chopped. Add oil and process until creamy. Season with pepper and add a few tablespoons of water if a thinner consistency is desired.

2. Place dip in a serving bowl and serve alongside fresh cut vegetables for dipping. It's best enjoyed fresh, but may be kept for 2-3 days in the refrigerator before significant browning occurs. To minimize browning when stored, place in an airtight container with a layer of parchment paper pressed tightly against the dip to seal out air.

AIP adaptation: Omit hemp seeds and miso.

Nutrients: A(BETA), B₆, C, E, Ca, Cu, Fe, Mg, Mn, Gl, Ly, O3, Pr

SPINACH, ARTICHOKE, AND AVOCADO DIP

This plant-based recipe is super easy to make and can be used as a dip for fresh vegetables or organic corn chips, or stuffed into a lettuce wrap. Nutritional yeast provides a subtle cheesy flavor and a boost of B vitamins.

Serves 4

Ingredients

1 large avocado

¼ cup fresh basil

1 tablespoon fresh lemon juice

1 small clove garlic

1½ teaspoons onion powder

2-3 tablespoons nutritional yeast (optional)

½ teaspoon sea salt

1 cup canned artichoke hearts, drained and chopped

1 cup packed fresh spinach, finely chopped

Black pepper to taste

Serving ideas:

Any fresh vegetables are great for dipping, but try something new like thinly sliced jicama, golden beets, Chioggia beets, or watermelon radish, using endive leaves for scooping, or romaine and butter lettuces for wrapping.

Preparation

1. Scoop the flesh from the avocado into a food processor affixed with an S-blade. Add basil, lemon juice, garlic, onion powder, nutritional yeast (if using), and salt. Process for 1-2 minutes, until completely smooth and creamy. Transfer avocado cream to a medium-sized bowl. Set aside.

2. Place artichoke hearts and spinach into the bowl of the food processor and pulse a few times, being careful not to over-process. Don't worry about cleaning the avocado residue out of the bowl first.

3. Transfer the artichoke and spinach mixture to the bowl with avocado cream and stir well to combine. Adjust salt and pepper to taste.

4. Place dip in a serving bowl and serve alongside fresh vegetables or corn chips.

Cook's note: This dip is best enjoyed right away, but may be kept for up to 1 day in the refrigerator before significant browning occurs. To minimize browning when stored, place in an airtight container with a layer of parchment paper pressed tightly against the dip to seal out air.

Nutrients: A(BETA), B₁, B₂, B₆, C, E, Ca, Cu, Fe, Mg, Mn, Se, Zn, Gl, Ly

CHILI SPICED PUMPKIN SEEDS

These protein and mineral-rich chili spiced kernels are sure to satisfy any cravings for a wholesome, salty, and crunchy snack. Make a batch to fuel you on the go, or simply sprinkle over chili and salads for an earthy crunch.

Makes 2 cups

Ingredients

- 2 cups raw pumpkin seeds
- 1 tablespoon chili powder
- 1½ tablespoons fresh lime juice
- 1 teaspoon avocado oil
- 1 teaspoon sea salt

Preparation

1. In a small bowl, combine pumpkin seeds, chili powder, lime juice, oil, and salt. Toss well to coat.

2. Heat a large skillet over medium heat. Add seasoned pumpkin seeds to pan and toast in dry skillet for 3-5 minutes, until pumpkin seeds become aromatic and begin to puff up. Lower heat if necessary to prevent burning and be careful not to overcook seeds.

3. Cool and enjoy immediately or store in a tightly sealed container in the refrigerator for up to 2 months.

Cook's notes: Use chipotle chili powder if you'd like to try a hotter, spicier, smokier version.

Nutrients: B₂, B₆, C, E, Cᴀ, Cᴜ, Fᴇ, Mɢ, Mɴ, Sᴇ, Zɴ, Lʏ

CONDIMENTS, SAUCES, AND SEASONINGS

GINGERY QUICK PICKLED CARROTS AND CAULIFLOWER

Pickling is a great way to stock up and preserve vegetables that you may have scored from a great sale or when in seasonal abundance from the farmers' market. Pickling is easier than many people realize. Jazz up any meal with a side of these flavor-packed pickled veggies, and reap their healthful digestive properties to boot.

Makes 1 pint

Ingredients

½ cup filtered water

⅓ cup apple cider vinegar

2-3 tablespoons local honey

¾ teaspoon sea salt

½ cup carrot coins, sliced thinly (approximately 1 carrot)

½ cup cauliflower florets

½ small red onion, sliced thinly

2-3 teaspoons peeled and chopped fresh ginger

½ teaspoon coriander seeds

¼ teaspoon red pepper flakes (optional)

Preparation

1. Make the pickling brine by combining water, vinegar, honey, and salt in a small saucepan. Heat on medium-high, stirring occasionally, until mixture comes to a boil. Remove from heat.

2. Pack the carrot, cauliflower, onion, ginger, coriander, and optional red pepper flakes into a pint-sized canning jar.

3. Pour brine into jar over vegetable mixture and let cool to room temperature. Cover and transfer cooled jar to the refrigerator until ready to eat. Pickles will store well for 3-4 weeks in the refrigerator.

Cook's notes: Carrots can easily be swapped out with thinly sliced beets or radishes. Beets will turn everything purple. Use orange cauliflower in this recipe, if available, to add additional color and carotenoids.

AIP adaptation: Omit coriander seeds and red pepper flakes.

Elimination/Provocation Diet adaptation: Omit red pepper flakes.

Nutrients: A(BETA), B$_6$, C, E, Mn, Ly, Gl

KALE WALNUT PESTO

Pesto is a versatile condiment that can be enjoyed as a sandwich spread, mixed into eggs, tossed with gluten-free noodles or spiralized vegetables, or mixed into whole grain salad dishes. The nutritional profile of this pesto is amplified by the unique addition of kale.

Makes approximately 1 cup

Ingredients

- 1 cup kale leaves
- 1 cup fresh basil leaves
- 1 cup shelled walnuts
- 1-2 cloves garlic
- ¼ cup extra virgin olive oil, plus a few tablespoons to reach desired texture
- 1 medium lime, juiced (approximately 2 tablespoons)
- 2 teaspoons chickpea miso or mild white miso (optional)
- ¾ teaspoon sea salt
- ½ teaspoon black pepper

Preparation

1. Place all ingredients in the bowl of a food processor affixed with an S-blade. Process for 30-60 seconds. With the processor running, slowly pour a few additional tablespoons of oil if a creamier, less rustic texture is desired.

2. Serve right away or store pesto in the refrigerator or freezer with a thin film of oil on top to seal out oxygen that may cause browning.

Cook's notes: You can experiment using different herbs in this pesto like parsley and/or mint in place of or in addition to basil. Pistachios make a delicious substitution for walnuts.

Miso adds the savory umami flavor usually created by Parmesan cheese traditionally found in most pesto recipes.

To freeze, scoop into a freezable container leaving 1 inch of space at the top to allow pesto to expand as it freezes.

Paleo adaptation: Omit miso.

AIP adaptation: Substitute one pitted avocado for walnuts and omit miso.

Nutrients: A(beta), B$_1$, B$_6$, C, Ca, Cu, Mg, Mn, Se, Gl, Ly, O3, Pr

PUMPKIN SEED CILANTRO PESTO

This amazing pesto combines protein-rich pumpkin seeds and liver detoxifying cilantro into a delicious pesto that can be used as a dip for vegetables or a sauce for spaghetti squash.

Makes approximately 1 cup

Ingredients

1¼ cups pumpkin seeds

1 cup packed fresh cilantro (approximately 1 bunch)

¾ cup baby spinach

2 cloves garlic

2 tablespoons fresh lime juice

2 teaspoons chickpea miso paste (optional)

¼ cup extra virgin olive oil

½ teaspoon sea salt

¼ teaspoon black pepper

Preparation

1. To toast pumpkin seeds, heat a dry skillet over medium and spread pumpkin seeds evenly in the pan. Heat seeds for 2-3 minutes until they become fragrant and begin to pop.

2. In the bowl of a food processor, combine pumpkin seeds, cilantro, spinach, garlic, lime juice, miso, oil, salt, and pepper and process until smooth. Thin with additional oil, if desired.

Cook's notes: Try parsley in place of cilantro, if desired. Sunflower seeds make a delicious substitution for pumpkin seeds.

Chickpea miso adds the savory umami flavor usually created by Parmesan cheese traditionally found in most pesto recipes.

To freeze, scoop into a freezable container leaving 1 inch of space at the top to allow pesto to expand as it freezes.

Nutrients: B₁, B₆, C, Ca, Cu, Fe, Mg, Mn, Se, Zn, Gl, Pr

Nutrients: B_1, B_6, C, Ca, Cu, Fe, Mg, Mn, Se, Zn, Gl, Pr

COCONUT PEANUT SAUCE

This is an amazingly flavorful sauce that can be used over grilled meat, steamed or roasted vegetables, and Asian-inspired rice bowls. Try it with the Asian Lettuce Wraps in the Main Dishes *chapter. It will keep for at least a week in the refrigerator, but I promise it won't even last that long.*

Makes 1 cup

Ingredients

- ½ cup full fat or light coconut milk
- ½ cup unsweetened, natural peanut butter
- 3-4 tablespoons reduced sodium tamari soy sauce or coconut aminos
- 1½ tablespoons pure maple syrup
- 1 tablespoon brown rice vinegar
- 1 clove garlic
- 1 teaspoon freshly grated ginger
- ¼ teaspoon red pepper flakes (optional)
- Sriracha hot pepper sauce to taste (optional)

Preparation

1. Place all ingredients into a blender and puree on high until smooth and creamy.
2. Store in an airtight jar for up to 7 days in the refrigerator.

Cook's notes: Substitute almond butter, sunflower seed butter, or cashew butter for peanut butter, if desired. To make soy-free, use coconut aminos in place of soy sauce.

Paleo adaptation: Substitute any nut or seed butter in place of peanut butter. Substitute coconut aminos for soy sauce.

Elimination/Provocation Diet adaptation: Substitute sunflower seed butter for peanut butter. Substitute coconut aminos for soy sauce. Omit chili pepper flakes and hot pepper sauce.

Nutrients: B$_6$, E, Cu, Fe, Mg, Mn, Zn, Rv

MAPLE MISO TAHINI SAUCE

This take on lemon tahini sauce rounds out the flavor with rich sweetness from the maple syrup and a touch of savory saltiness from the miso. It's absolutely delicious over stir-fried, steamed, or roasted vegetables or as a salad dressing over raw veggies.

Makes approximately 1 cup

Ingredients

- ½ cup sesame tahini
- 1 teaspoon lemon zest
- ½ cup fresh lemon juice (about 4 lemons)
- 2 tablespoons extra virgin olive oil
- 1-2 tablespoons pure maple syrup
- 1 tablespoon chickpea or light white miso
- 2 cloves garlic, minced
- ¼ teaspoon sea salt
- ¼ teaspoon black pepper
- ¼-½ cup filtered water (more or less to desired consistency)

Preparation

1. Place all ingredients in a small bowl and whisk until well blended. Thin with water, if desired, by adding 1 tablespoon at a time until desired consistency is reached.

2. Store in an airtight jar for up to 7 days in the refrigerator.

Cook's notes: Both roasted and raw tahini are great in this recipe. Roasted tahini has a deeper, richer flavor, but its thinner, oilier consistency requires less water to thin the sauce.

Paleo adaptation: Omit miso.

Nutrients: B₂, B₆, C, Ca, Cu, Fe, Mg, Mn, Se, Zn, Gl, Pr

HEMP SEED CHIMICHURRI

Chimichurri is an easy yet flavorful South American sauce that can provide a zesty kick to chicken, fish, pork, or beef. Add a dollop of this antioxidant-rich sauce to season your proteins. It's also great stirred into pasta dishes and spiralized veggies or drizzled over baked spaghetti squash.

Makes ¾ cup

Ingredients

1 cup fresh flat-leaf Italian parsley, tightly packed

½ cup extra virgin olive oil

3 tablespoons hemp seeds

2 tablespoons fresh lemon juice

2 cloves garlic

1 teaspoon dried oregano

½ teaspoon sea salt

¼ teaspoon black pepper

⅛-¼ teaspoon red pepper flakes

Preparation

1. Combine all ingredients in the bowl of a food processor affixed with an S-blade and process until coarsely chopped.

2. Use immediately or store in a tightly sealed glass container in the refrigerator.

Cook's notes: Double the recipe and freeze any extra in a freezer safe container like a mason jar. Leave about 1 inch of space at the top of container to allow sauce to expand as it freezes.

Nutrients: B$_6$, C, E, C$_A$, C$_U$, F$_E$, M$_G$, M$_N$, S$_E$, G$_L$, O3

CLASSIC MARINARA SAUCE

Homemade marinara is surprisingly easy to make from a few basic pantry ingredients – and tastes remarkably better than even the best supermarket sauce. Stir in some shredded carrot to add natural sweetness. Try this with the Grass-Fed Beef Quinoa Meatballs found in the Main Dishes *chapter.*

Makes approximately 3 cups

Ingredients

1 tablespoon extra virgin olive oil

4-6 cloves garlic, minced

1 (28-ounce) can no salt added whole or diced tomatoes

1 medium carrot, shredded (optional)

3 tablespoons tomato paste

2 teaspoons coconut sugar or Sucanat (optional)

2 teaspoons dried basil

2 teaspoons dried oregano

½ teaspoon sea salt

⅛ teaspoon red pepper flakes

⅛ teaspoon black pepper

Preparation

1. Heat oil over low heat in a 10-inch skillet and sauté garlic for 1-2 minutes, until it begins to soften. Be sure not to heat oil any higher than low, otherwise it may oxidize.

2. To prevent splattering, carefully and quickly pour entire contents of canned tomatoes into skillet and increase heat to medium. Stir in shredded carrot, tomato paste, sweetener, basil, oregano, salt, red pepper flakes, and pepper. Cover and bring to a gentle boil. Reduce heat to low and simmer for 20 minutes to allow sauce to thicken.

3. Use an immersion blender to puree sauce while still in the pan or carefully transfer to a blender and puree to desired consistency. If a chunky, more rustic texture is desired, skip this step.

Cook's notes: Using a large skillet in place of a saucepan allows the sauce to thicken quicker and easier.

Double recipe and freeze in a mason jar leaving about 1 inch of space at the top to allow sauce to expand as it freezes.

Nutrients: A(BETA), B$_6$, C, E, CA, Cu, FE, MN, LY

COCOA INFUSED ENCHILADA SAUCE

I grew up eating my grandma's homemade enchiladas with sauce prepared from chili peppers she ground herself. While this isn't my grandma's exact recipe, it definitely has an authentic Mexican flavor and evokes plenty of nostalgia. It's delicious simply drizzled over eggs, a baked sweet potato, or chicken.

Makes approximately 2½ cups

Ingredients

- ¼ cup chili powder
- 2-3 tablespoons unsweetened cocoa powder
- 1 teaspoon garlic powder
- ½ teaspoon ground cumin
- ½ teaspoon dried oregano
- ½ teaspoon sea salt
- 2 tablespoons ghee, avocado oil, or refined coconut oil
- 2 tablespoons gluten-free all-purpose flour
- 2 cups low-sodium vegetable broth or chicken broth
- 1 cup tomato sauce or 2 tablespoons tomato paste

Preparation

1. Mix chili powder, cocoa powder, garlic powder, cumin, oregano, and salt in a small bowl. Measure out broth and tomato sauce or paste. Set aside.

2. Heat ghee or oil in a large saucepan over medium-high heat. Add flour, reduce heat to medium-low, and whisk for approximately 1 minute. Flour will become well dissolved into the oil and the mixture will be bubbly.

3. Stir in spice mixture from small bowl. Gradually stir in broth, then tomato sauce or paste. Break up any lumps using the whisk. Continue to whisk until mixture comes to a gentle boil. Reduce heat to low and simmer for 10-15 minutes, stirring occasionally.

4. Remove from heat and use immediately or transfer to a glass mason jar.

Cook's notes: Can be stored in the refrigerator for up to 2 weeks. To freeze, transfer cooled sauce to a glass mason jar, leaving 1 inch of space at the top to allow for sauce to expand. Seal with a lid and store in the freezer for 3-4 months.

Vegan adaptation: Use vegetable broth in place of chicken broth.

Nutrients: B₂, B₆, C, E, Ca, Cu, Fe, Mg, Mn, Se, Zn, Ly, Pr

MELISSA'S HOMEMADE MAYO

This indispensable mayo recipe was created by our friend, Melissa Joulwan. Most commercial mayonnaises are full of highly processed ingredients that we recommend avoiding (e.g. soybean oil), so this makes a great alternative.

Melissa is the author of the best-selling Well Fed *cookbook series and the blog www.MelJoulwan.com, where she writes about her triumphs and failures in the gym, in the kitchen, and in life. Be sure to check out her newest cookbook:* Well Fed Weeknights: Complete Paleo Meals in 45 Minutes or Less.

Makes 1½ cups

Ingredients

1 large egg

2 tablespoons fresh lemon juice

¼ cup plus 1 cup avocado oil, divided

½ teaspoon dry mustard

½ teaspoon sea salt

Preparation

1. Place the egg and the lemon juice in a blender or food processor. Put the lid on your appliance and allow the liquids to come to room temperature, about 20-30 minutes.

2. Add ¼ cup oil, dry mustard, and salt to the canister and blend on medium until the ingredients are combined. With the motor running, slowly drizzle in the remaining 1 cup oil until it's smooth and thick. Transfer the mayo to an airtight container. It can be stored in the refrigerator until the expiration date of the egg.

Cook's notes: This recipe can also be made with an immersion or stick blender. Place all ingredients in a wide-mouth, 1-pint mason jar. Insert the immersion/stick blender and blend until smooth and thickened. Transfer the mayo to an airtight container.

Nutrients: A(RET), B$_2$, B$_6$, B$_{12}$, D, SE

MAPLE ALMOND DRIZZLE

Adding almond butter to maple syrup is a simple way to reduce the glycemic effect of the syrup because of the protein and wholesome fats in the nut butter. Drizzle over pancakes, waffles, or oatmeal to increase the yum factor.

Makes 6 tablespoons

Ingredients

- ¼ cup plus 2 tablespoons pure maple syrup
- 3-4 tablespoons raw, unsalted almond butter
- ½ teaspoon almond extract (optional)
- ¼ teaspoon sea salt

Preparation

1. Whisk all ingredients together in a small bowl until well combined.

   Cook's notes: Double or triple recipe and store in the refrigerator for up to 7 days.

Nutrients: B$_2$, E, Ca, Cu, Fe, Mg, Mn, Zn

RASPBERRY ORANGE CHIA JAM

This lovely jam is so good and such a cinch to make that it's bound to become a weekly staple. It turns anything it's dolloped on into a decadent treat. Eat it with a spoon straight from the jar (like me), or spread on pancakes, waffles, and toast.

Makes 1 cup

Ingredients

1¼ cups (6 ounces) fresh raspberries

1½-2 tablespoons local honey

1 teaspoon orange zest

2 tablespoons fresh orange juice

1½ tablespoons chia seeds

Preparation

1. Add raspberries, honey, orange zest, and juice to a blender and pulse a few times to break up the berries and incorporate the liquid. The mixture should be chunky and not too liquefied, so don't over-blend.

2. Pour mixture into a jar, stir in chia seeds, and place in the refrigerator to chill for at least 30 minutes. The chia seeds will cause the jam to thicken as it chills.

Elimination/Provocation Diet adaptation:
Omit orange zest and juice. Add 1-2 tablespoons filtered water.

Nutrients: C, Ca, Mg, Mn, O3

SESAME SEAWEED SPRINKLE

This simple condiment is a great substitute for table salt and a must-have on the kitchen table for thyroid health. Make a batch to sprinkle on anything that you would like to add a little nuttiness and iodine-rich sea vegetables to. I find it goes well on sautéed greens, steamed or roasted vegetables, avocado toast, and spaghetti squash.

Makes approximately 1 cup

Ingredients

1 cup sesame seeds

2-3 tablespoons kelp granules or dulse flakes

2 teaspoons sea salt

1 teaspoon granulated garlic

Preparation

1. Toast sesame seeds in a dry skillet over medium heat for 2-3 minutes. Set aside to cool.

2. Mix kelp granules or dulse flakes, salt, and garlic together in a small bowl. Add cooled sesame seeds and mix well.

3. Transfer to a small jar with a lid and keep on your kitchen table to use daily.

Cook's notes: Double recipe and store extra in the refrigerator for up to 6 months.

Nutrients: B$_2$, B$_6$, C, CA, CU, FE, I, MG, MN, SE, ZN, GL

BRAZIL NUT "PARMESAN"

This is an easy, 4-ingredient recipe that can be used most anywhere you'd normally sprinkle Parmesan cheese. Brazil nuts deliver a dose of selenium, an important mineral that helps drive thyroid hormone production. Try it with the Lemony Kale "Parmesan" Salad from the Salads chapter.

Makes 1 cup

Ingredients

- 1 cup Brazil nuts
- ¼ cup nutritional yeast
- 1 teaspoon sea salt
- ½-1 teaspoon garlic powder

Preparation

1. Add all ingredients to the bowl of a food processor and pulse until coarsely ground.
2. Transfer mixture to a glass jar with a lid and store in the refrigerator.

Elimination/Provocation Diet adaptation:
Substitute sunflower seeds for Brazil nuts.

Nutrients: B$_6$, C, C$_A$, C$_U$, M$_G$, M$_N$, Z$_N$, G$_L$

ZA'ATAR SPICE BLEND WITH SEA KELP

This simple yet flavorful seasoning can infuse a little Eastern Mediterranean flair into your meals. Sprinkle over fish, lamb, chicken, or pork or enjoy on hummus, cooked vegetables, or salads. Kelp is a sea vegetable that can be found in a shaker bottle at most natural food stores. It provides a unique source of the trace mineral iodine, an important building block of your thyroid hormones.

Makes approximately ½ cup

Ingredients

¼ cup sesame seeds

2 tablespoons dried thyme

2 tablespoons ground sumac

½ tablespoon ground cumin

2 teaspoons kelp granules

1 teaspoon sea salt

¼ teaspoon black pepper

Preparation

1. Toast sesame seeds in a dry skillet over medium heat for 2-3 minutes. Set aside to cool.

2. Combine all ingredients together in a small bowl and stir to mix well.

3. Transfer to an airtight container and store for up to 6 months.

Cook's notes: Dulse flakes, another sea vegetable variety, can be substituted for kelp granules, if desired.

Nutrients: B$_2$, B$_6$, C, Ca, Cu, Fe, I, Mg, Mn, Se, Zn

PLANT-BASED SIDES

SIMPLE ASPARAGUS WITH LEMON WALNUT GREMOLATA

Gremolata is an Italian condiment that typically contains garlic, parsley, and lemon zest. This version incorporates walnuts to provide extra nutrition and a nutty crunch.

Serves 4-6

Ingredients

Gremolata

½ cup walnuts

½ cup finely chopped fresh flat-leaf parsley

2 cloves garlic, minced

Zest of one large lemon

Asparagus

1½ pounds asparagus, trimmed

Sea salt to taste

Black pepper to taste

1 tablespoon fresh lemon juice

1 tablespoon extra virgin olive oil

Preparation

1. Finely chop the walnuts, parsley, garlic, and lemon zest together on a cutting board, until well combined. Transfer to a bowl.

2. Steam or boil the asparagus in salted water until tender, 4-5 minutes. Remove from heat and toss with the gremolata in a serving bowl or platter. Season with salt and pepper to taste.

3. Whisk together the lemon juice and oil and drizzle over the asparagus and gremolata mixture.

AIP adaptation: Omit walnuts.

Nutrients: B₁, B₂, B₆, C, E, Cu, Fe, Mn, Se, Gl, Ly, O3

SUN-DRIED TOMATO AND BASIL SPAGHETTI SQUASH

Spaghetti squash has a tender texture and mild flavor that allows the bolder flavors it's paired with to shine through. This recipe features sun-dried tomatoes, basil, and parsley to deliver deliciousness in every bite. This dish can be enjoyed as a side or entrée. For a hearty bowl of goodness, simply stir in cooked chicken, shrimp, or chickpeas.

Serves 2 as an entrée or 4 as a side

Ingredients

1 spaghetti squash

Filtered water

½ cup pine nuts or sunflower seeds

2 tablespoons ghee or avocado oil

3-4 cloves garlic, minced

¼ cup olive oil packed sun-dried tomatoes, chopped

½ cup chopped fresh basil

½ cup chopped fresh parsley

1 teaspoon lemon zest

Fresh lemon juice to taste

Sea salt and black pepper to taste

Preparation

1. Preheat oven to 400°F.

2. Carefully cut squash in half horizontally and remove the seeds with a spoon. Place squash cut side down in a baking pan filled with ½-inch of water and bake for approximately 30-35 minutes or until fork tender. Using a spoon, loosen the squash strands and scrape away from the shell into a medium-sized bowl. Drain off any liquid.

3. Meanwhile, toast pine nuts or sunflower seeds in a dry skillet over medium heat for 3-4 minutes while stirring frequently. Be careful not to burn. Remove from heat and set aside.

4. Heat ghee or oil over medium heat in a skillet and sauté spaghetti squash strands with garlic and sun-dried tomatoes for 3-4 minutes. Add in basil, parsley, and lemon zest and sauté for 1-2 more minutes.

5. Season with a squeeze of lemon juice and salt and pepper to taste. Garnish with toasted pine nuts or sunflower seeds and serve.

AIP adaptation: Use coconut or avocado oil instead of ghee. Omit sun-dried tomatoes and pine nuts or sunflower seeds.

Nutrients: A(BETA), B₆, C, E, CA, CU, FE, MG, MN, SE, GL, LY

SPIRALIZED ZUCCHINI NOODLES

Spiralized zucchini noodles are simply made from zucchini that has been mechanically shredded and trans-formed into a noodle-like shape using a kitchen appliance called a spiralizer. These "noodles" are delicious served with the Grass-Fed Beef Quinoa Meatballs found in the Main Dishes *chapter.*

Serves 4

Ingredients

- 2 large zucchini (or summer squash)
- 2 tablespoons ghee, avocado oil, or coconut oil

Preparation

1. Slice each end off of the zucchini or summer squash, flatly. If the zucchini is large, consider cutting in half once, crosswise.

2. Align the flat cut surfaces of the zucchini onto spiralizer tongs and press snugly to secure in place. Start to slowly and gently spin the handle clockwise to spiralize the zucchini. Place zucchini noodles in a bowl and roughly trim the noodles with kitchen shears into shorter strands.

3. Heat ghee or oil in a large sauté pan. Add zucchini noodles and sauté for 2-3 minutes, until noodles are tender. Zucchini has a high water content and will become mushy when overcooked.

4. Serve with desired seasonings.

Cook's notes: An even simpler and more cost-effective approach is to use a julienne vegetable peeler to achieve noodle-like zucchini strands. Read more about the julienne peeler, spiralizer, and other kitchen gadgets in Part Two: Essential Thyroid Kitchen of this cookbook.

Vegan, Elimination/Provocation Diet, and AIP adaptations: Use avocado or coconut oil instead of ghee.

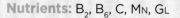

Nutrients: B$_2$, B$_6$, C, M$_N$, G$_L$

EASY GREEN BEANS WITH MUSHROOMS AND SHALLOTS

Crisp, vibrant green beans pair nicely with savory shallots and earthy mushrooms in this easy stovetop dish. It delivers the delightful flavors of a classic green bean casserole, but in a lightened variation.

Serves 4

Ingredients

½ cup raw slivered almonds

1 tablespoon olive oil or avocado oil

1 tablespoon ghee

½ cup shallots, sliced thinly

8 ounces crimini or button mushrooms, de-stemmed and sliced thinly

¼ teaspoon sea salt

⅛ teaspoon black pepper

1 pound green beans, ends trimmed

¼ cup low-sodium chicken or vegetable broth

Preparation

1. Preheat oven to 350°F. Spread almonds out on a sheet pan and place in the oven until toasted, approximately 3-4 minutes. Remove from oven and set aside.

2. Heat oil and ghee in a large skillet over medium heat. Add shallots, mushrooms, salt, and pepper. Sauté for about 6-8 minutes, until the liquid released from the mushrooms has evaporated and they begin to brown. Deglaze pan with a few tablespoons of water if mushrooms and shallots begin to stick.

3. Add green beans to the pan and spread out evenly with shallots and mushrooms. Pour broth over vegetables and cover pan. Let cook, covered, until green beans are tender, about 5-7 minutes.

4. Remove from heat, top with toasted almonds, and serve warm.

Cook's notes: Substitute ½ cup chopped onion if shallots are difficult to come by. Mushroom stems can be used for making homemade broth; clean, dry, and freeze until ready to use.

AIP and Elimination/Provocation Diet adaptations: Omit ghee and almonds.

Vegan adaptation: Omit ghee.

Nutrients: B$_2$, B$_6$, C, D, C$_A$, C$_U$, M$_G$, M$_N$, S$_E$, Z$_N$

GOLDEN CAULIFLOWER "RICE"

Cauliflower "rice" is simply made from cauliflower florets that have been ground into fine, rice-like crumbs in a food processor. It provides a lighter grain-free base to rice pilaf style dishes and is loaded with antioxidant nutrition. This recipe gets its golden color from curry powder, which contains the anti-inflammatory spice, turmeric.

Serves 2

Ingredients

- ¼ cup raw slivered almonds
- 2 cups chopped cauliflower
- 2 tablespoons ghee or coconut oil
- ½ yellow onion, chopped
- 3 cloves garlic, minced
- 2 teaspoons curry powder
- ½ teaspoon sea salt
- ¼ cup currants
- ¼ cup chopped fresh cilantro

Preparation

1. Preheat oven to 350°F. Spread almonds out on a sheet pan and place in the oven until toasted, approximately 3-4 minutes. Remove from oven and set aside.

2. Place cauliflower in the bowl of a food processor affixed with an S-blade. Pulse a few times until it's coarsely chopped and resembles the texture of rice. Set aside.

3. Heat ghee or oil in a large skillet over medium heat. Add onions and sauté for 3-4 minutes, until they begin to soften. Add garlic, cauliflower, curry powder, and salt and cook for an additional 4-5 minutes, stirring frequently.

4. Remove from heat and stir in almonds, currants, and cilantro.

Cook's notes: Use orange cauliflower in this recipe, if available, to add additional color and carotenoids. If you don't have a food processor, use the medium to large holes on a box grater to coarsely grate. Raisins can be substituted for currants, if desired.

AIP adaptation: Use coconut oil instead of ghee. Omit curry powder because it contains some spices derived from nightshades. Season with lemon or lime juice to taste.

Nutrients: B₂, B₆, C, E, Ca, Cu, Fe, Mg, Mn, Zn, Gl

ROASTED BRUSSELS SPROUTS WITH BALSAMIC DRIZZLE

Brussels sprouts are a cruciferous vegetable that possess powerful detoxifying properties. If you're in need of an easy go-to recipe so that they make a weekly appearance on your dinner plate, this is the one! Roasting to perfection brings out their natural sweetness and drizzling with little balsamic reduction amplifies their flavor to a whole new level.

Serves 4

Ingredients

Brussels Sprouts

1 pound Brussels sprouts

2 tablespoons extra virgin olive oil

2-3 cloves garlic, minced

½ teaspoon sea salt

¼ teaspoon black pepper

Balsamic Drizzle

1 cup balsamic vinegar

Preparation

1. Preheat oven to 400°F. Line a sheet pan or baking dish with parchment paper.

2. Wash and trim Brussels sprouts, then cut in half (or quarter if sprouts are large). Pat dry.

3. Toss Brussels sprouts with oil, garlic, salt, and pepper in a large bowl until well coated. Spread evenly on the sheet pan and place on middle rack in oven. Roast for 20-30 minutes, until tender and caramelized, stirring once or twice while roasting.

4. While Brussels sprouts are roasting, heat balsamic vinegar in a small, heavy-bottomed saucepan over medium heat until it begins to boil. Reduce heat to low and simmer for 15-18 minutes. Stir frequently and set timer to prevent burning. Remove pan from heat and let cool.

5. To serve, drizzle balsamic reduction over Brussels sprouts to taste.

Cook's notes: Store any remaining balsamic reduction in a tightly sealed glass container for up to a month in the refrigerator.

Nutrients: B_1, B_6, C, Ca, Cu, Mg, Mn, Se, Gl

ROASTED CAULIFLOWER AND CARROTS WITH MAPLE MISO TAHINI

Roasting cauliflower is a simple way to transform this cruciferous superstar into something addictively delicious. Carrots add contrasting color and natural sweetness. Drizzle with Maple Miso Tahini from the Condiments, Sauces, and Seasonings *chapter for the perfect flavor combination.*

Serves 4-6

Ingredients

- 1 head cauliflower, trimmed and cut into bite-sized florets
- 1 pound medium carrots, peeled and chopped
- 2 tablespoons extra virgin olive oil or avocado oil
- ½ teaspoon sea salt
- ¼ teaspoon black pepper
- Maple Miso Tahini from the *Condiments, Sauces, and Seasonings* chapter

Preparation

1. Preheat oven to 400°F. Line a large sheet pan with parchment paper.
2. Toss chopped cauliflower and carrots in oil with salt and pepper until well coated. Spread on sheet pan and place in oven for 30-35 minutes.
3. While cauliflower and carrots are roasting, make the Maple Miso Tahini.
4. Serve roasted carrots and cauliflower with a drizzle of Maple Miso Tahini.

Cook's notes: Use orange cauliflower in this recipe, if available, to add additional color and carotenoids.

AIP and Elimination/Provocation Diet adaptations: Omit Maple Miso Tahini sauce.

Nutrients: A(BETA), B$_6$, C, E, Mn, Gl, Ly

ORANGE GINGER MASHED BUTTERNUT SQUASH

This comforting recipe is a great change of pace for a healthy, yet flavorful side dish. The citrus adds brightness while warming ginger helps to soothe the digestive tract.

Serves 4

Ingredients

- 1 butternut squash (approximately 2-2½ pounds), peeled and cut into large chunks
- ¼ cup pure maple syrup
- 2 teaspoons orange zest
- ¼ cup plus 2 tablespoons fresh orange juice
- ¾ teaspoon fresh lemon juice
- 1 teaspoon freshly grated ginger
- ½ teaspoon ground cinnamon
- ¼ cup coconut butter (manna) or coconut oil
- Sea salt, to taste

Preparation

1. Place butternut squash in a large pot. Cover with water and boil for 20 minutes or until tender. Drain thoroughly and set aside.

2. Combine the maple syrup, orange zest, orange juice, lemon juice, ginger, cinnamon, and coconut butter or oil in a saucepan. Bring the mixture to a quick boil over high heat, being careful not to burn. Quickly lower to a simmer and cook about 2-3 minutes or until syrupy. Remove pan from heat.

3. Place drained butternut squash in a large bowl and pour orange mixture over the top. Mash together with a potato masher and season with salt. If a creamier texture is desired, transfer mixture to a food processor and pulse until smooth.

Cook's notes: Substitute peeled sweet potatoes for butternut squash, if desired.

AIP adaptation: Reduce the amount of maple syrup to 2 tablespoons or omit completely.

Elimination/Provocation Diet adaptation: Omit orange zest, orange juice, and lemon juice.

Nutrients: A(BETA), B₆, C, E, Mɴ, Gʟ

BASIC ROASTED WINTER SQUASH

Winter squash comes in several varieties: butternut, buttercup, acorn, delicata, kabocha, pumpkin, and spaghetti squash. It's a great cold weather pantry staple because it can be stored up to a few months and provides the body with an important source of immune-supportive carotenoids during cold and flu season.

Serves 4-6

Ingredients

1 winter squash

Filtered water

Sea salt and black pepper to taste

Preparation

1. Preheat oven to 400°F.
2. Carefully cut squash in half and remove the seeds with a spoon.
3. Place squash cut side down in a baking pan filled with ½-inch of water.
4. Bake for approximately 40 minutes or until brown. It's ready when it can easily be pierced by a fork.
5. Serve in the shell or scoop out.

Cook's notes: Roasted winter squash stores well and is great to batch cook for an easy, ready-to-eat complex carbohydrate later in the week. It is versatile enough to include in omelets or frittatas, tossed salads, or soups. You can also simply reheat it and enjoy as a side dish. It can be stored in the refrigerator for up to 5 days.

Nutrients: A(BETA), B$_6$, C, E, MN, GL

MAPLE ROASTED ACORN SQUASH

This is a quintessential autumn or winter side dish that's fairly effortless to prepare. These beautiful wedges make an eye-appealing side dish or salad topper.

Serves 4

Ingredients

1 acorn squash

2 tablespoons melted ghee or coconut oil

2-3 tablespoons pure maple syrup

1 teaspoon sea salt

¼ teaspoon black pepper

1-2 teaspoons ground cinnamon

Preparation

1. Preheat oven to 425°F. Line a large baking sheet with parchment paper.

2. Cut the acorn squash in half and scoop out the seeds with a spoon. Place cut side down on a cutting board and slice the squash into ½-inch thick half-moons. Toss in a large bowl with ghee or oil, maple syrup, salt, and pepper, making sure there is enough to thoroughly coat.

3. Spread out in a single layer on the baking sheet and sprinkle with cinnamon. Roast for 35-40 minutes, flipping halfway through, until the squash is fully cooked and lightly browned on top.

Cook's notes: The skin is edible and a great source of additional nutrients, but can be easily trimmed away after roasting, if desired.

Vegan, AIP, and Elimination/Provocation Diet adaptations: Use coconut oil in place of ghee.

Nutrients: A(BETA), B$_6$, C, E, MN, GL

GARLICKY ASIAN SWISS CHARD WITH SESAME SEAWEED SPRINKLE

Dark greens, such as Swiss chard, are among the most nutrient-dense foods we can eat. Greens are powerful blood purifiers and liver detoxifiers, making them an important everyday superfood. This simple recipe will quickly become a go-to for enjoying Swiss chard or other dark green leafy vegetables like kale.

Serves 2-3

Ingredients

- 1 bunch or approximately 6-8 leaves of Swiss chard
- 2 tablespoons coconut oil or ghee
- 4-6 cloves garlic, minced
- 1 tablespoon reduced sodium tamari soy sauce or coconut aminos
- 2 teaspoons brown rice vinegar
- 2 tablespoons Sesame Seaweed Sprinkle from the *Condiments, Sauces, and Seasonings* chapter

Preparation

1. Separate the stem of the chard from the leafy portion, thinly slice, and set aside. Bisect the leaves in half, then stack, tightly roll together, and chop into 1-inch pieces.

2. Heat oil or ghee in a medium-sized sauté pan over medium-high heat and sauté sliced stems with garlic for 2 minutes.

3. Add chopped leaves and sauté for 3-4 minutes until they become wilted and vibrant green.

4. Turn off heat and season with tamari or coconut aminos and brown rice vinegar.

5. Plate and garnish with Sesame Seaweed Sprinkle.

Cook's notes: Kale, collards, bok choy, beet greens, mustard greens, or turnip greens can be substituted for Swiss chard, if desired. Discard stems if using kale or collards.

Vegan adaptation: Use coconut oil instead of ghee.

Paleo adaptation: Substitute soy sauce with coconut aminos.

Elimination/Provocation Diet adaptation: Use coconut oil instead of ghee and coconut aminos instead of soy sauce.

Nutrients: A(BETA), B$_2$, B$_6$, C, E, CA, CU, FE, MG, MN, SE, GL

ROASTED ROOT VEGETABLE MEDLEY

Roasting vegetables deepens their flavor and draws out their natural sweetness. Double this recipe for leftovers that you can incorporate into your meals throughout the week.

Serves 4-6

Ingredients

2 pounds of any root vegetables (sweet potatoes, yams, carrots, parsnips, turnips, rutabagas, beets)

1 medium onion, peeled and cut into thin wedges

1 head garlic, separated into cloves and peeled

2 tablespoons extra virgin olive oil or melted coconut oil

Chopped fresh herbs like rosemary, thyme, or sage (optional)

Sea salt and black pepper to taste

Preparation

1. Preheat oven to 400°F.

2. Toss the root vegetables, onion, and garlic with oil, herbs, salt, and pepper and spread evenly on a roasting pan. Avoid crowding the vegetables to allow for even cooking.

3. Roast for 45-50 minutes, stirring about halfway through.

Cook's notes: With the exception of beets, leave the peel on your vegetables to retain some additional fiber, B vitamins, and minerals.

Nutrients: B$_6$, C, C$_A$, C$_U$, M$_G$, M$_N$, S$_E$

SOUPS AND STEWS

FORTIFYING CHICKEN BONE BROTH

Not only is bone broth an amazing way to load up on gut-healing nutrients like collagen, it's a great way to use up leftover chicken bones from whole roasted chickens – just freeze the bones along with your vegetable scraps until you're ready to make the broth. Add the sea vegetable, kombu, for extra trace minerals like iodine.

Makes approximately 3 quarts

Ingredients

2 pounds chicken bones (approximately two carcasses)

1 onion, rough chopped

1 head garlic, sliced open horizontally

2 carrots, rough chopped

2 stalks celery, rough chopped

1-2 tablespoons apple cider vinegar

1 bunch fresh parsley

1 tablespoon sea salt

1 teaspoon black peppercorns

1 bay leaf

1 (4-inch) strip of kombu (optional)

12 cups filtered water

Preparation

1. Place chicken bones, vegetables, vinegar, parsley, spices, and kombu (if using) in a large stockpot.

2. Fill pot with water and bring to a boil. Reduce heat and simmer on low heat for 24 hours.

3. Remove from heat and let cool. To strain broth, place a fine mesh strainer over a large pot or bowl and carefully pour contents of stockpot over strainer. Transfer broth into quart-sized mason jars and seal with a lid.

Cook's notes: If planning to freeze any of the broth, carefully pour into a quart-sized mason jar, leaving 2 inches of space at the top, as broth will expand as it freezes.

Nutrients: A(BETA), B$_6$, C, E, Ca, Cu, Mg, Mn, Se, Gl, Ly

HUG IN A MUG

When you're low on energy or not feeling well, this soothing soup will feel like a warm hug. I've made this many times for my husband when he's had a cold and now he returns the favor. Make this for yourself or a loved one when in need of a nourishing boost.

Serves 2

Ingredients

16 ounces chicken, lamb, or
beef bone broth

3-4 cloves garlic, finely minced

2 scallions, sliced thinly

2 teaspoons fresh ginger, finely grated

2 teaspoons fresh turmeric, finely
grated or ½ teaspoon dried turmeric

1-1½ tablespoons miso paste, divided

Sea salt and black pepper to taste

Squeeze of lemon

Preparation

1. Gently simmer bone broth with garlic, scallions, ginger, and turmeric for 5 minutes.

2. Place ½ to ¾ tablespoon of miso in the bottom of two mugs, 10-12 ounces in size. Pour a small amount of the broth mixture into each mug and stir to dissolve miso paste. Once miso is well dissolved, top off mug with the rest of the broth mixture.

3. Add salt and pepper to taste and brighten with a squeeze of lemon.

Cook's notes: If you're seeking a shortcut for homemade bone broth, you can use a pre-made store-bought version. Just make sure it says "bone broth." When comparing bone broth to other types of broth, you'll notice that bone broth is significantly higher in protein.

Vegan adaptation: Substitute low-sodium vegetable broth for bone broth.

AIP adaptation: Omit miso paste.

Elimination/Provocation Diet adaptation: Omit miso paste and lemon juice.

Nutrients: B$_6$, C, C$_A$, C$_U$, M$_G$, M$_N$, S$_E$

MOROCCAN CHICKPEA AND VEGETABLE STEW

This flavorful stew is seasoned with a prized Moroccan spice blend called Ras el Hanout. It creates a well-balanced curry-like flavor that's anti-inflammatory, warming, and slightly sweet. You may be able to find this blend at Whole Foods or Williams Sonoma, or you can make your own spice blend using recipe on next page.

Serves 6

Ingredients

2 tablespoons ghee or coconut oil

1 onion, diced

3 cloves garlic, minced

1 tablespoon freshly grated ginger

2 carrots, chopped

2 celery stalks, chopped

1½ cups cauliflower, chopped

4 cups low-sodium vegetable or chicken broth

1 (15-ounce) can coconut milk

1-2 cups filtered water

1 cup dry quinoa, rinsed

2-3 tablespoons Ras el Hanout (see next recipe)

1 (15-ounce) can chickpeas, drained and rinsed

Sea salt and black pepper

3 cups chopped Swiss chard

Toasted coconut (optional)

Fresh cilantro (optional)

Preparation

1. In a large soup pot, heat ghee or oil over medium heat and sauté onion, garlic, ginger, carrots, celery, and cauliflower for 5-6 minutes.

2. Add broth, coconut milk, water, quinoa, and Ras el Hanout and bring to a simmer. Simmer for 15 minutes to allow quinoa to cook thoroughly.

3. Add chickpeas and cook for an additional 2-3 minutes to allow chickpeas to warm. Season with salt and pepper.

4. To serve, place about ½ cup of chopped Swiss chard on the bottom of each soup bowl and cover with soup. Stir well to allow chard to wilt. Garnish with toasted coconut or fresh cilantro, if desired.

Cook's notes: Use orange cauliflower in this recipe, if available, to add additional color and carotenoids. To make your own Ras el Hanout spice blend, see recipe on next page.

Paleo adaptation: Omit quinoa and chickpeas. Add cooked chicken (optional).

Elimination/Provocation Diet adaptation: Use nightshade-free adaptation of spice blend on next page.

Nutrients: A(beta), B_2, B_6, C, E, Ca, Cu, Fe, Mg, Mn, Se, Zn, Ly

RAS EL HANOUT SPICE BLEND

The name of this prized Moroccan spice blend implies that it's "top-shelf" or the best a spice seller has to offer. It's not a fiery hot blend, but it is warming in flavor. The cinnamon, cloves, and nutmeg also add pleasing sweet notes.

Makes 3 tablespoons

Ingredients

2 teaspoons ground cumin

1 teaspoon ground coriander

1 teaspoon ground ginger

1 teaspoon ground turmeric

1 teaspoon sea salt

1 teaspoon ground cinnamon

¾ teaspoon paprika

¾ teaspoon black pepper

½ teaspoon cardamom powder

½ teaspoon ground allspice

¼ teaspoon ground nutmeg

¼ teaspoon ground cloves

½ teaspoon cayenne pepper (optional)

Preparation

1. Combine spices and stir until well mixed.

Cook's note: Double or triple recipe to keep on hand for marinades, as a rub for chicken, fish, or lamb, and as a seasoning for stews.

Elimination/Provocation Diet adaptation: Omit paprika and cayenne pepper.

SUPER IMMUNITY SOUP

This is a great soup to make whenever you're in need of an immune-boosting kick. Astragalus root is an optional ingredient that can typically be found at stores where herbal medicines are sold; add for its deep immune-supportive properties, if desired.

Serves 4-6

Ingredients

- 2 tablespoons ghee or coconut oil
- 1 yellow onion, chopped
- 5 cloves garlic, minced
- 2 tablespoons freshly grated ginger
- 3 celery stalks, diced
- 2 carrots, diced
- ¾ teaspoon sea salt plus more to taste
- 2 chicken breasts, chopped
- 4 cups chicken bone broth
- 1-2 cups filtered water
- 1 cup chopped cauliflower
- 1 bay leaf
- ⅛-¼ teaspoon cayenne pepper
- 1 slice of astragalus root (optional)
- 1-2 tablespoons fresh lemon juice
- Black pepper to taste
- 2-3 cups finely chopped greens (spinach, kale, chard)

Preparation

1. In a large stockpot, heat ghee or oil over medium heat and sauté onion, garlic, ginger, celery, carrots, and ¾ teaspoon salt for 3-4 minutes. Add chicken and continue to sauté for an additional 3-4 minutes, until chicken becomes mostly opaque.

2. Add broth, water, cauliflower, bay leaf, cayenne, and optional astragalus. Simmer for 10-20 minutes. Turn off heat and remove bay leaf and astragalus. Stir in lemon juice and add salt and pepper to taste.

3. To serve, place ⅓-½ cup of finely chopped greens in the bottom of each soup bowl and cover with a ladleful of soup. Stir well to help greens wilt.

Cook's notes: Use orange cauliflower in this recipe, if available, to add additional color and carotenoids.

Vegan adaptation: Use coconut oil instead of ghee. Substitute low-sodium vegetable broth for chicken bone broth. Add 1 can drained and rinsed chickpeas in step 2 in place of chicken breast.

AIP adaptation: Omit cayenne.

Elimination/Provocation Diet adaptation: Omit cayenne and lemon juice.

Nutrients: A(BETA), B$_1$, B$_2$, B$_6$, B$_{12}$, C, D, E, CA, CU, MG, MN, SE, GL, LY, TY

SENSATIONAL SEAFOOD STEW

This delicious stew delivers as much nutrition as it does flavor. Seafood is among the richest food source of trace minerals like iodine and zinc, which are more difficult to get from land-based foods.

Serves 6

Ingredients

- 2 tablespoons ghee or avocado oil
- 1 medium onion, chopped
- 1 fennel bulb, sliced thinly
- 2 small red potatoes, diced
- 4 cloves garlic, minced
- 1½ teaspoons dried thyme
- 1 teaspoon sea salt
- ¼ teaspoon red pepper flakes
- 1 bay leaf
- 1 (28-ounce) can crushed tomatoes in juice
- ¼ cup tomato paste
- 2 cups filtered water
- 1 cup dry white wine
- 1 (8-ounce) bottle clam juice
- 1 pound skinless cod or halibut, cut into 1-inch chunks
- ¾ pound mussels, scrubbed and de-bearded
- 1 pound uncooked large shrimp, peeled and deveined

Preparation

1. Heat ghee or oil in a large soup pot over medium heat. Add onion and fennel and sauté about 5 minutes, until onion is translucent. Stir in red potatoes, garlic, thyme, salt, and red pepper flakes and sauté for 2 more minutes.

2. Add the bay leaf, crushed tomatoes with their juices, tomato paste, water, wine, and clam juice. Cover and bring to a gentle boil. Reduce heat to medium-low, keep covered, and simmer for at least 20 minutes to allow flavors to blend and potatoes to cook through.

3. Add cod or halibut, mussels, and shrimp and allow seafood to cook over a gentle simmer for 5-6 minutes. Mussels will be opened wide, cod will be cooked through, and shrimp will be curled into a C-shape.

4. Before serving, discard bay leaf and any mussels that have not opened.

Cook's notes: Broth can cook longer at the end of step 2, if desired, but wait to proceed to step 3 until 5-6 minutes before serving to prevent overcooking seafood.

Nutrients: A(RET), B$_2$, B$_6$, B$_{12}$, C, E, CA, CU, FE, I, MG, MN, SE, ZN, O3, GL, LY, TY

GINGER MISO RAMEN WITH WAKAME

This Asian-inspired recipe is a veggie- and noodle-rich version of miso soup. Its savory warmth will provide you with comforting nourishment.

Serves 4-6

Ingredients

- 1 bunch baby bok choy
- 4 cups low-sodium chicken or vegetable broth
- 2 cups filtered water
- 4-6 cloves garlic, minced
- 1-2 tablespoons finely chopped ginger
- 1-2 carrots, julienned
- 4-6 green onions, sliced thinly
- 2 tablespoons dried wakame
- 1 (10-ounce) package gluten-free ramen noodles
- 3-4 tablespoons miso, or more to taste
- 1 tablespoon reduced sodium tamari soy sauce or coconut aminos (optional)
- 2 teaspoons brown rice vinegar (optional)

Preparation

1. Separate bok choy stems from leaves. Chop stems and leaves separately. Set aside.

2. Place broth and water in a large soup pot and bring to a low simmer. Add chopped bok choy stems, garlic, ginger, carrots, green onions, wakame, and gluten-free ramen noodles. Cook for another 4-5 minutes, until noodles are done.

3. Place miso in a small bowl and add some warmed broth. Whisk until smooth, then transfer mixture into soup pot along with bok choy leaves. Stir well.

4. Taste and add more miso and/or soy sauce and rice vinegar, if desired. Serve warm.

Cook's notes: For a soy-free variation, select chickpea miso and substitute coconut aminos for soy sauce.

Vegan adaptation: Use vegetable broth instead of chicken broth.

Paleo and AIP adaptation: Omit miso. Substitute ramen noodles with spiralized zucchini noodles and soy sauce with coconut aminos.

Elimination/Provocation Diet adaptation: Omit miso. Substitute soy sauce with coconut aminos.

Nutrients: A(BETA), B₂, B₆, C, E, CA, CU, FE, I, MG, MN, SE, ZN, GL, LY, PR

SOUTHWEST BLACK BEAN, SWEET POTATO, AND AMARANTH STEW

Southwestern vegetables and seasonings come together in this flavorful, plant-powered dish. Amaranth is a tiny, power-packed gluten-free whole grain with a remarkable nutrition profile that's very easy to sprinkle into soups and stews.

Serves 4

Ingredients

2 tablespoons ghee or avocado oil

1 yellow onion, chopped

2 celery stalks, chopped

3 cloves garlic, minced

1 medium sweet potato, diced

1 medium zucchini or yellow squash, chopped

1 medium poblano pepper, diced

2 teaspoons ground cumin

1½ teaspoons ground coriander

1 teaspoon sea salt

⅛ teaspoon cayenne pepper

4 cups low-sodium chicken or vegetable broth

1-2 cups filtered water

1 (15-ounce) can black beans, drained and rinsed

⅓ cup amaranth

Suggested toppings

Radish

Cilantro

Lime Juice

Preparation

1. Heat ghee or oil in a large soup pot over medium heat. Add the onion and sauté for 5 minutes, until softened and translucent. Add celery, garlic, sweet potato, zucchini, poblano pepper, cumin, coriander, salt, cayenne pepper, and 1 cup of broth. Sauté for 3 to 4 more minutes.

2. Add the remaining broth and water to cover vegetables. Stir in black beans and amaranth. Cover and simmer for 15 minutes.

3. Ladle into a bowl and top with thinly sliced radish, cilantro, and a squeeze of lime.

Cook's notes: Quinoa can be substituted for amaranth, if desired.

Elimination/Provocation Diet adaptation: Omit poblano pepper, cayenne, and lime juice.

Nutrients: B₂, B₆, C, Ca, Cu, Fe, Mg, Mn, Se, Zn, Gl

TUSCAN WHITE BEAN AND QUINOA MINESTRONE

This light soup features quinoa in place of pasta for a delicious gluten-free variation. Fennel bulb adds an aromatic sweetness as well as some digestive easing properties.

Serves 6-8

Ingredients

2 tablespoons ghee or avocado oil

1 large onion, chopped

4 cloves garlic, minced

3 celery stalks, chopped

3 carrots, chopped

1 small fennel bulb, chopped

2 teaspoons dried basil

1 teaspoon dried oregano

4 cups low-sodium chicken or
   vegetable broth

2 cups filtered water

1 (28-ounce) can diced tomatoes

3-4 tablespoons tomato paste

1 cup dry quinoa, rinsed

2 (15-ounce) cans cannellini beans,
   drained and rinsed

Sea salt and black pepper to taste

½ cup chopped fresh parsley

Preparation

1. Heat ghee or oil in a large soup pot over medium heat. Add the onion, garlic, celery, carrots, fennel, basil, and oregano. Sauté for 5 minutes until softened and translucent.

2. Add broth, water, diced tomatoes, tomato paste, and quinoa and bring to a boil. Lower to a simmer and cook for 15 minutes. Add cannellini beans during the last 5 minutes of cooking. Season with salt and pepper to taste.

3. Serve warm, garnished with chopped parsley.

Vegan adaptation: Use oil in place of ghee and vegetable broth instead of chicken broth.

Nutrients: A(BETA), B_6, C, E, CA, CU, FE, MG, MN, SE, ZN, LY

GRASS-FED BEEF, RED BEAN, AND QUINOA CHILI

This hearty chili is great on its own, balanced with a salad, or served over a baked sweet potato for an even heartier meal. Grass-fed beef is nutritionally superior to grain-finished beef and the quinoa adds an additional healthful twist.

Serves 6

Ingredients

- 1 tablespoon ghee or avocado oil
- 1 medium yellow or white onion, diced
- 2 cloves garlic, minced
- 1 pound 90% lean ground grass-fed beef
- 2 tablespoons chili powder
- 1 tablespoon ground cumin
- 1½ teaspoons sea salt
- ½ teaspoon ground cinnamon
- 1 (14.5-ounce) can diced tomatoes
- 1 (15-ounce) can tomato sauce
- ½ cup dry quinoa, rinsed and drained
- 1 cup filtered water, plus more to thin, if desired
- 2 (15-ounce) cans no salt added kidney beans, drained and rinsed
- 1 cup frozen organic corn (optional)

Preparation

1. Heat ghee or oil over medium heat in a large heavy pot. Sauté the onion and garlic for 3-4 minutes, until onion is translucent.

2. Add the beef, salt, and spices. Using a wooden spoon or spatula, work to break up beef into smaller pieces and continue to sauté an additional 3-4 minutes, until browned.

3. Stir in tomatoes, tomato sauce, quinoa, water, beans, and optional corn. Cover and simmer for 15-20 minutes. The chili will thicken as it cooks. Thin with additional water if desired.

Cook's notes: Grass-finished bison or organic ground turkey can be substituted for beef.

Nutrients: B_2, B_6, B_{12}, C, E, Ca, Cu, Fe, Mg, Mn, Se, Zn, Ly, Gl, O3, Ty

30 min

CURRIED COCONUT RED LENTIL STEW WITH WILTED GREENS

Red lentils tend to lose their shape and become comfortingly creamy when fully cooked. Their neutral flavor makes them a blank palette for absorbing whatever delicious seasonings you choose. This hearty stew relies on curry powder for some exotic flavor and anti-inflammatory properties.

Serves 6

Ingredients

- 2 tablespoons ghee, coconut oil, or avocado oil
- 1 yellow onion, chopped
- 2 tablespoons minced garlic
- 1 tablespoon freshly grated ginger
- 1 tablespoon curry powder
- 2 teaspoons ground cumin
- 1 (14.5-ounce) can fire-roasted diced tomatoes
- 1¾ cups red lentils
- 1 quart low-sodium vegetable or chicken broth
- 1 can coconut milk
- 1 teaspoon sea salt
- ¼ teaspoon black pepper
- 3 cups finely chopped kale, spinach, collards, or Swiss chard

Preparation

1. Heat ghee or oil over medium heat in a large stockpot. Sauté onion for 3 minutes, until it begins to soften. Add garlic, ginger, and spices and sauté for an additional 2-3 minutes. If ingredients begin to stick to the pan, use a few tablespoons of water or broth to deglaze.

2. Add tomatoes, red lentils, broth, and coconut milk. Simmer for 25-30 minutes, until lentils are fully cooked.

3. Season with salt and pepper. It's important to wait until lentils are fully cooked to add salt, otherwise salting early can harden the lentils and keep them from cooking properly.

4. Optional: Using an immersion blender, puree soup to desired consistency. Or carefully transfer a few ladles of the soup to a blender and puree. Stir the pureed portion back into the soup pot.

Nutrients: A(BETA), B$_6$, C, CA, CU, FE, MG, MN, SE, GL, LY

5. When ready to serve, place approximately ½ cup finely chopped greens at the bottom of each soup bowl and pour soup over greens. Stir to allow greens to disperse evenly throughout and give them time to wilt before eating.

Cook's notes: This soup freezes well, but don't add the greens until you're ready to thaw and reheat. To freeze, cool soup completely before transferring into a glass mason jar. Fill the jar, leaving approximately 2 inches of space at the top to allow the soup to expand while cooling.

Vegan adaptation: Use oil in place of ghee and vegetable broth instead of chicken broth.

ROASTED BELL PEPPER AND TOMATO SOUP

This soup is a flavorful fusion that is perfect to enjoy year-round. Roasting the peppers and tomatoes delightfully deepens and sweetens their flavor. The soup's creamy texture is accomplished by incorporating a handful of raw cashews in place of heavy cream.

Serves 4-6

Ingredients

¼ cup raw cashews, soaked 1-2 hours

1 yellow onion, chopped

4 cloves garlic

4 medium vine-ripened tomatoes, stemmed, seeded, and chopped

2 large red bell peppers, stemmed, seeded, and chopped

1 medium carrot, peeled and rough chopped

2-3 tablespoons extra virgin olive oil

1¼ teaspoons sea salt plus more to taste

¼ teaspoon black pepper plus more to taste

3-4 cups low-sodium vegetable broth

3 tablespoons tomato paste

⅛ teaspoon cayenne pepper (optional)

2 teaspoons nutritional yeast (optional)

Preparation

1. Preheat oven to 400°F.

2. Toss all vegetables with oil, salt, and pepper and spread evenly on a large rimmed sheet pan lined with parchment paper. Use two sheet pans, if necessary, to avoid crowding. Place in the oven and roast for 30-40 minutes.

3. Once vegetables are done roasting, heat vegetable broth, tomato paste, cashews, optional cayenne, and nutritional yeast in a large soup pot over medium-high heat. Carefully transfer the roasted vegetables into the pot and simmer for 5 minutes.

4. Puree the soup in the pot using an immersion blender or carefully transfer to a blender and puree a few cups at a time, until smooth and creamy. If a thinner consistency is desired, add water or additional broth a little at a time. Season with additional salt and pepper to taste.

Cook's notes: This soup freezes well. To freeze, be sure to cool soup completely before transferring into a glass mason jar. Fill the jar, leaving approximately 2 inches of space at the top to allow the soup to expand while cooling.

Nutrients: A(BETA), B$_6$, C, E, CA, CU, FE, MG, MN, ZN, GL, LY

CREAMY BROCCOLI SOUP

This creamy and delicious soup won't have you missing the dairy that's typically used to achieve richness in cream-based soups. It gets its luscious creaminess from the nutritious combination of Yukon gold potatoes and raw cashews.

Serves 4-6

Ingredients

2 tablespoons ghee or avocado oil

1 large onion, chopped

2-3 cloves garlic, minced

2 medium Yukon gold potatoes, chopped

1½ pounds broccoli, chopped

4 cups low-sodium chicken or vegetable broth

⅓ cup raw cashews

1½ tablespoons nutritional yeast (optional)

½ teaspoon ground nutmeg

⅛ teaspoon red pepper flakes

1-2 cups filtered water

1½ teaspoons sea salt

¾ teaspoon black pepper

Preparation

1. Heat ghee or oil in a large soup pot over medium heat. Add the onion and sauté for 5 minutes, until softened and translucent. Add garlic, potatoes, broccoli, and 1 cup of the broth. Sauté for 3-4 more minutes, then add remaining broth, cashews, optional nutritional yeast, nutmeg, and red pepper flakes. Add 1-2 cups of water, as needed, to ensure vegetables are completely covered. Cover pot and simmer for 15-20 minutes, until potatoes, broccoli, and cashews are tender.

2. Use an immersion blender to puree soup in the pot. Or carefully transfer soup to a blender and puree in batches. Pour soup back into the pot. Season with salt and pepper before serving.

Vegan adaptation: Use oil in place of ghee and vegetable broth instead of chicken broth.

Nutrients: B₂, B₆, C, E, Cₐ, Cᵤ, Fₑ, I, Mɢ, Mɴ, Zɴ, Gʟ

SALADS

ASIAN FORBIDDEN RICE SALAD WITH MANGO AND JICAMA

Forbidden rice is an unusual black rice that contains the richest amount of disease-fighting antioxidants than any other rice. It cooks up faster than brown rice and has a slightly nutty flavor that pairs well with creamy mango, crisp jicama, and an irresistible toasted sesame vinaigrette.

Serves 6

Ingredients

Salad

½ cup raw cashews

2 cups filtered water

½ teaspoon sea salt

1 cup forbidden rice

2 fresh mangos, diced

1 small jicama, peeled and diced

1 red bell pepper, diced

¼ cup chopped fresh cilantro

¼ cup chopped fresh mint

1 lime, cut into wedges

Dressing (Makes almost ½ cup)

3 tablespoons brown rice vinegar

1½ tablespoons toasted sesame oil

1½ tablespoons pure maple syrup

1 tablespoon reduced sodium tamari soy sauce or coconut aminos

Preparation

1. Preheat oven to 350°F. Spread cashews out on a sheet pan and place in the oven until toasted, approximately 6-8 minutes. Remove from oven and set aside.

2. Combine water, salt, and rice in medium-sized saucepan. Bring to a boil, then lower heat to medium and simmer for 35-40 minutes, until all liquid has been absorbed. Fluff the rice with a fork, then spread evenly on a parchment lined sheet pan and allow to cool.

3. Combine dressing ingredients together in a small bowl. Set aside.

4. When rice has cooled to the touch, transfer to a large bowl and combine with mango, jicama, bell pepper, cilantro, and mint. Add dressing to taste and toss until well-coated.

5. Garnish with toasted cashews and serve with lime wedges.

Cook's notes: Substitute soy sauce with coconut aminos for soy-free variation.

Nutrients: B_6, C, E, Cu, Fe, Mg, Mn, Se, Zn, Ly

SPINACH, STRAWBERRY, AND ASPARAGUS SALAD WITH LEMON POPPYSEED VINAIGRETTE

Tender spinach, sweet strawberries, and crisp asparagus blend well with a sweet and tangy vinaigrette in this classic salad. It's perfect for taking to a party.

Serves 4

Ingredients

Salad

¾ cup pecans

5-6 asparagus stalks

6-8 cups baby spinach

2 cups organic strawberries, sliced

2 cooked chicken breasts, sliced thinly (optional)

Lemon Poppyseed Vinaigrette (Makes ⅔ cup)

¼ cup extra virgin olive oil

¼ cup apple cider vinegar or champagne vinegar

Zest of 1 lemon

3 tablespoons fresh lemon juice

1½ tablespoons local honey or pure maple syrup

1 teaspoon poppyseeds

¼ teaspoon sea salt

Dash of black pepper

Preparation

1. Preheat oven to 350°F.

2. Spread pecans out on a cookie sheet and toast for 6-8 minutes. Be sure to set a timer so the pecans don't burn.

3. Trim woody end from each asparagus spear and using a vegetable peeler (preferably a Y-shaped peeler), shave spears into thin ribbons. Alternately, cut into ½-inch pieces.

4. Toss baby spinach, strawberries, optional chicken, asparagus, and pecans together in a large bowl.

5. Prepare dressing by whisking ingredients together in a small bowl.

6. Toss salad with enough dressing to lightly coat spinach. Add more to taste.

Cook's notes: Store remaining dressing in the refrigerator for up to 2 weeks.

Vegan adaptation: Omit chicken.

AIP adaptation: Omit poppyseeds and pecans.

Nutrients: A(BETA), B₁, B₂, B₆, C, E, CA, CU, FE, MG, MN, ZN, GL, LY

MANGO AVOCADO CHICKEN SALAD

This jazzed up chicken salad takes on a tropical twist. Leftover Easy Oven-Baked Chicken from the Main Dishes *chapter is great in this dish. Serve with a lettuce wrap, over a bed of salad greens with a balsamic vinaigrette, or with gluten-free crackers.*

Serves 2

Ingredients

¼ cup raw slivered almonds

1 tablespoon extra virgin olive oil

3 tablespoons fresh lime juice

1 (4-ounce) cooked chicken breast, diced

1 mango, diced

1 avocado, diced

1 red bell pepper, diced

¼ cup chopped fresh cilantro or parsley

½ teaspoon sea salt

Preparation

1. Preheat oven to 350°F. Spread almonds out on a sheet pan and place in the oven until toasted, approximately 3-4 minutes. Remove from oven and set aside.

2. In a medium-sized bowl, whisk the olive oil and lime juice together.

3. Add diced chicken, mango, avocado, bell pepper, cilantro or parsley, almonds, and salt and toss gently.

4. May be kept in the refrigerator for 1-2 days, but it's best enjoyed immediately due to rapid browning of avocado.

Vegan adaptation: Substitute 1 cup no salt added canned black beans (drained and rinsed) for chicken.

AIP adaptation: Omit red bell pepper and almonds. Add diced jicama, if desired.

Nutrients: B$_2$, B$_6$, B$_{12}$, C, D, E, C$_A$, C$_U$, F$_E$, M$_G$, M$_N$, S$_E$, Z$_N$, G$_L$, L$_Y$, T$_Y$

EARTH AND SEA SALAD WITH ROASTED SHRIMP AND TOASTED SESAME VINAIGRETTE

This salad beautifully combines nutrient-dense ingredients from the land and sea. The deeply flavorful toasted sesame dressing perfectly marries everything together into a delicious dish.

Serves 4

Ingredients

Toasted Sesame Dressing/Marinade
(Makes approximately 1 cup)

- ¼ cup plus 2 tablespoons brown rice vinegar
- 2 tablespoons reduced sodium tamari soy sauce or coconut aminos
- 3 tablespoons toasted sesame oil
- 3 tablespoons pure maple syrup
- Zest of 1 lime
- 2 limes, juiced (approximately 4 tablespoons)
- 1-2 tablespoons chickpea miso (optional)
- Dash of Sriracha or hot pepper sauce to taste (optional)

Shrimp

- 1 pound medium-sized (17-21 count) raw shrimp, peeled and deveined
- ¼ cup Toasted Sesame Dressing/Marinade
- ¾ teaspoon sea salt
- ¼ teaspoon black pepper

Salad

- 2 teaspoons arame (sea vegetable)
- ½ cup toasted cashews
- 3 cups micro greens and/or watercress
- 3 cups spinach, spring mix, or baby kale
- 4 radishes, sliced thinly
- 2 carrots, shredded

Nutrients: A(BETA), A(RET), B₁, B₂, B₆, B₁₂, C, E, CA, CU, FE, I, MG, MN, SE, ZN, GL, TY

Preparation

1. Preheat oven to 400°F.

2. For the marinade, whisk vinegar, soy sauce, oil, maple syrup, lime zest and juice, and optional chickpea miso and Sriracha together in a small bowl until well combined. Set aside.

3. Place shrimp in a small bowl. Measure approximately ¼ cup of dressing/marinade and pour over shrimp. Add salt and pepper and toss until well-coated. Allow to marinate for 5-10 minutes. Set aside the remaining dressing/marinade to be tossed with salad greens later. Be sure the extra dressing doesn't come in contact with raw shrimp.

4. While shrimp are marinating, spread cashews evenly on a sheet pan and toast in the oven for 6-8 minutes. Soak arame in 1 cup of water for 5 minutes. Remove the cashews from the oven, drain the arame, and set both aside.

5. Spread the marinated shrimp evenly in a single layer on a baking sheet or thread on skewers for easier flipping. Place in the oven on the middle rack and bake for 6-8 minutes, flipping halfway through. Shrimp will turn from blue-grey and translucent to white and pink and opaque when done. Remove from the oven and set aside.

6. Wash greens and spin or pat dry. Combine greens in a large bowl with arame, radishes, and carrots. Fold in roasted shrimp and toss with ¼ cup of the dressing. Add more to taste, if needed. Garnish with cashews.

Cook's Notes: Store extra dressing in a tightly sealed mason jar in the refrigerator for up to 2-3 weeks.

Vegan adaptation: Omit shrimp.

Paleo adaptation: Use coconut aminos in place of soy sauce.

SWEET CORN AND TOMATO SUCCOTASH WITH CHAMPAGNE VINAIGRETTE

Vibrant, colorful, and bursting with summer's freshest flavors, this crowd-pleasing recipe is great for a picnic or a potluck. The champagne vinaigrette has a light, crisp taste that complements this dish beautifully.

Serves 4

Ingredients

Salad

1 cup frozen lima beans

1 cup halved cherry tomatoes

1 cup organic corn kernels

2-3 tablespoons finely chopped fresh basil

2-3 tablespoons finely chopped fresh parsley or dill

4 scallions, sliced thinly

Dressing
(Makes approximately ¼ cup)

2 tablespoons extra virgin olive oil

2 tablespoons champagne vinegar

1 clove garlic, minced

1 teaspoon fresh lemon juice

1 teaspoon local honey

½ teaspoon Dijon mustard

¼ teaspoon sea salt

¼ teaspoon black pepper

Preparation

1. Cook lima beans according to package instructions (usually 12-16 minutes). While beans are cooking, prepare a bowlful of water with ice. When lima beans are tender, remove from heat, strain, and immerse in bowl of ice water for 60 seconds to cool them quickly.

2. Drain lima beans and place in a large bowl with tomatoes, corn, herbs, and scallions. Set aside.

3. In a separate bowl, whisk the dressing ingredients together, then transfer to the large bowl and toss gently with vegetable mixture. Serve immediately or store in the refrigerator for up to 4-5 days.

Cook's notes: Use frozen, thawed corn kernels or fresh corn cut from approximately 2 large ears. Substitute cooked edamame (shelled) for lima beans, if desired. Use red or white wine vinegar in place of champagne vinegar, if necessary.

Nutrients: A(BETA), B$_6$, C, CA, CU, FE, MG, MN, SE, GL, LY

RAINBOW COBB SALAD WITH RED WINE VINAIGRETTE

This beautifully colorful, eye-appealing salad is crisp, light, and refreshing, yet hearty and satisfying. It makes a complete well-balanced lunch or dinner. Use the Easy Oven-Baked Chicken from the Main Dishes *chapter or shredded rotisserie chicken.*

Serves 4-6

Ingredients

**Red Wine Vinaigrette
(Makes approximately ¾ cup)**

¼ cup plus 2 tablespoons extra virgin olive oil

¼ cup red wine vinegar

1-2 cloves garlic, minced

1½ tablespoons fresh lemon juice

1 tablespoon local honey or pure maple syrup

1½ teaspoons Dijon mustard

½ teaspoon sea salt

¼ teaspoon black pepper

Salad

1 head romaine lettuce, sliced crosswise into ¾-inch strips (about 6 cups)

1 cup watercress (or substitute baby kale)

1 cup shredded red cabbage

1 (4-ounce) cooked chicken breast

4 ounces cubed organic ham or cooked bacon

2 hard boiled eggs, peeled and chopped

1 large or 2 small tomatoes, diced

1 avocado, diced

Preparation

1. In a small bowl, whisk all dressing ingredients together. Set aside.

2. In a large bowl, toss the salad greens with ¼ cup of dressing, reserving the remainder for later. Spread greens on a platter or individual salad plates and decorate the top by assembling the remaining ingredients in rows of color. Drizzle with additional dressing over the top to taste.

Cook's notes: Leftover dressing can be stored in a small mason jar in the refrigerator for up to 2 weeks.

Nutrients: A(BETA), A(RET), B₁, B₂, B₆, B₁₂, C, D, E, CA, I, MG, MN, SE, ZN, GL, LY, TY

MASSAGED KALE SALAD WITH CREAMY CUMIN-LIME DRESSING

Kale's nutrition profile and versatility makes it a wonderful green to keep on regular rotation for fresh salads. When eaten raw, it's important to massage its dense leaves by hand to make them easier to digest; this will tenderize the leaves, allowing improved availability of kale's key nutrients. Tossing the leaves in this delightfully creamy dressing will help to balance bitter tones often found in kale.

Serves 4-6

Ingredients

Dressing (Makes ⅔ cup)

¼ cup plus 2 tablespoons sesame tahini

2 small limes, juiced

1½ tablespoons extra virgin olive oil

1½ tablespoons pure maple syrup

1 clove garlic, minced

1 teaspoon ground coriander

½ teaspoon ground cumin

¼ teaspoon sea salt

2-3 tablespoons filtered water
   to thin (optional)

Salad

½ cup raw sunflower seeds

1 large bunch kale

1-2 teaspoons extra virgin olive oil

2 carrots, julienned

½ cup shredded red cabbage

1 red bell pepper, julienned

4-6 radishes, sliced into thin rounds

½ cup dried cranberries

Preparation

1. Whisk all dressing ingredients together in a small bowl. Thin with water, if necessary. Set aside.

2. Toast the sunflower seeds in a dry skillet over medium heat for 3-4 minutes while stirring frequently. Be careful not to burn. Remove from heat and set aside.

3. Remove the stem from each kale leaf by holding the end of the stem in one hand while running your index finger and thumb from your other hand closely along where the leaf meets the stem. Chop or tear de-stemmed leaves into bite-sized pieces. Wash and dry leaves thoroughly, using a salad spinner, if possible, which will prevent salad from getting too soggy. Place in a large bowl.

4. Add 1-2 teaspoons olive oil to the bowl and gently massage into the kale leaves for approximately 2 minutes. Kale will begin to wilt and slightly brighten in color.

5. Add in the carrots, cabbage, bell pepper, and radishes. Toss with desired amount of dressing to taste. Garnish with cranberries and sunflower seeds and enjoy right away.

Cook's notes: This salad is best enjoyed immediately, but if you're planning for leftovers, massage and dress just the amount of kale you're ready to eat. Store the torn kale leaves, other prepped vegetables, and leftover dressing separately in the refrigerator until ready to combine. Extra dressing should keep for up to 2-3 weeks.

Nutrients: A(beta), B₁, B₆, C, E, Ca, Cu, Fe, Mg, Mn, Se, Zn, Gl, Ly

LEMON "PARMESAN" KALE SALAD

The simplicity of this lemony green salad makes it the perfect light supper or side dish. The lemon adds brightness while the sprinkling of Brazil Nut "Parmesan" offers a slightly cheesy and nutty crunch. Top with grilled chicken, if desired.

Serves 2-4

Ingredients

1 large bunch kale

Zest of 1 lemon

2 lemons, juiced (approximately 3½-4 tablespoons)

¼-⅓ cup extra virgin olive oil

½ teaspoon sea salt

¼ teaspoon black pepper

⅓ cup Brazil Nut "Parmesan" from *Condiments, Sauces, and Seasonings* chapter

Preparation

1. Remove the stem from each kale leaf by holding the end of the stem in one hand while running your index finger and thumb from your other hand closely along where the leaf meets the stem. Chop or tear de-stemmed leaves into bite-sized pieces. Wash and dry leaves thoroughly, using a salad spinner, if possible, which will prevent salad from getting too soggy. Place in a large bowl.

2. To make the dressing, whisk the lemon zest, juice, oil, salt, and pepper together in a small bowl.

3. Pour a few tablespoons of the dressing onto the kale and massage into the leaves with your hands. Continue massaging for about 1-2 minutes to ensure thorough coating of the leaves with dressing. Add additional dressing to taste.

4. Sprinkle the Brazil Nut "Parmesan" over the salad and toss well to distribute evenly. Enjoy right away.

Cook's notes: This salad is best enjoyed immediately, but if you're planning for leftovers, massage and dress just the amount of kale you're ready to eat. Store the torn kale leaves and leftover dressing separately in the refrigerator until ready to combine. The undressed kale should keep for several days, while the dressing should keep up to 3-4 weeks.

Nutrients: A(BETA), B₁, B₂, B₆, C, Ca, Cu, Mn, Gl

CITRUSY QUINOA AND ROASTED BROCCOLI SALAD

This zesty salad is full of bright flavors and layers of interesting textures. Roasting broccoli intensifies its flavor. Pair this dish with a nutritious plant or animal protein for a well-balanced meal.

Serves 6

Ingredients

- ¾ cup raw walnuts
- 1¼ cups dry quinoa, drained and rinsed
- 2⅓ cups filtered water
- Pinch of sea salt
- 2½ cups broccoli, chopped into bite-sized pieces
- 2 tablespoons extra virgin olive oil
- 1 cup grapes, cut in half
- 1 orange cut into segments
- ½ cup chopped fresh parsley and/or mint

Dressing (Makes 6 tablespoons)

- 1 teaspoon orange zest
- 1 teaspoon lemon zest
- 1 orange, juiced (approximately 3 tablespoons)
- 1 lemon, juiced (approximately 2 tablespoons)
- 2 tablespoons red wine vinegar
- 3 tablespoons extra virgin olive oil
- 1 tablespoon local honey
- 1 teaspoon ground coriander
- ½ teaspoon sea salt
- ¼ teaspoon black pepper

Preparation

1. Preheat oven to 350°F. Spread walnuts out on sheet pan and toast in the oven for 6-8 minutes. Be careful not to burn. Remove from heat and set aside. Increase oven temperature to 400°F for step 3.

2. Pour quinoa and water into a small saucepan with salt. Heat pan over medium-high heat to bring to a boil. Reduce heat, cover, and simmer for approximately 15 minutes, until all water has been absorbed. Do not stir quinoa while it's cooking or it will not cook evenly. To tell when it's done, carefully tilt pan to see if any water is pooling at the bottom. Pull from heat and set aside to cool for a few minutes. To expedite cooling, quinoa can be dumped onto a sheet pan and spread out evenly to help dissipate heat faster.

3. Ensure chopped broccoli is well dried, then toss with oil and spread evenly on a sheet pan lined with parchment paper. Roast in the oven for 10-12 minutes. Pull from the oven and set aside to cool.

4. In a small bowl, whisk together orange and lemon zests and juices, vinegar, oil, honey, coriander, salt, and pepper until well combined.

5. In a large bowl, toss quinoa with roasted broccoli, grapes, orange segments, walnuts, herbs, and dressing.

Nutrients: B_2, B_6, C, E, Ca, Fe, Mg, Mn, Se, Gl, O3

WILD SALMON & ARUGULA SALAD WITH MAPLE TOASTED PECANS AND APPLE CIDER VINAIGRETTE

With all of its delicious textures and flavors, this robust salad is satisfying enough to be a complete supper. The ingredients can also be prepped ahead of time to make packing a healthy lunch a breeze.

Serves 4

Ingredients

Wild Salmon

4 (4-ounce) wild salmon fillets

Coconut oil or ghee for greasing

4 teaspoons lemon zest, divided

1 teaspoon coarse sea salt

½ teaspoon black pepper

Maple Toasted Pecans

1 cup raw pecans

2 tablespoons pure maple syrup

¼ teaspoon sea salt

⅛ teaspoon cayenne pepper

Coconut oil or ghee for greasing (optional)

Apple Cider Vinaigrette

½ cup raw apple cider vinegar

¼ cup fresh lemon juice

¼ cup local honey

2 tablespoons Dijon mustard

⅔ cup extra virgin olive oil

½ teaspoon sea salt

¼ teaspoon black pepper

Salad

3 cups arugula

3 cups mixed greens

1 cup shredded carrot

1 cup halved cherry tomatoes

½ cup shredded red cabbage

Avocado slices

Nutrients: A(BETA), B₁, B₂, B₆, B₁₂, C, D, E, CA, CU, FE, MG, MN, SE, ZN, LY, GL, O3, TY

Preparation 🥣

1. Preheat oven to 425°F.

2. Place the salmon in a baking dish greased with coconut oil or ghee, skin side down. Sprinkle with lemon zest, salt, and pepper. Cook for 10-12 minutes per inch of thickness or until internal temperature reaches 145°F. Remove from the oven and once fish has cooled, carefully remove skin, if desired. Set aside.

3. Reduce oven temperature to 350°F. Mix pecans, maple syrup, salt, and cayenne pepper together in a small bowl. Spread evenly on a greased baking pan or a pan lined with parchment paper and toast in the oven for 6-8 minutes. Be sure to set timer to avoid burning the pecans. Remove from heat and set aside to cool.

4. Place vinaigrette ingredients in a small bowl in the order listed and whisk olive oil in slowly, until well combined. Season with salt and pepper. Transfer to a mason jar with a lid. Can be stored up to 1 month in the refrigerator.

5. In a large bowl, toss the arugula and mixed greens with the carrot, tomatoes, and cabbage. Dress with apple cider vinaigrette to taste. Arrange on 4 dinner plates with avocado, salmon, and maple toasted pecans.

Cook's Notes: Store leftover vinaigrette in a tightly sealed glass jar with a lid in the refrigerator for up to 3-4 weeks.

AIP adaptation: Omit Maple Toasted Pecans, Dijon mustard, and tomatoes.

MAIN DISHES

ASIAN LETTUCE WRAPS

These delightfully flavorful lettuce wraps are a cinch to prepare, making them a great option for a nutrient-dense weeknight meal. For an extra burst of flavor, drizzle with Coconut Peanut Sauce from the Condiments, Sauces, and Seasonings *chapter.*

Serves 4

Ingredients

- ½ cup raw cashews
- 2 tablespoons coconut or avocado oil
- 2 tablespoons sliced shallots
- 2 cloves garlic, finely chopped
- 2 tablespoons freshly grated ginger
- ½ cup chopped crimini or shiitake mushrooms
- 2 tablespoons filtered water or broth
- 1 pound ground chicken
- 3 tablespoons fresh lime juice
- 1 tablespoon reduced sodium tamari soy sauce or coconut aminos
- ¼ teaspoon red pepper flakes
- 1 head butter lettuce, washed and patted dry
- 1 cup shredded cabbage
- 1 large carrot, shredded
- Coconut Peanut Sauce from the *Condiments, Sauces, and Seasonings* chapter

Preparation

1. Preheat oven to 350°F. Spread cashews out on a sheet pan and toast in the oven for 6-8 minutes. Be careful not to burn. Remove from heat and set aside.

2. Heat oil in a medium-sized skillet over medium heat and sauté shallots, garlic, ginger, and mushrooms for 3-4 minutes until softened and lightly browned. If ingredients begin to stick to the pan, add water or broth to deglaze. Add ground chicken and cook thoroughly, for about 4-5 minutes, while using a wooden spoon to break into smaller pieces.

3. Remove pan from heat. Add lime juice, soy sauce or coconut aminos, and red pepper flakes. Mix well and adjust seasonings as desired.

4. To serve, spoon several tablespoons of chicken mixture into the center of a lettuce leaf and top with shredded cabbage, carrot, and cashews. Drizzle with Coconut Peanut Sauce.

Paleo adaptation: Substitute coconut aminos for soy sauce. Use Paleo adaptation for Coconut Peanut Sauce recipe.

AIP adaptation: Substitute coconut aminos for soy sauce and omit toasted cashews and Coconut Peanut Sauce.

Nutrients: A(BETA), B$_2$, B$_6$, B$_{12}$, C, D, E, CA, CU, FE, MG, MN, SE, ZN, GL, LY, TY

LEMON THYME WHOLE ROASTED CHICKEN

Aromatic herbs and lemon make this whole roasted chicken a dinner mainstay. Roasting a whole chicken is also an economical way to ensure delicious leftovers for days to come. Add it to fresh salads, stir into soup, or chop up into chicken salad using Melissa's Homemade Mayo from the Condiments, Sauces, and Seasonings *chapter.*

Serves 4-6

Ingredients

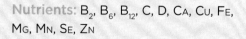

3½-4 pounds whole organic chicken

1 lemon

1 bunch fresh thyme or 2 tablespoons dried thyme

1 head garlic, halved crosswise

2-3 tablespoons olive oil

1½ tablespoons poultry seasoning

Sea salt and black pepper to taste

Preparation

1. Preheat oven to 400°F.

2. Place the chicken in a large baking dish or roasting pan. Slice lemon in half and squeeze juice over the outside of the chicken. Place squeezed halves into the cavity with thyme and garlic. Drizzle outside of chicken with oil and generously season with poultry seasoning, salt, and pepper.

3. Roast chicken for approximately 60-90 minutes to an internal temperature of 165°F. The thermometer should be inserted into the thickest part of the thigh. Skin should be golden brown and juices should run clear.

4. Remove from oven and let rest for at least 10 minutes before carving.

Cook's notes: Because chickens can vary in size, cooking time can vary up to 15-30 minutes. I recommend investing in an instant-read thermometer for the safest and easiest way to check for doneness. Insert into the thickest part of the thigh; it should read 165°F when done.

AIP adaptation: Omit poultry seasoning (usually contains nutmeg).

Elimination/Provocation Diet adaptation: Omit lemon.

Nutrients: B₂, B₆, B₁₂, C, D, Cᴀ, Cu, Fᴇ, Mɢ, Mɴ, Sᴇ, Zɴ

"PARMESAN" CHICKEN TENDERS

These savory chicken tenders get their delicious, selenium-rich breading from the Brazil Nut "Parmesan." Enjoy these tenders over sautéed zucchini noodles with my Classic Marinara Sauce from the Condiments, Sauces, and Seasonings *chapter.*

Serves 4-6

Ingredients

Brazil Nut "Parmesan"

1½ cups Brazil nuts

½ cup almond flour

½ cup nutritional yeast

2 teaspoons garlic powder

2 teaspoons sea salt

"Parmesan" Chicken Tenders

2 large eggs

½ cup gluten-free all-purpose flour

2 cups Brazil Nut "Parmesan" (above)

1½ pounds boneless, skinless chicken breasts, cut into tenders

Preparation

1. Preheat oven to 400°F. Line a large baking sheet with parchment paper.

2. For the "Parmesan," add Brazil nuts, almond flour, nutritional yeast, garlic powder, and salt in the bowl of a food processor affixed with an S-blade. Pulse until coarsely ground. Transfer mixture to a flat, shallow bowl or container for easy dipping.

3. Whisk eggs in a bowl. Set aside.

4. Add the all-purpose flour to a flat, shallow bowl or container for easy dipping.

5. Set up an assembly line for coating the chicken tenders and transferring to the baking sheet. First, dip chicken tenders one by one into the flour, then the egg, and lastly the Brazil Nut "Parmesan." Place each tender on the baking sheet once completely coated.

6. Bake for approximately 10-12 minutes, or until chicken is cooked thoroughly, flipping the tenders once halfway through. The chicken will no longer be pink inside and will read 165°F on an instant-read thermometer when ready.

Nutrients: A(RET), B$_2$, B$_6$, B$_{12}$, C, D, Ca, Cu, I, Mg, Mn, Se, Gl, Ty

EASY OVEN-BAKED CHICKEN

By following a few simple techniques inspired by thekitchn.com, it's easy to achieve oven-baked chicken that's juicy and flavorful, instead of dry and bland. The chicken can be seasoned very simply with salt and pepper, or feel free to experiment with your favorite additive-free seasoning blends. Batch cook several breasts at a time in advance to easily incorporate into soups, salads, sandwiches and wraps, and other dishes.

Serves 4-6

Ingredients

1-2 tablespoons olive oil or ghee

2-4 (4-ounce) boneless, skinless chicken breasts

Sea salt and black pepper

Favorite seasonings (optional)

Preparation

1. Preheat oven to 400°F. Line the bottom of a sheet pan or baking dish with parchment paper and lightly grease the parchment with oil or ghee.

2. Gently pat the chicken breasts dry using paper towels. Lay each breast evenly on the baking pan and season with a small amount salt, pepper, and favorite seasonings, if desired.

3. Cover chicken by pressing a separate sheet of parchment paper firmly against the breasts and tucking it snugly to make a nice seal. Be sure to completely cover all of the chicken.

4. Place pan in the oven on center rack and bake for approximately 20-30 minutes, or until the chicken reaches an internal temperature of 165°F.

5. Remove from oven and let rest for 5 minutes. Discard parchment paper and enjoy right away or cool thoroughly and store for up to 3-4 days in the refrigerator.

Cook's notes: Sealing the chicken in parchment paper is key for creating tender and juicy meat because it acts like the chicken's skin and prevents it from drying out. An instant-read thermometer is the safest and easiest way to check for doneness. Insert into the thickest part of the breast; it should read 165°F when done.

AIP and Elimination/Provocation Diet adaptations: Use olive oil instead of ghee and opt for nightshade-free seasonings. For AIP, also select seasonings not derived from seeds.

Nutrients: B_2, B_6, B_{12}, D, Se, Ty

MELISSA'S BANH MI MEATBALLS

This recipe was shared with us by our friend, Melissa Joulwan, when we were exploring palate-pleasing ways to feature nutritious chicken livers. These exotically flavorful meatballs immediately won our vote. Liver is among the most concentrated sources of B vitamins, iron, and Vitamin A. When consumed regularly, liver can support energy levels and immunity. Melissa recommends serving these meatballs in a lettuce wrap with a dollop of her Homemade Mayo from the Condiments, Sauces, and Seasonings *chapter.*

Melissa is the author of the best-selling Well Fed *cookbook series and the blog www.MelJoulwan.com, where she writes about her triumphs and failures in the gym, in the kitchen, and in life. Her newest cookbook is* Well Fed Weeknights: Complete Paleo Meals in 45 Minutes or Less.

Serves 4

Ingredients

¼ teaspoon baking soda

½ teaspoon cream of tartar

2 tablespoons filtered water

½ pound organic chicken livers

1 pound ground pork

1 tablespoon fish sauce

1 tablespoon hot sauce

2 cloves garlic, minced

10-12 fresh basil leaves, minced

4 scallions, sliced thinly

1 teaspoon black pepper

¾ teaspoon sea salt

1 head butter lettuce

1 carrot, shredded

2-3 tablespoons chopped fresh cilantro

Melissa's Homemade Mayo from the *Condiments, Sauces, and Seasonings* chapter

1 lime, cut into wedges

Preparation

1. Preheat oven to 400°F.

2. In a small bowl, mix baking soda and cream of tartar with the water. Set aside.

3. Place the chicken livers in the bowl of a food processor and pulse until minced. Place them in a large mixing bowl, then add the baking soda mixture, pork, fish sauce, hot sauce, garlic, basil, scallions, pepper, and salt. Mix well to combine.

4. Roll the meat into 1-inch meatballs and place them on a baking sheet. Bake 20-25 minutes until browned and sizzling.

5. Serve in lettuce wraps topped with carrot, cilantro, a dollop of mayo, and a squeeze of lime.

AIP adaptation: Omit hot sauce and mayo.

Elimination/Provocation Diet adaptation: Omit hot sauce, fish sauce, mayo, and lime.

Nutrients: A(BETA), A(RET), B₆, B₁₂, C, D, CA, CU, FE, MG, MN, SE, ZN, GL, LY, O3, TY

LEMON GARLIC SHRIMP AND SPINACH SAUTÉ

Shrimp is one of the fastest cooking proteins, taking just minutes to prepare. This dish is especially good when served over a bed of brown rice, quinoa, or roasted spaghetti squash.

Serves 4

Ingredients

- 1 tablespoon extra virgin olive oil or ghee plus more if needed
- 5 cloves garlic, minced
- 1 pound raw shrimp, peeled and deveined
- 2 teaspoons lemon zest
- ½ teaspoon sea salt
- 3-4 cups baby spinach
- Black pepper to taste
- 2-3 teaspoons fresh lemon juice

Preparation

1. Heat oil or ghee in a large sauté pan over low-medium heat. Add garlic, shrimp, lemon zest, and salt and sauté for approximately 1 minute.

2. Add spinach and continue to cook for an additional minute to allow spinach to wilt. Add a small amount of additional oil or ghee, if needed.

3. Shrimp will become opaque and curl into a C-shape when fully cooked. Pull from heat to prevent overcooking. Add pepper and brighten with a spritz of lemon juice before serving.

Cook's notes: Keeping frozen shrimp on hand for a fast and easy dinner solution is a smart idea because it thaws quickly – simply place in a colander under a very slow stream of cold water for 5 minutes.

AIP adaptation: Use olive oil in place of ghee.

Nutrients: A(BETA), A(RET), B₁, B₂, B₆, B₁₂, C, E, CA, CU, FE, I, MG, MN, SE, ZN, GL, TY

TOMATO BASIL SHRIMP PASTA

This light pasta dish comes together quickly, making it perfect for a weeknight meal. The white wine rounds out the flavors in the sauce and adds some depth, but this dish is equally delicious without it. Serve over your favorite gluten-free pasta noodle, or for a grain-free option, opt for the Spiralized Zucchini Noodles from the Plant-Based Sides *chapter.*

Serves 4

Ingredients

- 8 ounces whole grain gluten-free pasta noodles
- 1 tablespoon avocado oil or ghee
- ½ medium yellow onion, finely chopped
- 4-6 cloves garlic, minced
- 1 (28-ounce) can diced tomatoes
- ¼ cup dry white wine (optional)
- 1-2 tablespoons extra virgin olive oil
- ½ cup fresh basil, sliced thinly
- 1 pound raw shrimp, peeled and deveined
- 1 teaspoon sea salt
- ½ teaspoon black pepper

Preparation

1. Cook pasta noodles according to directions on the package. Drain and set aside.

2. Heat oil or ghee over medium heat in a large sauté pan. Add onion and sauté 3-4 minutes, until softened. Add garlic and sauté an additional 2 minutes. Carefully stir in tomatoes, optional wine, oil, and basil. Using a wooden spoon, gently mash diced tomatoes into smaller pieces while heating. Allow mixture to simmer for 4-5 minutes while stirring frequently.

3. Add shrimp and allow to cook for 2-3 minutes on each side in simmering tomato mixture. Shrimp will be finished cooking when they coil into a C-shape and turn from being slightly translucent to more opaque.

4. Divide pasta noodles into 4 servings and top with tomato basil sauce and shrimp.

Paleo adaptation: Substitute Spiralized Zucchini Noodles or roasted spaghetti squash in place of gluten-free pasta. These simple recipes can both be found in the *Plant-Based Sides* chapter.

Nutrients: A(BETA), A(RET), B₆, B₁₂, C, E, CA, CU, FE, I, MG, MN, SE, LY, TY

GRASS-FED BEEF QUINOA MEATBALLS

This unique meatball recipe features nutrient-dense grass-fed beef along with whole grain quinoa and shredded carrots to further enhance the nutrition profile. They're great over Spiralized Zucchini Noodles (see Plant-Based Sides chapter) and topped with my Classic Marinara (see Condiments, Sauces, and Seasonings chapter). I recommend making a double batch of sauce. If you don't own a spiralizer don't fret–simply serve with your favorite gluten-free pasta.

Makes 18 meatballs

Ingredients

½ cup dry quinoa

½ teaspoon sea salt plus a pinch, divided

1 pound 90% lean ground grass-fed beef

3 cloves finely minced garlic

1 egg

½ cup grated carrot

2 tablespoons finely chopped onion

2 tablespoons tomato paste or unsweetened ketchup

1 tablespoon reduced sodium tamari soy sauce or coconut aminos

¼ teaspoon dried oregano

¼ teaspoon dried thyme

¼ teaspoon black pepper

Preparation

1. To cook quinoa, rinse and drain in a fine mesh strainer then add to a small saucepan with 1 cup water and a pinch of salt. Cover and bring to a boil. Reduce heat to low, keep covered, and simmer for approximately 10-12 minutes, until all water has been absorbed. Remove from heat and let stand for 5 minutes, then fluff with a fork.

2. Preheat oven to 450°F. Line a large baking sheet with parchment paper.

3. In a large bowl, mix all ingredients together, including the remaining salt and cooked quinoa, until well combined. Shape into 18 golf ball sized meatballs and transfer to the baking sheet.

4. Place in the oven and roast until cooked through and golden brown, about 15 minutes. Serve hot with Classic Marinara.

Cook's notes: Organic ground turkey can be substituted for grass-fed beef, if desired.

Paleo adaptation: Omit quinoa. Substitute soy sauce with coconut aminos.

Nutrients: A(BETA), B₂, B₆, B₁₂, C, E, Ca, Cu, Fe, Mg, Mn, Se, Zn, Gl, Ly, Ty, O3

GRASS-FED BEEF BURGERS WITH CARAMELIZED ONIONS AND SHIITAKES

Nutrient dense grass-fed beef is an exceptional choice for your burger. Topped with a mouthwatering layer of caramelized onions and mushrooms, this recipe boasts extra selenium and B_{12}. Enjoy on a gluten-free bun or form smaller patties and eat as a wrap using butter lettuce.

Serves 4

Ingredients

Caramelized Onions and Mushrooms

2 tablespoons coconut oil or ghee

1 medium onion, sliced into half-moons

½ teaspoon sea salt plus a pinch, divided

8 ounces shiitake mushrooms, sliced
  (or substitute criminis or white buttons)

2 tablespoons sherry vinegar (optional)

¼ teaspoon black pepper

Burgers

1 pound grass-fed beef

1-2 cloves garlic, minced

2 tablespoons minced onion

2 tablespoons tamari soy sauce or
  coconut aminos

2 tablespoons organic
  unsweetened ketchup

1 teaspoon sea salt

½ teaspoon black pepper

1 head butter lettuce or 1 package
  gluten-free buns

Nutrients: B_2, B_6, B_{12}, D, Cu, Mn, Se, Zn, O3, Ty

Preparation

1. To caramelize onions, heat oil in a large skillet over medium-high heat. Add onion and a pinch of salt. Cover with a lid and cook over medium-low heat for 6-8 minutes to sweat the onions. Remove lid, add the mushrooms, and continue to cook over medium-low heat for another 10-15 minutes, stirring occasionally, until mixture is golden brown. Season with optional vinegar, remaining salt, and pepper.

2. Preheat grill to medium-high heat. If using a grill pan on the stove, do step 3 first.

3. Mix all burger ingredients together (except for the butter lettuce or buns) in a medium-sized bowl. Once meat is well combined with seasonings, form into 4 equal patties (or 8 smaller patties for sliders).

4. Grill burgers on preheated grill for 2-3 minutes per side, then move to a lower-heat spot on grill. Cook for an additional 3-4 minutes for medium, or 5-6 minutes for well-done. An instant-read thermometer inserted in the center of the meat should read 160°F when done.

5. Remove from heat and serve on a gluten-free bun or lettuce wrap topped with onions and mushrooms.

Cook's notes: If burgers are made into smaller, slider size patties, they will take approximately half the amount of time to cook. Adjust accordingly.

Paleo, AIP, and Elimination/Provocation Diet adaptations: Substitute soy sauce with coconut aminos and serve in a butter lettuce wrap. For AIP and Elimination/Provocation diet, also omit ketchup.

ZESTY OVEN-BAKED FISH

Quality wild fish is full of flavor and doesn't need much embellishing. This recipe provides a basic template for preparing a variety of different types with very simple seasoning. Wild salmon, halibut, Icelandic cod, and trout are my favorites. Top with Kale Walnut Pesto or Pumpkin Seed Cilantro Pesto from the Condiments, Sauces, and Seasonings *chapter, if desired.*

Serves 4

Ingredients

4 (4-ounce) fish fillets

1 tablespoon lemon zest, divided

1 teaspoon coarse sea salt

¼ teaspoon black pepper

Preparation

1. Preheat oven to 425°F. Line baking sheet with parchment paper.

2. Place fish skin side down on baking sheet. Sprinkle each fillet evenly with lemon zest, salt, and pepper.

3. Bake in the oven for about 10-12 minutes per inch of thickness or an internal temperature of 140°F. To check for doneness, separate flesh in the thickest part of the fish with a fork; it should flake easily.

Cook's notes: Fresh seafood should be consumed within 2 days of purchase, otherwise store in the freezer until ready to cook.

Elimination/Provocation Diet adaptation: Omit lemon zest.

Nutrients: B$_2$, B$_6$, B$_{12}$, D, S$_E$, O3, T$_Y$

BLACKBERRY SAGE SALMON

Salmon is rewarding to prepare for its anti-inflammatory Omega-3s, as well as its flaky texture and rich flavor. Topping it with this succulent blackberry sage sauce will send your taste buds soaring.

Serves 4

Ingredients

Blackberry Sauce (Makes ¾ cup)

2 tablespoons ghee, coconut oil, or avocado oil

½ cup chopped shallots

2 cloves garlic

½ cup filtered water

¼ cup plus 2 tablespoons balsamic vinegar

2 cups blackberries

2 tablespoons chopped sage

1 tablespoon local honey

¼ teaspoon sea salt plus more for seasoning

¼ teaspoon black pepper plus more for seasoning

Salmon

4 (4-ounce) wild salmon fillets, deboned

1 teaspoon coarse sea salt

¼ teaspoon black pepper

Preparation

1. Preheat oven to 425°F. Line baking sheet with parchment paper.

2. Heat ghee or oil over medium heat in a medium-sized saucepan. Add shallots and garlic and sauté for 2-3 minutes, until lightly browned.

3. Add in water, vinegar, blackberries, sage, honey, salt, and pepper. Bring to a boil then reduce to a simmer. Simmer for 15 minutes until liquid is reduced by approximately half.

4. Place fish skin side down on baking sheet. Sprinkle each fillet evenly with salt and pepper.

5. Bake in the oven for about 10-12 minutes per inch of thickness or an internal temperature of 140°F. Remove from oven and serve topped with warm blackberry sauce.

AIP and Elimination/Provocation Diet adaptations: Use coconut or avocado oil in place of ghee.

Nutrients: A(RET), B$_2$, B$_6$, B$_{12}$, C, D, CA, CU, MG, MN, SE, GL, O3, TY

PAN-SEARED CARIBBEAN LIME HALIBUT WITH PINEAPPLE RAINBOW SALSA

A denser, meatier fish like halibut is delicious when marinated before cooking. Pan-searing the fish first helps to lock in flavor. If halibut is unavailable, substitute with a dense fish like turbot or mahi mahi. Top with Pineapple Rainbow Salsa from the Appetizers *chapter.*

Serves 4

Ingredients

1 tablespoon reduced sodium tamari soy sauce or coconut aminos

3 tablespoons extra virgin olive oil

1 tablespoon freshly grated ginger

3 tablespoons fresh lime juice (approximately 2 limes)

1 teaspoon coconut palm sugar

3 cloves garlic, minced

1 pound halibut, turbot, or mahi mahi

2 tablespoons coconut oil or ghee

Pineapple Rainbow Salsa from the *Appetizers* chapter

Preparation

1. Whisk soy sauce or coconut aminos, oil, ginger, lime juice, sugar, and garlic together in a shallow baking dish. Place fish in baking dish with marinade and coat evenly. Allow fish to marinate 25-30 minutes in the refrigerator, flipping and redistributing marinade halfway through.

2. Preheat oven to 425°F.

3. Heat oil or ghee in an oven-proof skillet. Place fish in the pan, starting with skin side up. Sear for approximately 1 minute on each side. Leave fish in skillet and carefully transfer into preheated oven. Be sure to use oven mitts to prevent getting burned.

4. Bake fish for approximately 10-12 minutes per inch of thickness or until it reaches an internal temperature of 140°F. Using an oven mitt, carefully remove fish from oven and let rest for 3-4 minutes.

5. Top with Pineapple Rainbow Salsa.

Cook's notes: If you don't have a stainless steel or cast iron skillet that can easily be transferred to the oven, simply transfer your fish to a greased baking dish after searing and place in the oven.

AIP adaptation: Substitute coconut aminos for soy sauce and omit coconut sugar if no added sugar is desired. Use AIP adapted version of Pineapple Rainbow Salsa found in the *Appetizers* chapter.

Nutrients: B$_2$, B$_6$, B$_{12}$, C, Ca, Cu, Mg, Mn, Se, Ly, O3, Ty

MAPLE DIJON PORK TENDERLOIN

The combination of maple and mustard provides a sweet and savory tang to this simple pork tenderloin dish. Take care not to overcook, as pork tenderloin can easily dry out.

Serves 4

Ingredients

- ¼ cup reduced sodium tamari soy sauce or coconut aminos
- 3 tablespoons Dijon mustard
- 2 tablespoons olive oil or avocado oil
- 2-3 tablespoons pure maple syrup
- 1-2 cloves garlic, minced
- 1 tablespoon chopped shallots
- 2 teaspoons onion powder
- 2 teaspoons garlic powder
- 1 pound pork tenderloin

Preparation

1. Whisk the soy sauce or coconut aminos, Dijon mustard, oil, maple syrup, garlic, shallots, and spices together in a bowl. Place pork tenderloin in a shallow baking dish and cover with marinade. Cover and refrigerate, allowing tenderloin to marinate at least 20-30 minutes.

2. Preheat oven to 400°F.

3. Pull baking dish from the refrigerator and pour marinade off into a small saucepan. Set saucepan aside. Place baking dish in preheated oven and roast for approximately 15-25 minutes, depending on the thickness of the tenderloin. Tenderloin will be done when it reaches an internal temperature of 145°F.

4. While tenderloin is roasting, bring marinade to a boil, then lower to a simmer and cook for 10-15 minutes over low heat. The marinade will reduce and thicken slightly.

5. Remove tenderloin from oven. Keeping the meat in the baking dish, cover with foil and allow it to rest for 5-10 minutes.

6. Slice meat and serve drizzled with reduced marinade.

Cook's notes: An instant-read thermometer is the safest and easiest way to check for doneness. Insert into the thickest part of the tenderloin; it should read 145°F when done.

Paleo and Elimination/Provocation Diet adaptations: Use coconut aminos in place of soy sauce.

Nutrients: B$_6$, C, Ca, Cu, Mg, Mn, Se, Zn, Ty

(P) (EP)

PAN-SEARED PORK CHOPS

Pan-searing may sound like a fussy, time-consuming cooking technique, but it's quite simple. It helps to build deeper flavor by caramelizing the surface of the meat and will have you licking your chops. This recipe is superb topped with the Hemp Seed Chimichurri from the Condiments, Sauces, and Seasonings *chapter.*

Makes 2-4 pork chops

Ingredients

1-2 tablespoons ghee or avocado oil

2-4 pork chops, bone-in

Sea salt and black pepper to taste

Preparation

1. Preheat oven to 400°F.

2. Heat a thin layer of ghee or oil in a large oven-proof skillet over medium heat on the stove. Season each side of the pork chops with salt and pepper and lay in hot skillet without crowding. Pan-sear the bottom of chops for 3 minutes until they begin to brown. Turn chops with tongs and sear the other side another 3 minutes then transfer skillet to oven. Be sure to use oven mitts to prevent getting burned.

3. Roast the chops in the oven for approximately 6-8 minutes, depending on the thickness of the chop. They should be done when they reach an internal temperature of 145°F.

4. Remove skillet from the oven and allow chops to rest for 3-4 minutes before serving. Plate and top with Hemp Seed Chimichurri, if desired.

Cook's notes: A cast iron skillet is best for pan-searing and transferring to the oven, but you may also try an oven-safe stainless steel pan, or simply transfer the meat to a baking dish after pan-seared. An instant-read thermometer is the safest and easiest way to check for doneness. Insert into the thickest part of the chop; it should read 145°F when done.

Nutrients: B$_6$, C, E, C$_A$, C$_U$, F$_E$, M$_G$, M$_N$, S$_E$, Z$_N$, G$_L$, O3, T$_Y$

SWEETS AND TREATS

FLOURLESS TRIPLE CHOCOLATE WALNUT BROWNIES

Everyone loves a decadent chocolate brownie and these are no exception. They feature magnesium-rich chocolate three different ways: as cocoa powder, dark chocolate chips, and cacao nibs. Perfectly moist and gooey combined with a satisfying crunch, just go ahead and double the batch!

Makes 12-16 brownies

Ingredients

Coconut oil, for greasing pan

1 cup packed almond butter

¼ cup plus 2 tablespoons unsweetened cocoa powder

1 egg

½ cup pure maple syrup

2 tablespoons melted coconut oil or ghee

1 teaspoon vanilla extract

½ teaspoon baking soda

¼ teaspoon sea salt

¼ cup walnuts, chopped

¼ cup dark chocolate chips

2 tablespoons cacao nibs

Preparation

1. Preheat oven to 350°F. Lightly grease an 8-inch square baking dish with oil.

2. Place almond butter, cocoa powder, egg, maple syrup, melted oil or ghee, vanilla, baking soda, and salt in bowl of a stand mixer. Mix on medium speed for 30-60 seconds until ingredients are well combined. Using spatula, scrape batter out of bowl and spread evenly in pan. Sprinkle walnuts, chocolate chips, and cacao nibs evenly over the top, gently pressing into batter until partially covered.

3. Place baking dish in oven and bake for 30 minutes. Remove from oven and let cool slightly for 5 minutes before cutting into 12-16 brownies. They will continue to firm up as they cool.

Cook's notes: This recipe features almond butter but could just as easily be made with sunflower seed butter if tree nuts are a problem. If either nut or seed butter is runny or oily, then omit additional coconut oil or ghee.

Paleo adaptation: Omit dark chocolate chips if concerned about small amount of cane sugar.

Nutrients: B$_2$, B$_{12}$, D, E, Cu, Fe, I, Mg, Se, Zn, Gl, O3, Ty

FLOURLESS ALMOND BUTTER CHOCOLATE CHIP COOKIES

Full of flavor and chewy softness, no one will miss the flour in these grain-free cookies. Feel free to substitute peanut butter or sunflower seed butter for the almond butter, if preferred.

Makes 15 cookies

Ingredients

1 cup unsweetened almond butter

½ cup coconut sugar

1 large egg, whisked

1 teaspoon vanilla extract

1 teaspoon baking soda

¼ teaspoon sea salt

½ cup 70% dark chocolate chips

Preparation

1. Preheat oven to 350°F. Line a large cookie sheet with parchment paper.

2. In a large bowl, combine almond butter, sugar, egg, and vanilla and stir until well mixed.

3. Add in the baking soda, salt, and chocolate chips and stir until well combined.

4. Form dough into balls, about 1½ tablespoons each. Place on cookie sheet, about 2 inches apart, and press down gently to partially flatten.

5. Bake for 8-10 minutes. Cookies are done when they begin to brown around the edges. It's normal for them to appear slightly unbaked in the center.

6. Remove from oven and allow to cool on cookie sheet for 5 minutes before transferring to a wire rack to cool completely.

Paleo adaptation: Omit dark chocolate chips if concerned about small amount of cane sugar.

Nutrients: B$_2$, B$_{12}$, D, E, Ca, Cu, Fe, I, Mg, Mn, Se, Zn, Ty

GRAIN-FREE PUMPKIN CHOCOLATE CHIP MUFFINS

These pumpkin muffins are a great treat for fall, but pumpkin's nutrition profile makes them perfectly fine to enjoy year-round. If you can't do the chocolate chips, chopped apples would make them equally delicious.

Makes 12 muffins

Ingredients

2½ cups almond flour

¼ cup coconut sugar

¼ cup ground flaxseeds

1 teaspoon baking soda

½ teaspoon ground cinnamon

½ teaspoon sea salt

3 eggs

¼ cup pumpkin puree

2 tablespoons pure maple syrup or local honey

½ teaspoon vanilla extract

½ cup 70% dark chocolate chips

Preparation

1. Preheat oven to 375°F. Line a muffin tin with paper muffin cup liners.

2. Mix dry ingredients (flour, sugar, flaxseeds, baking soda, cinnamon, and salt) together in a large bowl with a whisk or a fork. Ensure that any lumps in the flour are broken up.

3. In a separate bowl, whisk eggs, pumpkin puree, maple syrup or honey, and vanilla together until well combined.

4. Combine the wet and dry mixtures and stir with a rubber spatula until well mixed. Gently fold in chocolate chips, taking care to avoid over-mixing. Batter will be thicker than most muffin batters, but will be spoonable.

5. Spoon batter into muffin cups until approximately ¾ full. Place muffin tin in the oven and bake for 20-22 minutes, until tops are golden. Test doneness by inserting a toothpick into the center of a muffin. If it comes out clean, the muffins are done.

Cook's notes: Maple sugar, Sucanat, or any other unrefined granulated sweeteners can be substituted for coconut sugar.

Paleo adaptation: Omit dark chocolate chips if concerned about small amount of cane sugar.

Nutrients: A(BETA), A(RET), B$_1$, B$_2$, B$_6$, B$_{12}$, C, D, E, Ca, Cu, Fe, I, Mg, Mn, Se, Zn, Gl, O3, Pr, Ty

GRAIN-FREE BLUEBERRY MUFFINS

One of the best ways to enjoy plump and juicy blueberries is baked into muffins. This recipe provides a gluten-free, grain-free alternative to a timeless classic. Add a little lemon zest for a bright twist.

Makes 12 muffins

Ingredients

2½ cups almond flour

¼ cup coconut sugar

½ teaspoon baking soda

½ teaspoon ground cinnamon

¼ teaspoon sea salt

3 eggs

2 tablespoons avocado oil or melted coconut oil

2 tablespoons pure maple syrup or local honey

½ teaspoon vanilla extract

Zest of 1 lemon (optional)

¾ cup fresh blueberries

Preparation

1. Preheat oven to 375°F. Line a muffin tin with paper muffin cup liners.

2. Mix dry ingredients (flour, sugar, baking soda, cinnamon, and salt) together in a large bowl with a whisk or fork. Ensure that any lumps in the flour are broken up.

3. In a separate bowl, whisk together the eggs, oil, maple syrup or honey, vanilla, and optional lemon zest, until well combined.

4. Combine the wet and dry mixtures and stir with a rubber spatula until well mixed. Gently fold in blueberries, taking care to avoid over-mixing. The batter will be thicker than typical muffin batter, but spoonable.

5. Spoon batter into muffin cups until approximately ¾ full. Place muffin tin in oven and bake for 20-22 minutes, until tops are golden. Test doneness by inserting a toothpick into the center of a muffin. If it comes out clean, the muffins are done.

Cook's notes: Maple sugar, Sucanat, or any other unrefined granulated sweetener can be substituted for coconut sugar.

Nutrients: A(ʀᴇᴛ), B₂, B₁₂, C, D, E, Cᴀ, Cᴜ, Fᴇ, I, Mɢ, Mɴ, Sᴇ, Zɴ, Tʏ

GRAIN-FREE ALMOND BANANA FLAX MUFFINS

These egg-free muffins use Omega-3-rich flaxseeds as a binder, making them a delicious vegan option. Naturally sweet and nutty, they're great with or without the chocolate chips.

Makes 12 muffins

Ingredients

- 1 tablespoon ground flaxseeds
- 3 tablespoons warm, filtered water
- 2 cups almond flour
- ¼ cup coconut sugar
- ½ teaspoon baking soda
- ¼ teaspoon sea salt
- 3 medium bananas, peeled and mashed (approximately 1 cup)
- 2 tablespoons avocado oil or melted coconut oil
- 1 tablespoon local honey or pure maple syrup
- 1 teaspoon vanilla extract
- ½ cup 70% dark chocolate chips (optional)

Preparation

1. Preheat oven to 375°F. Line a muffin tin with 12 muffin cup liners.
2. In a small bowl, whisk flaxseeds together with water. Set aside for 5-10 minutes to allow to thicken.
3. In a large bowl, mix dry ingredients (flour, sugar, baking soda, and salt) together. Use a fork or whisk to break up any lumps.
4. In a separate medium-sized bowl, add the mashed bananas, oil, honey or maple syrup, vanilla, and flax mixture and whisk until well combined.
5. Combine the wet and dry mixtures and stir with a rubber spatula until well mixed. Gently fold in the optional chocolate chips, taking care to avoid over-mixing.
6. Spoon batter into muffin cups until approximately ¾ full. Place muffin tin in the oven and bake for 20-22 minutes. Test doneness by inserting a toothpick into the center of a muffin. If it comes out clean, the muffins are done.
7. Allow to cool for at least 15 minutes to allow them to firm up.

Cook's notes: Maple sugar, Sucanat, or any other unrefined granulated sweetener can be substituted for coconut sugar. Do not use overly ripened bananas.

Paleo adaptation: Omit dark chocolate chips if concerned about small amount of cane sugar.

Nutrients: B₁, B₂, E, CA, CU, FE, MG, MN, ZN, O3

BERRY PARFAITS WITH VANILLA CASHEW CREAM AND NUTTY CHIA DATE CRUMBLE

This delightful treat is healthy enough to serve for breakfast, but goes over just as well as a dessert. The Vanilla Cashew Cream is so good that you'll want to lick the bowl!

Serves 4

Ingredients

3-4 cups fresh mixed berries

Vanilla Cashew Cream

1 cup raw cashews, soaked for 2-4 hours

½ cup filtered water, plus more to thin as desired

2-3 tablespoons pure maple syrup

1 teaspoon vanilla extract

⅛ teaspoon sea salt

Nutty Chia Date Crumble

½ cup raw pecans

½ cup raw walnuts

¼ cup chia seeds

¾ cup pitted dates

1 teaspoon vanilla extract

¼ teaspoon sea salt

Preparation

1. Wash and drain berries. If including strawberries, remove the stem and cut or quarter into bite-sized pieces. Set aside.

2. For the cream, drain and rinse soaked cashews and place in a blender with water, maple syrup, vanilla, and salt. Blend on high for 45-60 seconds, until smooth and creamy. Set aside.

3. For the crumble, place pecans, walnuts, chia seeds, dates, vanilla, and salt in a food processor and pulse until coarsely ground. Set aside.

4. To assemble, take 4 short glasses and portion ⅓-½ cup of berries into each. Spoon a tablespoon or two of the Vanilla Cashew Cream into each glass, on top of the berries. Add a few tablespoons of the Nutty Chia Date Crumble. Repeat another layer of berries, cashew cream, and crumble until you've reached the top of each glass. Serve immediately.

Cook's notes: The Vanilla Cashew Cream can be made in most blenders, but is best when made in a Vitamix, Blendtec, or other high-powered blender.

Nutrients: B$_6$, C, C$_A$, M$_G$, M$_N$, S$_E$, G$_L$, O3

CHOCOLATE "GANACHE" WITH STRAWBERRIES

Chocolate and strawberries have long been a match made in heaven. This dairy-free chocolate ganache is smooth and rich, while juicy strawberries provide a burst of fruity flavor. This decadent dessert is simple, yet satisfying.

Makes approximately 1 cup

Ingredients

4 pitted Medjool dates, softened in filtered, hot water for 5-10 minutes

¼ cup reserved soaking water from dates

⅓ cup full fat coconut milk

¼ cup unsweetened cocoa powder

⅓ cup raw almond butter

1 tablespoon pure maple syrup

½ teaspoon vanilla extract

Pinch of sea salt

1 pint fresh strawberries

Preparation

1. Strain dates (reserving the soaking water) and transfer to a high-speed blender.

2. Add ¼ cup of soaking water, coconut milk, cocoa powder, almond butter, maple syrup, vanilla, and salt. Secure lid and blend on high for approximately 60 seconds or until mixture is smooth and creamy. Add additional water, 1 tablespoon at a time, if thinner consistency is desired.

3. Pour into a bowl and dip with strawberries.

Cook's notes: The chocolate ganache is best made in a Vitamix, Blendtec, or other high-powered blender. If you don't have a high-powered blender, you may want to soak dates for 3-4 hours before blending. For a lighter variation, use light coconut milk in place of full fat coconut milk.

Nutrients: B_2, E, Ca, Cu, Fe, Mg, Mn, Zn, Pr

AVOCADO SORBET

Greens are the most important food you can incorporate into your diet on a daily basis, but have you ever tried them for dessert? In this recipe, the sometimes bitter taste of the greens is masked by the sweetness of the honey and banana, the brightness of the lemon, and the creaminess of the avocado. This recipe was inspired by my dear friend and nutrition colleague, Traci Carpenter.

Makes 2 cups

Ingredients

- 1 large ripe avocado
- 1 cup greens (kale, spinach, collards, etc.)
- 1 large lemon or lime, peeled and seeded
- 1 frozen banana
- 2 cups ice
- 3 tablespoons local honey

Preparation

1. Place all ingredients in a high-powered blender and slowly increase speed to high. Blend for approximately 30-60 seconds. Be careful not to over-mix or melting will occur.

2. Enjoy right away.

Cook's notes: This sorbet is best made in a Vitamix, Blendtec, or other high-powered blender.

Nutrients: A(BETA), B$_1$, B$_6$, C, E, CA, CU, MG, MN, GL

WARM APPLE CRISP

Apple crisp is an all-time favorite dessert that is simple enough to be enjoyed year-round. Feel free to adapt this recipe with seasonal fruits. Peaches, cherries, or fresh berries are great in the summer or swap the apples with pears in the fall and winter.

Makes 12 servings

Ingredients

Filling

7 cups chopped apples
(approximately 6 large apples)

¼ cup pure maple syrup

2 tablespoons lemon juice

2 tablespoons arrowroot starch or organic cornstarch

1 teaspoon ground cinnamon

Topping

1¾ cups certified gluten-free rolled oats

¾ cup almond flour

¾ cup chopped walnuts, pecans, or hazelnuts

⅓ cup pure maple syrup

¼ cup melted coconut oil or ghee

1 teaspoon ground cinnamon

½ teaspoon sea salt

Preparation

1. Preheat oven to 350°F.
2. To make the filling, place chopped apples in a 9x13 inch baking dish. Pour the maple syrup, lemon juice, arrowroot starch or cornstarch, and cinnamon over the apples and toss gently until thoroughly coated. Spread the apples evenly in the dish.
3. To make the topping, combine oats, almond flour, nuts, maple syrup, coconut oil or ghee, cinnamon, and salt together in a small bowl.
4. Spoon the topping mixture evenly over the apples. Cover and bake for 40-45 minutes. Uncover and bake for an additional 10-15 minutes to make the topping crisp.
5. Let apple crisp rest for 5-10 minutes before serving.

Cook's notes: When in season, substitute 7 cups of chopped peaches, cherries, or berries for the apples. Reduce baking time to 30 minutes covered, 10 minutes uncovered.

Vegan adaptation: Use coconut oil in place of ghee.

Nutrients: B$_2$, B$_6$, E, Ca, Cu, Fe, Mg, Mn, Zn

HOMEMADE PUMPKIN APPLESAUCE WITH GOLDEN FLAXSEEDS

If you've never had or made your own applesauce, you're truly missing out. It's so much better than store bought and is easy to make. This version incorporates pumpkin and ground flaxseeds to increase the nutrition. It's perfect alone or you can serve a dollop over the Multigrain Breakfast Bowl found in the Breakfasts *chapter.*

Makes 2 cups

Ingredients

6 medium apples
(approximately 2½ pounds)

½ cup filtered water

1 teaspoon ground cinnamon

1 teaspoon freshly grated ginger

½ cup canned pumpkin puree

1 tablespoon fresh lemon juice

4 teaspoons ground golden flaxseeds

Preparation

1. Peel, core, and slice the apples into bite-sized chunks.

2. Combine apples with water, cinnamon, and ginger in a large pot and cook over medium heat, stirring occasionally, for 20 minutes.

3. Remove from heat and stir in pumpkin puree and lemon juice. Mash the apple mixture with a potato masher for a chunky, rustic texture. For a smoother texture, use an immersion blender to break up chunks or carefully transfer mixture to a regular blender and puree until smooth.

4. Divide evenly into 4 individual servings and stir 1 teaspoon of ground flaxseeds into each.

Cook's notes: Leftovers can be stored in the refrigerator in a tightly sealed glass container for up to a week.

AIP adaptation: Omit flaxseeds.

Elimination/Provocation Diet adaptation:
Omit lemon juice.

Nutrients: A(BETA), B₁, B₆, C, E, Cu, Mg, Mn, Gl, O3

PUMPKIN CUSTARD WITH HAZELNUT PECAN DATE CRUMBLE

This recipe gives you all of the flavors of pumpkin pie without the fuss of making a crust. Perfectly portioned and easy to make, it would be a shame if you reserved this nourishing sweet treat solely for Thanksgiving.

Serves 6

Ingredients

Custard

3 large eggs

1 (15-ounce) can pumpkin puree

½ cup full fat coconut milk

⅓ cup pure maple syrup

¼ cup cashew butter or raw cashews, soaked 4 hours, then drained

1-2 tablespoons blackstrap molasses (optional)

1 tablespoon ground pumpkin pie spice

Pinch of sea salt

Crumble

½ cup raw pecans

½ cup hazelnuts

½ cup pitted Medjool dates

½ teaspoon sea salt

Preparation

1. Preheat oven to 350°F.

2. Place all of the custard ingredients into a blender and puree until smooth and well mixed.

3. Pour mixture evenly into six 6-ounce (¾ cup) custard cups. Place custard cups in a large baking dish. Pour boiling water into baking dish around custard cups to a depth of 1 inch. Place baking dish on oven rack in the center of the oven.

4. Bake for 45 minutes or until centers are almost set. Carefully remove custard cups from baking dish and cool on wire rack.

5. To make the crumble, place pecans, hazelnuts, dates, and salt into the bowl of a food processor and process until nuts are finely chopped and incorporated with the dates to create a sticky, granular consistency. Crumble on top of custard cups.

Cook's notes: If you don't have pumpkin pie spice, use 2 teaspoons ground cinnamon, ½ teaspoon ground nutmeg, and ¼ teaspoon dried ground ginger.

Nutrients: A(BETA), A(RET), B₂, B₆, B₁₂, C, E, D, Ca, Cu, Fe, I, Se, Mn, Gl, Ty

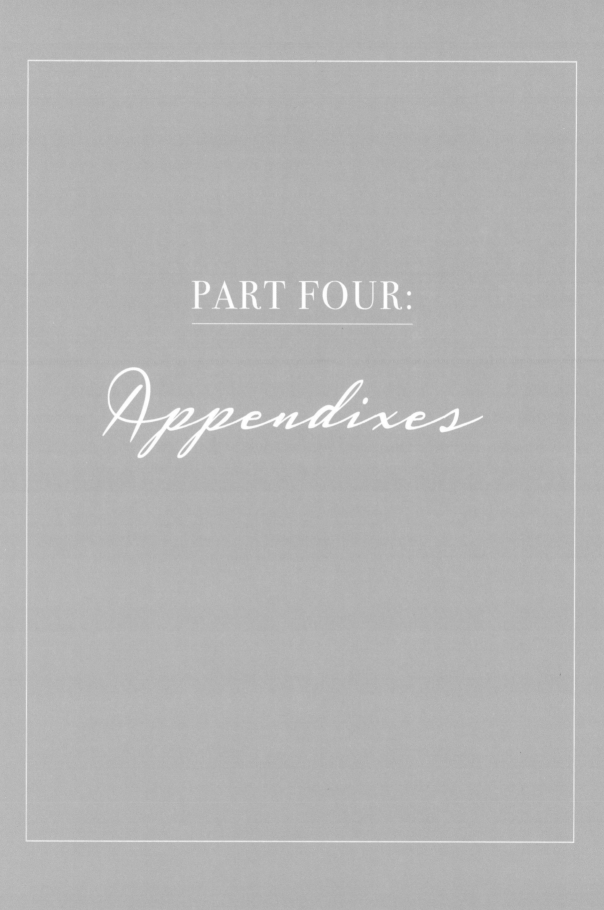

PART FOUR:

Appendixes

APPENDIX A

The Nutritional Springboard for This Cookbook

The link below provides a visual representation of the information provided in the *Our Springboard* and *Our Methodology* chapters. The Essential Hypothyroidism and Hashimoto's Nutrition Guide is an easy-to-read chart that displays the detailed research on whole foods sources of the thyroid- and immune-supportive nutrients that ultimately determined what ingredients we highlighted in this cookbook.

Lisa and I realize that not everyone wants to geek out with us on this nitty-gritty information, but we're very proud of our research and put a lot of effort into making this chart as pretty as possible. We think you'll enjoy looking at it.

The Essential Hypothyroidism and Hashimoto's Nutrition Guide:

www.thyroidcookbook.com/nutrition_guide

APPENDIX B

Suggested Supplements

While I often caution my clients and students against the slippery slope of over-supplementation, supplements can, when taken correctly and judiciously, be instrumental in healing. I frequently recommend many of the products listed below, *but I do not recommend all of these supplements for all Hashimoto's sufferers.*

Please see our website for links to all of these supplements (www.thyroidcookbook.com).

Dietary Supplement Disclaimer:

This book makes reference to various commonly available dietary supplements. The FDA is not authorized to review dietary supplement products for safety and effectiveness before they are marketed. As such, the FDA requires that dietary supplements sold in the U.S. include a statement that they are not intended to treat, diagnose, prevent, or cure diseases. Absent unique circumstances, dietary supplements may not be linked to specific disease-states. Any statements made in this work about dietary supplements have not been evaluated by the FDA and are not approved to diagnose, treat, cure, or prevent disease.

We reference dietary supplements for informational purposes only. Neither Blue Wheel Press nor the authors of this work are acting in the capacity of a doctor, nurse, licensed dietitian-nutritionist, or herbalist by providing such information and are not prescribing or advising any treatment, herb, or supplement for the treatment, cure, or prevention thereof, or otherwise suggesting changes to any treatment protocol already in place.

For the foregoing reasons, the charts below do not include any recommendations for dosing. It's your responsibility to consult with an appropriate healthcare practitioner for dosing requirements and potential contraindications with any other supplementation or pharmaceutical use before commencing any program. Work with a qualified thyroid specialist or other healthcare provider to determine your specific needs. Neither Blue Wheel Press nor the authors will be held responsible for any adverse reaction or contraindication of any supplement suggested in this book. You can visit the National Institutes of Health's Office of Dietary Supplements to strengthen your knowledge and understanding of dietary supplementation (https://ods.od.nih.gov).

Digestive support:

Supplement:	Manufacturer:
Glutamine	Metagenics: Glutagenics
Probiotics	Bio-Kult Bio-Kult contains the soil-based organism, Bacillus subtilis, which is recommended for those with autoimmunity. MegaFood: MegaFlora Plus (14 strains) MegaSporeBiotic
Collagen/gelatin	Vital Proteins
Digestive enzyme	Pure Encapsulations: Digestive Enzymes Ultra
Digestive enzyme for accidental gluten and dairy ingestion	Pure Encapsulations: Gluten/Dairy Digest
Omega-3 fatty acids	Metagenics: OmegaGenics EPA-DHA 1000

I recommend all of the above supplementation when doing an Elimination/Provocation diet. (One possible exception is the Gluten/Dairy Digest.)

Thyroid support:

Supplement:	Manufacturer:
Multi-mineral	MegaFood: Balanced Minerals MegaFood: Thyroid Strength[a]
Magnesium	MegaFood: Magnesium For anxiety and sleeplessness, additional magnesium is sometimes needed over and above a multi-mineral.
Copper	Pure Encapsulations: Copper (glycinate) I rarely make a recommendation for a stand-alone copper supplement; you can likely get your needs met with MegaFood's Balanced Minerals or Thyroid Strength, mentioned above.
Selenium	MegaFood: Selenium Additional selenium is sometimes needed over and above a multi-mineral, given selenium's ability to increase T3 and lower thyroid antibodies.

Iron	MegaFood: Blood Builder This product also contains folate and Vitamins B_{12} and C. Additional iron is sometimes needed over and above a multi-mineral for hair loss and/or anemia.
Ferritin (iron storage protein, often low for those with Hashimoto's)	Pure Encapsulations: OptiFerin-C Vital Proteins encapsulated liver (grass-fed)
Zinc	MegaFood: Zinc Additional zinc is sometimes needed over and above a multi-mineral for hair loss.
Tyrosine	Pure Encapsulations: l-Tyrosine It's easy to get tyrosine if you eat meat, fish, and eggs. I only recommend tyrosine for my vegan/vegetarian clients.

[a] *I don't typically suggest "thyroid supplements." Many of them are a combination of questionable ingredients, including bovine and porcine glandulars, which I'm wholeheartedly against due to their ability to over-stimulate the adrenals. Or perhaps they're high in iodine. But I stand behind this MegaFood product, which is a combination of food-based, thyroid-supportive minerals (iodine (low dose), zinc, selenium, and copper), tyrosine, and adaptogenic herbs, which are adrenal-supportive.*

Adrenal support:

See *The Essential Thyroid Cookbook Lifestyle Companion Guide* for our Restore Your Adrenals guide. You can download it for free on our website (www.thyroidcookbook.com/companion).

Supplement:	Manufacturer:
Adaptogenic herbs	Herb Pharm: Ashwagandha Herb Pharm: Holy Basil MegaFood: Adrenal Strength[a]
B Vitamins	MegaFood: Balanced B Complex[b]
Vitamin C	MegaFood: Complex C
DHEA	Metagenics: BioSom spray[c]

[a] *I typically recommend single herbs for adrenal health (e.g. ashwagandha, holy basil). But I also like this MegaFood product; it's a combination of a few adaptogens, along with Vitamin C, B_5 (pantothenic acid), magnesium, and reishi mushrooms.*

[b] *B Vitamins are nicknamed "the anti-stress vitamins" and B_5 (pantothenic acid) is particularly nourishing to the adrenals.*

[c] *DHEA is an adrenal hormone and I recommend supplementation with caution. Never supplement with DHEA unless you know that you're deficient. Don't blindly take DHEA. Even when you're known to be deficient, supplementation should be low dose. Otherwise, you risk aggression, facial hair, and acne. This product offers a mere 5 mg/spray. As with all supplements, talk with your doctor about proper dosing.*

The combination of the above four products is considered "the magic formula" for adrenal restoration. Again, be judicious with DHEA supplementation.

Immune modulators and anti-inflammatories:

Supplement:	Manufacturer:
Vitamin D[a]	Metagenics: D3 10,000 with K2 Metagenics: D3 5000 Metagenics: D3 2000 Complex
Turmeric	Gaia: Turmeric Supreme Life Extension: Super Bio-Curcumin
Omega-3 fatty acids	Metagenics: OmegaGenics EPA-DHA 1000
Glutathione	Seeking Health: Optimal Liposomal Glutathione (Some have difficulty with the flavor of this product.) Pure Encapsulations: Liposomal Glutathione (Softgel caps, but contains soy.)
Moducare	Thorne
Blackseed oil	Panaseeda

[a] *Get tested for your D level and take the above according to need and per your doctor's instructions. You can also find Dr. Frank Lipman's dosing guide (www.drfranklipman.com/vitamin-d-faq).*

Liver support:

See *The Essential Thyroid Cookbook Lifestyle Companion Guide* for more tips on supporting liver function. You can download it for free on our website: www.thyroidcookbook.com/companion.

Supplement:	Manufacturer:
Liver support	Herb Pharm: Liver Health
N-acetylcysteine (NAC)	Pure Encapsulations
Powdered fiber	Metagenics: MetaFiber (Take between meals.)
B Vitamins	MegaFood: Balanced B Complex
Vitamin C	MegaFood: Complex C
Multi-mineral	MegaFood: Balanced Minerals
Di-indolylmethane (DIM)	Designs For Health: DIM-Evail[a]

[a] *It's not recommended to take DIM without confirmation of high estrogen or estrogen dominance, as DIM can lower estrogens.*

Anti-candida/anti-yeast:

See *The Essential Thyroid Cookbook Lifestyle Companion Guide* for more information on addressing candida. You can download it for free on our website: www.thyroidcookbook.com/companion.

Supplement:	Manufacturer:
Biocidin	Bio-Botanical Research
Candibactin AR	Metagenics
Candibactin BR	Metagenics
InterFase Plus This product is for dissolving biofilm.	Klaire Labs
Activated charcoal This product is for mitigating the symptoms of a detox or Herxheimer reaction.	Integrative Therapeutics

Replenishing stomach acid:

See Appendix G for how to do a hydrochloric acid challenge.

Supplement:	Manufacturer:
Hydrochloric acid	Metagenics: SpectraZyme Metagest

APPENDIX C

The Important Role of Fats in the Diet

S aturated fats and cholesterol have been vilified for decades, but they're essential for good health and a necessary component of every cell in your body.

Fat and cholesterol help to regulate insulin levels, convert food into energy, protect liver function, and monitor the body's innate cholesterol production, which is generated by the liver and makes up about 75 percent (depending on heredity) of the cholesterol our bodies need.

Cholesterol is not the major culprit in heart disease. And saturated fat does not raise cholesterol levels. These theories have been proven repeatedly, but mainstream medicine continues to heavily promote low-fat diets and the multi-billion dollar statin drug industry.

"The diet-heart hypothesis—which holds that eating cholesterol and saturated fat raises cholesterol in our blood—originated with studies in both animals and humans more than half a century ago. However, more recent (and higher quality) evidence doesn't support it," states Chris Kresser, a globally recognized leader in the field functional and integrative medicine.[1]

Dr. Frank Lipman states, "For years, mainstream medical organizations such as the American Heart Association have demonized saturated fat as a root cause of cardiovascular disease. And, for years, progressive docs—backed by meta-analyses and other studies—have shouted from the rooftops that it's refined carbs and processed sugars—NOT saturated fat—that drive heart disease (and so many other chronic diseases). Now, comes big news that the sugar industry bribed scientists in the 1960s to downplay the relationship between sugar and heart disease and point the finger at saturated fat instead."[2]

In Dr. Lipman's interview with Dr. Mark Pettus, Pettus stated, "We spent most of the last generation looking at total cholesterol and LDL as if to suggest that those two values give you an accurate reflection of what we know to be a much more complex and nuanced issue with lipids. But, when you give people fat from a quality source and lower their carbohydrates, generally you see their triglycerides come down. That's a good thing. You see their good cholesterol, the HDL, go up. That's a really good thing."[3]

According to OB/GYN nurse practitioner and women's health expert, Marcelle Pick, "Cholesterol is the mother of all fat molecules in our bodies. We literally run on the stuff. It maintains neurotransmitter and brain function, builds brain and nerve tissue, and nourishes the immune system. It provides the insulation around nerves that transmit electrical impulses. It is a keystone of normal cell function and mood regulation and helps us digest fat-soluble vitamins like A, D, E, and K. Importantly for women, many of our most important hormones, including estrogen and progesterone, are made from cholesterol."[4]

It's not necessary to understand each of the hormones in the chart below—the important takeaway is that they're all made from cholesterol, which has been villainized. No wonder we see so many hormonal imbalances in women who shy away from dietary fat. In my mind, the criminalization of dietary fat has been a train wreck for many women and their hormonal health.

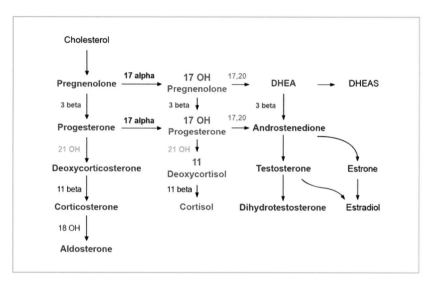

Chart by: Endocrine doctor (Own work) [CC BY-SA 4.0 (http://creativecommons.org/licenses/by-sa/4.0)], via Wikimedia Commons

Additionally, we need fat to burn fat. Fat is what helps us feel full and satiated and without it, there's no real feeling of satisfaction, which makes us eat more than necessary. It also helps to balance blood sugar by slowing the release of carbohydrates into our system and levels the ratio of two hormones, insulin to glucagon, which is critical for giving stored fat the heave-ho. The short story is that the right kinds of healthful fats help to make us hotter metabolic burners.

The myth-busting that's taken place the last several years about fat and cholesterol has been head-spinning; we've learned that a diet in the right types of healthful fats doesn't cause heart disease and doesn't make us fat. If you'd like to learn more, I suggest:

- Chris Kresser's report, The Diet-Heart Myth, found here: www.chriskresser.com/ebook/the-diet-heart-myth

- Dr. Mark Hyman's book, *Eat Fat, Get Thin* (Boston: Little, Brown and Company, 2016).

APPENDIX D

Eco-Label Reading Guide

The key to an eco-label's credibility and legitimacy is if the certifying organization employs independent, third-party inspections.

A 1st party label is issued by the producer without independent review. *"Trust us, we raise free-range chickens."*

A 2nd party label is issued by an industry, trade, or membership association. *"Trust us, our dairy farmers have pledged to not use growth hormones."*

There are problems with these two labels. According to Marion Nestle, Professor in the Department of Nutrition, Food Studies, and Public Health at New York University, "Anyone can put any kind of eco label on a product. Each of these groups sets its own rules. With the exception of organic, which for all its flaws does have a government agency behind it, you have to trust the labels are honest and honestly monitored."[5]

A 3rd party label/certification is issued by an organization independent from the product/producer. *"Our coffee is Fair Trade Certified."*

An independent, neutral, third party entity has exhaustively inspected the operation, based on predefined criteria. The third party reports back to the certification organization, allowing no conflict of interest to muddy the waters. And thus, consumers can be assured that the claims are meaningful, verifiable, consistent, clear, transparent, open to public comment, and independent with no conflict of interest.

Authentic, third party claims offer:

- Traceability: What/where is the source?

- Transparency: What are the standards?

- Accountability: Have the standards been met?

Some examples of authentic third party labels are: Non-GMO Project, American Grassfed Association, Animal Welfare Approved, Fair Trade Certified, Food Alliance Certified, Demeter Certified Biodynamic, Certified Humane, Bird Friendly, Marine Stewardship Council Certified, Rainforest Alliance Certified, Salmon-Safe, and USDA Certified Organic.

Some claims that are slippery and misleading are:

Antibiotic-Free: This is difficult to verify. It's often seen on milk and meat products and implies that the cows or chickens were never given antibiotics. But perhaps we should seek out more specific terminology such as "raised without antibiotics." Otherwise, the beef may have at one point been given antibiotics, even though they don't appear in its system right before slaughter. Terms like "no subtherapeutic use of antibiotics used in feed" are useful, since this can be tracked via paper trail by the USDA or certification organization.

Cage-Free and Free-Range: With cage-free, the birds are kept out of cages and have continuous access to food and water but don't necessarily have access to the outdoors. It could mean the animal lives in a barn with 10,000 other birds. With free-range, the birds must have continuous access to the outdoors, unless there's a health risk present. There are no standards, though, for what that outdoor area must be like—a concrete lot could do. The definition is vague, requiring only access to outdoors for an undefined time period each day, which could be five minutes or no access at all. Though widely used, this label is only defined by the USDA for poultry products, but not eggs.

Below are among the *least-reliable labels.*

Cruelty-free: There's no official definition for this label, so it's not regulated in any way.

Grass-fed (uncertified): This label sounds straightforward, but watch out. Even on some conventional farms, cows are fed grass for the first few months of their lives before being switched to grain, which can cause health problems in cattle and lead to the use of antibiotics.

Grass-finished: This refers to the last 90-160 days before slaughter. The term "grass-finished" may or may not mean that the cattle were raised on grass all of their lives, both as calves and during the finishing phase.

Hormone-free: This is difficult to verify. Besides, giving hormones to pigs and poultry is illegal, so when you see these products with a "no added hormone" label, know that the company is playing an unethical marketing game.

Pasture-raised: This term is unregulated. But we can assume that the animals haven't been confined to CAFOs (confined animal feeding operations). It implies that hens got at least part of their food from foraging on greens and bugs, which adherents say can improve flavor. Some studies have found that pasture-raised eggs contain more nutrients.

Natural: This label has absolutely no legal meaning except for fresh meats. The USDA declares that "natural" meats must not have any artificial ingredients, such as colors or preservatives, and must be minimally processed, meaning no further processing other than chopping, grinding, smoking, etc. It has no bearing on the production methods or standards of care for animals. A processed food claiming to be "natural" may still contain stuff you don't want. And what's troubling is that a Consumer Reports survey found that nearly 9 out of 10 consumers assume that meat labeled "natural" comes from animals that were raised without drugs or chemicals.

One way to get around misleading claims is to get to know your farmers and food producers personally through your local food co-op, farmers' market, CSA (community supported agriculture), or community garden.

Go here for Food Alliance's Eater's Guide to Food & Farm Sustainability: bit.ly/2cyxrV0

Go here for Food Alliance's frequently asked questions about sustainable farming: www.foodalliance.org/about/faqs

I'm good friends with Jack and Betsy McCann of TC Farm, a pasture-based farm raising beef, pork, chicken, and eggs. Jack is a sustainable farming expert and a consultant to farmers on sustainable practices. Go here to read his advice for sourcing the best meat and eggs: bit.ly/2c8EK7s

APPENDIX E

Sustainably-Sourced Seafood

The three resources below are the go-to for learning about fish that's responsibly farmed and caught, in ways that have the least impact on the environment; can be traced to a sustainable source; are richest in Omega-3 fatty acids; and are lowest in mercury contamination.

- Environmental Working Group's Good Seafood Guide: www.ewg.org/research/ewgs-good-seafood-guide
- Monterey Bay Aquarium's Seafood Watch: www.seafoodwatch.org
- Marine Stewardship Council, certified sustainable: www.msc.org

In addition to fish, mercury is found in cosmetics, pesticides, vaccines, and dental fillings and coal-burning plants pump out tens of thousands of mercury into the atmosphere yearly.

We cannot adequately cover the concerns around mercury exposure here, but as discussed in the *Selenium* subchapter, it has been shown to bind to the thyroid, which is very adept at absorbing mercury, and inhibit proper thyroid function. It can displace selenium, a critical thyroid mineral.

Mercury can also put you at risk for autoimmunity; as your immune system goes to work trying to get rid of it, its gets overtaxed and can lose its ability to recognize self from non-self and attack our tissues, including the thyroid. Additionally, a study in 2011 showed a link between mercury exposure and thyroid antibodies in women.[6]

See *The Essential Thyroid Cookbook Lifestyle Companion Guide* for our Biological Dentistry guide. You can download it for free on our website: www.thyroidcookbook.com/companion.

APPENDIX F

Affordable Organic and Sustainably-Grown
Food and How to Prioritize

Buying food that's organic, sustainably-grown, local, and grass-fed doesn't have to be all or nothing. Fruits and vegetables carry different pesticide loads and produce raised conventionally is an acceptable choice in many cases. Lisa and I don't suggest conventionally-raised pork, organ meat, eggs, chicken, or dairy, but lamb that's not organic or 100% grass-fed is likely fine. (Our cookbook is dairy-free; some with Hashimoto's cannot tolerate dairy but can reintroduce after digestive healing has taken place. See the chapter, *Dairy and Your Thyroid*.)

The Environmental Working Group has established "The Dirty Dozen," identifying the most contaminated fruits and vegetables and "The Clean Fifteen," the foods least likely to hold pesticide residues. You can find these guides at www.ewg.org/foodnews/summary.php.

We can't say enough good things about The Environmental Working Group and we're regular, monthly financial supporters. Their slogan is, "Know your environment, protect your health." They offer not only the above-mentioned food-buying guides, but also a Food Scores database that rates 80,000 products. They've created guides on safe seafood, sunscreens, water filters, cleaning products, and skincare and cosmetics, via their ever-popular Skin Deep Database. They've also created the "Dirty Dozen Endocrine Disruptors" resource as well as resources on non-GMO food and safe cellphone use. You can find all of these at www.ewg.org.

Check out their Good Food on a Tight Budget guide (www.ewg.org/goodfood).

Tips for saving:

- Cook from scratch as often as you can.

- Make a shopping list and stick to it.

- Prior to creating your list, take a visual inventory of your pantry and fridge. Did you know that 40 percent of our food ends up in a landfill? Tuning in to what you already have on hand helps you save money and reduce waste.

- After you've taken inventory, think of 2-3 complete meals you'd like to make and determine what you need to add to your list. Consider ways that you can cook once, but eat multiple meals from that cooked meal. You may want to reuse leftovers in new ways throughout the week.

- Batch cook so that you have go-to meals, alleviating the temptation to eat out.

- Buy more foods in bulk, especially beans, lentils, whole grains, and nuts. Grains and dried beans double or triple in size when cooked and can be prepared in large quantities and frozen.

- Avoid buying larger, value-sized options if you don't have a large household. It's likely that you won't use them before they expire and you may end up throwing away more money than you're saving.

- During the growing season, shop at your local farmers' market.[a]

- Join a CSA (community-supported agriculture).[a]

- Join your local food co-op. As a member/owner, you get special sales and discounts and also receive a yearly dividend, based on your spending.[a]

- Share the cost—join others in a CSA or go in together on a whole or half cow. Pound for pound, the cost of cuts of meat from whole or half animals is often a fraction of what you'll pay at the store.[a]

- Look for the leanest cuts of meat.

- While we recommend pastured meat as often as possible, it can get pricy. Look for the cheaper cuts, like chuck roast or chuck steak, which can be just as nutritious.

- When a product you normally buy is on sale, stock your pantry and freezer.

- Buy fresh fruits and vegetables when they're in season.

- Don't be afraid of frozen and canned vegetables.[b]

- Opt for canned fish instead of fresh. Salmon, sardines, and herring are good choices.

- Limit your trips to once a week, which decreases overall spending (and can save on gas money).

- Stick to the basics. Buy items that are versatile and can be used in a variety of ways. For example, forget the exotic spices that you may use infrequently.

- Don't waste money on things you can live without, like fancy bottled water. Identify your nonessentials.

- Shop online for the ease and convenience of buying certain staples in bulk. We suggest Barefoot Provisions. While they claim to be "primal" (aka Paleo), and we don't necessarily adhere to or suggest a pure Paleo lifestyle, they feature so many of the products that we love and recommend.

- It's hip to clip. Use coupons for items that fall within the context of a healthful diet—but be aware that many coupons are for highly processed junk foods.

[a] *Use these resources to find retail food co-ops, farms, farmers' markets, CSAs, farm-to-table restaurants, and other sources of local, sustainable food in your area:*

- *Local Harvest: www.localharvest.org*

- *Eat Wild: www.eatwild.com*

- *Eat Well Guide: www.eatwellguide.org*

[b] *Frozen and canned fruits and vegetables can be a healthful and economical choice. They can be just as nutritious and have a longer shelf life than fresh produce. Often, quality frozen and canned produce is packaged not long after harvesting, offering better nutritional value than the "fresh" produce that was harvested prematurely, warehoused, and then shipped to the store. Make sure that you only purchase canned foods from cans with BPA-free liners and opt for no salt or low-sodium products when available. (See the* Pantry Staples and Ingredients *chapter for more information.)*

A surefire way to spend too much on groceries is to purchase processed and packaged foods. You're paying for not only the processing, but also the slick and shiny boxes and bags. If this weren't enough of a rip-off, many of these foods often represent empty calories, offering flavor with little to no nutritional value.

APPENDIX G

Increasing Stomach Acid (Hydrochloric Acid Challenge)

Our digestive system is meant to be highly acidic so that we can thoroughly digest our food, especially protein-rich foods. An acidic environment is also necessary for the adequate absorption of important vitamins and minerals, including calcium, magnesium, zinc, iron, and Vitamin B_{12}, all of which the thyroid is wholly dependent upon.

Adequate gastric acid also provides a protective barrier against pathogens and in the presence of an acid deficiency, candida overgrowth and/or SIBO (small intestine bacterial overgrowth) are likely.

Here's a mind-bender: If you have any of the following symptoms, you may have a *deficiency* in stomach acid, not excess. The idea that these could be caused by low stomach acid is contrary to what you'll often hear from a conventional/Western doctor. Walk in and complain of these symptoms, and you'll likely be prescribed a PPI (proton pump inhibitor), which is the opposite of what you'd need.

- Excessive burping
- Bloating
- Constipation
- Gas
- Heartburn
- Acid reflux

Low hydrochloric acid (HCl) is also a critical consideration for those with hair loss; without adequate gastric acid, we're unable to efficiently digest and absorb proteins, including the amino acids for protein production, which is a major contributor to hair loss.

Instructions:
Take one capsule of SpectraZyme Metagest (betaine HCl and pepsin) at the end of your **protein-containing meal**.

1. If you don't feel a mild warming sensation in your stomach or mild nausea, take two at the end of your next protein-containing meal. (Each meal should contain some protein.)

2. Continue increasing the dosage by one capsule until you notice a slight warming or feelings of discomfort or nausea. Your maximum dose will be six pills at each meal. Anything beyond six has shown no therapeutic benefit. If you need to, stay with six capsules for several meals, until you feel discomfort.

3. Once you feel discomfort, your therapeutic dose is one capsule below when discomfort occurred.

4. As your stomach heals, your therapeutic dose will continue to decrease. Over time, you'll begin to feel discomfort at your therapeutic dose. When this occurs, decrease your dose by one capsule. This is your new therapeutic dose.

5. Continue this pattern until you feel warming, nausea, or discomfort with one capsule. Then decrease to half a capsule.

6. Once symptoms begin at the dosage of half a capsule, you've now reestablished the optimal level of HCl and have completed the challenge.

Note: When having a meal containing only a small amount of protein, you may need to take only half your current therapeutic dose of HCl.

Alternately, instead of the HCl pills, you can take one tablespoon of apple cider vinegar in as little water as it takes to get it down. Increase the tablespoons as you would the pills in the above instructions. I feel that the preferable way to do this experiment is with HCl.

NOTES

PREFACE

Introduction

1. Mark Hyman, *The Diabesity Prescription* (Lenox, MA: UltraWellness Center, 2010), 1, http://drhyman.com/downloads/Diabesity.pdf.

Farm Huggers

1. Jack Hitt, "Michael Pollan on the Links Between Biodiversity and Health," *Yale Environment 360,* May 28, 2013, accessed March 2015, http://e360.yale.edu/mobile/feature.msp?id=2655.

2. Dan Charles, "Are Organic Vegetables More Nutritious After All?," Minnesota Public Radio, *All Things Considered* (July 11, 2014), accessed January 2016, http://www.npr.org/sections/thesalt/2014/07/11/330760923/are-organic-vegetables-more-nutritious-after-all.

3. M. Barański, D. Srednicka-Tober, N. Volakakis, et al., "Higher Antioxidant and Lower Cadmium Concentrations and Lower Incidence of Pesticide Residues in Organically Grown Crops: A Systematic Literature Review and Meta-analyses," abstract, *British Journal of Nutrition* 112, no. 5 (September 14, 2014), doi:10.1017/S0007114514001366.

4. Daria Brambilla, Cesare Mancuso, Mariagrazia Rita Scuderi, et al., "The Role of Antioxidant Supplement in Immune System, Neoplastic, and Neurodegenerative Disorders: A Point of View for an Assessment of the Risk/Benefit Profile," abstract, *Nutrition Journal* 7, no. 29 (2008), doi:10.1186/1475-2891-7-29.

5. Virginia Worthington, "Nutritional Quality of Organic Versus Conventional Fruits, Vegetables, and Grains," *Journal of Alternative and Complementary Medicine* 7, no. 2 (2001), accessed February 2016, http://ucanr.edu/datastoreFiles/608-794.pdf.

6. Joseph Mercola, "New Analysis Concludes Organic Food Really Is Healthier," July 29, 2014, accessed March 2016, http://articles.mercola.com/sites/articles/archive/2014/07/29/organic-food-healthier.aspx.

7. Richard Shames, *Thyroid Power* (New York: HarperCollins, 2005), 158.

8. Carolyn Dean, "Balancing Adrenals and Thyroid," *Uncensored Natural Health Blog,* December 28, 2013, accessed November 2015, http://drcarolyndean.com/2013/12/balancing-adrenals-and-thyroid.

9. D. Srednicka-Tober, M. Barański, C. Seal, et al., "Composition Differences Between Organic and Conventional Meat: A Systematic Literature Review and Meta-analysis," abstract, *British Journal of Nutrition* 115, no. 6 (March 28, 2016), doi:10.1017/S0007114515005073.

10. A. J. McAfee, E. M. McSorley, G. J. Cuskelly, et al., "Red Meat from Animals Offered a Grass Diet Increases Plasma and Platelet n-3 PUFA in Healthy Consumers," abstract, *British Journal of Nutrition* 105, no. 1 (January 2011), doi:10.1017/S0007114510003090.

Both/And: Organic and Sustainable Farming

1. Rodale Institute, "Transition to Organic," February 24, 2014, accessed March 2015, http://rodaleinstitute. org/transition-to-organic.

2. The George Mateljan Foundation, "What Is Sustainable Agriculture?," *The World's Healthiest Foods*, accessed February 2016, http://www.whfoods.com/genpage.php?tname=george&dbid=230.

What This Means for You

1. Richard Shames, *Thyroid Power* (New York: HarperCollins, 2005), 184.

2. Mark Hyman, "Fat, Tired and Inflamed—Could it be your Thyroid?," June 5, 2015, accessed December 2015, http://drhyman.com/blog/2015/06/05/when-this-master-metabolism-hormone-malfunctions-you-become-fat-tired-and-inflamed.

3. Mark Hyman, "6-Steps to Heal Your Thyroid," June 10, 2015, accessed November 2015, http://drhyman. com/blog/2015/06/10/a-comprehensive-6-step-strategy-to-heal-your-thyroid.

4. E. Sloter, M. Nemec, D. Stump, et al., "Methyl Iodide-Induced Fetal Hypothyroidism Implicated in Late-Stage Fetal Death in Rabbits," abstract, *Inhalation Toxicology* 21, no. 6 (May 2009), doi:10.1080/08958370802596942.

5. A. O. Farwell and J. L. Leonard, "Effect of Methyl Iodide on Deiodinase Activity," abstract, *Inhalation Toxicology* 21, no. 6 (May 2009), doi:10.1080/08958370802597577.

6. Whitney S. Goldner, Dale P. Sandler, Fang Yu, et al., "Pesticide Use and Thyroid Disease Among Women in the Agricultural Health Study," abstract, *American Journal of Epidemiology* 171, no. 4 (February 15, 2010), accessed June 2015, http://aje.oxfordjournals.org/content/171/4/455.abstract.

7. Jill Grunewald, "Estrogen and Your Thyroid," *Healthful Elements*, January 10, 2013, accessed January 2015, https://www.healthfulelements.com/blog/2013/01/estrogen-and-your-thyroid.

8. P. Allain, S. Berre, N. Krari, et al., "Bromine and Thyroid Hormone Activity," abstract, *Journal of Clinical Pathology* 46, no. 5 (May 1993), http://www.ncbi.nlm.nih.gov/pmc/articles/PMC501258.

9. Organic Consumers Association, "Take Genetically Engineered Bovine Growth Hormone off the Market!," accessed October 2015, https://www.organicconsumers.org/old_articles/rBGH/cfsrbghlegal.php.

10. "Report on the Food and Drug Administration's Review of the Safety of Recombinant Bovine Somatotropin," U.S. Food and Drug Administration, updated April 23, 2009, accessed October 2015, http://www.fda.gov/AnimalVeterinary/SafetyHealth/ProductSafetyInformation/ucm130321.htm.

11. Susan Blum, *The Immune System Recovery Plan* (New York: Scribner, 2013), 243-244.

12. Ibid., 244.

13. Consumers Union, "The Overuse of Antibiotics in Food Animals Threatens Public Health," accessed October 2015, http://consumersunion.org/news/the-overuse-of-antibiotics-in-food-animals-threatens-public-health-2.

14. Randall S. Singer, Roger Finch, Henrik C. Wegener, et al., "Antibiotic Resistance—the Interplay Between Antibiotic Use in Animals and Human Beings," abstract, *Lancet: Infectious Diseases* 3, no. 1 (January 2003), doi:http://dx.doi.org/10.1016/S1473-3099(03)00490-0.

15. Centers for Disease Control and Prevention, "Antibiotic Use in Food-Producing Animals; Tracking and Reducing the Public Health Impact," accessed November 2015, http://www.cdc.gov/narms/animals.html.

16. Thomas Jefferson University, "Can Antibiotics Cause Autoimmunity?," *ScienceDaily*, March 31, 2014, accessed October 2015, https://www.sciencedaily.com/releases/2014/03/140331153520.htm.

17. J. Karczewski, B. Poniedziałek, Z. Adamski, and P. Rzymski, "The Effects of the Microbiota on the Host Immune System," abstract, *Autoimmunity* 47, no. 8 (December 2014), doi:10.3109/08916934.2014.938322.

PART ONE: ESSENTIAL THYROID NUTRITION

About the Thyroid

1. Mark Hyman, *Ultra-Metabolism* (New York: Simon and Schuster, 2008), 179.

2. Aviva Romm, "The Thy-Gap: Why Your Thyroid Labs Might Be Normal When You Really Have Hashimoto's," *Own Your Health, Change the World*, accessed February 2016, http://avivaromm.com/thyroid-labs-gap.

3. Alan Christianson, "Top 10 Myths of Thyroid Disease," April 7, 2016, accessed April 2016, http://drchristianson.com/top-10-myths-of-thyroid-disease.

What Causes Hypothyroidism?

1. Amy Myers, "Do Cruciferous Vegetables Cause Hypothyroidism?," April 7, 2014, accessed May 2014, http://www.amymyersmd.com/2014/04/do-cruciferous-vegetables-cause-hypothyroidism.

2. Richard Esquivel, "Autoimmune Disease in the U.S., Part 1: Introduction to Autoimmune Disease," San Jose Functional Medicine, accessed January 2016, http://sanjosefuncmed.com/autoimmune-disease-u-s-part-1-6-part-series/#_edn5.

3. Chris Kresser, "The Most Important Thing You May Not Know About Hypothyroidism," June 28, 2010, accessed October 2013, http://chriskresser.com/the-most-important-thing-you-may-not-know-about-hypothyroidism.

We Are the 3 Percent: Non-Autoimmune Hypothyroidism

1. Chris Kresser, telephone interview, March 2012.

2. Jill Grunewald, "Your Thyroid and Your…Mattress?," *Healthful Elements*, August 20, 2015, accessed August 2015, https://www.healthfulelements.com/blog/2015/08/your-thyroid-and-yourmattress.

The Role of Nutrition in Thyroid Function

1. Mark Hyman, *The Ultra Thyroid Solution* (Lenox, MA: UltraWellness Center, 2008), 33, http://mywellnessrevolution.com/wp-content/uploads/2013/03/Thyroid-Report-1.pdf.

The Thyroid/Digestion Connection

1. Datis Kharrazian, "Good Thyroid Health Depends on Good Gut Health," *Dr. K. News*, September 6, 2010, accessed February 2013, https://drknews.com/good-thyroid-health-depends-on-good-gut-health.

2. Mark Hyman, "How Hidden Food Sensitivities Make You Fat," February 22, 2012, accessed June 2013, http://drhyman.com/blog/2012/02/22/how-hidden-food-sensitivities-make-you-fat.

Gluten and Your Thyroid

1. C. Sategna-Guidetti, M. Bruno, E. Mazza, et al., "Autoimmune Thyroid Diseases and Coeliac Disease," abstract, *European Journal of Gastroenterology and Hepatology* 10, no. 11 (November 1998), http://www.ncbi.nlm.nih.gov/pubmed/9872614.

2. Amy Myers, "Do Cruciferous Vegetables Cause Hypothyroidism?," April 7, 2014, accessed May 2014, http://www.amymyersmd.com/2014/04/do-cruciferous-vegetables-cause-hypothyroidism.

3. M. N. Akçay and G. Akçay, "The Presence of the Antigliadin Antibodies in Autoimmune Thyroid Diseases," abstract, *Hepatogastroenterology* 50 (December 2003), Supplement 2, http://www.ncbi.nlm.nih.gov/pubmed/15244201.

4. Sategna-Guidetti et al., "Autoimmune Thyroid Diseases and Coeliac Disease."

5. M. Hakanen, K. Luotola, J. Salmi, et al., "Clinical and Subclinical Autoimmune Thyroid Disease in Adult Celiac Disease," abstract, *Digestive Diseases and Sciences* 46, no. 12 (December 2001), http://www.ncbi.nlm.nih.gov/pubmed/11768252.

6. Chris Kresser, "The Gluten-Thyroid Connection," July 18, 2010, accessed July 2013, http://chriskresser.com/the-gluten-thyroid-connection.

Dairy and Your Thyroid

1. Amy Myers, "The Dangers of Dairy," April 12, 2013, accessed October 2014, http://www.amymyersmd.com/2013/04/the-dangers-of-dairy.

Why This Is Not Another Paleo or AIP Cookbook

1. Chris Kresser, "5 Steps to Personalizing Your Autoimmune Paleo Protocol," January 23, 2015, accessed January 2015, https://chriskresser.com/5-steps-to-personalizing-your-autoimmune-paleo-protocol.

2. Ljudmila Stojanovich, "Stress and Autoimmunity," abstract, *Elsevier Autoimmunity Reviews* 9, no. 5 (November 27, 2009), accessed August 2014, https://www.csub.edu/~kszick_miranda/stress.pdf.

3. Mark Hyman, "How to Stop Attacking Yourself: 9 Steps to Heal Autoimmune Disease," July 30, 2010, accessed November 2014, http://drhyman.com/blog/2010/07/30/how-to-stop-attacking-yourself-9-steps-to-heal-autoimmune-disease.

4. Judy Dutton, "Conserve Your Willpower: It Runs Out," October 6, 2012, accessed May 2014, http://www.wired.com/2012/10/mf-willpower.

5. Shahid Umar, "Intestinal Stem Cells," abstract, *Current Gastroenterology Reports* 12, no. 5 (October 2010), doi:10.1007/s11894-010-0130-3.

6. Sean Croxton (producer), "How to Fix Your 'Bathroom Woes,'" *Underground Wellness* audio blog post, accessed April 2015, retrieved from http://underground1452.rssing.com/browser.php?indx=29758951&item=1.

7. Chris Kresser, "7 Things Everyone Should Know About Low-Carb Diets," September 2, 2014, accessed October 2014, http://chriskresser.com/7-things-everyone-should-know-about-low-carb-diets.

8. Andrew Weil, answer to question, "Should I Eat Like a Caveman?," Weil Q&A Library, February 20, 2002, accessed June 2014, http://www.drweil.com/drw/u/QAA36527/eat-like-a-caveman-paleolithic-diet.html.

9. Marc David, "Is There Anything New in Nutrition Worth Talking About?," Institute for the Psychology of Eating, 2014, accessed July 2015, http://psychologyofeating.com/is-there-anything-new-in-nutrition-worth-talking-about.

Spotlight: In Defense of Grains

1. John Douillard, "5 Paleo Myths," *John Douillard's LifeSpa*, March 12, 2015, accessed March 2015, http://lifespa.com/5-paleo-myths.

2. Andrew Weil, foreword to *The Good Gut,* by Justin Sonnenburg and Erica Sonnenburg (New York: Penguin Press, 2015), xii.

3. Justin Sonnenburg and Erica Sonnenburg, *The Good Gut* (New York: Penguin Press, 2015), 112.

Spotlight: In Defense of Legumes

1. Stephan Guyenet, "Beans, Lentils, and the Paleo Diet," *Whole Health Source,* November 23, 2013, accessed August 2014, http://wholehealthsource.blogspot.com/2013/11/beans-lentils-and-paleo-diet.html.

2. F. M. Lajolo and M. I. Genovese, "Nutritional Significance of Lectins and Enzyme Inhibitors from Legumes," abstract, *Journal of Agricultural and Food Chemistry* 50, no. 22 (October 23, 2002), http://www.ncbi.nlm.nih.gov/pubmed/12381157.

3. Susan Blum, *The Immune System Recovery Plan* (New York: Scribner, 2013), 210.

4. Ibid., 276.

5. Donna Jackson Nakazawa, *The Autoimmune Epidemic* (New York: Touchstone, 2008), 234.

6. John Douillard, "Beans: Spring's Unexpected Superfood," *John Douillard's LifeSpa*, April 26, 2016, accessed April 2016, http://lifespa.com/beans-springs-unexpected-superfood.

7. Justin Sonnenburg and Erica Sonnenburg, *The Good Gut* (New York: Penguin Press, 2015), 103.

Low-Carb: A Disaster for Those with Hashimoto's

1. Lara Briden, "Gentle Carbs for GABA, Cortisol, and Adrenal Health," *Lara Briden's Healthy Hormone Blog*, February 10, 2013, accessed October 2014, http://www.larabriden.com/gentle-carbs-for-gaba-cortisol-and-adrenal-health.

2. P. H. Bisschop, H. P. Sauerwein, E. Enders, and J. A. Romijn, "Isocaloric Carbohydrate Deprivation Induces Protein Catabolism Despite a Low T3-Syndrome in Healthy Men," abstract, *Clinical Endocrinology* (Oxford) 54, no. 1 (January 2001), http://www.ncbi.nlm.nih.gov/pubmed/11167929.

3. Cara B. Ebbeling, Janis F. Swain, Henry A. Feldman, et al., "Effects of Dietary Composition on Energy Expenditure During Weight-Loss Maintenance," abstract, *Journal of the American Medical Association* 307, no. 24 (June 27, 2012), doi:10.1001/jama.2012.6607.

4. R. Markus, G. Panhuysen, A. Tuiten, and H. Koppeschaar, "Effects of Food on Cortisol and Mood in Vulnerable Subjects under Controllable and Uncontrollable Stress," abstract, *Physiology and Behavior* 70, no. 3–4 (August 2000), http://www.ncbi.nlm.nih.gov/pubmed/11006432.

5. M. K. Poddar, B. C. Bandyopadhyay, and L. Chakrabarti, "Dietary Protein Alters Age-Induced Change in Hypothalamic GABA and Immune Response," abstract, *Neuroscience* 97, no. 2 (2000), http://www.ncbi.nlm.nih.gov/pubmed/?term=10799772.

Fiber: The Other Low-Carb Casualty

1. Monica Reinagel, "Benefits of Fiber," *Quick and Dirty Tips,* July 25, 2008, accessed August 2015, http://www.quickanddirtytips.com/health-fitness/healthy-eating/benefits-of-fiber.

2. David McKeon and William Bonificio (producers), "Episode 5: Diet and Its Impact on Our Microbiota and Health with Drs. Erica and Justin Sonnenburg," American Microbiome Institute audio blog post, April 21, 2015, accessed April 2016, retrieved from http://www.microbiomeinstitute.org/podcast/episode5.

3. Justin Sonnenburg and Erica Sonnenburg, *The Good Gut* (New York: Penguin Press, 2015), 112.

4. Jill Grunewald, "Estrogen and Your Thyroid," *Healthful Elements*, January 10, 2013, accessed January 2015, https://www.healthfulelements.com/blog/2013/01/estrogen-and-your-thyroid.

Our Springboard

1. Michael Pollan, "Unhappy Meals," *New York Times Magazine,* January 28, 2007, accessed August 2013, http://www.nytimes.com/2007/01/28/magazine/28nutritionism.t.html.

Minerals

1. Richard Shames, *Thyroid Power* (New York: HarperCollins, 2005), 158.

2. Carolyn Dean, "Balancing Adrenals and Thyroid," *Uncensored Natural Health Blog,* December 28, 2013, accessed January 2016, http://drcarolyndean.com/2013/12/balancing-adrenals-and-thyroid.

Minerals: Calcium

1. Richard Shames, *Thyroid Power* (New York: HarperCollins, 2005), 57.

2. Robert M. Sargis, "Thyroid Gland Overview," *EndocrineWeb*, updated November 12, 2015, accessed November 2015, http://www.endocrineweb.com/endocrinology/overview-thyroid.

3. University of Bristol, "Calcium Is Initial Trigger in Our Immune Response to Healing," *ScienceDaily*, February 14, 2013, accessed December 2015, http://www.sciencedaily.com/releases/2013/02/130214111608.htm.

4. Margherita T. Cantorna, Yan Zhu, Monica Froicu, and Anja Wittke, "Vitamin D Status, 1,25-Dihydroxyvitamin D3, and the Immune System," abstract, *American Journal of Clinical Nutrition* 80, no. 6 (December 2004), accessed May 2014, http://ajcn.nutrition.org/content/80/6/1717S.

5. J. H. Izquierdo, F. Bonilla-Abadía, C. A. Cañas, and G. J. Tobón, "Calcium, Channels, Intracellular Signaling and Autoimmunity," abstract, *Reumatología Clínica* 10, no. 1 (January–February 2014), doi:10.1016/j.reuma.2013.05.008.

6. Thomas Levy, *Death by Calcium* (Henderson: Medfox Publishing, 2013), 196.

Minerals: Copper

1. Richard Shames, *Thyroid Power* (New York: HarperCollins, 2005), 158.

2. G. J. Brewer, "The Risks of Free Copper in the Body and the Development of Useful Anticopper Drugs," abstract, *Current Opinion in Clinical Nutrition and Metabolic Care* 11, no. 6 (November 2008), doi:10.1097/MCO.0b013e328314b678.

3. Chris Kresser, "Could Copper-Zinc Imbalance Be Making You Sick?," January 11, 2012, accessed August 2014, http://chriskresser.com/rhr-could-copper-zinc-imbalance-be-making-you-sick.

4. Ann Louise Gittleman, *Why Am I Always So Tired?* (New York: HarperCollins, 2010), 15.

5. Laurie Warner, "Copper-Zinc Imbalance: Unrecognized Consequence of Plant-Based Diets and a Contributor to Chronic Fatigue," The Weston A. Price Foundation, February 14, 2008, accessed September 2015, http://www.westonaprice.org/modern-diseases/copper-zinc-imbalance-unrecognized-consequence-of-plant-based-diets-and-a-contributor-to-chronic-fatigue.

Minerals: Iodine

1. Chris Kresser, telephone interview, March 2012.

2. Richard Shames, *Thyroid Power* (New York: HarperCollins, 2005), 175.

3. Ibid., 176.

4. Amy Myers, "Thyroid Health Part VI: The Iodine-Thyroid Connection," August 21, 2015, accessed August 2015, http://www.amymyersmd.com/2015/08/thyroid-health-part-vi-the-iodine-thyroid-connection.

5. Mario Renato Iwakura, "Iodine and Hashimoto's Thyroiditis, Part 2," *Perfect Health Diet*, May 26, 2011, accessed September 2015, http://perfecthealthdiet.com/2011/05/iodine-and-hashimotos-thyroiditis-part-2.

6. Chris Kresser, "RHR: Chris Masterjohn on Cholesterol and Heart Disease (Part 3)," February 8, 2012, accessed September 2015, http://chriskresser.com/chris-masterjohn-on-cholesterol-and-heart-disease-part-3.

7. Shames, *Thyroid Power*, 176.

8. "Nutrients for Thyroid & Adrenal Health," *Integrative Health*, accessed August 2015, http://www.integrativehealthcare.com/nutrients-for-thyroid-adrenal-health.

9. Guy E. Abraham, "Iodine Study #5: The Safe and Effective Implementation of Orthoiodosupplementation in Medical Practice," *Optimox*, accessed July 2015, http://www.optimox.com/pics/Iodine/IOD-05/IOD_05.html.

10. Alan Christianson, "Iodine: The Goldilocks Mineral," *Huffington Post*, May 28, 2015, updated May 28, 2016, accessed June 2015, http://www.huffingtonpost.com/alan-christianson/iodine-health_b_7455316.html.

11. Alan Christianson, "Why I Discourage High-Dose Iodine," *Integrative Health*, accessed June 2015, http://www.integrativehealthcare.com/why-i-discourage-high-dose-iodine.

Minerals: Iron

1. M. B. Zimmermann and J. Köhrle, "The Impact of Iron and Selenium Deficiencies on Iodine and Thyroid Metabolism: Biochemistry and Relevance to Public Health," abstract, *Thyroid* 12, no. 10 (October 2002), http://www.ncbi.nlm.nih.gov/pubmed/12487769.

2. M. T. Bertero and F. Caligaris-Cappio, "Anemia of Chronic Disorders in Systemic Autoimmune Diseases," abstract, *Haematologica* 82, no. 3 (May–June 1997), http://www.ncbi.nlm.nih.gov/pubmed/9234597.

3. Richard Shames, *Thyroid Power* (New York: HarperCollins, 2005), 27.

Minerals: Magnesium

1. Carolyn Dean, "The Magnesium Miracle," accessed May 2014, http://drcarolyndean.com/magnesium_miracle.

2. Frank Lipman, "Support Your System—With Magical Magnesium," April 10, 2016, accessed April 2016, http://www.drfranklipman.com/support-your-system-with-magical-magnesium.

3. F. C. Mooren, S. W. Golf, and K. Völker, "Effect of Magnesium on Granulocyte Function and on the Exercise Induced Inflammatory Response," abstract, *Magnesium Research* 16, no. 1 (March 2003), http://www.ncbi.nlm.nih.gov/pubmed/12735483.

4. Lawrence Wilson, "Thyroid Disease and Its Healing," November 2015, accessed May 2016, http://www.drlwilson.com/articles/thyroid.htm.

5. John Douillard, "Your Vitamin D Needs Magnesium," *John Douillard's LifeSpa*, February 3, 2013, accessed March 2015, http://lifespa.com/your-vitamin-d-needs-magnesium.

Minerals: Manganese

1. Aaron K. Holley, Vasudevan Bakthavatchalu, Joyce M. Velez-Roman, and Daret K. St. Clair, "Manganese Superoxide Dismutase: Guardian of the Powerhouse," *International Journal of Molecular Sciences* 12, no. 10 (October 21, 2011), doi:10.3390/ijms12107114.

2. E. Blaurock-Busch, "The Clinical Effects of Manganese (Mn)," *Townsend Letter for Doctors & Patients*, 2010, accessed June 2015, http://www.tldp.com/issue/180/Clinical Effects of Mn.html.

Minerals: Selenium

1. M. B. Zimmermann and J. Köhrle, "The Impact of Iron and Selenium Deficiencies on Iodine and Thyroid Metabolism: Biochemistry and Relevance to Public Health," abstract, *Thyroid* 12, no. 10 (October 2002), http://www.ncbi.nlm.nih.gov/pubmed/12487769.

2. David Brownstein, *Overcoming Thyroid Disorders* (West Bloomfield: Medical Alternatives Press, 2008), 257.

3. Roberto Negro, "Selenium and Thyroid Autoimmunity," abstract, *Biologics: Targets and Therapy* 2, no. 2 (June 2008), http://www.ncbi.nlm.nih.gov/pmc/articles/PMC2721352.

4. Andrew Weil, "This Mineral Is Essential for Healthy Aging," Dr. Andrew Weil's Daily Health Tip, December 15, 2012, accessed November 2014, http://www.drweilblog.com/home/2012/12/15/this-mineral-is-essential-for-healthy-aging.html.

5. I. Vasiliu, C. Preda, I. L. Serban, et al., "Selenium Status in Autoimmune Thyroiditis," abstract, *Revista medico-chirurgicală a Societății de Medici și Naturaliști din Iași* 119, no. 4 (October–December 2015), http://www.ncbi.nlm.nih.gov/pubmed/26793846.

6. Chris Kresser, "Selenium: The Missing Link for Treating Hypothyroidism?," February 3, 2012, accessed March 2014, http://chriskresser.com/selenium-the-missing-link-for-treating-hypothyroidism.

7. Brownstein, *Overcoming Thyroid Disorders,* 137.

8. Zimmermann and Köhrle, "The Impact of Iron and Selenium Deficiencies."

9. Mario Renato Iwakura, "Iodine and Hashimoto's Thyroiditis, Part 2," *Perfect Health Diet*, May 26, 2011, accessed September 2015, http://perfecthealthdiet.com/2011/05/iodine-and-hashimotos-thyroiditis-part-2.

10. Kresser, "Selenium: The Missing Link."

11. Brownstein, *Overcoming Thyroid Disorders,* 256.

Minerals: Zinc

1. S. Nishiyama, Y. Futagoishi-Suginohara, and M. Matsukura, "Zinc Supplementation Alters Thyroid Hormone Metabolism in Disabled Patients with Zinc Deficiency," abstract, *Journal of the American College of Nutrition* 13, no. 1 (February 1994), http://www.ncbi.nlm.nih.gov/pubmed/8157857.

2. A. H. Shankar and A. S. Prasad, "Zinc and Immune Function: The Biological Basis of Altered Resistance to Infection," abstract, *American Journal of Clinical Nutrition* 68, no. 2, Supplement (August 1998), http://www.ncbi.nlm.nih.gov/pubmed/9701160.

3. David Brownstein, *Overcoming Thyroid Disorders* (West Bloomfield, MI: Medical Alternatives Press, 2008), 87.

4. Suzy Cohen, *Drug Muggers* (Emmaus: Rodale Books, 2011), 13.

Vitamins and Other Nutrients: Vitamin A

1. David Brownstein, *Overcoming Thyroid Disorders* (West Bloomfield, MI: Medical Alternatives Press, 2008), 88.

2. Mark Hyman, *Ultra-Metabolism* (New York: Simon and Schuster, 2008), 33.

3. Sally Fallon and Mary G. Enig, "Vitamin A Saga," The Weston A. Price Foundation, March 30, 2002, accessed February 2014, http://www.westonaprice.org/health-topics/abcs-of-nutrition/vitamin-a-saga.

4. E. Hedrén, V. Diaz, and U. Svanberg, "Estimation of Carotenoid Accessibility from Carrots Determined by an In Vitro Digestion Method," abstract, *European Journal of Clinical Nutrition* 56, no. 5 (May 2002), http://www.ncbi.nlm.nih.gov/pubmed/12001013.

5. Sarah Pope, "Busting the Beta Carotene Vitamin A Myth," *Healthy Home Economist*, accessed July 2016, http://www.thehealthyhomeeconomist.com/beta-carotene-vitamin-a-myth.

6. Michelle Kmiec, "Which Form of Vitamin A Is the Best: Beta-Carotene or Retinol?," *Online Holistic Health*, revised from 2011, accessed July 2015, http://www.onlineholistichealth.com/betacarotene-retinol.

Vitamins and Other Nutrients: B Vitamins

1. K. M. Shakir, S. Kroll, B. S. Aprill, A. J. Drake, and J. F. Eisold, "Nicotinic Acid Decreases Serum Thyroid Hormone Levels While Maintaining a Euthyroid State," abstract, *Mayo Clinic Proceedings* 70, no. 6 (June 1995), http://www.ncbi.nlm.nih.gov/pubmed/7776715.

Vitamins and Other Nutrients: Vitamin B$_1$ (thiamin)

1. A. Costantini and M. I. Pala, "Thiamine and Hashimoto's Thyroiditis: A Report of Three Cases," abstract, *Journal of Alternative and Complementary Medicine* 20, no. 3 (March 2014), doi:10.1089/acm.2012.0612.

2. Josh Axe, "Hypothyroidism Diet + Natural Treatment," *Dr. Axe: Food Is Medicine*, accessed May 2016, http://draxe.com/hypothyroidism-diet-natural-treatment.

3. Alan Christianson, "Supplements to Take for Hashimoto's," November 4, 2015, accessed January 2016, http://drchristianson.com/supplements-to-take-for-hashimotos.

Vitamins and Other Nutrients: Vitamin B$_2$ (riboflavin)

1. Sara Gottfried, *The Hormone Cure* (New York: Scribner, 2013), 140.

2. J. A. Cimino, S. Jhangiani, E. Schwartz, and J. M. Cooperman, "Riboflavin Metabolism in the Hypothyroid Human Adult," abstract, *Proceedings of the Society for Experimental Biology and Medicine* 184, no. 2 (February 1987), http://www.ncbi.nlm.nih.gov/pubmed/3809170.

3. R. F. Grimble, "Effect of Antioxidative Vitamins on Immune Function with Clinical Applications," abstract, *International Journal for Vitamin and Nutrition Research* 67, no. 5 (1997), http://www.ncbi.nlm.nih.gov/pubmed/9350472.

Vitamins and Other Nutrients: Vitamin B$_6$ (pyridoxine)

1. Sara Gottfried, *The Hormone Cure* (New York: Scribner, 2013), 140.

2. R. F. Grimble, "Effect of Antioxidative Vitamins on Immune Function with Clinical Applications," abstract, *International Journal for Vitamin and Nutrition Research* 67, no. 5 (1997), http://www.ncbi.nlm.nih.gov/pubmed/9350472.

Vitamins and Other Nutrients: Vitamin B$_{12}$ (cobalamin)

1. David Brownstein, *Overcoming Thyroid Disorders* (West Bloomfield, MI: Medical Alternatives Press, 2008), 88.

2. Ibid.

3. Jill Grunewald, "Estrogen and Your Thyroid," *Healthful Elements,* January 10, 2013, accessed January 2015, https://www.healthfulelements.com/blog/2013/01/estrogen-and-your-thyroid.

Vitamins and Other Nutrients: Vitamin C

1. Richard Shames, *Thyroid Power* (New York: HarperCollins, 2005), 157.

2. David Brownstein, *Overcoming Thyroid Disorders* (West Bloomfield, MI: Medical Alternatives Press, 2008), 87-88.

3. Sara Gottfried, *The Hormone Cure* (New York: Scribner, 2013), 135.

4. William Jubiz and Marcela Ramirez, "Effect of Vitamin C on the Absorption of Levothyroxine in Patients With Hypothyroidism and Gastritis," abstract, *Journal of Clinical Endocrinology and Metabolism* March 6, 2014, accessed May 2016, doi:http://dx.doi.org/10.1210/jc.2013-4360.

Vitamins and Other Nutrients: Vitamin D

1. Frank Lipman, "Vitamin D: FAQ," September 24, 2009, accessed October 2015, http://www.drfranklipman.com/vitamin-d-faq.

2. Mark Hyman, *The Ultra Thyroid Solution* (Lenox, MA: UltraWellness Center, 2008), 35, http://mywellnessrevolution.com/wp-content/uploads/2013/03/Thyroid-Report-1.pdf.

3. F. Baeke, T. Takiishi, H. Korf, C. Gysemans, and C. Mathieu, "Vitamin D; Modulator of the Immune System," abstract, *Current Opinion in Pharmacology* 10, no. 4 (August 2010), doi:10.1016/j.coph.2010.04.001.

4. S. Chaudhary, D. Dutta, M. Kumar, et al., "Vitamin D Supplementation Reduces Thyroid Peroxidase Antibody Levels in Patients with Autoimmune Thyroid Disease: An Open-Labeled Randomized Controlled Trial," abstract, *Indian Journal of Endocrinology and Metabolism* 20, no. 3 (May–June 2016), doi:10.4103/2230-8210.179997.

5. Greg Plotnikoff, telephone interview, August 2016.

6. Mark Hyman, "The Sunshine Vitamin: A Closer Look at Vitamin D," accessed May 2016, http://drhyman.com/blog/2010/06/18/the-sunshine-vitamin-a-closer-look-at-vitamin-d.

Vitamins and Other Nutrients: Vitamin E

1. Richard Shames, *Thyroid Power* (New York: HarperCollins, 2005), 157.

2. J. Yu, Z. Shan, W. Chong, et al., "Vitamin E Ameliorates Iodine-Induced Cytotoxicity in Thyroid," abstract, *Journal of Endocrinology* 209, no. 3 (June 2011), doi:10.1530/JOE-11-0030.

Vitamins and Other Nutrients: Omega-3 Fatty Acids

1. E. S. Abd Allah, A. M. Gomaa, and M. M. Sayed, "The Effect of Omega-3 on Cognition in Hypothyroid Adult Male Rats," abstract, *Acta Physiologica Hungarica* 101, no. 3 (September 2014), doi:10.1556/APhysiol.101.2014.3.11.

2. Susan Blum, *The Immune System Recovery Plan* (New York: Scribner, 2013), 55.

Vitamins and Other Nutrients: Tyrosine

1. Richard Shames, *Thyroid Power* (New York: HarperCollins, 2005), 8.

Vitamins and Other Nutrients: EGCG

1. M. Pae and D. Wu, "Immunomodulating Effects of Epigallocatechin-3-Gallate from Green Tea: Mechanisms and Applications," abstract, *Food and Function* 4, no. 9 (September 2013), doi:10.1039/c3fo60076a.

2. Medical College of Georgia, "Green Tea and EGCG May Help Prevent Autoimmune Diseases," *ScienceDaily*, April 20, 2007, accessed November 2015, https://www.sciencedaily.com/releases/2007/04/070419140910.htm.

3. Emily Ho, "Health Benefit of Green Tea: Mechanism Discovered, New Approach to Autoimmune Disease," *Medical News Today*, June 3, 2011, accessed November 2015, http://www.medicalnewstoday.com/releases/227420.php.

4. Susan Blum, *The Immune System Recovery Plan* (New York: Scribner, 2013), 59.

Vitamins and Other Nutrients: Glutathione

1. Mark Hyman, "Essential Glutathione: The Mother of All Antioxidants," accessed May 2015, http://drhyman.com/blog/2010/05/19/glutathione-the-mother-of-all-antioxidants.

2. Datis Kharrazian, *Why Do I Still Have Thyroid Symptoms When My Lab Tests are Normal?* (Carlsbad, CA: Elephant Press, 2010).

3. Susan Blum, *The Immune System Recovery Plan* (New York: Scribner, 2013), 58.

4. Datis Kharrazian, "Glutathione Recycling for Autoimmune Disease," *Dr. K. News*, August 18, 2011, accessed December 2014, https://drknews.com/glutathione-recycling-for-autoimmune-disease.

5. Blum, *The Immune System Recovery Plan*, 249, 250.

6. Ibid., 250.

Vitamins and Other Nutrients: Lycopene

1. Mana Abdul-Hamid and Marwa Salah, "Lycopene Reduces Deltamethrin Effects Induced Thyroid Toxicity and DNA Damage in Albino Rats," *Journal of Basic and Applied Zoology* 66, no. 4 (August 2013), doi:10.1016/j.jobaz.2013.08.001, retrieved from *ScienceDirect*, accessed November 2015, http://www.sciencedirect.com/science/article/pii/S2090989613000283.

2. Eze Ejike Daniel, Aliyu Mohammed, and Yusuf Tanko, "Effects of Lycopene on Thyroid Profile in Streptozotocin-Induced Diabetic Wistar Rats," *European Journal of Biotechnology and Bioscience* 3, no. 1 (January 2015), accessed February 2016, http://www.biosciencejournals.com/vol3/issue1/pdf/17.1.pdf.

Vitamins and Other Nutrients: Probiotics

1. Susan Blum, *The Immune System Recovery Plan* (New York: Scribner, 2013), 177.

2. Sarah Pope, "Fermented Foods Need This Probiotic Boost to Heal the Gut," *Healthy Home Economist*, accessed April 2016, http://www.thehealthyhomeeconomist.com/soil-based-probiotics-plus-fermented-foods-heal-gut.

Vitamins and Other Nutrients: Resveratrol

1. Susan Blum, *The Immune System Recovery Plan* (New York: Scribner, 2013), 41-42.

2. Amy Myers, "5 Foods and 5 Supplements to Reduce Inflammation," August 16, 2013, accessed December 2014, http://www.amymyersmd.com/2013/08/5-foods-and-5-supplements-to-reduce-inflammation.

3. Datis Kharrazian, *Why Do I Still Have Thyroid Symptoms When My Lab Tests are Normal?* (Carlsbad, CA: Elephant Press, 2010).

The Myth of "Goitrogens"

1. Datis Kharrazian, "Goiter, Goitrogens, and Thyroid Enlargement," *Dr. K. News*, November 12, 2013, accessed December 2013, https://drknews.com/goiter-goitrogens-and-thyroid-enlargement.

2. Jane Higdon, "Cruciferous Vegetables," Linus Pauling Institute, Oregon State University, 2005, updated December 2008 by Victoria J. Drake, accessed November 2014, http://lpi.oregonstate.edu/mic/food-beverages/cruciferous-vegetables.

3. Joel Fuhrman, article about cruciferous vegetables and thyroid function, formerly at https://www.drfuhrman.com/library/cruciferous_vegetables_and_thyroid.aspx, accessed October 2013, used with permission from Dr. Joel Fuhrman, per email on August 22, 2016.

4. Amy Myers, "Do Cruciferous Vegetables Cause Hypothyroidism?," April 7, 2014, http://www.amymyersmd.com/2014/04/do-cruciferous-vegetables-cause-hypothyroidism.

5. Chris Kresser, "Iodine for Hypothyroidism: Crucial Nutrient or Harmful Toxin?," July 5, 2010, accessed May 2014, http://chriskresser.com/iodine-for-hypothyroidism-like-gasoline-on-a-fire.

A Word About Soy

1. Mark Hyman, "How Soy Can Kill You and Save Your Life," accessed April 2014, http://drhyman.com/blog/2010/08/06/how-soy-can-kill-you-and-save-your-life.

2. Richard Shames, *Thyroid Power* (New York: HarperCollins, 2005), 168.

The Autoimmune Epidemic

1. Donna Jackson Nakazawa, *The Autoimmune Epidemic* (New York: Touchstone, 2008).

2. Moises Velasquez-Manoff, "An Immune Disorder at the Root of Autism," *New York Times,* August 25, 2012, accessed November 2014, http://www.nytimes.com/2012/08/26/opinion/sunday/immune-disorders-and-autism.html.

3. Dr. Robert Rountree, e-mail message to author, July 14, 2016.

4. Frank Lipman, "FAQs on Epigenetics," accessed June 2014, http://www.drfranklipman.com/faqs-on-epigenetics.

The Basics of Mitigating the Autoimmune Response

1. Susan Blum, *The Immune System Recovery Plan* (New York: Scribner, 2013).

2. Amy Myers, *The Autoimmune Solution* (San Francisco: HarperOne, 2015).

3. Donna Jackson Nakazawa, *The Autoimmune Epidemic* (New York: Touchstone, 2008).

4. J. B. Furness, W. A. Kunze, and N. Clerc, "Nutrient Tasting and Signaling Mechanisms in the Gut. II. The Intestine As a Sensory Organ: Neural, Endocrine, and Immune Responses," abstract, *American Journal of Physiology* 277, no. 5, part 1 (November 1999), http://www.ncbi.nlm.nih.gov/pubmed/10564096.

5. Nakazawa, *The Autoimmune Epidemic*, 230.

6. Katherine Erlich, "MTHFR Basics from Dr Erlich," March 1, 2012, accessed July 2014, http://mthfr.net/mthfr-basics-from-dr-erlich/2012/03/01.

7. Mary Ruebush, "Dirt, Germs, and Other Friendly Filth," *Experience Life*, September 2012, accessed September 2014, https://experiencelife.com/article/dirt-germs-and-other-friendly-filth.

Elimination Provocation Diet Instructions

1. Tom Malterre and Alissa Segersten, *The Elimination Diet* (New York: Grand Central Life & Style, 2015).

2. Andrew Weil, answer to question, "Best Test for Food Intolerance?," Weil Q&A Library, accessed June 2014, http://www.drweil.com/drw/u/QAA400354/Best-Test-for-Food-Intolerance.html.

Conclusion

1. Aviva Romm, *Thyroid Insights* (Aviva Romm M.D., 2015), 5, 19, https://avivaromm.leadpages.co/thyroid-ebook.

PART TWO: ESSENTIAL THYROID KITCHEN

1. Hiromitsu Watanabe, "Beneficial Biological Effects of Miso with Reference to Radiation Injury, Cancer and Hypertension," abstract, *Journal of Toxicologic Pathology* 26, no. 2 (June 2013), doi:10.1293/tox.26.91.

2. Jill Grunewald, "Kicking the Can – The Dangers of BPA," *Healthful Elements*, October 2011, accessed August 2016, https://www.healthfulelements.com/sites/default/files/bpa.pdf.

3. Andrea Winquist and Kyle Steenland, "Association Between Cumulative PFOA Exposure and Thyroid Disease in Community and Worker Cohorts," abstract, *Epidemiology* 23, (September 2012), doi:10.1097/01.ede.0000416721.10292.47.

4. Leah Zerbe, "Nonstick Cookware + Teflon Dangers," *Rodale's Organic Life*, February 14, 2013, accessed October 2014, http://www.rodalesorganiclife.com/home/nonstick-cookware-teflon-dangers.

PART FOUR: APPENDIXES

Appendixes

1. Chris Kresser, "The Diet-Heart Myth: Cholesterol and Saturated Fat Are Not the Enemy," April 19, 2013, accessed April 2014, https://chriskresser.com/the-diet-heart-myth-cholesterol-and-saturated-fat-are-not-the-enemy.

2. Frank Lipman, "The Truth About Saturated Fat: An Interview with Mark Pettus, MD," September 14, 2016, accessed September 2016, http://www.drfranklipman.com/truth-saturated-fat/#more-27877.

3. Ibid.

4. Marcelle Pick, "The Truth About Cholesterol and Fat," *Women to Women*, accessed May 2016, https://www.womentowomen.com/healthy-weight/the-truth-about-cholesterol-and-fat/2.

5. Jennifer Salerno, "Food Expert Marion Nestle on 'Green' Food Choices," *Food & Wine*, accessed August 2014, http://www.foodandwine.com/articles/food-expert-marion-nestle.

6. Carolyn M. Gallagher and Jaymie R. Meliker, "Mercury and Thyroid Autoantibodies in U.S. Women, NHANES 2007–2008," abstract, Environment International 40 (April 2012), accessed March 2016, http://www.sciencedirect.com/science/article/pii/S0160412011002716.

INDEX

Page references followed by n refer to notes. Page references followed by t refer to tables.

RECIPE AND INGREDIENT INDEX

ABOUT THE AUTHORS
Lisa Markley, MS, RDN & Jill Grunewald, HNC

Lisa Markley, MS, RDN of Nourish Yourself Nutrition and Wellness created, developed, and wrote each recipe in this cookbook, with the exception of the three noted.

Lisa is a dietitian and nutritional wellness expert with over a decade of experience working passionately towards improving the health of others. She has diverse experience in the fields of integrative nutrition, health education, clinical counseling, clinical research, and community wellness.

Lisa is also a seasoned culinary educator, food writer, and recipe developer with a deep love of cooking, eating, and advocating for local, seasonal, organic, and sustainably-produced foods. Her mission is to help others translate seemingly complex nutrition recommendations into simple, actionable steps using health-supportive ingredients prepared in ways that taste delicious.

She began her education at Northern Arizona University with a Bachelor of Science in Health Education. Later, she received a Master of Science in Nutrition from Bastyr University in Kenmore, WA. She then returned to her hometown, Kansas City, to complete her Certificate in Dietetics from the University of Kansas Medical Center.

As a lifelong learner, Lisa has continued her professional development with ongoing continuing education from the Integrative and Functional Nutrition Academy, the Institute for Functional Medicine, and Field to Plate.

She currently consults for the University of Kansas Hospital and Healthful Elements. She also teaches nutrition classes at Johnson County Community College and Turning Point: The Center for Hope and Healing. Lisa has been featured frequently as a nutrition and cooking expert in the Kansas City media.

Lisa knows first-hand the struggles of chronic illness. She was diagnosed with Hashimoto's thyroiditis in 2008, chronic Lyme disease in 2012, and mycotoxin illness in 2014. Although she's experienced challenges and limitations from these illnesses, Lisa has used a combination of conventional as well as functional medicine to address her situation head-on. Therapeutic nutrition has been one of Lisa's greatest allies on her healing path. It's her desire to help empower and inspire you to become an advocate for your own health and learn how to harness the healing power of food and healthful lifestyle changes through the practical tips and recipes provided in this cookbook.

She lives in Kansas City with her husband, Jim, and son, Evan. As of this writing, Lisa is expecting the arrival of a baby girl, due in August of 2017.

Jill Grunewald, HNC, Integrative Nutrition and Hormone Coach, is a thyroid health and autoimmunity specialist and wrote the educational component of this cookbook. For nearly a decade, she has successfully guided her clients and students with hypothyroidism and Hashimoto's to health and vitality.

She's a 2006 graduate of the Institute for Integrative Nutrition and a member of the Minnesota Natural Health Coalition. Since graduating from nutrition school, Jill has taken part in many courses from the functional medicine community specifically for healthcare practitioners. In 2017, she will graduate with a certificate from the Functional Medicine Coaching Academy, in partnership with the prestigious Institute for Functional Medicine.

Jill has suffered from alopecia (autoimmune hair loss), off and on, since 1982 and in early 2008, was diagnosed with Hashimoto's thyroiditis (the same year as Lisa). Jill knew that starting thyroid drugs right out of the chute and taking them "for life," with no consideration for why her thyroid was under-functioning or what to do about her immune dysregulation was not the answer. She immersed herself in learning everything she could about autoimmunity and hypothyroidism and how to manage these conditions with whole foods, botanicals, lifestyle modifications, and other natural therapies.

Jill's Hashimoto's has been successfully managed since late 2008 without the use of thyroid drugs. And unlike many with alopecia, her now-infrequent bald spots always grow back.

In her coaching practice, Healthful Elements, Jill not only specializes in hypothyroidism and Hashimoto's, but also other autoimmune conditions (especially alopecia and Graves'), adrenal dysfunction/HPA axis dysfunction, polycystic ovary syndrome (PCOS), perimenopause/menopause, and pre-diabetes/diabetes.

Jill has written for various publications, blogs, and online magazines, including Huffington Post, MindBodyGreen, and Experience Life magazine and has contributed to articles in Self and Shape magazines.

She lives in Minneapolis with her husband, Mark, and daughter, Harriet.